SEXUAL ABUSE OF YOUNG CHILDREN

SEXUAL ABUSE OF YOUNG CHILDREN

Evaluation and Treatment

KEE MACFARLANE
and
JILL WATERMAN
with
SHAWN CONERLY
LINDA DAMON
MICHAEL DURFEE
SUZANNE LONG

Foreword by Roland Summit

THE GUILFORD PRESS

New York   *London*

© 1986 The Guilford Press
A Division of Guilford Publications, Inc.
200 Park Avenue South, New York, N.Y. 10003

Printed in the United States of America

Library of Congress Cataloging in Publication Data

MacFarlane, Kee.
  Sexual abuse of young children.

  Includes bibliographies and index.
  1. Sexually abused children—Mental health.
2. Child psychotherapy.   3. Sexually abused children—
Family relationships.   I. Waterman, Jill, 1945–
II. Title.   [DNLM: 1. Child Abuse.   2. Family Therapy.
3. Incest.   4. Sex Offenses.   WA 320 M143s]
RJ507.S49M33   1986   618.92′89   85-30539
ISBN 0-89862-675-7

To my parents: for the gifts of an abuse-free childhood, the encouragement to think for myself and the freedom to do it. They don't come any better than you.—K.M.

To my sons, Justin and Aaron, who were part of the process of this book, both in the womb and in the world. I hope they and their generation will experience love and caring, free from all abuse.—J.W.

To my children who taught me the best of what I know about kids.—S.C.

To Frank and our family who put up with my many weekends away from home while I met with the Book Club.—L.D.

To my father, the child psychiatrist. He would be proud.—M.D.

To my parents who stimulated curiosity, tolerated stubbornness and accepted individuality. To my husband, Jim, and sons, Casey and Brady, who have been encouraging, loving, and supportive in this long process.—S.L.

AUTHORS

KEE MACFARLANE, MSW, Children's Institute International, Los Angeles, California

JILL WATERMAN, PhD, Department of Psychology, University of California at Los Angeles, Los Angeles, California

SHAWN CONERLY, Orange County Child Protective Services, Santa Ana, California

LINDA DAMON, PhD, San Fernando Valley Child Guidance Clinic, Northridge, California

MICHAEL DURFEE, MD, Los Angeles County Department of Health Services, Los Angeles, California

ASTRID H. HEGER, MD, Children's Institute International, Los Angeles, California

ROBERT J. KELLY, PhD, Department of Psychology, University of California at Los Angeles, Los Angeles, California

SANDY KREBS, Children's Institute International, Los Angeles, California

SUZANNE LONG, LCSW, Private Practice, Irvine, California

ROBERT LUSK, MA, Department of Psychology, University of California at Los Angeles, Los Angeles, California

MERILLA MCCURRY SCOTT, MA, Department of Psychology, University of California at Los Angeles, Los Angeles, California

BRUCE WOODLING, MD, Private Practice, Ventura, California

ACKNOWLEDGMENTS

The Book Club would like to acknowledge a number of people who assisted and supported us in various ways throughout this endeavor. First, we want to thank our colleagues in each of our agencies who learned with us about this emerging field of study, participated with us in the development of the ideas, techniques, and clinical models presented in the book, and who shared with us many useful insights. Second, we are most grateful to our publisher, Seymour Weingarten, who deserves a lot of credit for his remarkable patience and restraint in dealing with us over this 3-year period. Like a benevolent coach of a predominantly female junior varsity soccer team, Seymour alternately provided much needed doses of encouragement, support, advice, ultimatums, and limits.

Third, we want to acknowledge David Corwin and Roland Summit for providing the original impetus that brought some of us together to work on the development of interview protocols and for their continuing contributions and leadership in the area of sexual abuse of the young child. Fourth, Bob Burdick provided the desperately needed technical know-how with computers and word processing to allow us to endlessly revise some of our chapters and even typed much of the final version of our longest chapter. The support of Mary Emmons and others at Children's Institute International also helped to produce these materials. We also are grateful to Deanne Tilton for supporting Michael Durfee through all of this and for her work with the ICAN agencies which have supported us all.

Finally, we offer our heartfelt thanks to our families and "significant others" who put up with us, with having draft chapters spread all over our respective houses, and with the Book Club's weekend meetings ("What? Not *another* Saturday for that damn book") over the years.

The Book Club

FOREWORD

The unprecedented emergence of child sexual abuse has created the psychological equivalent of a disaster for victims, parents, and professionals alike. It is a disaster played in slow motion. It is a nightmare of exposure, fear, confusion, helplessness, and paralysis. The scream won't come out and the flight reflexes are petrified. The nightmare is made all the more Kafkaesque by the legions of spectators who serenely pass by as if nothing is happening. But this is no dream that ends with simple awakening. Anyone who is touched by the reality of child sexual abuse moves into a new world from which there is no deliverance. Old comforts like justice, fairness, decency, self-worth, power, autonomy, and free will take on new meaning there. Even those who weather the change successfully will feel isolated and alienated from friends and colleagues. In this nightmare the desperate paralysis is real, as is the desperate indifference of unbelieving friends.

If this metaphor seems lurid and inappropriate for a scholarly textbook, I can only say that it is mild and inadequate to the reality of working with the victimized preschool-age child. What must be understood first, before discussing the arcane and intellectual facts, are the primitive and fundamentally devastating feelings that dominate every attempt to understand why and how anyone would violate such a young and precious soul.

Child sexual abuse is an intensely controversial, deeply divisive subject. It splits children from parents, mothers from fathers, and families from their friends, neighbors, and relatives. It divides social workers against psychiatrists, therapists against investigators against prosecutors against judges against jurors, and every player against society itself. Any traditional or potential alliance is threatened, and every nascent distrust is exaggerated. Each question becomes a dispute and every answer an insult. Here in the midst of the flowering of 20th-century reason and scientific enlightenment is a neglected relic of mythic and superstitious issues almost untouched by mainstream adult consciousness. This is the stuff of nightmares, fairy tales, comic books, illegal pornography, and the tabloids nobody admits to reading in the supermarket checkout lines. This is little against big, child versus adult, the simple engulfed by the profound, feeling overpowered by reason, abject helplessness provoking inexcusable power, prototypical innocence as a foil for grandiose corruption, and, simply, a battle between good and evil.

What makes the issues so difficult is not their power but their paradox. Most of us are survivors of childhood. We are intimidated and embarrassed by the shadows of our past. It was good to become enlightened, imperative to become strong and sure, vital to replace fearful feelings with comforting beliefs. It is normal to be an adult. It is healthy to take charge. It is necessary to *know*. Who can dare slip back to experience the feelings and vulnerabilities of a dependent child? Who will fight for the wretched, soiled, uncertain little kid against all those adult spectators who *know* the child is lying? Child advocacy is not only not reasonable, it is not *professional*. And it's not smart. Those who fight for power are courageous. Those who crusade for the underdog are called hysterical.

Besides all those basic growth and power issues, each of us is challenged in our personal beliefs and loyalties. If we are loyal and respectful to the memorial image of our own parents, and if we are protective of appropriate hierarchies of enlightenment and power, can those securities stand the test of believing that a pediatrician has molested a patient or that a father has sodomized his own 3-year-old? If mothers are vital to our experience of caring and being cared for, can we contemplate that a woman could enjoy forcing feces into the mouth of her infant? And could such a woman be at the same time the trusted organizer of a parent cooperative preschool? Most of us insist that she would be found, if at all, only in Bedlam.

Even beyond the challenge to positive anchors of security, sexual abuse of young children assaults our pathological defenses. Anyone betrayed and molested by loving caretakers in childhood will try to establish a protective mythology: "They were right and good; I was bad and provoked my own suffering (and if I could only learn to be good they would love me)." By learning to be hyperalert and intuitively sensitive to clues of displeasure, abused children can learn to protect adults and to scapegoat themselves, making reasonable order out of intolerable chaos. An adult survivor of such a childhood may be very good at helping others in distress even while despising the child who elicits that distress. Many practitioners in the helping professions are themselves victims, hidden even from themselves. Some will be incapable of empathy with abused children. Others, further along in their partial recovery from abuse, can feel only for the children and against the offenders. Child sexual abuse gives new meaning to the old adage "Physician, heal thyself."

To effect any change in the bewildering conflicts that surround the subject, the practitioner must learn to be both comfortable in dealing with and knowledgeable about the sexual and psychological abuse of very young children. Before building experience in the field, the clinician deserves the benefit of the best available preparation and training from those most experienced in the field. This truism is all the more inescapable in light of the runaway progress (or explosive chaos) that defines the field. The expert in child sexual abuse today may be an ignoramus tomorrow. One way to separate the wheat from the chaff in a quest for training is to seek out those who have weathered the strongest winds and who have endured the longest thrashing.

The authors of this volume have demonstrated their substance over time and travail. They have withstood the winnowing gales of disbelief and distrust. By pioneering and by persisting so long, each represents an exception to the norm, someone who has stayed in the center of controversy long enough to establish a measure of comfort and authority. Their authority is born not of books alone, but of professional and personal experience. Their understanding has grown with the field, evolving and shifting to cope with each reversal and each contradictory excursion into an expanding turf. They are adults who speak as children. Many even speak *with* children.

Contrary to popular belief, molested preschool children are not unknown or newly discovered. As early as 1979, ages ago by present reckoning, Mike Durfee organized in Los Angeles a large and vigorous group of professionals who were working with preschool-age molested children. Most of the founding members of that group brought in years of experience with incest and other forms of sexual child abuse. Members shared their views and endorsed and expanded fledgling efforts at diagnosis, therapy, forensic interaction, prevention, and research. The best of those efforts has matured into corresponding chapters in this book. Parallel membership in the Los Angeles County Interagency Council on Child Abuse and Neglect (ICAN) strengthened bridges of credibility and priority planning to governmental, educational, community, and justice system agencies. The Child Sexual Abuse Project, initiated by ICAN in 1978, discovered ever younger children, thanks in part to the prophetic warnings of Dr. Durfee. Parents Anonymous, born in Southern California in 1969, drew many professionals into direct experience with abusive parents. Jolly K, the parent founder of Parents Anonymous, literally forced both Kee MacFarlane and me to own up to the reality of sexual abuse of young children. Parents United and the affiliated professional sexual abuse treatment models established in the early 1970s by Hank and Anna Giarretto provided a melting pot for participants and professionals, as well as a resource for training, all of which has continued to support and open windows of credibility. Kee convened the National Child Sexual Abuse Consultation Meeting in Washington, D.C., on August 9, 1978, and initiated among those invited pioneers dialogues and affiliations that flourish even today.

When Kee moved to Los Angeles, after leaving Washington in January 1982, she began working immediately with a group of professionals who had formed for the express purpose of developing the use of videotape for interviewing molested children. David Corwin, who provided the impetus, the setting, and the snacks for those late-night seminars, is perhaps the first child psychiatrist ever to be trained and supervised within a university treatment setting specialized for child sexual abuse: the Family Support–Parents United Program at UCLA. Kee also began working with Jean Matusinka, head of the District Attorney's vertical prosecution unit for child abuse and a founding veteran of both Parents Anonymous and ICAN, to bring legal advocacy to the child victim. That coalition between clinician and prosecutor, unlikely except in the context of deliberate and dedicated networking, provided the tools for exploring ways to prevent systemic trauma of young children.

Although this narrative omits many players equally deserving of mention and does no justice to the richness of expertise even in Los Angeles County, let alone the rest of the country, it does provide, I hope, a glimpse of the seedbed of this volume. Far from incidental or impulsive, it is the logical and eventual outcome of many years and thousands of hours of collective, collegial experience. Each chapter reflects the state of the art as well as the humility and the humiliations of imperfect knowledge.

We, the professional practitioners for tiny victims, still don't know as much as the victims themselves, and we can't hope to share the intimate omniscience of the successful, well-hidden perpetrators. But we're trying, and we're learning. And we know already, at this moment, more than ordinary adults have ever dared to guess about this long-avoided subject. This book contains the most responsible, the most reliable, the most immediate, and the most useful experience ever compiled for the benefit of very young victims of child sexual abuse.

Roland Summit, M.D.

PREFACE

The seeds of these writings grew from a small group of community professionals who met bimonthly for many years in Los Angeles to explore the then little-known topic of molestation of preschool age children. The group, organized by Michael Durfee, met in order to share experiences and expertise concerning our young clients. At the time, there were few resources available other than ourselves. The evolution of this book from conception to birth took more than 4 years. The evolutionary process for its six authors (who came to call ourselves "The Book Club") was, at times, as arduous as the development of the book itself. When Michael Durfee mobilized five of his colleagues from the Preschool Age Molested Children's Professional Group to work together on this effort, and they all happened to be motivated, strong-willed, and opinionated women, he quickly found himself with more than he'd bargained for. Fortunately, his ego-strength and inherent good nature seem to have remained intact, even if the book's resemblance to his initial vision did not.

At the time that we began talking about putting some of our thoughts and experiences into writing, we weren't sure we knew enough about the subject matter to presume to write about it, and the prospect of producing an entire book about the rape and molestation of little children seemed both depressing and formidable. But, as Judith Herman said in the preface to her book *Father-Daughter Incest*, "Incest is not a topic that one embraces; one backs into it, fighting every step of the way" (Herman, 1981). And so it was with this examination of this subject as well.

As we began discussing what might go into such a book we realized that, while we didn't have all (or even many) of the answers to the dilemmas we raised, we did, collectively, have many years of experience working with very young victims of sexual abuse. We also knew that we had learned many things the hard way—through trial and error, estimates of outcomes, and projections of what would be best for our young clients. We felt that we might be able to help others avoid inventing some of the same lessons by writing about them, and we were able to go forward with the book once we allowed ourselves to view it as a working product, a state-of-our-collective-knowledge document which, like many of our clients and the field in general, is still in its infancy. We hope that its readers will regard it similarly.

One of the reviewers of our drafts, in deference to our vulnerability on witness stands, said that he hoped we had never done any of the things we advised against in the book or, conversely, had never failed to do the things we advised. In reply, we could only ask how he thought we had learned much of what we know, and reaffirm our sense of obligation to pass along those hard-earned lessons.

Much has changed in the field of child protection in the 4 years since we began this book. There has been an explosion in public awareness concerning child sexual abuse and a marked increase of reported cases across the country involving abuse of preschool age children by their caretakers. Some of what we wrote several years ago we would rewrite now, but for the fact that it would probably take 2 more years and need revising after that. If, as they say, the road to success is always under construction, we can at least take heart in the fact that our road has never remained static and that its continual renovation is consistent with the continual additions to our own knowledge.

The Book Club devoted considerable effort to motivating, encouraging, pleading with, and sometimes, threatening one another to produce written results. Dozens of Saturdays and Sundays were devoted to Book Club activities, and innumerable late nights found us amidst piles of paper, food, and wine as we engaged in earnest debate over what we felt confident enough to commit to writing and how the information should be presented. Throughout this process we underwent our own evolutions. Within the ranks of the Book Club there was a divorce, a marriage, an engagement, a disengagement (none of these between us), and a few members even managed to remain relatively stable, all things considered. Midway through the book some of us found ourselves caught up in several cases involving large numbers of children in child care settings. Our frustrating and difficult involvement in these cases stretched all of us to our limits and forced us to reexamine some of our previous experiences and assumptions in light of situations that were entirely different from any we had previously encountered. What we have learned from them, particularly about the legal system, could fill another book.

But there was also a bright spot midway through our journey because, during the process, more than a book was born. In 1984, consistent with the fact that she devoted more time and effort into getting this book completed than any of us, Jill gave birth to twin boys, constituting the only aspect of the process that was ever completed ahead of schedule. The Book Club, a group of hopeless baby addicts if there ever was one, immediately incorporated the twins into the endeavor, feeding, burping, and cuddling them at every subsequent meeting. Whatever the advantages or disadvantages to the twins of being nurtured by a crowd of child therapists, their gentle presence in our midst as we discussed their less fortunate counterparts was a poignant reminder of why we continue to remain involved in this difficult and discouraging aspect of human behavior.

CONTENTS

SEXUAL ABUSE OF YOUNG CHILDREN

INTRODUCTION

SCOPE OF THE PROBLEM

Jill Waterman
Rob Lusk

Sexual abuse among preschoolers is a problem that nobody wants to admit or discuss. The thought of babies, toddlers, and preschoolers as sexual objects is abhorrent to most people, and has led to denial of the possibility that such abuse exists in any but the most rare and pathological situations. In the last few years, society has come to recognize that sexual abuse of children in general is a problem of large proportions in the United States today. Only in the past year or so has there been recognition that such abuse is not confined to budding adolescent girls but affects very young children as well, boys and girls alike, even including babies. In this introductory chapter, definitional issues in child sexual abuse are discussed; figures about the incidence of child sexual abuse in general and sexual abuse of preschoolers in particular are presented; and problems with knowing the true incidence of abuse are reviewed. Additionally, some major dimensions of sexual abuse of children are given.

DEFINITIONAL ISSUES

The number and variety of definitions of child abuse in general have caused many problems in interpretation of case findings and research:

1. The definitions lack comparability; there are literally thousands of definitions of child abuse in use.
2. They are imprecise, causing problems in measuring degree of abuse reliably.

3. They lack "taxonomic delineation"; many different types of
child abuse are often lumped together without allowing for
or specifying differences (Besharov, 1981).

These points are particularly true with regard to child sexual
abuse. There is huge variability in the sexual acts included in various
definitions of sexual abuse; in fact, in 1980, 34 states that included
sexual abuse in their child abuse statutes did not even attempt to
define what it meant. In general, both legal and medical definitions
are thought to be too restrictive; they frequently rely on physical
evidence of molestation, which is usually not present (Mrazek, 1980).
This is especially true for preschool victims, where penetration occurs
less frequently than with older children.

Research on incest has probably suffered most from definitional
problems. Here, definitions have ranged from fantasied sexual acts
with relatives (Gordon, cited in Rosenfeld, Nadelson, & Krieger, 1979)
to fondling, masturbation, or oral copulation, to Bixler's (1981) highly
restrictive definition of "heterosexual intercourse between post pu-
bescent consanguinous nuclear family members." It is obvious that
with such divergence in definitions, there is bound to be much variability and disagreement about the incidence, dynamics, and effects
of sexual abuse.

Thus, it seems important to specify some factors that vary in
sexual abuse, and to keep them in mind when looking at case studies
or research data. These include the type of sexual act involved; the
nature of the relationship between the participants; the duration of
the abuse; the degree of violence and threats; the ages and relative
developmental level of the participants; and the familial and cultural
context in which the actions have occurred.

What types of sexual abuse occur with preschoolers? Basically,
almost every type of abuse identified for older children has been
reported to occur with preschoolers as well. Perhaps fondling is most
common, and vaginal or anal intercourse least common, with oral
copulation in between. One common pattern seen in incestuous sexual
abuse is behavior that begins as affectionate fondling in the preschool
years, then moves to more overt sexual activity such as oral copulation
or mutual masturbation in the early school years, and progresses to
full intercourse in the preadolescent and adolescent years.

INCIDENCE OF CHILD SEXUAL ABUSE

How many children are sexually abused? What proportion of these are preschoolers? These questions are difficult to answer, for reasons spelled out below. In looking at the astronomical increases in reported cases of child abuse over the last 5 to 8 years, one might conclude that there is a current epidemic of child molestation that is only getting worse and worse. However, this increase seems related to greater public awareness and acceptance of the existence of the phenomenon, rather than to a great explosion in the number of acts of sexual molestation. It has been noted that when a community opens a child sexual abuse hotline, begins advertising treatment services, or gives great media exposure to the issue of child sexual abuse, reports increase dramatically. In any event, despite disagreements about actual incidence, there is virtually unanimous agreement that sexual abuse is the fastest-growing form of reported child abuse (Finkelhor, 1983).

Estimates of the incidence of sexual abuse tend to come from one of two sources—either documented or reported cases received by various agencies, or survey studies of adults that ask about previous molestation experiences. In reviewing reports received by the American Humane Society's Clearinghouse on Child Abuse, it has been estimated that 60,000 to 100,000 children are sexually abused annually in the United States; with this incidence, it would appear that 10–14% of American families are affected by child sexual abuse each year (Bander, Fein, & Bishop, 1982a).

However, there are many reasons to call into question incidence figures based on reported cases of child sexual abuse. First, in 1978, only 31 states and territories submitted information on sexual abuse to the American Humane Society's Clearinghouse; this fact renders their data incomplete and inaccurate (Finkelhor, 1983). Second, it appears that a huge number of cases go unreported each year. Some of the reasons for this involve difficulties in documenting abuse; without physical evidence, a child frequently is not believed, or the suspicion is so vague that it is not reported. Additionally, in cases of abuse within the family, the possibility of separation from parents or other disruption of the family may cause a child to give a false retraction or to deny a valid complaint. Preschoolers may not be able to communicate effectively events or behaviors that may have occurred with molesters, or may be unaware that the behavior is anything unusual, unexpected, or negatively sanctioned. Also, states differ greatly in relevant laws and reporting criteria.

Finally, studies have documented from several points of view that many, if not most, cases of sexual abuse go unreported. For example, a survey of convicted child molesters revealed that these men committed between two and five times as many crimes as they were actually apprehended for (Groth, Longo, & McFadin, 1982). Similarly, of physicians in the Seattle area who responded to an anonymous questionnaire, only 42% indicated that they would report all cases of sexual abuse, despite mandatory reporting laws (James, Womack, & Strauss, 1978). These doctors asserted that they were mainly concerned that reporting would be harmful to the family or that the cases could be better handled without social services intervention. Finally, in Russell's (1983) random survey, in only 2% of cases of women who had experienced sexual abuse within the family and in 6% of cases of those abused by someone outside the family were the incidents reported.

Given the factors just mentioned, it is hardly surprising that estimates of the incidence of sexual abuse vary dramatically. Some estimate that the "hidden incidence" of child sexual abuse is 5 to 10 times the reported incidence (Tsai & Wagner, 1978). In terms of absolute numbers, current reliable estimates range from 100,000 to 500,000 cases per year. Sarafino's (1979) estimate of 336,200 cases annually, derived from a variety of sources, is perhaps reasonably accurate.

As mentioned earlier, the other major source of data about the incidence of sexual abuse comes from surveys of adults who are asked about sexual experience in childhood. In questionnaires administered to college students and other nonclinical populations, proportions of people reporting sexual contact with an adult prior to puberty or late adolescence range from about 8% to 35%. For example, in a frequently quoted study, Finkelhor (1979a) gave an anonymous questionnaire to 795 undergraduates in New England and found that 9% of the men and 19% of the women reported being victimized as children. It is important to note that the data were self-reports and therefore subject to potential bias; also, the sample is obviously nonrepresentative of the nation as a whole.

The survey by Russell (1983), referred to briefly earlier, was noteworthy because the 930 women interviewed were randomly selected from adult women in San Francisco. She found that 16% of those interviewed had experienced sexual abuse by a family member and 31% had been molested by someone outside the family before age 18. In a literature review of the survey studies done on nonclinical populations, Mrazek (1980) suggests that one-fourth to one-third of all children have at least one sexual experience with an adult. Although results from these surveys are retrospective and rely solely on the person's memory of the events, they suggest that children in the United States are at great risk for some form of sexual abuse.

How many of the cases of child sexual abuse involve children of preschool age or younger? This incidence is especially hard to pinpoint, for some of the reasons mentioned earlier that relate to a child's credibility and the developmental level of the child's cognitive and communication skills. Additionally, crime statistics often do not differentiate victims by age. While many believe that the peak age for child sexual abuse is generally 8 to 13 years, the duration of the abuse, particularly in cases of incest, may cause the ages reported to be artificially high. For example, if the abuse is ongoing for several years before discovery or disclosure, the age listed as the age of abuse is almost always the child's age at the time a report is made. Many long-term victims of child sexual abuse do not remember exactly when the abuse began. This is partly a function of the gradual manner in which much sexual abuse begins, and partly due to the poor time sense of preschool and young school-age children.

Several authors have noted that small but significant proportions of the sexually abused children they have encountered are preschoolers (Landis, 1956; MacFarlane, 1979) or even infants (Finkelhor, 1983). Current statistics are actually quite alarming. According to the Los Angeles County Health Department, the most common age of report of sexual abuse by health professionals in Los Angeles County currently is 4 years, and in a 3-month period in 1984, 21 1-year-olds and 64 2-year-olds were reported as having been sexually abused. In 1983, Los Angeles County Mental Health reported that 21.4% of their sexual abuse cases involved children under 5 years of age, according to the Interagency Council on Child Abuse and Neglect. Additionally, the incidence of gonorrhea in children under 12 years of age in Los Angeles County consistently peaks between ages 2 and 7 years.

DIMENSIONS OF SEXUAL ABUSE

Sexual abuse of children varies along several dimensions, which are delineated here.

NATURE OF PARTICIPANTS' RELATIONSHIP: INSIDE VERSUS OUTSIDE THE FAMILY

There is general agreement that children are sexually abused by people close to them—relatives, step-relatives, friends of the family, neighbors, and authority figures. The perverted stranger in a trench-coat offering candy to children is clearly not the culprit in the sexual abuse of most young children. It has been found that 75–80% of sexual abuse occurs within "affinity systems"—families, relatives, friends, and neighbors (Finkelhor, 1979a; Tsai & Wagner, 1978). In surveying women who were molested as children, Tsai, Feldman-Summers, and Edgar (1979) found that only 6.7% were molested by strangers. Despite agreement that most abuse is perpetrated by someone known to a child, there is considerable disagreement about what proportion of children are abused by family members. Estimates range from 10% of sexual abuse cases (Schecter & Roberge, 1976) to 50% of those abused (Finkelhor, 1979a; Russell, 1983). Typically, studies that have looked at clinical populations who are seeking help for reactions to the abuse or who are experiencing significant emotional problems have reported higher proportions of incest victims than have investigations of nonclinical groups; this seems to indicate that in general, the effects of ongoing sexual involvement with an adult family member may be more harmful to a child than involvement with someone outside the home. These dynamics and effects are discussed in more detail later.

WHO ABUSES AND WHO IS ABUSED WITHIN THE FAMILY

Brother–sister incest is thought by many to be the most common form of incest; it is probably greatly underreported, due to its transient nature and generally less harmful effects (Dixen & Jenkins, 1981). Two preschoolers playing doctor, or sex between mutually consenting adolescents at roughly the same developmental level, is typically not considered sexual abuse. However, if there is a large discrepancy between the ages, developmental stages, or relative power of the siblings, the dynamics and effects may be more similar to those of parent–child incest (Finkelhor, 1980b). There is considerable variation in estimates of the percentage of children abused by their fathers. While Finkelhor's survey found that 6% of the incestuous relationships involved a father or stepfather, Schecter and Roberge (1976) concluded that about 78% of reported incest involves fathers and daughters.

Father–daughter incest is certainly the best-documented form of incest. Incest involving fathers and sons, as well as other male adult relatives, seems to be relatively common, but still considerably less so than brother–sister or father–daughter incest. The rarest and least-discussed form of incest is mother–daughter incest, and sexual relationships between same-sex siblings are also rarely reported. Mother–son incest is reported relatively infrequently, and it used to be assumed that it only happened with severely disturbed or psychotic mothers; however, we are finding more cases of mother–son incest recently, and new evidence suggests that there may be several types of relationship patterns involved (MacFarlane & Summit, personal communication).

SEX OF PERPETRATOR AND OF CHILD

The large majority of sexual perpetrators appear to be males (Herman & Hirschman, 1981; Lindholm & Willey, 1983), and, traditionally, girls were felt to be abused considerably more often than boys. However, it has recently emerged that boys may be abused much more frequently than previously supposed. Surveys of child molesters have revealed that as many as 85% of them (who are predominantly male) were themselves abused as children (Groth, 1982). However, sex-role norms and homophobia are likely to be responsible for severe underreporting of sexually abused boys. Swift (1979) has stated:

> A conspiracy of silence surrounds the boy who is sexually victimized. His victimization is proof that he has failed in one of the primary mandates of the masculine role—to defend himself. To share his trauma is to advertise his defeat and invite not only immediate humiliation, but continuing stigmatization. (p. 134)

Some authors now believe that boys may be sexually abused as commonly as girls (Groth, 1978; O'Brien, 1980); this may be especially true for preschoolers. Further evidence for the hidden incidence of abuse of boys comes from the fact that most confirmed pedophiles who abuse many children outside the family prefer young males (Groth & Birnbaum, 1978).

TYPE OF SEXUAL ACT INVOLVED

As noted earlier, acts may vary from fondling through oral copulation to sodomy and intercourse. Fraser (1981) suggests that the type of act is likely to have a considerable differential impact on the child; he believes they can be separated into nontouching acts (e.g., exhibitionism), nonviolent touching acts, and violent touching acts (e.g., rape). Groth (1982) has differentiated between the child rapist, who uses force, power, and threats in the sexual abuse, and the child molester, who is more likely to coax and cajole the child, moving slowly and often with considerable affection. Clearly, the effects on the child would be quite different in these two situations. While it is difficult to make generalizations, the preschool-age child is probably somewhat more likely to encounter a "molester" than a "rapist."

SOCIOECONOMIC FACTORS

Information on socioeconomic status and ethnicity of those involved in child sexual abuse is very sketchy and confusing. For one thing, the topic is so sensitive that many agencies have chosen not to collect systematic data about class or ethnicity of the families they work with, in order to avoid controversy. While some have concluded that sexual abuse is a lower-class phenomenon, this seems largely due to the disproportionate overrepresentation of lower-socioeconomic-status persons in documented cases. More affluent families are likely to have more resources to handle the experience without letting it come to the attention of governmental sources, despite mandatory reporting laws. Certainly, child sexual abuse occurs in all strata of society, and cannot be considered exclusively a lower-socioeconomic-status phenomenon.

With regard to ethnicity, results from several large-scale surveys are contradictory. While some conclude that blacks are overrepresented in sexual abuse cases (De Francis, 1970; Finkelhor, 1983), others have found the exact opposite—that blacks are underrepresented in sexually abused samples (Adams-Tucker, 1981; Lindholm & Willey, 1983)! It is also important to consider the cultural context in which the sexual activity occurs: In some societies, sexual initiation of a young person by a specified older relative may be an accepted cultural ritual, while such activity would clearly constitute sexual abuse in our society. Sociocultural issues are explored in more depth in Chapter 8.

CONCLUSIONS AND CAUTIONS

It is clear from the contradictory figures presented above that our actual knowledge about the incidence of child sexual abuse and of factors involved in specifying precisely who is involved is sketchy at best. Conclusions drawn from documented cases are suspect, because the information is clearly not representative. On the other hand, while survey data tap into unreported cases, they are always retrospective and therefore subject to selective and faulty recall, social desirability, and demand characteristics. To date, the only survey using random sampling is Russell's (1983); this also was retrospective, and suffered from a 50% rate of refusal by those requested to participate. Information from studies of family members who are receiving clinical treatment is also tainted with selection biases; therefore, estimates of incidence and data about the participants cannot be considered representative. These are additionally subject to biases on the part of clinicians. These methodological problems, coupled with widespread disagreement about definitions of sexual abuse, suggest that any conclusions about the incidence of sexual abuse or demographic factors involved should be viewed very tentatively.

As the recognition that preschool children are sexually abused in significant numbers becomes more accepted, it may be hoped that more carefully controlled research will be carried out to clarify some of the disagreements and controversies discussed above. In this book, we attempt to share our clinical knowledge and our understanding of previous investigations regarding the evaluation and treatment of molested preschool children and their families; the dynamics involved when such young children are victims (from the perspective of the family and of societal systems); the effects (both short- and long-term) on the children; and some ideas for preventing sexual abuse from happening to our babies, toddlers, and preschoolers at all.

In Section II of this book, issues in evaluation of preschool children suspected of having been sexually abused are addressed. Developmental considerations are examined; methods of assessing suspected abuse are reviewed; the medical assessment is discussed; techniques for interviewing and evidence gathering are described; and, finally, the effects of sexual abuse on children are considered. In Section III, the broader societal and legal context of sexual abuse of very young children is examined. Issues discussed include abuse allegations in relation to divorce proceedings; sociocultural factors; and considerations in the taping of interviews and testimony. Section IV, on treatment, follows. It includes chapters dealing with general, treatment issues; family dynamics found with sexually abused preschoolers; guidelines for treating preschool children individually and in parallel groups with their mothers; and suggestions for helping parents deal with extrafamilial molestation. The final section deals with conclusions, implications, and ideas for prevention of sexual abuse of our youngest children.

EVALUATION OF
YOUNG CHILDREN

DEVELOPMENTAL CONSIDERATIONS

Jill Waterman

Preschool children are in a period of rapid development along a variety of dimensions. They learn to play with others; develop sex roles; expand their language and communication skills tremendously; and develop a repertoire of preacademic skills, such as discriminating and naming colors, and learning numbers and letters. Because of the great changes that occur in this age range, it is very important to be aware of certain aspects of the child's development and to take them into account when evaluating a child who is suspected of having been sexually abused. Particular attention needs to be paid to developmental issues in three areas: (1) the child's developmental level, relative to other children of the same age; (2) developmental aspects of sexuality in the preschool child; and (3) aspects of preschool development relevant to successful interviewing techniques and to court testimony. Each of these areas is explored in depth.

THE CHILD'S DEVELOPMENTAL LEVEL

Assessing the child's developmental level is important for several reasons. First, it is necessary to ascertain whether the abuse may be one sign of an inadequately stimulating and caring environment, or whether the child may have regressed in development as a result of the abuse or of the aftermath of abuse. Second, one must know the child's developmental level in order to make sure that the interview questions and procedures are appropriate. Mrazek (1981) also points out that it is necessary to assess the developmental age of the child in order

to make a judgment of the child's capacity to deal directly with the
abusive incident, and in order to propose the most appropriate form
of psychotherapy (e.g., play vs. verbal approaches). Third, knowing
the child's developmental level can be helpful in guiding law enforcement authorities to take appropriate actions regarding court testimony for the child.

There are many different levels of sophistication for assessing a
child's development. For purposes of evaluating a child suspected of
having been sexually abused, a rough screening of developmental
level is generally adequate. If this rough screening leads to questions
about the adequacy of the child's development along a particular
developmental line (A. Freud, 1965), then formal screening tests such
as the Denver Developmental Screening Test should be given. If the
results of such a formal screening test are abnormal or questionable,
then a psychologist should administer a standardized test of development or intelligence.

For children under $2\frac{1}{2}$ years of age, the Bayley Scales of Infant
Development are probably the best means of making an in-depth
assessment. For children over $2\frac{1}{2}$ years of age, either the McCarthy
Scales of Children's Abilities or the Kaufman Assessment Battery for
Children (K-ABC) are very appropriate. The Wechsler Preschool and
Primary Scale of Intelligence (WPPSI) can be used if the child is over
4 years of age. It is important when referring a preschool child to a
psychologist for developmental or intellectual evaluation to make sure
that the psychologist is experienced in working with very young children and is familiar with the appropriate testing material.

A few other tests are worthy of mention because they assess specific abilities in preschoolers and because they are in wide use. The
Peabody Picture Vocabulary Test—Revised (PPVT-R) is a measure
of receptive language skills (how well a child understands language
concepts) and is sometimes used as a screening test for intelligence.
The Beery Visual Motor Integration Test is also a screening test, but
measures eye–hand coordination and fine motor development through
drawings. The Leiter International Performance Scale is a nonverbal
test of concept formation that can be very helpful for children who
have a hearing loss, speak a different language, or have delayed language development for any reason. If one's main source of information about the child's development is the parent, then the Vineland
Adaptive Behavior Scales can be used to estimate developmental level.

In order to help evaluators of preschool children suspected of having been sexually abused to make a rough assessment of the child's developmental level, a guide has been prepared; it is shown in Figure 2-1. It may be used to decide whether or not a child needs to be referred for further developmental assessment, and includes items from the Denver Developmental Screening Test, the Gesell Scales, and the Stanford–Binet Scale of Intelligence. The materials needed to make this rough screening are a set of 10 one-inch square blocks, paper and pencil or crayon, a doll of some sort, and two sets of colored circles or squares cut out of construction paper (red, yellow, blue, and green).

If the child is consistently behind the age levels indicated on the guide in most or all of the areas, then further evaluation is needed. If the child shows a mild delay in one or two of the areas, then the child should probably just be watched, since there are wide variations in the age at which children attain various developmental milestones; the ages listed on the guide represent average ages of achievement for the various tasks. If there is a significant delay in one area (e.g., language), then the child should probably be referred to a specialist in that area for in-depth evaluation.

The blocks and drawings cover the area of fine motor development and eye–hand coordination; the language items deal with both understanding of language and spoken language; and the body parts and colors involve cognitive development and concept formation, as well as some language skills. It should be stressed that the guide in Figure 2-1 is only a rough screening device, and that any potential abnormalities need to be checked out by a trained specialist before any conclusions are reached.

DEVELOPMENTAL ASPECTS OF SEXUALITY IN THE PRESCHOOL CHILD

The development of sexuality has received very little attention in research and literature, perhaps because, until recently, the myth that children were basically asexual prior to adolescence prevailed. Two different aspects of sexual development are discussed in this section. First, data about preschoolers' interest in and knowledge of sexuality are talked about, and then theory relating to developmental trends in sexuality is touched upon.

FIGURE 2-1. *Developmental screening guide.*

Age	Blocks	Body parts	Language	Drawing	Colors	Social and self
1½	Builds two-cube tower	Points to three body parts on doll or self	Knows 10 words	Scribbles		Uses words to make wants known
2	Builds six-cube tower	Identifies four or more body parts	Uses three-word sentences; pronouns (I, me, you)	Imitates vertical and circular strokes		Refers to self by name; imitates domestic tasks
2½	Builds nine-cube tower	Identifies six body parts		Imitates vertical and horizontal strokes	Matches one color	Parallel play with other children; identifies self in mirror
3	Builds ten-cube tower; imitates bridge of cubes 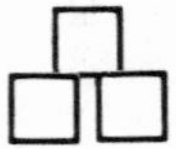		Uses plurals; understands two prepositions[a]; answers one comprehension question[b]	Copies circle; imitates cross	Sorts four colors to match sample; matches four or more colors	Knows own sex ("Are you a boy or a girl?")
3½	Builds three-cube bridge from model alone		Answers two comprehension questions; understands three prepositions			Cooperative play with other children

Age					
4	Imitates five-cube structure	Understands four prepositions[a]	Copies cross; draws person with two parts	Names three or more colors	Plays assigned or chosen role; dresses and undresses with supervision
4½	Builds five-cube structure from model alone	Knows two of three composition questions[c]	Copies square		Bosses and criticizes
5	Builds three steps		Copies triangle; draws human with body		Counts fingers correctly and knows number; asks meaning of words
6			Copies diamond; draws person with neck, hands, clothes, two-dimensional legs		Knows left and right

[a] Prepositions: on, in, under, behind, in front of ("Put the block on the table, in front of the chair," etc.)
[b] Comprehension questions: "What do you do when you are cold? hungry? tired?"
[c] Composition questions: "What is a house made out of? window? book?"

Our scant information on development of childhood sexuality comes from three sources. There have been a few studies involving interviews with children of different ages. A second source involves retrospective accounts by adults of when they first experienced certain sexual activities or experiences. (Of course, these surveys suffer from the distortion of retrospection, and this is particularly of concern when examining information from as far back as the preschool years.) The third source involves observations of children by parents or teachers.

One excellent study of children's sexual knowledge was carried out by Anne Bernstein (1976). She asked 60 boys and girls at three age levels, "How do people get babies?", and then analyzed their responses to yield six levels of maturity that showed a consistent sequence of development. Level I children, mostly 3- and 4-year-olds, answered in terms of geography; they believed that babies have always existed, and you simply need to know where they have been before they come out. Some answers these children gave included "You go to a baby store and buy one," "From tummies," and "From God's place."

At Level II, children believed that babies are manufactured as if they were refrigerators or cars. They knew that babies have not always existed, but believed they must be built. One 4-year-old at this level, according to Bernstein, when asked how babies start to be in mommies' tummies, replied: "Maybe from people. They just put them in an envelope and fold them up and the mommy puts them in her 'gina and they just stay in there." A few children at level II were reported to connect a father with the birth process, but they saw his role as part of the mechanical process.

At Level III, with children from about 4 to 8 years of age, there was a state of transition; procreation was seen as a mixture of physiology and technology. These children may have known that three things are necessary for making babies (social relationships such as love and marriage; sexual intercourse; and the union of sperm and egg), but their ability to combine these factors into a coherent whole was limited. By the age of 8 or so, Level IV was reached, where explanations in terms of concrete physiology were given. Levels V and VI in Bernstein's study were more sophisticated, but are not discussed in detail here, since they do not apply to preschoolers.

Based on play interviews with 4- and 5-year-olds, Cohen and Parker (1977) found that almost all knew the general facts of intrauterine growth of babies and childbirth. However, over half of the children felt that the baby had always been inside of the mother (Bernstein's Level I). While almost none had knowledge of sexual intercourse, 90% felt that the father had some role; most often this was brought up in terms of his babysitting, changing diapers, or providing transportation.

In another sort of investigation, Janus and Bess (1981) analyzed the drawings and essays of 3200 children aged 5 to 12. They found that 97% of both boys and girls in kindergarten and first grade had a sense of their maleness or femaleness (sexual identity), while 74–78% had developed the accompanying sex-role identification (gender identity). At this age, only 15% of the boys and 24% of the girls mentioned sexual activities, including kissing and holding hands as well as more overtly sexual material. This figure rose to about 55% for the sixth-graders in the sample.

Victor (1980) reported on a study of 3- to 6-year-old nonabused children where only 14% of the girls could offer any word for the female genitals, while over 50% of the boys could give a name for their genitals. More girls had a word for penis than for their own genitals.

Probably the most famous retrospective account of development of sexuality comes from Kinsey's large-scale work of several decades ago (e.g., Kinsey, Pomeroy, & Martin, 1948; Kinsey, Pomeroy, Martin, & Gebhard, 1953). The males in his sample reported that by age 12, 20% had masturbated, 30% had been involved in homosexual play, 40% had experienced heterosexual play (including exhibition and looking, as well as touching), and about 15% had attempted intercourse with a girl. Among female respondents, about 15% reported masturbating, about 20% had had homosexual experiences, and 30% reported heterosexual experience (including looking and exhibition).

In an analysis of unpublished Kinsey data and a small current college sample, Gebhard (1977) looked at acquisition of basic sex information. He found that less than 1% of both samples reported knowledge of intercourse under the age of 5 years, and only about 2% reported they knew about it under 7 years of age. While only about 2% of respondents in Kinsey's sample knew about pregnancy under the age of 5, in the more recent sample, 10% of males and

25% of females reported knowing about pregnancy before they were 6 years old.

In a study of women hospitalized for mental problems and a healthy control group, Landis (1963) did not find many significant differences in early sexual experiences or interest between the groups. Between 10% and 15% of the women reported curiosity about sex before age 6; this was usually stimulated by the birth of babies in their own families or in friends' families. Curiosity about the origin of babies usually came before interest in the physical differences between boys and girls. If the women had had brothers or boy playmates, they tended to have early knowledge of sex differences, but this area did not arouse interest in the way that where new babies came from did.

Sketchy information from nursery schools is available from Norway and from the United States. Sixty Norwegian preschool teachers were interviewed about sexual behavior in children (Gundersen, Melas, & Skar, 1981). The majority felt that sex-role behavior was clearly established by age 3. Fifty percent reported that sexual words were used "occasionally," while the other 50% felt they were used "often" or "very often." Most teachers thought that the children did not really understand the words if they were under 4 years of age. Boys used the words more frequently, but both sexes used the same words.

The children did not ask many sexual questions of the teachers, and those questions that were asked tended to center around pregnancy and birth. All the teachers observed some family role playing, and 50% of them said that this play contained some direct sexual behavior, such as exploring bodies and genitals. Almost all the respondents said that the children showed marked interest in their own genitals, indicated by fondling and showing them to others. Both boys and girls showed more interest in male genitalia. Masturbation was observed "seldom" or "now and then" by 76% of the participants in the study, while 24% felt masturbation occurred "often" or "very often" among preschoolers.

In an investigation in the United States based on observations in nursery schools and Head Start centers, Broderick (1969) concluded that many preschool children show interest in sex differences, both physical and behavioral. They also are interested in where babies come from, especially if a new baby is part of their experience. He felt that preschoolers are rarely concerned with questions of sexual intercourse or conception, unless these are raised by older children or adults.

From the information presented above, skimpy though it may be, it is clear that certain issues regarding sex crop up naturally during the course of development in the preschool years. It will be helpful for the evaluators of children suspected of being sexually abused to keep these in mind, in order to assess other areas of sexual interest such children may exhibit against a background of common sexual issues. For example, from the information presented above, it appears that where babies come from is probably the most common area of sexuality that preschoolers wonder about. Some are mildly interested in physical differences between boys and girls, and most become very aware of sex-role differences by the end of the preschool years. Occasional masturbation is quite frequent. In contrast, concern about sexual intercourse or other forms of adult sexual behavior appears to be very rare in children who have not been involved in or exposed to such behaviors.

THEORY RELATING TO DEVELOPMENTAL TRENDS IN SEXUALITY

Since Freud's theory of psychosexual development is the only psychological theory dealing with development of sexuality, aspects of the theory that are relevant to the preschool years are mentioned briefly here. According to his psychosexual theory, children from approximately ages 2 to 4 are in the anal stage, where they struggle for bowel and bladder control. In fact, control in general is the issue during this stage, with the children working to develop a sense of self and to exert control over aspects of their environment.

Between ages 4 and 6, the children enter the phallic stage, during which they become increasingly aware of their genitals and of the differences between boys and girls (Leaman & Knasel, 1980). Masturbation and playing "doctor" or other exploratory games with friends and siblings may be seen during this period. According to Freud, as children develop a clear sense of sex roles in this age range, they deal with their sexual feelings toward their parents through the Oedipal conflict in boys and the Electra conflict in girls. A child develops a romantic attachment to the parent of the opposite sex and is disappointed when the parent does not respond to his or her overtures. The child then identifies with the parent of the same sex in order to become more attractive to the desired parent. Children in this stage may show versions of adult behavior, such as strutting and teasing in little boys and coy or flirtatious behavior in little girls. The identification with their same-sex parents helps children strengthen their own sexual image (Leaman & Knasel, 1980). After the preschool years, the latency period was postulated by Freud to occur between ages 6 and 12. Interest in sexuality is less overt during this period, with a decrease in sex play, but dirty words and jokes hold considerable appeal.

If Freud was right about the stages of psychosexual development, it can be seen that the behavior of preschoolers in the phallic stage of development may raise issues that relate to possible sexual abuse. For one thing, it is natural during this time (approximately ages 4 to 6) for a child to flirt with the parent of the opposite sex, express feelings of wanting to marry that parent, and perhaps even work to leave the same-sex parent out of activities in which the child and the opposite-sex parent participate. If a parent is very needy and has trouble with boundaries in the family, he or she could easily misinterpret the child's Oedipal/Electra behavior as sexual attraction and might act on this misinterpretation in a way that leads to sexual exploitation of the child. A second thing to keep in mind when evaluating a preschool child is that some flirtatious behavior may be normal during this stage; however, it is generally reserved for the familiar opposite-sex parent, and if the behavior is indiscriminate, the possibility of sexual abuse must be considered.

DEVELOPMENTAL ISSUES IN INTERVIEWING

While the details of successful interviewing of preschool children suspected of having been sexually abused are discussed in the following chapters, certain aspects of interviewing that relate to developmental considerations are mentioned in this chapter as well. Developmental issues relevant to giving court testimony are also highlighted. The most obvious point is that the interview material must be pitched to a level that is comfortable and understandable to the particular preschool child. There are two major implications of this:

1. The main medium through which information can be obtained is play; during the preschool years, play is the work of the child, through which he or she masters the environment.

2. Suspected sexual abuse must be viewed through the filter of the child and examined from the child's point of view. The game that Daddy played with Sammy may not be viewed as either sexual or abusive by Sammy, who may only be able to say that he does not like that game at all.

Some characteristics of preschool children's thinking and abilities are discussed below; the discussion is based partially on information compiled by Shawn Conerly of the Orange County Child Abuse Registry. First, such children's thinking is very concrete. Only toward the end of the preschool period do the children begin to understand concepts such as "animal," "fruit," and "family" as including several objects or people within the concept. Their ability to think abstractly is very minimal, and irony, metaphor, and analogy are concepts far beyond their grasp. Some preschoolers are even concrete in terms of feelings; when asked "How do you feel now?", some will answer "hot" or "thirsty."

It is important to be very careful not to assume that a child understands concepts presented. This must be checked out thoroughly, as some children will agree with the examiner without really understanding, while others will use their verbal skills in such a way that they seem on the surface to understand when, in reality, they have no understanding at all.

In addition, children between about 3 and 5 years of age have a tendency to answer "yes" to most questions, striving to please the adult involved. For example, a child may answer "yes" to the lawyer's question, "Do you like to make up stories like this one?", in order to gain the approval of a frightening authority figure. Similarly, the child may answer affirmatively when asked whether the sexual abuse happened last week, when in actuality it happened last month. While such "yes–no" questions are necessary to begin exploring an area, it is important to get further elaboration or to ask the question in several different ways to assess the child's level of understanding.

Second, preschoolers do not logically organize their thinking or speech. Instead, they say whatever enters their mind at the moment, without much censoring or prethought. Therefore, their narratives and descriptions tend to be disjointed and rambling; the examiner must sort out relevant information from irrelevant data, because it is beyond the children's cognitive capacities to do this alone. A child giving court testimony must be prepared carefully, as such developmentally appropriate rambling may cause the truth of the child's statements to be questioned. For instance, rather than asking the child, "Tell me what happened last Christmas," which may elicit a list of gifts gotten, food eaten, and stomach aches experienced, it would be more effective to say, "Do you remember when Grandpa came to visit you last Christmas? Tell me what Grandpa did at bedtime." While such a question may be considered leading in legal circles, it is necessary to phrase queries in similar ways when dealing with children at a preschool developmental level.

As a consequence of preschool children's concreteness and illogical thinking, they do not have the ability to keep two concepts in mind at the same time, and cannot easily look at two concepts at once. Additionally, cause and effect are understood at only a primitive level. For example, Johnny may know that telling Mother that his sister hit him will make her mad, but may not have any conception that telling Mother that someone touched his pee-pee will cause great upset (unless, of course, the child has been threatened by the perpetrator about the negative consequences of telling). In other words, the child learns only from direct personal experience and can make few inferences or generalizations to other situations.

Third, a preschool child's understanding of space, distance, and time is nonlogical and nonlinear. The preschooler's memory will not work chronologically, and he or she has not yet learned units of measurement and their meaning. Therefore, the child cannot recall information sequentially. When an examiner is asking about significant events related to possible abuse, the questions must be phrased in a way to help the child organize thinking according to developmentally appropriate landmarks, rather than to adult standards. Most preschoolers would be at a loss to answer a doctor or lawyer who asks, "When did this occur?" To help place the time of an incident, reference points such as birthdays, holidays, summer, night or day, lunchtime, bedtime, and the like need to be used; a more appropriate question might be, "Did it happen when it was hot outside, or during the winter, when it was cold?" If asked in court what date the incident occurred on, no preschooler will be able to answer to the satisfaction of the judge without such landmarks.

Similarly, asking where the incident occurred can be easier for the child to grasp if the question is phrased in terms of whether it occurred in a house or outside, at whose house, and so forth. Children can memorize some strings of information, but will not necessarily comprehend what has been memorized. Therefore, questions about something memorized but not experienced will result in stereotyped, noninformative answers.

Fourth, issues of truth versus lying are complex in the preschool years. Children in this age group may tell lies under two circumstances: in order to avoid a problem or punishment (e.g., "Susie was the one who did it, not me") and in order to impress adults or get attention (e.g., telling tall tales, such as that there was a hippopotamus in the back yard last night). However, children cannot manufacture stories based on information that they have not learned or experienced. For example, children will not make up a story about the comings and goings of Eskimos if they have never been exposed to any learning about Eskimos, and will not say someone attempted oral copulation with them if they have not had either direct or vicarious experience with that act.

Preschoolers see issues as black and white, since they think very concretely. Therefore, they think parents and other adults are all-powerful and all-knowing. They feel that adults do not lie, and would be able to tell easily if a child were lying. Despite their occasional tendency to tell untrue stories, children in the preschool years do know the difference between fact and fantasy, between the truth and a lie. While they may stand by a lie, further gentle probing will reveal their understanding of what is true and what is false. A complicating factor is that some young children's memories of events may become distorted over time by dreams and fantasies; in their attempts to work out the trauma, their memory of the facts may change, or different aspects may become more salient.

Fifth, preschool children are egocentric in their perceptions of the world and in their reactions to it. They think the world revolves around them, and they relate all that happens to personal issues. Similarly, these children do not think of what effect their actions will have on others, nor do they worry about what others think. As a result, a child may be emotionally spontaneous in ways that are occasionally very disconcerting to adults. For example, if a preschooler is asked in court to look at the judge, who happens to be obese, the child may very un-self-consciously and without any malice say, "Oh, that big fat man in the dress?"

Sixth, a preschool child's attention span is limited. Long interviews are often not possible, for the child simply cannot concentrate or sit in one place for long periods of time. The interviewer must be flexible—conducting several short sessions over a period of time if necessary, or allowing the child frequent breaks to play nonthreatening games or to go see his or her parents in the waiting room. Anxiety is often expressed through fidgeting, distractibility, and running around; interviewers need to keep this in mind and to view such behavior as a necessary defense rather than as "bad."

It is also important to educate court personnel about these characteristics of preschoolers if court testimony is required (Berliner, Canfield-Blick, & Bulkley, 1983). Long waiting periods, continuances after a child is prepared to talk, and long sessions of cross-examination are unproductive and potentially abusive to the child. Testimony of young children should always be scheduled in the morning, when they are most alert and when it does not conflict with their usual naptime. Therapists and attorneys should be willing to ask the child frequently if a break is needed, or to provide one if the child's behavior or affect indicates that a break is overdue.

Seventh, and most relevant to toddlers and early preschoolers, a child's ability and comfort with strangers must be taken into account. Many developmentally normal 2- and 3-year-olds will not separate comfortably from their parents, and the interviewer must work slowly and sensitively to help the child separate gradually, if possible. Meeting a child in the waiting room and immediately suggesting that the child alone come to the interviewer's office will almost certainly elicit tears and reluctance in a young preschool-age child. If the child will not separate comfortably, the interview may have to begin with the parent present, with the goal of seeing the child alone later when he or she is more familiar with the examiner, or of interviewing the child alone in a separate session at a later date. This is also of concern when children must talk to strangers in the court situation; helping them become familiar ahead of time with the cast of characters involved can be invaluable.

SUMMARY

In summary, considering developmental aspects of preschoolers' thinking and experiencing is necessary when evaluating young children or when working with them in a court situation. For purposes of evaluation for suspected sexual abuse, three facets of preschool development have been highlighted as significant factors. First, the child's developmental level must be roughly assessed. Second, the interviewer must have a sense of normal and deviant sexual development and interest patterns for this age group, against which to compare a specific child's sexual knowledge, activity, and interaction style. Third, the evaluator must take into account the unique thinking patterns of preschool children and develop an interviewing style compatible with a particular child's needs and developmental level.

ASSESSMENT OF SUSPECTED CHILD SEXUAL ABUSE

Shawn Conerly

INTRODUCTION

Conducting evaluations of young children suspected of being sexually abused is a task that requires special people with special skills. It requires, among other things, imagination; a willingness and ability to be childlike and un-self-conscious; knowledge of the dynamics of child sexual abuse; and an extraordinary amount of patience. No one should be required to conduct such evaluations as part of a larger job requirement if he or she is uncomfortable with the subject matter, unable to try unconventional approaches to communicating, or uneasy with young children. The task of diagnosing sexual abuse is difficult enough without such hurdles to overcome; with them, it becomes exceptionally difficult for evaluators and unfair to children.

This chapter describes a number of techniques and approaches that may be unorthodox, in the sense that they are rarely taught in the professional training programs that traditionally prepare clinicians and law enforcement personnel for their future careers. However, these approaches increasingly are being utilized and advocated by those who work with young abused or traumatized children. They represent an effort to reach children on their own level—to give children both permission and the opportunity to communicate with the adult world in their own verbal and nonverbal languages, rather than demanding that they try to translate their feelings and experiences into ours.

There is a growing awareness of the problem of sexual abuse

among young children, and reports of cases in the preschool-age group are increasing dramatically all over the country. As a consequence, awareness of the difficulty of evaluating, substantiating, and prosecuting these cases has also increased. Many professionals who have been quickly recruited into conducting assessments of suspected preschool-age victims soon learn that they lack the background and perspective necessary to communicate successfully with this special population of youngsters. The number of reports for this age group requiring investigation is not likely to decrease dramatically in the near future. The need is to increase the pool of professionals in every community who can develop the skills and experience necessary to promote competent evaluation of these very young children. It is hoped that this chapter will contribute to that process.

INFORMATION GATHERING PRIOR TO EVALUATION OF THE CHILD

It is very important for the evaluator to gather as much information as possible about the child, the family, and the background leading to the suspicion of sexual abuse. This information serves as a baseline against which to interview and assess the responses of the child. It is very unlikely that a child will make a spontaneous declaration about sexual abuse, and the evaluator can use the information obtained prior to the interview process to help the child communicate.

In an ideal setting, the evaluator would be able to interview all of the family, the babysitter, the preschool teacher, and any others who might have knowledge of the child and the family. This is not the usual situation. Sometimes the child must be interviewed before the parents are contacted. Sometimes the parents are not available, and the evaluator must fill in with what information is available from other sources. The parents and the child should be interviewed separately, and the evaluator should never confront the parent if the child is present or within hearing distance.

In each interview with each significant member of the child's family group, the evaluator should obtain the following:

1. A personal history, including psychosexual development.
2. A family history.

3. History of the child's development.
4. A list of all persons having access to the child.
5. A list of what the child calls each member of the family group, including pets.
6. A list of what the child calls the genitals and elimination functions.
7. Basic idea of the child's daily routine.
8. Observations of usual and unusual behavior.

This may seem like a huge amount of material, but it can be obtained quite rapidly with experience. The parents should also be asked about their marital history, custody, visitation, and what limits they set on their own sexual behavior in the presence of the child.

If possible, others with information about the situation should be contacted in a low-keyed manner, in order to learn as much as possible about the child. The evaluator should compile and become familiar with a list of people having access to the child; it is helpful to learn the names by which the child calls each of these people, and to get some brief idea of what each looks like. Several times this type of information has allowed an evaluator to identify the abuser indirectly from drawings and remarks a child has made. It is useful for the evaluator to have the impressions of those people who may have witnessed the child's unusual behavior, such as genital grabbing, masturbation, or posturing.

TOOLS FOR EVALUATION

Evaluation of the preschool child requires different tools and skills from those used with older children and adolescents. The evaluator needs to be comfortable playing with children. This sounds simple, but often professionals feel that it is not "appropriate" to get down on the floor and romp with a 3-year-old. They would rather talk to the 3-year-old because they are more comfortable talking then playing, but usually a 3-year-old would rather play than try to understand what the adult wants to talk about. Often, 3-year-olds will talk after they have had a chance to play with an adult who likes to play. It is also important to realize that the need for activity is very normal for this age group and really necessary if a child is feeling anxiety or tension. Enjoying oneself while playing with a young child is a good way to demonstrate acceptance of the child. It is critical that the evaluator do whatever is necessary to reach the child on the child's level. If the child is sitting on the floor, the interviewer must sit on the floor with the child. If the child wants to talk while sitting under the table, the interviewer should eagerly come to the child and sit under the table. Evaluating young children is a difficult job, and the best tool the evaluator has is himself or herself. The willingness to be "childlike" and to really enjoy doing "childish" things in less than optimal situations is necessary in order to work with very young children effectively.

DOLLS

The most common tools used in these cases are dolls and doll families. Under ideal conditions, the evaluator would have a large assortment of dolls and toys in a room especially designed for interviewing little children. In reality, an evaluator usually carries all of the dolls and other materials used in interviewing young children with him or her. This does limit the number of dolls, but it is still important for the child to have a selection of types and sizes to choose from. Dolls that have been successfully used vary from dollhouse-size families to large soft-body rag dolls that are almost child-sized. Children really do have preferences, and they relate better to some dolls than to others.

If possible, the evaluator should have a set of anatomically correct dolls. Observing a child play with dolls with correct genitalia is a good way to observe the child's reaction to sexual material and the child's knowledge and level of sophistication about sexual behaviors. It is not unusual for an anxious child to throw a doll across the room upon discovering that the doll has a penis. Often this same child will return to the same doll that was thrown later on in the interview period or at another session. Sometimes the child takes a peek to ascertain that the doll really does have a penis. Sometimes the child won't say a word but will go to the doll and be physically abusive with the part of the doll's anatomy that is offensive or has caused the child pain.

Dolls are also useful as "action agents in play therapy" (Oaklander, 1978). Given enough time, a child may actually act out a situation with the dolls that he or she could never describe to the interviewer. The evaluator must pay a great deal of attention to the child's play—

in Oaklander's (1978) words, "watching the body postures, gestures, expressions and breathing" of the child and "determining patterns in the process that I see unfolding before my eyes." While the child plays with the dolls, the evaluator can say, "Show me what happens next," instead of "Tell me." "Show me" is one very possible way to get around the threats of violence or prohibitions children experience in regard to not ever telling the secret. When the evaluator is not clear about what the child is trying to communicate, the dolls can make it possible for the child to demonstrate positions or types of contact that the child does not have words to describe. A child may demonstrate sexual behavior, such as oral–genital contact, suddenly without any preliminaries. If the evaluator asks the child about what the dolls are doing, the child may reply, "They're playing the wiener game," which is the opening the evaluator has been waiting for. Small doll families can be used to obtain a child's version of his or her daily routine. Learning that "Uncle Charlie always makes us girls take a bath when he babysits for us" may be important.

Anatomical dolls are useful, but some children do not like hardbody dolls, and the soft-body types may not have all the openings necessary for children to demonstrate genital, anal, and oral contacts with adults. A small set of baby twins has been very useful in learning from children about their perceptions of the differences between boys and girls. The baby twins are a natural approach to this area, since even little children know about changing diapers. Another type of doll that has been very helpful is a "Sascha" doll. This little girl doll has very long, lifelike hair. Children like to brush the doll's hair; the act of brushing the doll's hair seems to have a smoothing effect on them, and they seem more willing to talk while engaged in this manner.

ART MATERIALS AND DRAWING PICTURES

Art materials are very useful, but once again possibilities for their use are somewhat limited because they must be carried around by the evaluator and sometimes used in places where spilled paint might be disaster. Some things that are easy to carry around include the following:

1. Paper and multicolored felt-tip pens
2. Wide markers and lined paper
3. Brown paper bags

4. Yarn
5. Scissors
6. Tape and paper clips

Clay is very useful in working with young children, but it is difficult to carry and it tends to stick where it is not wanted.

Asking a child to draw a picture of his or her family is a good beginning activity. Some children are hesitant to begin, but can be encouraged to "make a present" for Mom or another person. A very young child can make a scribble, and the evaluator may use that drawing to talk about the family. Some interviewers draw along with children to reduce the anxiety level, but for some children this is too distracting. By encouraging the child to talk about the drawing, the interviewer can gain much valuable information about the child and the family.

Another technique is to ask the child to draw a picture and then dictate a story to the evaluator. A child who gets caught up in an art-related activity is not too anxious, and can often begin to talk more freely to the interviewer.

Paper dolls, felt boards, paper to cut and paste with scissors and tape, and other art materials serve dual purposes. They help the child and the evaluator begin to establish some kind of a relationship, and they also produce materials that are helpful in evaluating the child's developmental level.

PUPPETS

Brown paper bags used for lunches can be decorated by the child to represent the members of the family. The bag puppets can then be used to talk about what is happening in the home. Other types of puppets are useful, and boys in particular like animal puppets who can talk for them. Fingers and thumbs can also become puppets who speak for the child, saying the things which the child is not supposed to tell anyone.

THE BAG PERSON

An easy way to carry all the material around is in a large, colorful bag. If the evaluator puts the dolls, puppets, and art materials into a bag, along with a small blanket and a few other toys, the evaluator is

able, upon sensing the child's boredom or frustration, to pull something new out of the bag. This involves the child in the process, and
provides naturally occurring pauses for time outs. An evaluator may
find it useful and comfortable to become the "Bag Lady" or the "Bag
Man" when working with young children.

THE INTERVIEW PLAN

Once information and materials have been gathered, it is often helpful
to make an interview plan before making contact with the child. A
plan helps the interviewer make sure that all the areas are covered
during the time available. The plan should be thought of as a series
of modules that can be used in the order in which the child seems
most interested or as they fit into the flow of the interview.

The plan is always modified by the circumstances under which
the child must be evaluated. Under ideal conditions, the plan might
be to interview the child in three sessions of 1 hour each to allow
adequate time to develop rapport with the child. However, other
situations call for other plans. The assessment of the child cannot be
squeezed into less than 2 hours, and it would benefit everyone involved to have 6 hours. Usually the interview must be done in a limited
time period. Children and the adults who interview them are unique
individuals. There can be no exact formula, but the interview plan
provides a structure to work from.

There are three distinct phases in the interview process with the
child who may have been sexually abused: initial contact, getting information, and closure. Within each of the phases there are a number
of things that may be tried, and issues that may need to be dealt with
by the evaluator. Awareness of the phases should help the interviewer
plan what techniques will be most useful.

PHASE I: INITIAL CONTACT

Children who have been sexually exploited by adults are often reluctant to talk to strangers. They may have been told not to talk to anyone
except the family, and they generally appear very shy. This needs to
be taken into consideration when deciding which contact approach is
best for a particular child.

The "Bag Lady" or "Bag Man"

In the "Bag Person" approach, mentioned above, the evaluator approaches the child with a large colorful bag and a smile and introduces himself or herself, taking care to address the child by name and making sure to give the child a business card. The evaluator will explain what the card says. For example, "I'm Joan Smith, and I'm a Child Protective Service Worker. Do you know what 'protection' means? Someone called me because they thought you might need protection!" The child is invited to "play" and examine the contents of the bag.

"In the Corner"

If the evaluator has learned that a child is very reluctant to talk to anyone or has demonstrated withdrawal behavior, such as running away from strangers, a more indirect approach, such as "In the Corner," may be needed.

The evaluator, with the bag in hand, enters the room where the child is waiting and walks to the corner most distant from the child. The evaluator may say "Hi" to the child in passing, but does not look directly at the child. The evaluator sits down (at the same level as the child) and takes a toy or object from the bag. The evaluator begins to play with the toy without paying any particular attention to the child. After a short while the child will make some moves toward the evaluator. It is important that the interviewer remain friendly, but detached; he or she should let the child make the moves and should not react greatly to tentative approaches by the child. The child may be invited to choose something from the bag to play with, if he or she seems interested. Usually there is a period of parallel play, after which the child is ready for more contact. This is a good point to ask the child to draw or play a game. Gradually, the evaluator can attempt conversation, saying "My name is Candy" and asking simple questions such as "Are you a boy or a girl?" Any response from the child should be positively reinforced. It is important for the interviewer to risk being "silly" and "playful" when the child begins to respond.

Creative Contact

If many unsuccessful attempts have been made to elicit information from a child by several adults, the evaluator may have to take a novel or creative approach from the first time contact is attempted. Some approaches that have been successfully used in this situation are the following.

The Crawl-In.   The evaluator crawls into the room on all fours and if possible, sits under a piece of furniture, such as a table. By this maneuver, the evaluator usually gets the child's attention. Often contact can begin rapidly in a nonverbal manner. Waving, making faces, and pantomime are good ways of beginning; mirroring the child's gestures, with the interjection of lots of smiles and giggles on the part of the evaluator, can be an opening to game playing and interaction. Verbal overtures by the child can be responded to in kind. The evaluator should proceed very carefully to establish contact at a verbal level.

Mask or Costume.   The evaluator can enter while wearing a funny hat, mask, or cape, and then offer the child a mask, hat, or cape to wear. This provides a nonverbal invitation to play a pretend game.

Reaching the Very Reluctant Child

If one approach does not appear to be working, the evaluator should try something else. If that does not work, he or she should stop trying, sit very quietly for some time, and then say, "Julie, I would really like to be your friend and play with you!" If the child does not respond, the evaluator can say, "It seems like you don't feel like playing now, so I'm leaving for a little while, but I'll come back to see if you want to play later." The evaluator can leave for 5 to 10 minutes, and can then ask the child to play again. If the child wants to play, he or she should be encouraged to choose something from the bag. If the child still does not respond, the evaluator should say good-bye and leave.

Some children have a need to test adults. They want to know that a person is genuinely interested in them before they talk to him or her. One of the ways in which young children who have been sexually molested test adults is by seeing whether an adult is willing to make more than one attempt to reach them. Sometimes setting up several interviews with a child is enough to demonstrate caring. Remember, many of these children have been repeatedly disappointed by adults. Just because a child does not talk about something does not mean that it did not happen, and that the child was not hurt.

One very frustrating experience everyone encounters from time to time is the child who can't be reached. it is very easy to be hard on oneself for failing to reach children who need to tell about sexual abuse. But this happens, and it is no one's failure. Sometimes children are just not ready to talk, and nothing the evaluator does can change that. Some children are in such pain that only with long-term therapy do they begin to tell.

One case like this was very difficult for an experienced evaluator. Two little girls were interviewed shortly after being placed in a foster family because of physical abuse by their mother and stepfather. They were 4 and 6 years of age. Shortly after they were placed, the older girl made several attempts to grab the penis of the foster father She also tried to get into the bathroom every time he was in there. There had been no previous indications of sexual molestation. A child protective service worker interviewed both of the children. After several sessions, the older child was able to demonstrate with dolls, and later to talk about, the oral copulation she had been forced to perform with her stepfather. The younger child refused to talk and withdrew from all attempts to reach her. The caseworker had treatment ordered for the children. After 1 year, the younger child began to have night terrors—she told the therapist that the "slide" hurt her and she was afraid of the "slide hurting her again." The caseworker was called to interview the child with the therapist. The little girl was finally able to demonstrate with drawings and the anatomical dolls how her stepfather had molested her. He had her "slide" down his body while he "pinched her pookie." She told the caseworker about some "pictures"; these were eventually found, and the stepfather was prosecuted.

PHASE II: GETTING INFORMATION

As soon as contact is established, the evaluator begins to gather information about many things, including the child's development level, verbal skills, gestures, and breathing. As the evaluator is able to engage the child in simple games, it is possible to assess the child's development. Asking a child to identify the color of the marking pens should be a fun game. Correct responses should be reinforced in a playful manner. The evaluator can ask the child to count the pens, and finally to use the pens to draw simple shapes, such as a circle, square, and triangle. It is then an easy transition to have the child use the pens to draw a picture of his or her family. It is important to remember what information has been gathered from others about the child's daily routine, and to note areas where the child is unable to give answers. There are often simple explanations for discrepancies, but they need to be noted and checked. Two areas that seem to be highly associated with molestation are bedtime and bathtime. Other areas are dressing and playing.

"Who Gives You a Bath?"

Having the child act out the bathtime routine can provide useful information and good opportunities to ask questions. The interviewer needs to ask questions like these:

- Who starts the bath?
- Who undresses the child?
- Who is in the bathroom?
- Do the people in the bathroom have their clothes on?
- Where are the places that get washed?

Some children get quite involved in acting out this bath play. They will say, "wash your face, Jennifer, it is still dirty!", often imitating their caretaker's tone and gestures. One $3\frac{1}{2}$-year-old recently told an interviewer while playing the role of the father, with the anatomically correct dolls, "Now we have to wash your winkie!" Then the father said very sternly, "Open up! We have to get winkie clean!" The child spread the doll's legs apart and put her index finger in the opening. "Now the wash cloth," she said. She grabbed the dolly wash cloth and began to rub the doll's genital area in front of her still-inserted finger in a rhythmic manner. The interviewer asked the child in a very matter-of-fact way, "Who washes your winkie?"

"Daddy!"

"Does your daddy use the wash cloth and his finger to wash your winkie?"

"Yes,"

"Where does your daddy wash you?"

(*Giggle.*) "Everywhere."

"In your house?"

"No, when I visit him."

This same little girl told the interviewer that Daddy washed her winkie so that he could kiss it goodnight, stating, "Mommies don't do that." The child added that she had accepted her father's explanation for his behavior without question. She did not realize that his behavior was not the same as that of all daddies.

Bedtime Is Another Story

Bedtime is another high-risk time for children. The evaluator needs to ask the child such questions as these:

- What do you wear to bed?
- Who kisses you goodnight?
- Where is the kiss placed?
- Does someone come into your room

One 5-year-old girl was fondled every time she spent the night at her grandparents' house. Grandfather would come into the bedroom a few minutes after Grandmother had tucked her in for the night. He would kiss her on the mouth, push her nightgown up, and "check to see if she had to go potty." This went on for a long time because it was so much a part of the routine that the child did not realize anything was wrong. The child asked the interviewer whether "grandfathers checked to see if little boys had to go potty in bed." The interviewer was able to pick up this clue and learn what happened when the child stayed with Grandfather.

If the evaluator notes hesitations or inconsistencies in connection with bedtime or bathtime, it is useful to go to a different medium (such as puppets) to talk out or act out what happens to the child at these times. Small dolls can be used to act out the family activities at these times. Sometimes just the topic of bathtime or bedtime makes children anxious; if a time-out activity and changing the medium do not help, the evaluator should try having the child brush a doll's hair or some other activity to relax the child. One technique that is sometimes effective is for the evaluator to say "Shush!" Don't tell me what happens, show me what happens." If the evaluator has narrowed down the molestation to a certain person and time, then reviewing the access list with the child may add useful information. The evaluator may prompt the child by stating, "Uncle Larry washes you at bathtime." This is sometimes enough to trigger a statement from the child. Such a response is at least partially due to the child's perception that if the evaluator has some information about Uncle Larry, he or she must know all about the things Uncle Larry does at bathtime.

The Secret Game

When the evaluator feels that a child is relating well, the time may be right to introduce the "secret game." This should not be tried to early in the informational phase, because it can misfire and cause the child to withdraw. Most children like to whisper, and they usually have an idea about what a secret is.

One 4-year-old wanted to play the secret game but would only play if she could sit on the evaluator's lap. The evaluator began by whispering, "I like jelly beans best of all." The child whispered back to the evaluator, "I like the candy my daddy gives me sometimes." The evaluator responded, "Sometimes I like my daddy, sometimes I don't." The child drew very close and whispered, "Sometimes does your daddy hurt you?" "Yes, sometimes he hurts me," the evaluator replied. The child said, "My daddy hurts me sometimes." The evaluator whispered, "Where does your daddy hurt you?" The child rolled backward, spread her legs, and pointed to her crotch: "Here. My daddy hurts me here." The child then told the evaluator that her father "hurt my potty. He hurts it with a stick with a nail on it." The evaluator was puzzled and concerned with the statement about the stick with a nail; she was aware of her own feelings about people who use instruments to hurt children. However, she tried several more questions about the stick. The child responded to the question "What color is the stick?" by pointing to the evaluator's hand. The evaluator suddenly knew what the nail and the stick were: They represented a finger to the child who was hurt. The finger became a "stick with a nail on it."

This is a good example of the kinds of puzzles that children present to interviewers. It often helps to remember that the interviewer is very much like a translator—sometimes it is hard to find the right words to describe something in another language. Children provide clues, and it is the evaluator's job to put them together so that they make sense to other adults.

Hitting the Mark

Sometimes an evaluator tries very hard to get a child to talk, but when the child does begin to talk about being sexually abused, the evaluator doesn't know exactly what to do first. This is very natural, and more experience brings more confidence. Sometimes as the child begins to disclose details surrounding the abuse, the evaluator reacts by beginning to question the child very directly about the abuse. If this happens, the child will usually clam up right away. When the child starts to confirm some of the evaluator's suspicions, it is a difficult transition point in the interview. One technique that helps the evaluator stay on target is to think of a poker player holding two aces. The evaluator should make very neutral comments; this matter-of-fact attitude seems to encourage the child. It is very important for the evaluator to remain calm. Most of these children have been threatened with dire consequences if they ever tell anyone about what has been happening to them. If the evaluator can be calm and accepting about the information the child is sharing, then the child is able to give more details and feel more secure about being with the evaluator.

It is also important for the evaluator to consider the importance of his or her response to the child's first disclosure. The child's willingness to share this information with other professionals, such as police officers and attorneys who must interview the child, may be partly dependent on the manner in which the evaluator behaves upon the first disclosure. Allowing the child to go slowly and disclose in his or her own way usually helps the child feels secure. While this information is being given, the child may need to get up and move around. This should not be interpreted as evasion. The child's tension is often so extreme that the only way for him or her to talk is to keep moving. Some children want to be held or rocked by the evaluator. There are several things that children need to be told by the evaluator (often again and again):

1. "I know this is difficult for you to do."
2. "You're doing a good job."
3. "You're just a little girl [little boy]. What happened to you wasn't your fault."
4. "I know you love your daddy [uncle, grandma, etc.], and I'm sure your daddy loves you." (This is important when a child has very loving feelings for the molester.)
5. "Sometimes big people get mixed up and do things they shouldn't to children. They need help to get better."

The evaluator should not make any promises to a child that he or she cannot personally guarantee. The child has trusted the evaluator enough to tell a secret; the evaluator should not promise something because it seems the easiest way to handle the situation.

Finally, the evaluator should give the child a business card with his or her phone number. These children need this whether or not they can read it. They need a token of the disclosure to know it really happened, and they need to be treated with respect. You helped them. A child may also want to reach an evaluator later to share more information.

PHASE III: CLOSURE

After spending time with and playing with a child, the evaluator must eventually close the interview; it is important to do this in a positive manner.

What about Feelings?

The first time a child shares information about sexual abuse with an interviewer, an incredible range of feelings can emerge. During the course of evaluation, the evaluator's emotions may vary from rage and frustration to excitement and profound sadness. The feelings of the child need to be acknowledged—especially those that are difficult for the evaluator to handle, such as loving or sexual feelings for the molester, anger at the evaluator, anger at being taken away from the molester, and fear of being separated from the family. It is critical that no judgmental statement regarding the alleged abuser be made to the child or around the child. The evaluator should try to remember that although most adults regard the sexual molestation or incest with horror and disgust, this is not what most young children experience. Children may be confused by the sexual behavior of adults whom they trust, but they do not form the same moral judgments as adults do. Young children often experience loving and caring feelings from the people who molest them, and do not usually experience "betrayal" in the same way that older abuse victims do. A young child may be angry with the person who molested him or her, or the person who did not make it stop, or the person who would not listen when the child tried to tell about the abuse. The evaluator needs to be sensitive to the emotions that the child is experiencing and to be as supportive of the child as possible.

The evaluator needs to acknowledge his or her own feelings regarding this particular child and this particular evaluation. People who work in this emotionally charged field need to have someone or a network of people with whom they can share their feelings.

What if Nothing Happens in Spite of the Best Efforts of the Interviewer?

Part of the problem in doing these interviews is always time pressure. Under ideal conditions, an evaluator would be able to see a child three times for about an hour or more, allowing time to really work with the child. Usually this is not the case, and situations where children must be evaluated without much preparation are bound to be less successful than those where adequate time and information are available. Some children will only disclose information after they have spent months or years working with the same person. The younger a child is, the more time it usually takes to evaluate the child. Sometimes there is just not enough time to reach a particular child, and the evaluator cannot change those circumstances. Timing is also a critical factor. If a child is not ready to share, nothing the interviewer can do will change that.

It helps to remember that in many ways children are just like adults. They may not respond to a particular evaluator for a variety of reasons:

1. The evaluator may remind the child of someone else.
2. The child may not like the way the evaluator looks.
3. The race, sex, and age of the evaluator may also be factors.

One of the hardest things about doing this work is that there are times when an interviewer believes a child is being molested and nothing can be done about it. Sometimes the child has to grow up more and become more verbal before anything can be done. This is particularly hard to accept when there are some indications of abuse but not enough to make a clear judgment. Occasionally it is possible to arrange for a child to be monitored so that a second evaluation can be done when the child is a little older.

On the positive side, to do an evaluation and discover that there is no abuse is nice. Where else does one get good feelings about being wrong? It is wonderful to find that a child has not been molested when there have been some indications of sexual abuse.

What if the Evaluator Doesn't Know?

If an evaluator interviews a child and comes to the conclusion that he or she really doesn't know whether the child was molested, the only thing to do is to say, "I don't know." There needs to be a report of any indications that were present and any factors complicating the finding (e.g., a child speaks only Spanish or is handicapped).

Sometimes there are strong indications of molestation (3-year-olds do not spontaneously learn to French-kiss, or make rocking motions and call it "humping"), but there is not enough evidence to make a clear judgment or take a child into protective custody. It is an uncomfortable situation for an evaluator to be in, and there are no easy ways out. There are a great number of things that are unknown about the sexual abuse of very young children. It may be hoped that as time goes on, knowledge will accumulate and the evaluation process will become easier. But for now, the best thing to do when a clear judgment cannot be made is to allow someone else to decide (such as a police officer or judge), or, at the least, to see whether the child can be followed. Any indications of abuse should be reported and kept on file with local and state agencies. Having this type of information on file often allows the establishment of baseline data and history documentation. A documented history of reports and good baseline data can be significant factors in a child's future. There have been several cases where intervention became possible because there was a history of abuse reports coupled with new information that demonstrated the existence of an ongoing problem, rather than an isolated incident.

SPECIAL ISSUES

During the evaluation process, the interviewer may be confronted with a number of issues that may be difficult to handle.

MALE CHILD AS VICTIM

A male child as the victim of abuse presents several different problems for the evaluator. The first thing one has to deal with is the myth that little boys are not sexually abused by anyone except "dirty old men who hang out in public parks." Little boys are often sexually victimized by members of their families (including parents, grandparents, aunts and uncles, siblings, and cousins), caretakers, neighbors, and teachers. Sexual abuse of little boys is not reported nearly as frequently as abuse of females of the same age; this is partly due to a lack of awareness on the part of professionals, and partly to a cultural bias that sexual activity cannot harm boys. Boys usually do not suffer the "damaged goods" syndrome, because there is no premium on male virginity. Little boys, however, are emotionally and developmentally injured by sexual abuse. Dr. Nicholas Groth, in his work with convicted sex offenders, has learned that a very large percentage of these men were molested as children (Groth, 1979).

There are impediments that make obtaining information from little boys more difficult. Little boys are taught very early that they should not be "crybabies," "tattletales," or "sissies." This means they are not as likely as girls to disclose information about molestation to caretakers or teachers. A second obstacle has to do with the gender confusion that often results from sexual abuse. Young boys may eventually tell the evaluator that they are "girls." Children learn very early that girls are the passive, penetrated ones. When a little older, an abused boy may fear that he is homosexual. This happens because he is often told something about this in order to enforce not telling anyone what is happening, or because he may feel there is something wrong with him, since otherwise he would not have been sexually abused.

Some small boys will work with the dolls, but often more information is elicited from them through drawing, storytelling, or especially the use of animal puppets. The evaluator needs to be aware that a sexually abused boy may tell or act out a story of a girl who is abused. Boys need lots of reassurance about the things they view as masculine, such as strength, agility, and building skills, before they can disclose. Oral copulation is common in reported cases of male victims; this means that the evaluator needs to carefully explore the situations where this would be a likely activity, such as going to the bathroom.

LYING

Among the most common questions asked of people who are experienced in interviewing and evaluating young children are these: "Do little children lie? Can they be taught to lie so that they incriminate innocent people? Do they fantasize and report this as truth?" Very young children do not make up complex lies. A young child may, on occasion, say "no" when the answer is "yes." (For example, a child may respond to the question "Did you wet your pants?" by saying "no" and giving a headshake, in spite of the fact that the front of his pants is soaking.) Sometimes a child will tease by repeatedly giving the wrong answer. In general, however, young children can be counted on to tell the truth except when there is a very strong need to deny. If a 4-year-old child is told, "Somebody's going to kill your dog and send you to jail if you tell the secret," then the child may feel compelled to deny the abuse. This is not the same kind of behavior that an older child may engage in to get someone else in trouble. It is important to remember during the interviewing process that the child may have a need to deny that anything happened; however, the evaluator should not be convinced just because the child denies, especially in the first part of the evaluation.

Another problem that adults often connect with lying is that, in young children, time and space concepts are not very well developed. This is frustrating to law enforcement officers, who must establish a time and location in order to determine that a crime took place. The evaluator needs to keep in mind that children do not necessarily remember things in chronological order. This does not mean that a child is lying or is being difficult. It just means that time is not important to children in the same way it is important to adults. Often a child can remember enough details for the evaluator to determine an approximate time, given careful questioning. Linking situations with special events (e.g., birthdays, Christmas, weekends, etc.) may be helpful.

One of the questions an evaluator may be asked regarding the evaluation of a child for sexual abuse is "How do you know the child didn't just make this up?" Ever since Freud changed his opinion and declared that most incest material was fantasy, this question has come up. It certainly is true that children fantasize, but they do not fantasize about sexual relationships with adults. A little girl may make a statement about wanting to marry Daddy when she grows up, but this is significantly different from saying she wants to have a sexual relationship with her father. A child may be "romantically" interested in Mommy, but that does not equate with a sexual relationship with the mother. The connection between romance and sexual activity is not found in young children who have not been sexualized by experience with someone older. There have been cases where parents said that their children became sexually interested in adults by watching X-rated movies on TV or by watching adults. There is certainly a possibility that a child exposed to some adult sexual activity by observing adults either accidentally or deliberately may talk about this. However, the information that children who have been molested give is detailed in ways that a child accidentally observing parents cannot give. Additionally, children who watch X-rated movies usually do not understand what is taking place. They may infrequently attempt to imitate gross behaviors, such as lying on top of another child; however, unless they have had direct experience, they will not understand exactly what happens or be able to give details (how things feel and taste, etc.).

CUSTODY

Particularly difficult situations are those where there are indications that the alleged sexual abuse is a custody ploy. Attorneys often believe that one parent can "brainwash" a child into giving incriminating evidence against the other parent. In some cases, one parent has actually tried this maneuver, but generally a young child cannot sustain the story well enough to convince the evaluators. One case demonstrated that a 4½-year-old child could be taught to parrot three responses to all the evaluator's questions. One way in which the evaluator can discern whether or not a response is valid is to look at the amount of detail that a child is able to give. A child who has not been sexually involved with adults will not be able to give many details, if any. It is always a good idea early in the evaluation process for the interviewer to establish the child's ability to distinguish reality from fantasy: Most children can say that some things are "make-believe" and other things are "real." They will also readily give examples of each. The evaluator can test this by making statements such as "Mommies are only make-believe"; usually the child will delight in telling the evaluator just how silly that is.

WHAT HAPPENS NEXT?

When a child tells an evaluator about being sexually abused, a number of things must be done, and lots of questions have to be answered. The child will want to know what will happen next. This is always a dilemma. The simplest answer seems to be "We will get help for the person who has been doing this to you." As noted above, the evaluator should explain to the child that sometimes big people have problems and they need someone to help them with the problem. How much to tell a child depends on the age of the child and his or her ability to understand the situation within these parameters. The child needs to be told as much of the truth as the evaluator feels the child can handle.

It is often tempting at this point to color the circumstances in such a way that the evaluator gains the child's cooperation; not "exactly" telling the child that he or she must be taken into custody may appear easier than dealing with the child's emotions and objections. The tears, fears, and anger of the child are real feelings in response to a real situation that *is* painful and traumatic. The evaluator can be a good role model by being truthful and allowing the child to express his or her emotions. These ways of interacting are not commonly found in families who become involved in sexual abuse. The children have usually been lied to and betrayed by their mother, father, and caretakers. They need to be told the truth and to have their feelings respected.

Often the evaluator does not know what will happen next. What happens frequently depends on the police or juvenile court judge. The evaluator can tell the child that he or she does not know what will happen next, while providing reassurance that the child will be protected.

PARENTS AND OTHERS

Parents are very interested in just what the child has told the evaluator. It is not in the child's best interest to discuss the child's statements with the mother, father, or any other family member. Sometimes children must be returned to the parents. If this happens, the children will need all the protection possible. One way to provide some protection for them is not to disclose to the parents. Later, if a court battle ensues, the parents will be able to learn some of the information, but this can protect a child when there is not enough evidence.

AFTERMATH

It is important to keep good notes on each child who is evaluated. Evaluators are often ordered to courtrooms, and it is important to be able to use notes to refresh one's memories of some events that may have taken place months or even years ago. It is helpful to contact each child after the intake process is completed. This provides continuity for the child and demonstrates caring. The evaluator should not be surprised if the child is not happy to see him or her. Children are often very angry with the people they have told. Allowing them to be angry is the best way to help, though it may be very difficult for the evaluator.

The evaluator is not a popular person with parents, attorneys, and sometimes the police. The act of evaluation may cause people to look at something they would rather not see. The need to deny that children are sexually abused is very common. Often those who are most enlightened in other areas will not believe that a child is sometimes an object of sexual and emotional gratification. As people become more aware of this, and more willing to work with these very young children, both evaluators and young children who have been sexually abused will have an easier time.

MEDICAL EVALUATION

Michael Durfee
Astrid H. Heger
Bruce Woodling

Recognition of sexual molestation in a child is entirely dependent on the individual's inherent willingness to entertain the possibility that the condition may exist.—Suzanne M. Sgroi (1975)

INTRODUCTION

Many physicians have contributed to the lack of awareness of the epidemic of child sexual abuse by their unwillingness to consider the possibility that children are sexually abused. Sexual abuse is a difficult diagnosis for most physicians, because they (1) experience personal internal discomfort, (2) are uncomfortable talking with children about sexuality, and (3) lack fundamental training and experience. When physicians' discomfort is obvious to child victims, they become reluctant to talk openly about their victimization (Kempe, 1978; Rosenfeld, 1978).

Many children with allegations of sexual abuse ultimately receive no medical examination whatsoever (Jason, 1982). Medical records on children who have been examined are often inadequate and may never become part of the legal evaluation. Additionally, the lack of physical evidence is sometimes taken as conclusive evidence that sexual abuse did not occur.

It is not clear which medical specialty should be the domain for evaluation of sexual abuse. Some would say that pediatricians should examine child victims, and gynecologists most postpubertal females. However, an inherent understanding and committed concern seems to be the most important function determining the type of physician who should perform a medical–legal assessment. If properly trained, gynecologists, urologists, family practitioners, and pediatricians may all be appropriate choices to perform such evaluations.

Many, if not most, cases of molestation pass through the system without any accurate or thoughtful history being taken. Histories may be taken repeatedly but ineffectively. The medical–legal examination itself may be the most overrated and most inadequately applied evaluation component of possible sexual assault. Significant trauma may be overlooked by an inexperienced examiner. Proceeding from this premise, this chapter has two purposes: to educate nonmedical professionals as to the general components of a medical–legal examination, and to provide medical practitioners with a general guideline for conducting adequate interviews and examinations.

THE MEDICAL INTERVIEW

Ideally, the initial therapeutic interview will be conducted by a knowledgeable, trained child advocate/therapist. It may be possible for the physician to participate in this validation process, either by being present during part of the therapeutic interview or by using information available from the interview to re-emphasize information essential for the medical examination. Sometimes these can be done more easily during the physical examination.

The medical interview is the medical history. This interview requires privacy and time, and includes a review of all pertinent information surrounding the nature of the assault and the identity of the assailant. With preschoolers, it is vital first to establish rapport by spending time playing and talking with them. The use of art materials, puppets, anatomically correct dolls, and other toys will greatly facilitate a medical interview. Anatomical drawings will establish a particular child's terminology for body parts.

It is important for the child to understand initially that the physician is comfortable talking about sexuality. For example, the physician may say, "I talk to a lot of kids about touching and things like that." Second, the physician needs to confront the child's guilt and fear: "It is never your fault when a grownup touches you in that way." Third, the physician can allow some distance and sense of control, when introducing the topic of sexual touching, through statements like these: "Sometimes kids tell me they get touched," or "Sometimes kids who tell me they hurt in their private places hurt because someone has touched them there." Fourth, the physician needs to acknowledge that genital touching feels good, and that people who touch kids may know how to make it feel good. This allows the child to accept his or her own ambiguous feelings about the perpetrator. Lastly, the physician, whether he or she is the initial interviewer or is following up on a disclosure interview, should continue to use the language of the child and to conduct the interview on the developmental level of the child. As noted, this can often be facilitated by the use of drawings, anatomical dolls, and puppets.

In conclusion, the physician conducting the interview is practicing the same art of history taking that he or she would with any sick child. And therefore, although it is possible to begin with less specific questions, it is frequently necessary to progress from the general to the specific, with questions such as these: "Did he touch you here on your pee-pee?", "Did he touch you with his pee-pee?", "Can you show me on the doll where you were touched?", "Can you show me on the doll what part of him touched you?" (Altchek, 1981; Anderson & Berliner, 1983; Burgess & Holmstrom, 1978; Herjanic & Wilbois, 1978; Kempe, 1978; May, 1977; Orr, 1979; Saries, 1982; Sgroi, 1978; Sgroi, Porter, & Blick, 1982). In many states, the physician's statement of what the child has said to him or her during the medical interview is admissible in court to substantiate the child's testimony.

THE PHYSICAL EXAMINATION

Most cases of sexual abuse present themselves as common pediatric problems. Of course, in cases where a child is being evaluated for genital injury and/or infection, the diagnosis of sexual abuse is more easily made (see Table 4-1 for medical indicators). More often, children's presenting symptoms may be stomach aches, nightmares, enuresis, encopresis, and the like, all of which are commonly associated with sexual abuse (see Table 4-2 for behavioral indicators).

Many cases of child sexual abuse have no demonstrable medical evidence. The legal system is reluctant to prosecute these cases. Both physicians and attorneys need an understanding that the validation

TABLE 4-1. *Medical Indicators of Child Sexual Abuse*

A. General	B. Males
1. Bruises	1. Pain on urination
2. Scratches	2. Penile swelling
3. Bites	3. Penile discharge
4. Sexually transmitted disease	
5. Blood stains on underwear	C. Females
6. Bruising or swelling of genital area not consistent with history	
7. Pain in anal, genital, gastrointestinal, and urinary area	1. Vaginal discharge
8. Genital injuries	2. Urethral inflammation
9. Petechiae	3. Lymph gland inflammation
10. Injury to lips	4. Pregnancy
11. Grasp marks	

of child sexual abuse has its foundation in what a child says, and that the medical examination, negative or positive, may be consistent with sexual abuse. This often difficult medical–legal interface mandates that we as physicians must meticulously document findings (of even suspected minor genital trauma) in descriptive terms, not in terms of conclusion.

Throughout the examination, the child's privacy and feeling of helplessness need to be respected. The child must have a sense of participation and control, and should be accompanied during the exam by a supportive adult of the child's choice. The purpose of the examination should be explained to the child at the beginning in language that the child will understand: "I am going to look you over from top to bottom to make sure that, even though that touching happened, you are perfectly okay." The child should remain clothed

TABLE 4-2. *Behavioral Indicators*

Dysfunctional behavior, especially any change in behavior
Acute reactions: clinging, fear, phobias
Regression: bedwetting, thumb sucking
Sleep: nightmares, won't sleep alone
Food: over- or undereating
School: poor performance or concentration; change in performance
Social: restricted social life, poor interpersonal relationships
Emotional: poor self-esteem, depression, suicidal statements or behavior
Acting out: running away, promiscuity
Sexual: behavior inappropriate for age, excessive masturbation
Substance abuse

TABLE 4-3. *Date Estimation of Bruising of the Abused Child*

Time elapsed	Characteristics
Less than 1 day	Reddish-blue or purple with margins
1–2 days	Bluish-brown to dark purple
3–5 days	Yellowish-green to brown
5–7 days	Yellow, fading
Past 1 week	Yellowish-brown, fading

until the time of the actual physical examination. In our office, we have colorful print gowns for children to choose. Two necessary therapeutic goals of the medical–legal examination are to allow children to have control and to assure them that they are not "damaged goods." One should never conduct a part of the examination that is refused or not consented to by the suspected victim.

The medical exam proceeds from the general to the specific. During the general examination, careful attention must be paid to any evidence of nongenital trauma. Bruising frequently accompanies sexual abuse. This bruising can be in the form of grip marks on the arms or legs, but there may also be bruising of the forehead in a child who has been forcefully sodomized, or bruising around the genital area. These bruises are then carefully evaluated for age (see Table 4-3), photographed, and documented on the traumagram.

For the medical practice or clinic committed to the evaluation of sexually abused children, it is important to establish an examining room that is suitably equipped and furnished in a way that will reduce a child's anxiety.

EXAMINING THE FEMALE CHILD

With the very young female child (aged 2–3), the examination is done with the child lying frog-legged in the mother's lap. The slightly older child can be examined lying on the examining table, with her advocate present to reassure and distract her. If a child is too anxious to be alone on the table, she can be placed supine on top of the mother, who is also supine on the table. This may be important if colposcopy is being utilized. With the legs in the frog-leg position, there is excellent visualization of the vaginal introitus. With slight lateral–posterior traction on the labia minora, it is possible to see beyond the hymen and into the vagina. Without any change in position, it is now also possible to evaluate the anus of the female child by having the child grasp her knees to her chest.

EXAMINING THE MALE CHILD

The classical knees-to-chest, face-down position has been abandoned by many examiners. This position is a possible re-enactment of the abuse of boys and is threatening to them. We place the boys in a left lateral decubitus position and ask them to grasp their knees "like a cannonball," which results in excellent visualization.

MEDICAL INDICATORS OF SEXUAL ABUSE

VAGINAL PENETRATION

Since preschool-age children have an unsophisticated idea of vaginal penetration, little girls may describe both vulvar and vaginal intercourse by stating, for example, that "He put his pee-pee in my front potty." In vulvar intercourse, the physical findings may be acutely limited to abrasion and erythema of the vulvar area and/or laceration of the posterior fourchette. Old vulvar coitus injuries may be in the form of small perihymenal scars, as well as scarring of the posterior fourchette. However, vaginal penetration of the prepubescent female will always result in abrasions and laceration of the hymen (Paul, 1977; Woodling & Kossoris, 1981; Wynne, 1980).

The normal prepubescent hymen has been described as being "thin like tissue paper," with a diameter of 0.4 (Cantwell, 1981; Cowell, 1981) to 1.0 cm. The lacerations to the hymen are most frequently found between three o'clock and nine o'clock, with the most frequent laceration being at six o'clock (Paul, 1977; Woodling & Kossoris, 1981; Wynne, 1980). This laceration may frequently extend across the posterior fourchette and may even involve the perineum itself. It has been our experience that it is also possible to visualize circumferential scarring lateral to the hymenal opening, running parallel.

Most transected hymens have borders altered in appearance, no longer appearing delicate and paper-thin. Rather, they become scarred and thickened, with rounded, redundant hymenal remnants. There may be adhesions binding the hymen laterally and distorting the opening. These adhesions or synechiae may also extend into the vagina.

In Cantwell's (1981) study, a vaginal opening that exceeded 0.4 cm correlated with sexual abuse in 75% of the cases evaluated. Our experience supports this finding. However, there are cases where the hymenal opening is within normal limits, but demonstrates extensive scar formation where the hymen appears to have been transected and healed.

The colposcope is useful in the evaluation of vaginal penetration (see "A Colposcopic Examination," below). This tool helps to delineate areas of scarring from normal anatomy.

In summary, signs of vaginal penetration include the following:

1. *Acute:* Abrasions, lacerations, contusions with hematomas, spasm of the pubococcygeal muscle, and positive laboratory workup for seminal products.
2. *Chronic:* Multiple well-healed hymenal scars, perpendicular to the hymenal opening; circumferential scars lateral to the hymenal opening and parallel; rounded hymenal remnants; large vaginal opening greater than 0.5-1.0 cm; laceration of the hymen and the posterior fourchette at six o'clock (this laceration may also involve the perineum).
3. *Soft signs* (Paul, 1977; Woodling & Kossoris, 1981): Easily relax puboccygeal muscle when the child is touched lateral to the vulva; vaginal discharge; distinct odor.

ANAL PENETRATION

Fifty percent of all sodomy cases manifest a normal-appearing anus. The anus is capable of accommodating without injury large, hard stools whose size may equal the average diameter of an adult erect penis (3.5 cm). Injuries vary, depending on the use of lubricants, force, and the number of penetrations.

Acute Anal Penetration

Within the first hour or two, the anal sphincter may be initially relaxed (Paul, 1977) and then shortly thereafter may go into spasm. There will be swelling of the anal verge, with abrasions, bruising, and localized hematomas; loss of the normal puckered appearance of the anus may transitorily develop. Rarely will there be overt tearing of the anal sphincter requiring surgical repair. Small tears and fissures are more common. In addition, there is a generalized erythema extending outward from the anus, with edema distorting the anal opening. Seminal products may be present if the assault is less than 24–48 hours old.

Chronic Anal Penetration

In chronic cases of assault, especially when the last incident occurred more than 2 weeks prior to the exam, more than 50% of the cases will have no physical findings (Paul, 1977; Woodling & Kossoris, 1981; Wynne, 1980). If the child is evaluated within 2–3 weeks of the last assault, it may be possible to elicit a reflex relaxation of the anal sphincter with gentle lateral traction of the buttocks. Complete or partial loss of sphincter control may be found in cases of chronic abuse. There is also a positive wink reflex (i.e., stroking the perianal tissue with a cotton-tipped applicator will result in a reflex relaxation). There is a progressive change with loss of normal puckered skin folds and progressive thickening of the skin and mucous membranes. The anal rugae become hypertrophied and distorted by the deposition of fibrous tissue. Old fissures and lacerations may heal with a cupping or coving effect and an obvious loss of perianal fatty tissue. Fissures may also heal leaving prominent skin tags. In preschool-age children, there can also be fan-shaped scars extending out from the anus, with the widest part being peripheral to the anus. Since most children are sodomized from behind, the preponderance of scarring appears in the six o'clock position, or ventrally.

LABORATORY FINDINGS, TREATMENT OF DISEASE, AND COLLECTION OF EVIDENCE

A careful, well-documented evaluation of specimens obtained from the oral pharynx, the vagina, and the anus is essential in the medical–legal evaluation. The insertion of anything into the vagina or anus of a sexually abused child is frightening. Therefore, it is important to limit intracavity probing to those children in which it is indicated and essential. Specimens should be obtained by using only premoistened cotton-tipped applicators or sterile glass droppers. It is possible when the sample is carefully obtained to use one sample for all culture and forensic studies. For oral sampling, a throat culture must be done.

Samples for seminal products are most productive if taken from between the upper molars and the cheek. The vaginal sample should
be taken from the posterior vaginal pool, whereas the anal sample is
taken from the rectal ampula (Harborview). One should carefully
cleanse the perianal skin prior to inserting a cotton-tipped swab rec-
tally to avoid external contamination of the swab.

Diagnosis of sexually transmitted disease requires that triple cultures be taken. In addition, the examining physician should smear
and stain any discharge. Neiserria gonorrhea cultures need to be
maintained under optimal environment conditions (gas and temper-
ature) to facilitate growth. The physician may also obtain a baseline
test for syphilis where appropriate. This blood test is indicated when
there is evidence of any other venereal disease.

A negative or positive culture for gonorrhea or syphilis does not
end the possibility of other venereal diseases or pathogens: genital
herpes, trichomoniasis, *Chlamydia trachomatis*, *Hemophilus hominues*,
Gardnerella vaginalis, and venereal warts (condylomata accuminata).
Testing for these, when suspected, may require special viral or bac-
terial cultures in addition to "wet-mount" examination. *C. trachomatis*
has been increasingly recognized as the most common sexually transmitted pathogen. Nonspecific urethritis caused by *C. trachomatis* is not
eradicated by the use of penicillin or ampicillin; it should be considered as a diagnosis in all children where there is a persistence of
inflamation and/or discharge without evidence of gonorrhea.

Infections from *C. trachomatis* and gonorrhea may clear spontaneously because of natural antibody response, or they may only appear
to clear. Treatment failure may be followed by continued evidence
of vaginal or urethral irritation and/or discharge. Chronic, nonvisible
cases of untreated infections may cause severe damage or infertility,
or may be a vector for the spread of infection. In all children, sexually
communicable diseases are transmitted via the same mechanisms as
are accepted for adults (Neinstein, Goldenring, & Carpenter, 1984;
Sgroi, 1977).

Concurrent with the detailed physical examination, and its special
emphasis on the genital exam, are specific medical tasks that the
physician must be aware of. It is the role of the physician to assess
injuries that may require surgical intervention.

Sophisticated laboratory tests for seminal fluid analysis, sperm,
and public hair have precedent in adult rape protocols. These tests

may have critical value as evidence in the examination of young children; they may be the *only* evidence in preverbal children. This evidence will have little value in the legal system, however, unless evidence collection protocol is adhered to and a chain of evidence is established. It is helpful for physicians to establish such a protocol with the assistance of the legal system in their communities.

Protocol needs to include detailed descriptions of the labeling and sealing procedures necessary to maintain a noncontaminated chain of custody. Next, protocol needs to include a description of the crime scene evidence. Pubic hair, blood stains, remnants of cloth, and dried saliva are important evidence for a forensic laboratory. Seminal fluid fluoresces, and scanning the body with a woods lamp can help the physician identify areas with seminal fluid stains for more careful analysis. Areas of the skin that fluoresce should be swabbed with saline-moistened swabs and air-dried or preserved, according to local crime laboratory protocol. The parents should be asked to bring all clothing that the child was wearing at the time of the assault. The physician should undress the child on a paper sheet and save the sheet and any debris. Damp clothing should be air-dried and saved in separate paper bags.

Samples should be collected and examined for seminal fluid. Forensic laboratories may test for acid phosphatase, phosphoglucomutase, spermine, or other chemicals found in seminal fluid. Also, 80% of males secrete their ABO blood type in the seminal fluid; ABO typing may be used to show that a suspect is or is not compatible with the sample found. Similar tests for saliva are necessary to confirm the secretory status of the assailant if an assailant is apprehended. Forensic laboratories can test for spermatozoa on dry slides taken from vaginal, anal, or oral secretions.

Microscopic examination of secretions for motile or nonmotile sperm needs to be done at the time of the child's original medical evaluation. Motile spermatozoa are the single most dramatic finding of a recent male sexual contact. They may be seen under a microscope using a "wet-mount" slide. A "wet mount" is made by mixing a drop of saline fluid with the suspected semen, placing that on a slide under a slide cover, and examining under a microscope. Motile sperm may last for up to 12 hours in a vagina and for more than 5 days in the endocervical canal. Nonmotile sperm may last for 3–5 days in the vagina and for up to 14 days in the endocervical canal. In addition to the "wet mount," a prepared, fixed slide should be made and sent to the laboratory for confirmation.

Traumagrams are useful to document bruising, abrasions, bites, and other signs that indicate force or coercion. When possible, the physician should photograph all injuries.

THE MEDICAL RECORD

The medical record is the documentation of the interview and physical examination. It will include all pertinent historical information, past and present. If possible, the history of the assault should be stated in the child's language and can include actual questions and answers from the interview. The written record of the medical examination may include diagrams and narrative description. The physician should describe the general appearance of the genital and anal regions, noting bruises, contusions, petechiae, lacerations, and size of vaginal opening (this description should not be stated in terms of "virginal" or "intact"). This record can also include photographs, both macroscopic and microscopic. Finally, any conclusions should validate the child's story and state clearly that presence or absence of physical findings is consistent with the history of sexual abuse (Anderson & Berliner, 1983).

A COLPOSCOPIC EXAMINATION

The colposcope is an instrument whose use is well-established in the gynecological community, primarily for the purpose of early detection of cervical cancer. It is essentially a binocular optical instrument with a 13× magnification potential. More recently, it has been introduced as a significant tool for the clarification of diagnostic findings in victims of sexual assault. When used for the diagnosis of sexual abuse, the colposcope is a noninvasive instrument. It is primarily important in clarifying patterns of scarring that may also be visible with the naked eye or with the use of magnifying lenses. At no time does the colposcope touch or penetrate the victim.

The photographic potential of some colposcopes is an important but nonessential component of the instrument. Although, the photographs are a true representation of what is visualized, recording a lasting document of what is visualized, they are primarily useful when correlated with the actual visualization. It is important to emphasize that the colposcope is not a magical instrument that makes the diagnosis of sexual abuse for the physician; it is only useful in the hands of a professional trained in the diagnosis of sexual abuse. If a physician is untrained in the macroscopic diagnosis of sexual abuse, such an examination will be of little value.

CONCLUDING THE MEDICAL EVALUATION— REASSURANCE

The final component of the medical evaluation is the reassurance of the child and the family. Even in the cases where children will require surgical repair, it is important to explain to the children that they will be perfectly normal. Reassurance of child victims is vital, since most victims of sexual abuse see themselves as "damaged goods"—different from other children. After we have checked a child carefully, a technique we have found helpful is to capture the child's attention with this: "I have looked you over from head to toe and I just want you to know that you are perfectly normal. Everything is exactly where it is supposed to be." The physician should never discuss extent of scarring damage with the child present.

HUMAN FACTORS FOR A SENSITIVE EVALUATION

GENERAL POINTS

The thoughtful human components of the medical–legal history and physical examination are difficult to describe and probably more difficult to deliver. Common sense, and common courtesy to victims, siblings, and families will help the legal and medical process and will demonstrate that medicine is a resource rather than a necessary evil.

  1. The physician should not avoid examination to protect adult anxiety. For most of these children, this assessment will be their first genital examination. For some of them, the examination may be more humiliating and frightening than the molestation itself. Avoiding examination of a frightened child may seem humane, but it may leave the child with unidentified medical problems. It may also leave care-takers and victims with a feeling that the victims are very "broken" and damaged. No examination should omit evidence collection that leaves a child unprotected.

2. *The physician should be calm and unhurried.*   An examiner should respond to the child's and the family's needs. Clearness, firmness, and positive reassurance should enable the physician to complete an adequate evaluation.

3. *An examination should never be forced on a child.*   Occasionally, a child may do well to return another day for an examination. The restrained, screaming youngster being "reraped" in the physician's office should be a thing of the past.

4.   *The physician should prepare and support the adults involved.*   The examiner should explain to the accompanying adults what will happen during the exam, and should clarify all findings. A reasonable place to sit, a reassuring touch, and the offer of a cup of coffee will result in more cooperation and less indignation. Parental cooperation at the time of the entry exam may make the rest of the legal and treatment process smoother and more effective.

5. *The physician should prepare and support the child.*   The child should be interviewed first with clothes on by a gently supportive staff person and with someone who will stay with the child. The physical examination should be explained. The child should be allowed control when possible. Having a family member present is reassuring, especially when that person remains calm and supportive.

6. *The physician should give the child an opportunity for closure.*   After the examination, the child should be affirmed and reassured again with clothes on. This gives the child, while in a less vulnerable position, a chance to be angry at the examiner and to ask any question of immediate concern. The child needs a forum to retain a sense of control and to feel a sense of closure and separation from the medical experience. Ultimately, children seem to appreciate regard for their feelings and any opportunity to feel some sense of control.

CHILD RESPONSES: VARIANCE WITH AGE

There have been numerous debates about the gender of the examiner, the race of the examiner, and the use of white coats. Children seem generally to respond to the quality of the person examining them.

The exceptions we have seen are that some young children are afraid of white coats, and that some adolescents may prefer a female (or a male) examiner. Most of the distinctions correlate primarily with a child's age.

Infants may seem bothered by rapid changes or pain. The genital examination parallels diaper changing and genital hygiene. Toddlers dislike lying down, ear speculums, and sudden movements. All in all, very young preschool children seem to respond well to a comfortable adult and can cooperate in a postmolestation examination as well as any other medical examination.

Verbal preschool-age children and early-elementary-school-age children seem the most responsive to being allowed to participate in the examination. They may want to see the culture tube. They almost invariably enjoy using a stethoscope to listen to their own hearts and the examiner's heart. They also are responsive to postexamination contact with clothes on, and to a reassuring apology for any pain or discomfort. All verbal children should be allowed the final word, if only to give them the chance to ask questions.

Elementary-school-age children have more of a problem with medical–legal assessment. The medical examination by a strange person may easily be more frightening than their molestation by a familiar adult. Extra time and effort, particularly with this age group, is necessary to minimize the possible examination trauma. Appropriate time and effort not only will lower trauma, but will make a competent examination more probable.

ADULT REACTIONS TO THE EXAMINATIONS

Adult professionals and family members add their own confusion and distress to the medical–legal examination process. This anxiety may correlate with the sex of the child, the extent or type of sexual contact, or the category of person identified as the alleged perpetrator.

Parents add their own confusion about the molestation and about the examination. A preschool-age girl may be seen as "no longer a virgin." Speaking with and listening to the child and parents after the examination can be extremely useful in clarifying misconceptions that can easily affect a lifetime.

The examiner is also affected by the examination. It is useful and probably necessary for the examiner to have a resource for sharing personal distress. Sensitive examiners often experience a great deal of confusion and distress, but this can ultimately result in personal and professional growth and development.

The primary obstruction to a competent and thorough medical examination of molested children is the irrational anxiety of responsible medical professionals. It becomes important to accept and deal with those anxieties, and to apply common sense and basic, natural empathic responses. The examination is ultimately a fairly simple and reasonable procedure when applied thoughtfully and with competence.

CONCLUSION

As professionals, it is our responsibility to recognize that sexual abuse is occurring in epidemic proportions. One of the most frequent complaints of child victims is that the worst part of the abuse "was when they took me to the doctor." As noted above, the restrained, screaming child being examined in the physician's office should be a thing of the past. Any complaints related to genital injury, pain discharge, or infection need to be carefully evaluated. However, these are usually disguised as common pediatric problems, and they require a sensitive private interview with a child. Physicians need to be fully acquainted with both medical and behavioral indicators of sexual abuse, and must understand the mandatory personal commitment of time and emotional support necessary to treat sexually abused children effectively. Along with the promotion of other preventive medical programs, physicians should encourage parents to discuss sexuality with their children and to establish those lines of communication that will facilitate "no more secrets."

TECHNIQUES FOR INTERVIEWING AND EVIDENCE GATHERING

Kee MacFarlane

Sandy Krebs

An interviewer may have to assume several different roles when conducting diagnostic evaluations of alleged victims of child sexual abuse. Regardless of the interviewer's professional affiliation, initial interviews with young children often involve a range of interactions that are both clinical and investigatory in nature. Even when an evaluation is conducted for purely therapeutic purposes, the information divulged by the child may necessitate the filing of a report of suspected child abuse, and could result in legal action. In such instances, the way in which the interview was conducted may be subject to legal scrutiny; it may call into question the validity of the interviewer's opinion or the child's statements; and it could affect the outcome of a case. Therefore, it is important to be knowledgeable about both aspects of the interviewing process: the ways in which preschool-age molested children act, react, and perceive the world; and the intricacies and requirements of legal, judicial, and law enforcement systems.

Coping with the dual roles of child evaluator and evidence gatherer is frequently very difficult for therapists and law enforcement personnel alike, and is often a source of conflict among local agencies. Nonetheless, it is not always possible or even always advisable to separate these functions. As community agencies continue to define their evolving roles and responsibilities, it is important to continue increasing our knowledge about all aspects of the complex process of communicating with young children. This chapter includes information that can be helpful in either role. It is written from the perspective of clinicians, but it owes a great deal to lessons learned from police officers and district attorneys. We all struggle with a variety of communication barriers, but we have much to learn from one another that will ultimately benefit children and case investigation.

LAYING THE FOUNDATION FOR AN INTERVIEW

The role of a children's interviewer is, in some ways, similar to that of an interpreter for a person who comes from another country or even another world. The fact that the interpreter once lived in that world is only helpful to the extent that he or she can remember what that world was like, or has managed to keep up to date with its customs, language, and current events. The interviewer is both a translator of another language to others in the adult world, and someone who helps small people communicate their thoughts and experiences in ways that can be understood by adults. The following are some thoughts and techniques that may help in that process.

ESTABLISHING COMMON TERMINOLOGY

Names for People and Things

It is essential when doing initial interviews with children to determine the exact words they use for the people who populate their worlds. Children often have many different nicknames for the people in their lives, and it is vitally important in interview conversations for the interviewer to be sure that he or she and the child are talking about the same person. This is true too for the names of pets, dolls, stuffed animals, and imaginary friends that children sometimes refer to as if they were people. Interviewers should encourage children to describe such characters before making assumptions about who or what they are. Interviewers should also be aware that abusers sometimes introduce themselves to young children by using the names of fictional or television characters (e.g., "My name is He Man. This person is my friend Skelator.") This ploy, of course, immediately reduces the disclosing child's credibility in the eyes of those who assume that he or she is confusing fantasy with reality (which is just what it is intended to do). Asking children how they know someone's name, where they met, what the person looked like, etc., will help to enlighten the interviewer and prevent false assumptions.

After determining the identities of people in a child's life, the interviewer should use the names that the child uses first, in order to avoid confusion as to the identity of someone. If, for example, the interviewer refers to a grandfather as "Grandpa" with a child who refers to the grandfather as "Papa" (a term the interviewer associates with the child's father), and the child reveals that he or she has been molested, it is possible that someone could be mistakenly suspected of child abuse. Even if the error is discovered in later interviews, it can have traumatic repercussions for all concerned. These usually can be avoided by careful attention to a child's terminology in the first interview.

Identifying who's who is especially important in cases where fathers, stepfathers, and mothers' boyfriends may all be referred to as "Daddy" at different points in time by young children. It is also important to follow the clues of children with regard to "strangers" whom children describe as having molested them. A child may be unable to name a person whom he or she (or the interviewer) thinks of as a "stranger," even though it is a person the child knows in some context and may be able to identify. In one case, a young child implicated a man she referred to as "Mr. Tickle," but insisted that she did not know his name and could not describe him. Upon further questioning, it was learned that she knew he was married to "Mrs. Tickle," her nickname for another suspect in the case whom she could identify. When shown a photographic lineup that included the suspect's husband, the child was able to identify the man she knew as "Mr. Tickle."

It can be helpful to have the child's caretaker bring photographs to the interview of people in the child's life. Referring to photographs of people the child knows (including, but not limited to, anyone suspected of having molested the child) can be a helpful way of making sure that the child and the interviewer are clear about who is being discussed. Asking children to identify everyone in the pictures is also a good way to instigate discussion concerning how they feel about those people. However, if clinicians use photographs in this way, they should be introduced early in the interview before any issues about abuse are raised. In that context, they serve as aids in determining who is familiar to a child, not aids in identifying suspected abusers. Because suspect identification is such a critical issue in sexual abuse cases, an interviewer should not single out someone in a photograph while asking a child if that person touched or hurt or molested him or her. The validity of such an identification process primarily rests on the child's independent ability to identify someone, without any suggestion from outside sources.

The issue of suspect identification when the abuser is not someone well known to a child (such as a family member) raises another set of problems concerning the cognitive abilities of young children. Some children do well in associating photographic images with people they know or have seen, while others try to make the cognitive translation according to familiar facial landmarks (e.g., a moustache, length and color of hair, etc.). When such things are missing in a black-and-white photograph that is not a good likeness of someone as the child remembers him or her, this recognition task may be a poor test of a young child's ability to identify an abuser. Similarly, if a child interprets the task to mean that he or she should pick someone out of a photographic lineup, the child may pick someone who looks like the abuser and may pick out more than one person for that reason. For these and other reasons relating to subsequent legal ramifications of a task that invariably is challenged in court, regardless of who participates or how carefully it is conducted, clinicians are probably better off leaving the process of suspect identification in the hands of law enforcement.

In cases where there may be multiple victims and/or multiple perpetrators (such as cases involving schools, Scout troops, summer camps, etc.), it can be helpful to have any group or class pictures that might be available. Along with using them initially for "who's who" identification purposes, they can be referred back to in order to verify a child's degree of certainty. If, for example, a child alleges something about one of the adults or names another child as having been victimized, the interviewer (in order to make sure the child is not confusing one person with another) might pick up the photograph and say, "Now, is that person in this picture?" The interviewer should be careful not to make assumptions about the names provided by a child, simply because the child has correctly identified someone once. It is better for interviewers to feign their own bad memories and ask children to repeat the identification process, rather than providing the link between a name and a face with such statements as, "Oh, that's Mr. So-and-So, isn't it?", or by pointing to someone in a photograph in response to a child providing someone's name.

Similarly, dolls identified as specific individuals in the child's life can be used by children to show and describe who did what to whom. In cases involving suspected multiple perpetrators, it can be helpful to use anatomical dolls from various manufacturers that look different in shape, color, and hair texture. Aside from the need to keep the age and gender of the dolls accurate (i.e., adult male, child female, etc.), it may be less important with young children that the dolls be of the proper ethnic persuasion than the fact that they are easy to differentiate from one another. This suggestion goes against one's usual tendency always to use dolls of the same ethnicity as the child being interviewed or as suspected abusers. However, with cases involving multiple suspects, the use of distinctly different-looking dolls provides children with simple, visible cues for staying clear about who they are describing (e.g., Uncle Harry is the skinny black doll; Miss Smith is the big fat white doll; the "Candy Man" is the brown doll with the curly hair). If a child points to a certain doll as having said or done something to him or her, the interviewer might ask, "And who is that, again?" As with the use of photographs, it is the child, not the interviewer, who should make the verbal identification of the person being discussed.

Names for Body Parts and Sexual Acts

Along with correctly identifying people, it is also important to be clear about children's terminology for body parts and for sexual acts. The surest way to do that is for the interviewer to determine and use whatever words a child uses. Parents or caretakers may be able to provide this information prior to interviews with children, but sometimes they either do not know their children's terminology, think their children have no words for genitalia, or provide terminology that is different from what their children may tell the interviewer in conversation. Therefore, it is important for the interviewer to try to obtain this information directly from the child. It may be easiest to do this in an anxiety-free context that is not associated with questions about sexual abuse, touching, or secrets; that is, relatively early in the interview, once the child becomes comfortable with the interviewer and has developed some level of rapport. Although talking about sexual body parts is not something most children are terribly comfortable with, it is not as difficult as it may seem; it can be turned into an activity that is nonthreatening or even fun, depending on the attitude and comfort level of the interviewer.

One of the easiest ways to do this is through drawings of human figures using colored marking pens (preferably water-based, or else the interviewer will soon need a new wardrobe!). Although preprinted anatomically correct drawings currently are available, artistic ability is optional for this exercise, and drawing together helps in building rapport. In fact, children often like it when adults cannot draw much better than they can. One way to engage children in this activity is for the interviewer to tell them, "If you can guess what I'm drawing, you can help me finish it." The interviewer then draws the outline of a person, face forward with arms and legs extended. Most children will figure it out right away, no matter how primitive or abstract the drawing, and the child and interviewer can laugh together at what a "crummy" artist the interviewer is. The child is then encouraged to help by picking a pen of his or her favorite color and giving the person a face. As the child draws each body part, such as eyes, nose, and so on, the interviewer can ask the child what it is called and write it down on the paper, drawing a line between the word and the part of the body indicated. The child can be given encouragement through this process through remarks on how smart he or she is for knowing the various parts of the body. At the point where a child is likely to begin drawing clothes on the figure, the interviewer can ask the child to draw the dot or "button" in the middle of the tummy—the one that everyone has, regardless of whether a person is a boy or a girl. The purpose of this is to establish that the figure is naked before the interviewer has to dissuade the child from drawing on clothes; it is also a nonthreatening part of the body, which is easy to draw, and which most children call a "belly button."

For some children, drawing the genitals will be no problem, while for others it may be an embarrassing task that they may be unsure they should be performing. The interviewer should try to keep the atmosphere light and nonchalant. Comments from the interviewer such as "See how easy this is?" or "Everyone has these parts, just like everyone has a nose," help to put a child at ease. Some children may say that they "can't" draw those parts, and may ask the interviewer to do it for them. If they simply won't do it or begin to get anxious at the prospect, it is better for the interviewer to suggest that the child draw a dot or an "X" on the correct place than to draw the body part for the child. It is more important to establish the child's terminology during a first interview than to produce an accurate rendition of genitalia. If children have trouble saying certain words or claim that they don't know what something is called, the interviewer can offer to have them whisper it in his or her ear, or to have a doll or puppet tell it; with children who can spell, the interviewer may suggest that they spell it or at least provide the first letter or two so that the interviewer can guess (based on names provided by parents).

It is not difficult to introduce anatomically correct dolls into an interview following the completion of the "body parts" drawing. The interviewer can reveal that he or she has some special dolls that look a lot like the drawing, with parts that look like real people. A humorous approach to undressing and getting acquainted with anatomical dolls can serve as a great tension reliever, and it helps children to mask any initial embarrassment and anxiety. Besides, some of these dolls are really quite funny-looking. Undressing the child doll of the same sex as the child seems to be the least threatening way to begin. Also, having the interviewer undress the first doll in a quick, casual way, and then inviting the child to help undress the others, can prevent self-conscious moments for children who sense that their reactions are being observed.

It is sometimes easiest to leave the clothes, or at least the underwear, off the dolls until such time when they may be used to help disclose abuse, unless a child is embarrassed or uncomfortable with them. Most children tend to ignore the nudity of the dolls once they have gotten over their initial interest in them. As the dolls are undressed, the interviewer can reiterate aloud the names a child has given to various parts of the body. This serves to verify the names on the drawing, as well as to show the child again how easy it is to say the names aloud. Regardless of whether the doll's clothes remain on or off during the interview, if a child reveals molestation, it is important to ascertain whether his or her clothes were on or off at the time. The same applies to the alleged abuser.

Use of anatomically correct dolls to help children become comfortable in talking about parts of their bodies is primarily a clinical, rather than an investigatory, technique. If the dolls are to be used at a later point in the interview to allow a child an opportunity to demonstrate what might have happened to him or her, it also helps to have introduced the dolls earlier so that the child can become accustomed to their uniqueness or get over any initial uncomfortable reactions or associations they might invoke. Early introduction can prevent distractions or necessary digressions during a critical moment of disclosure. On the other hand, the use of these dolls is becoming increasingly controversial as more and more court cases include defense claims that the dolls increase children's suggestibility to the degree that they will falsely allege sexual abuse. Although there are currently no data to support such claims, law enforcement personnel and others who use dolls as part of investigatory interviews are becoming more cautious of their use so as not to jeopardize the information obtained. They have introduced such precautions as: leaving the dolls dressed or even out of view until after a child has verbally described abuse; insuring that the child, not the interviewer, undresses or positions the dolls if that occurs; and arranging the dolls in such a way that the child must choose from an assortment, rather than being handed a doll or two by an interviewer. Some experienced investigators are even beginning to advocate interviews without anatomical dolls whenever possible in order to avoid some of the now predictable defense arguments they create when a case goes to court. Although it is important to be aware of and to minimize, the legal liabilities associated with using communication tools such as these, it would be clinically inadvisable (if not downright cowardly) to abandon them altogether simply because they require additional explanations and defense of their use in court. For very young children whose verbal skills are limited or whose fear of telling something ties their tongues, the words "show me" rather than "tell me" can be the first step towards unlocking secrets about sexual abuse.

Regardless of what words are provided by the child for various body parts, the interviewer should use the child's words throughout the interview when referring to those parts of the body. If the child uses the same word, such as "pee-pee" or "potty," to refer to all genitals of both sexes, the interviewer might try to clarify things—by saying, for example, "You mean the man's potty in the front here, or in the back where he sits down?" In our opinion, it is best not to provide children with new terminology for body parts, even if they are the clinically correct words to use. An initial interview is not necessarily the best place for a lesson in sex education. It may confuse the child, and it may unnecessarily upset some family members if a child comes home using words like "vagina" or "vulva" instead of the childish terminology that parents are accustomed to hearing. More importantly, it can add one more level of confusion to a case that may end up in criminal or juvenile court, and it may add fuel to accusations that the child was "coached" to allege sexual abuse during the initial interview.

Children are not usually asked to use the correct names for body parts when testifying in court, as long as the parts to which they refer can be clearly established and identified using dolls, drawings, or further description. There are simply two purposes to the exercises described here: first, to establish children's terminology for body parts, particularly genitalia; and, second, to demonstrate to children in a nonthreatening way that the interviewer is comfortable with this subject. While it can be helpful to verbally acknowledge a child's embarrassment or nervousness, the interviewer's own spoken and unspoken messages to a child should be the opposite (e.g., that he or she has no problems in discussing private parts of the body and can help kids talk about such things). By transmitting the message that he or she has heard it all before and is "unshockable," the interviewer can relieve children of the burden or the fear that what they have to say might be shocking and result in rejection. If interviewers are uncomfortable in this role, children will usually sense the discomfort and will respond accordingly. This is why it is important for beginning interviewers to role-play and practice their interviewing skills and to gain experience in communicating with average preschoolers before attempting to interview suspected child victims of sexual abuse.

OVERCOMING FEAR OF THREATS OR CONSEQUENCES

Addressing Fears Directly

If children have been sworn to secrecy, threatened not to tell, or given descriptions of consequences that will befall them or their families should they ever reveal abuse, it is important to try to help them get past their fears before beginning to elicit from them any details about alleged or suspected molestation. Therefore, if children acknowledge that they have secrets they can't tell or if they appear particularly frightened or avoidant in ways that are indicative of possible abuse, it is usually best to address their fears directly. This process entails trying to determine what, if anything, it is they think or have been told will happen to them should they tell. It also entails finding out who may have threatened them, since it may or may not be the same person who molested them. If the interviewer cannot get abused children over their initial fear of consequences, or if the interviewer is unable to convince them that he or she and others can protect them from the things they most fear, it is unlikely that they will feel safe enough in an interview to provide much information about abuse.

One way to deal with threats that seem very real to children is to redefine them as "tricks" that adults sometimes play on children in order to keep them from telling something. Even small children usually understand the concept of "tricks," and it is a way of recasting vague and frightening premonitions into an emotionally manageable concept that is less believable, and therefore less threatening. One way of trying to uncover threats is to ask children if there is anything or anybody who has scared them, or to comment that they seem to be scared of something. The interviewer might ask the child if there is someone they have talked about together, or somebody in a photograph they have looked at together, or someone else in the child's life who is scary. Another way is to invite the child to make a list (the interviewer can write it down) of all the people and things that are most scary to him or her. After the list is made, the interviewer and the child can figure out together why each one is considered scary. Children seem to respond well to making lists; it gives them options, and it gives the interviewer more data with which to work. Whether the child describes someone as scary because he happens to have big eyebrows, or because of something that may be more indicative of abuse, it provides the interviewer with an avenue for discussion and may give the child permission to acknowledge that he or she is afraid of something.

Puppets and Toys as Communication Aids

There are a number of techniques that can be used to lessen children's anxiety when talking about subjects that they find frightening or uncomfortable. We have found the use of hand puppets to be one of the most effective communication tools in working with very young children (and it has been used successfully with frightened children up to the age of 12). If a child becomes particularly fearful or non-responsive at some point during an interview, the interviewer can introduce puppets to the child as his or her helpers—helpers whose jobs are to assist children when they have to talk about difficult subjects. The interviewer can begin by talking with a puppet and by asking the other puppets if any of them are going to come over and talk to him or her on the child's hand. Children are usually quick to respond to this invitation. A conversation can then ensue between the two puppets, with the interviewer encouraging the child's puppet to talk for and about the child.

Although there has been some criticism about the use of puppets and dolls, which centers around the concern that they encourage fantasy in children, even young children know that hand puppets are not real and that they cannot talk unless someone talks for them. Children also know that it is they who are doing the talking when puppets on their hands speak to an adult or to other puppets. This is true even when children attempt to "back off" a statement by asserting, "The puppet said that, not me." What puppets provide to young children is a measure of *distance* from the adult interviewer and from material or information that the children may be too frightened or too reluctant to simply sit and discuss. They may also give very small children a feeling of safety from threatened consequences because it can be a puppet who "tells" the secrets initially, not a child. Establishing that the puppet's job is always to tell the truth about what happened to the child, and not to make anything up, can be a non-threatening way of getting a child to open up initially and talk about what he or she is really feeling.

The best puppets to use for interviewing young children are those with mouths that open and are easy for little hands to maneuver. Having a wide assortment of puppets allows children to change puppets according to their moods or as a way of releasing their anxiety. Children may even use different puppets to convey to an interviewer their feelings or reactions to certain questions. Examples of such responses are "It would take a braver puppet than this one to answer *that* question," or "Mr. Froggy is too embarrassed to tell about that," or "Big Bird promised never to tell that secret."

Puppets can also be used in interviews for more than just talking. For example, following disclosure by a child that someone touched

him or her in a way or in a place that he or she didn't like, the child's
puppet can be asked to help in figuring out exactly what happened.
Before the child has time to become more anxious, the puppet can
be asked if he or she is smart enough to be able to hold a pointer
(such as a pencil) in his or her mouth. This is a task that children
usually like to prove that they can do. The puppet can then be asked
to use the pointer to point to the part(s) on an anatomical (child) doll,
or on a drawing, or even on the child's body where the child was
touched. The puppet can also point to parts of the adult doll or
drawing that show what may have touched the child. Pointers in the
mouths of puppets, like puppets themselves, are one more way of
offering children a little distance between themselves and something
that may be too threatening to say at first.

   Again, if children initially are reluctant to verbally identify individuals who have hurt or molested them, but are willing to point
them out to the interviewer, it is important to try to guard against
error or accommodation by (1) providing them with the widest choice
possible among people in their lives (using either dolls, photographs,
lists of names, or some other device that provides options); and (2)
clarifying that the children know and can identify, by name or by
description, the individuals whom they have singled out.

   Toy telephones, one for the child and one for the interviewer,
can be used in a similar way to allow the child to describe things that
initially may be too threatening to say face-to-face. The child and
interviewer may even want to take the parts of other people in the
child's life, such as the child and the alleged perpetrator, in order to
re-enact conversations such as threats (which the child may repeat in
the voice of the perpetrator) or to allow the child to tell the perpetrator
the child's feelings about what he or she did. Children frequently use
toy telephones in this way to reveal feelings that are too frightening
or confusing for them to communicate without the distance provided
by the phone. Regardless of which adult role interviewers play on the
toy phone, they should take a neutral to friendly tone, ask open-ended
questions such as "How do you feel about me?", and avoid negative
or suggestive comments.

   Given encouragement to express their feelings in any way they
can, children will use a variety of toys creatively to communicate. One
little girl decided to use a toy doctor kit to tell her secrets. After placing

the toy stethoscope in the ears of the interviewer "doctor," she proceeded to whisper her descriptions of having been molested into the other end of the toy. A dollhouse is another useful tool for helping children describe their worlds, such as who sleeps where and what happens at bathtime. Boys (who sometimes are reluctant to use anything that isn't a "boy toy") have even used little toy trucks or airplanes to disclose abuse by making them park or land on the parts of anatomical dolls where the touching occurred. These represent first steps by children to show or tell what happened.

Puppets, dolls, and stuffed animals also can be helpful with children whose verbal skills are limited or who are too frightened or embarrassed to talk at all. Children can indicate "yes" or "no" by having a puppet nod or shake its head—as long as the head motions are very clear to the interviewer and/or are verified by the child. Children can also be told that it is okay to indicate when they get particularly scared or want to take a break from the interview, and that they can do so simply by having a puppet bite its tail or its foot to show the interviewer that the child is getting anxious. Children who are exhibiting avoidant reactions or feeling frightened will often take puppets off their hands, saying that their hands are getting "too hot to keep talking." They may even send the puppets off to work or to sleep to keep them from talking about sensitive subjects. If the interviewer keeps a close eye on what the puppets are saying and doing, he or she will soon recognize that they can be an excellent barometer of what is going on inside a child.

It is important, ultimately, to obtain much more than an affirmative nod from a puppet in order to establish that a child has been abused. But a child's acknowledgment, through a puppet, that sexual abuse has occurred, followed by an interviewer's nonjudgmental permission to talk further about it, may be the first step in unlocking the secrets of a frightened child. It is important to keep in mind that verbal skills are among the least developed skills of many young children; this is why one goal of interviewing is to give them a variety of avenues through which to communicate. Puppets, drawings, and toys merely provide a vehicle by which children can safely begin to communicate with an unfamiliar adult. One hopes that a child will eventually be able to put down the puppet and describe what, if anything, has occurred. This often takes longer than one interview and may only occur during the course of ongoing therapy. Nonetheless, puppets and other toys can represent a beginning in the process of establishing rapport between a child and a caring adult.

UNDERSTANDING CHILDREN'S DEFENSES

COMMON DEFENSE PATTERNS

Children have different ways of coping with abuse and with their belief that they are not supposed to talk about it. Giving abused children permission to tell secrets that they have been warned not to divulge puts them in an emotional bind virtually unknown to children who do not carry these kinds of secrets. As a consequence, they have various ways of defending themselves against the intrusiveness of this kind of questioning and against our requests for disclosure.

One of the ways in which they do this is to describe acts of sexual abuse but to deny that it ever happened to them. Sometimes children will tell an interviewer that the abuse occurred while they were asleep or that they "dreamed it." Frequently, the "everyone-but-me syndrome" occurs in cases where there is more than one victim. Although some children *have* been in the position of observing the molestation of other children (whether or not they themselves were abused), they also may describe the abuse of others or of an imaginary friend in order to rid themselves of the secret while attempting to avoid the potential repercussions of implicating themselves.

Avenues to overcoming a child's fear of personalizing an abuse incident include providing accepting, supportive responses to the information provided, and helping the child to talk through the situation in as much detail as he or she can tolerate. It frequently is the incredibly telling details about an abusive incident—the smells, the sounds, what people said, and how things felt—that serve as guideposts to our understanding of what has actually happened to a child.

Sometimes young children disclose abuse without their even realizing it. For example, if a child describes seeing something come out a man's penis, the interviewer might ponder aloud, "I wonder what that stuff tastes like. I wonder if it tastes like strawberries or maybe chocolate?" Children who have been the recipients of oral sex are frequently quick to contradict the interviewer by shaking their heads, making a face, or saying, "No way." The interviewer then might say, "Well, maybe I've got it wrong. I wonder what it does taste like?" Sexually abused children may go on to describe the graphic details of such an act. On the other hand, children who have not been exposed to oral sex are likely to look at the interviewer as if he or she is crazy and say something such as "That stuff doesn't go in your *mouth*, it goes in the potty."

In cases where children consistently deny abuse but where there are strong reasons to suspect its occurrence, some interviewers have tried to determine whether or not children know any details about abuse by asking them what they *think* an experience would have been like if it *had* happened to them. In some instances, this has provided the only credible information that has indicated whether or not a child has been molested. On the other hand, it carries the disadvantage of providing abused children with an "out" at the end of the interview: They are likely to reiterate their initial denial and to claim that they were merely "guessing." On the other hand, the contrived guessing of a nonabused young child may provide enough inaccurate information for the interviewer to determine that molestation did not occur. Nonetheless, it is a high-risk technique that relies heavily on the skills and experience of the interviewer—and the lack of sexual knowledge of a nonabused child. As a consequence, this technique should be used with caution, especially in cases where legal action could result. Despite the time pressures put on most interviewers to come up with answers concerning a child's possible victimization, we must ask ourselves whether the same child who can respond to a "what-if" hypothetical situation may be able to disclose in a more direct way, when given more time.

Similarly, we advise interviewers not to suggest to children that anything about the interview is "pretend," including any attempts at pretending to describe or show what may have happened to them. The "let's pretend game," although easy and nonthreatening for a child to participate in, will only serve to confound any information gathered; will cast doubt upon the credibility of the information if it is subjected to legal scrutiny; and will provide a sure avenue for the child to retract any statements made during the "pretend interaction." It is important to keep reiterating to children (and to their puppets) that this is the time to tell the truth and help everyone understand what really happened.

Children frequently tell what happened to them in small pieces, saving the "worst" parts until they see how the interviewer, their parents, or others react to the things they divulge first. This is one of the reasons why first interviews often only reveal a small portion of what really happened. Children have their own perceptions of what things are "worst." For some children, the hardest things to tell about are sexual acts themselves; for others, they are the threats of the consequences of telling; for still others, the "worst" thing may be their perception of their own responsibility for participating in their abuse or their perpetration of sexual acts on other children. The interviewer should watch closely for children's behavioral cues. High levels of anxiety or avoidance in regard to the material being discussed should signal the interviewer to go more slowly or to return to that particular material at a later time.

The process of telling what happened in small pieces frequently begins with denial of any involvement in any sexual acts or unwanted touching. Molested children often deny abuse when first questioned, in order to protect themselves and others. They also do so in order to test the interviewer's reactions, persistence, and willingness to take the matter further. Therefore, it is not always in a child's best interests for the interviewer to accept an initial denial at face value. Asking a denying child if something "may" have happened or if it happened "sometimes" is frequently a way of gleaning the first indications of acknowledgment of abuse. It has been astounding to see the number of children who have been willing to acknowledge that "sometimes" they were touched in sexual ways, and who later have fully described molestation, but who initially said, "no" without any qualifiers to an inquiry. This type of faltering acknowledgment, especially by a young child, has occurred so frequently that we have termed it the "no–maybe–sometimes–yes syndrome." Again, it is an interviewer's accepting reaction to a child's disclosure that "maybe it happened sometimes" that can give a child permission to acknowledge further what actually happened and how frequently it occurred.

Fragmented Memories and Repressed Material

Children's thoughts and memories are not well organized and frequently come out in fragments. In cases where molestation occurred some time in the past, the process of helping children to recapture negative memories is one that takes patience and some practice. Some memories are very vague and may only be experienced as primary feelings or physical sensations that are associated with the memories. Some memory fragments are very vivid and replete with graphic details, but cannot be connected by children to a broader picture of what occurred. Other memories may only be triggered when paired with associations that are presented to the child by an outside source, such as an interviewer's verbal cues, a picture, or other current reminder. This concept is not the same as the "power of suggestion," in that it is geared toward the reconstruction of actual events and feelings, rather than something derived from imagination or mere prompting. This process involves active communication on the part of the interviewer, creativity with regard to the images introduced, and close attention to any and all clues (usually in the form of brief, seemingly peripheral statements) provided by children. All statements made a child during interactions where the interviewer is attempting to help the child recall earlier events or to take him or her back to an earlier point in time should be pursued.

Some memories, which truly have been repressed, are rarely retrievable during short-term intervention, even when their presence may seem apparent in the form of avoidant reactions and negative associations to the certain material presented. Similarly, it is particularly frustrating to evaluate a young child who acts out detailed scenarios of his or her abuse but denies it verbally. While this behavior may be that of a highly avoidant or frightened child who needs more time in therapy to feel safe enough to disclose, it may also be that of a child who is demonstrating unconscious recall of sexual abuse but actually has no verbal access to that unconscious material.

It is important for the interviewer to understand that this phenomenon is different from the disclosure process previously described, in which children provide small pieces of information and wait to see how they will be received. The positive and negative functions of repression in sexually abused children and adults are only just beginning to be studied and understood. Repression of early childhood experiences of sexual assault appear to operate both as the "psychological time bomb" frequently described in the literature, and as an important survival mechanism for children who do not perceive disclosure as an option at the time of abuse (MacFarlane, 1978). By recognizing this material as simply unavailable to some children, interviewers will be less likely to regard them as resistant to the interview process and can take care not to push them into areas in which they are not emotionally defended. Children who we have reason to believe have repressed sexual abuse (i.e., where there are clear medical findings of abuse; where the child re-enacts molestation in play; where there are witnesses to the abuse; or where there is evidence to suggest that all other children in their circumstances, especially in their family, were abused) usually need time and the emotional support that only long-term treatment can provide.

SENSITIVITY TO TIMING AND PHYSICAL SPACE

Finally, an understanding of the importance of timing is critical to all aspects of successful interviewing. Children's sense of timing and interviewers' need for information often do not coincide, usually to the detriment of both the child and a diagnostic evaluation. While it is sometimes necessary to ask children for information several times or in several different ways during an interview, when the interviewer believes that the information is accessible to the child but is not forthcoming, the timing of certain inquiries can make a big difference in whether such an attempt is successful or disruptive. Paying close attention to a child's emotional state is critical at such points.

The issue of timing can relate to such factors as how long an anxious child has been kept waiting for an interview, or whether the interview is conducted during a child's regularly scheduled naptime (a good reason for interviewing preschoolers in the morning). Or it can have more subtle effects, such as not taking the time to help a child relax or asking for disclosure information before a child's fear of the interviewer or of retaliation by others has been reduced. After asking a child a series of questions about possible abuse, it is important to lesson the emotional climate and intensity of the moment by "backing off" the material and giving the child some time out to focus on less threatening and more enjoyable things.

In the same way that it is important to acknowledge and accept a child's sense of timing, it is important to recognize a child's sense of space and physical contact. Many interviewers are instinctively inclined to provide physical comfort or physical contact with preschool-age children. While this may be a natural inclination for many adults and children, we do not recommend that interviewers physically reach out to children suspected of having been sexually abused, unless a child seeks such comfort and contact, or touches the interviewer first. Of course, there are some children who readily seek such contact and appear to feel much safer when they receive it. In such cases, physical contact can be part of an interaction that positively benefits the interview process. Some small children instinctively seek physical comfort during discussions of things that are particularly anxiety-provoking to them.

However, there are many children who are understandably skittish and distrustful of physical contact, given what they may have been subjected to in the way of unwanted touch and betrayal of trust. In such cases, attempts at physical contact can serve to "clam up" a child at a time when the interviewer is trying to achieve exactly the opposite effect. Interviewers must put themselves in these children's position. An adult stranger, whom they have just met, takes them into a room alone without their parents and talks to them about having their private parts touched and about uncomfortable secrets. This prospect can be frightening enough to some children without adding the confusing fact that this adult is also attempting to touch them, regardless of how friendly and comforting that touch may be intended to be. Even if the fear of being remolested is not a conscious one, many sexually abused youngsters are overly cautious and hypersensitive about physical contact. Consequently, it is usually best to suppress most spontaneous gestures involving interviewer-initiated physical contact.

On the other hand, some young children are spontaneously physical and barely notice when they step across the interviewer's leg or crash into his or her arms. Some will even crawl into the interviewer's lap for extra security while they tell their secrets. Others, who have become highly sexualized or lack appropriate physical boundaries, may even attempt sexualized contact with the interviewer in the form of touching, rubbing, or disrobing, or they may masturbate excessively during the interview. Such behavior is usually a sign of high anxiety, or of testing to see how "safe" the interviewer is or how impervious he or she is to provocation.

All of these situations must be responded to with the interviewer's best judgment and sense of what the child needs at any given moment. It also depends on the comfort level of the interviewer with the situation. It is important to be physically relaxed and not appear stiff. This usually comes from experience in being with young children and from feeling prepared for all kinds of reactions from them. Some children will need to see that the interviewer does not come too close, while other children may need to be gently restrained or shown that there are boundaries to physical contact. If interviewers take their cues from children and maintain nonjudgmental attitudes, the interactions, whatever their nature, will usually go smoothly.

By keeping a close watch on children's emotional responses to what is being asked of them, an interviewer can usually avoid invoking an emotional reaction, such as tears or other signs of upset. This is important for two reasons: (1) A diagnostic evaluation need not and should not be a confusing or traumatic experience for a child; and (2) once an interviewer "loses" very young children to an emotional reaction, whatever its duration, it is extremely difficult to recover their original sense of safety and cooperation, and to re-establish the relationship where it left off. Sexually abused children should be able to leave a diagnostic interview feeling good about what occurred and feeling understood, validated, and safe in a newly established protective relationship. While, obviously, this is not always possible (depending on the circumstances of the abuse and the consequences to a child of disclosure), it is something that is achievable and should be recognized as an important goal of interviewing children.

CONSIDERATIONS ON EVIDENCE GATHERING

THE CONTROVERSY OVER CHILDREN'S SUGGESTIBILITY

Some professionals, especially those in legal and criminal justice systems, caution interviewers not to ask focused questions; not to suggest that information is already known; not to indicate any expectations of certain responses; and not to support children in any way for their statements or answers to inquiries. This may be generally sound advice regarding the desire to interject as little influence as possible into an interview, especially in those cases that may result in litigation. It is also reasonable advice when the persons being interviewed are adults. It may even be prudent advice when interviewing a child who is not suspected of having been sexually assaulted and/or threatened or warned not to tell about it. Unfortunately, such advice may not be in a child's best interest if the child is young, frightened, and sexually abused.

The controversial issues of children's suggestibility, the effects of reinforcement by interviewers, and the use of leading questions have become nemeses in the field of child sexual abuse. It is time to recognize that child sexual abuse is not comparable to other types of adult crimes, and should not be investigated as though it were. Children who have been frightened into silence about things that they do not comprehend, and may not even have the language to describe, represent a special population that demands specialized approaches. Questioning a young child about sexual abuse is not comparable to asking a burglary victim to enumerate items that were taken from his or her home. Asking a child what, if anything, unpleasant or unusual happened to him or her during a certain period of time may be an acceptably neutral way of framing a question, but if a young child has been molested and told not to tell, it is unlikely that the abuse will be revealed. Such a child might then become one of the thousands of adults who have reported that they never told anyone as a child because no one ever asked them (Finkelhor, 1979b; Herman, 1981; MacFarlane & Korbin, 1983; Russell, 1984).

Professionals without legal or law enforcement training are sometimes unfamiliar with the concept of "leading questions." A leading question is a question that, legally, is considered to be calculated to lead an individual to make a particular statement. They are questions that point an inquiry in a certain direction and suggest its answer. In the most technical sense, a leading question could even be defined as one that can be answered with a "yes" or "no" answer.

In the best of all possible worlds, it would be advisable not to ask children leading questions, in order to avoid the concern that children are responding to suggestions that certain things occurred or that they are being compliant and acquiescent to an adult authority figure. But, in the best of all possible worlds, children are not sexually assaulted in secrecy, and then bribed, threatened, or intimidated not to talk about it. In the real world, where such things do happen, leading questions may sometimes be necessary in order to enable frightened young children to respond to and talk about particular subjects. Although they may present legal problems later on, leading questions, on the other hand, should not be viewed as some form of illegal activity on the part of an interviewer. In California, as in many other states, the law specifically acknowledges the difficulty of questioning young children, especially in court, and allows attorneys to ask leading ques-

tions of child witnesses. Indeed, their questions, which are designed
to elicit particular responses, are usually far more leading than those
employed by clinicians. Nonetheless, interview settings and play rooms
are not courts of law; they are not and should not be subject to the
same formalities and rules of protocol. They are places where we
begin the slow process of piecing together and ferreting out the truth
of a child's experience—not where we attempt to prove something
beyond a reasonable doubt, especially in one initial interview.

At the same time, interviewers in this field have a grave obligation
to be responsible in their use of leading questions and verbal reinforcement, and to provide only as much direction as children may
need to overcome their fear and resistance to disclosure if they have
been abused. It is a difficult process to articulate, and often requires
a fine balance between intrusion and restraint. In addition, an interview style that may serve the best therapeutic interests of a child may
be contraindicated because of legal ramifications. On the other hand,
it is essential that information about abuse ultimately come from the
child, not the interviewer. "Yes" or "no" responses to directed questions are insufficient for making a complete diagnosis. Again, children
usually need time and security in order to talk more freely. There
are no easy answers when dealing with an issue that is both a crime
and a mental health problem for children. It is hoped that the following examples may aid in recognizing some of the kinds of leading
questions that range from useful to not recommended.

Overcoming Denial and Clarifying Terminology

In attempts to be avoidant, or as part of the developmental stage of
concrete thinking, children often will tell the very minimum that can
be said about something and still be responsive. They are also likely
to interpret a question in the narrowest, most literal way possible.
When an interviewer has a sense that this may be happening, it is
helpful to follow up with a more specific question, even if it is non-
responsive to the previous question. For example, if a child has been
asked, "And did he touch you any place else besides your winkie?",
and the answer was "no," the interviewer might want to go one step
further by asking a more directed question. For example, the interviewer might ask, "What about your mouth? Did anything ever touch
your mouth in a way that you didn't like?" If the answer is "yes," it

does not necessarily mean that the child was lying in the first response. Such seemingly contradictory answers on the part of children can be understood through a variety of explanations. One is children's natural tendency to deny or minimize things about which they are ashamed or afraid, or for which they think they will be blamed (Kerns, 1981). As with the previously described interaction we call the "no–maybe–sometimes–yes syndrome," some children may simply need encouragement in order to disclose in small, tentative steps.

For other children, a "no" answer to a general question followed by a "yes" answer to a more specific question may be indicative of the child's own literal translation of the words being used by the interviewer. For example, many children interpret the word "touched" to mean something that is done only with the hand or the fingers. A child who has been raped may not necessarily describe or think of the behavior as being "touched" in the vagina with a penis. Similarly, a child might not think of the mouth as a place that ever got "touched," unless someone put a finger in his or her mouth. Consequently, it may take much more direct questions in order to elicit information about oral sex.

Interviewers may also have communication problems centering around their use of the word "hurt." Although the first disclosures of many young children are sometimes misunderstood or overlooked because they *only* use the word "hurt" (i.e., "Uncle Jimmy hurt me"), it should not be assumed that all sexual abuse physically hurts young children or even that they regard all sexual acts as negative or upsetting (Mrazek, 1981). Sexual abuse in the guise of tickling, bathtub entertainment, games, or make-believe medical examinations usually does not "hurt," nor does oral sex when the child is the recipient of gentle contact.

Obviously, it is always the best approach to elicit children's own words and descriptions for what, if anything, has been done to them. However, if unsolicited descriptions are not forthcoming, it is useful to use a wide range of terminology during questioning. Examples of terms sometimes used by children include "touching" (with various parts), "kissing," "licking," "poking," "rubbing," "tickling," "playing with," "messing with," "hurting," "making a boo-boo" (or "ouwie"), "putting something inside," or "taking naked pictures" of private parts. Finding the right words and understanding a child's use of them are crucial to accountable interviewing. What may sound like an initial allegation of abuse ("Daddy poked my pee-pee") may be a child's description of an unwanted, but innocent, bathtime routine. On the other hand, it could be a child's first attempt at describing being raped.

The first step is to try to establish common terminology for acts that a child can either acknowledge or deny. The second step is to understand what that acknowledgment or denial means to the child (i.e., what is it that did or did not happen). The last and most important steps are (1) to elicit from the child enough of an explanation, description, and/or demonstration of what occurred to decipher the people and the circumstances surrounding the alleged incident(s); (2) to rule out whether the child could be making a statement at the direction of someone else; (3) to assess the feasibility and credibility of the child's statements; and (4) to make a preliminary determination as to whether or not sexual abuse has occurred. As stated previously, the completion of this process is not always possible in one interview, but it should be kept in mind, regardless of the necessity of a long investigatory or treatment process.

PROVIDING OPTIONS FOR ANSWERING

When children are given permission to answer questions in a variety of ways, they will be less likely to use certain answers, such as "I don't know," as protective mechanisms against things they are not ready to reveal. To accomplish this, the interviewer can begin by explaining that he or she is going to be asking a bunch of questions; some might sound silly or strange or scary, and some will be easy to answer. The process can then be explained to the child as follows:

- "You have a lot of choices in how to answer the questions."
- "The best choice is just to give the true answer, if you know it, or to tell me you don't know the answer if you don't. (If I asked you what your mother's favorite color was, and you didn't know—that's okay, I don't know my mother's favorite color either.)"
- "If I ask you a question about something that didn't happen ('Did anybody step on your foot today?'), it's fine to say 'No, that didn't happen.' We never want to say that something happened if it didn't."
- "On the other hand, if I ask you about something that did happen or something you know the answer to but you don't

want to tell me about it right now, you don't have to say it didn't
happen or that you don't remember. It's okay to tell me that
you don't feel like talking about it yet, or that it's too scary to
talk about, or that you don't like the question."

- "It is better not to answer than to say "no" when the answer is
really 'yes', or 'yes' when it is 'no.' If you get too scared or
embarrassed by my questions, just tell me or give me a sign and
we'll talk about other things for a while."

- "If I ask you a question that you don't understand, never try
to guess the answer or say 'yes' just because you think you
should. Just tell me, 'Hey, I don't know what you mean by
that.' "

Giving young children these kinds of options not only gives them
permission not to know or not to tell certain things that they might
otherwise deny or confirm; it also gives them more control over the
circumstances of the interview. If children disclose sexual abuse, helping them feel in control of the way they disclose will assist in coun-
terbalancing the helpless feelings engendered by their memories of
the abuse. If they have not been abused, their understanding that
they have options to using denial as a self-protective defense makes
the denial more credible.

Most of all, the giving of options reduces whatever pressure a
child might feel to answer questions in a certain way or to say things
that he or she may need to contradict later. Offering a "no response"
or "decline to respond" option to a child gives the interviewer the
opportunity to identify sensitive or frightening issues for the child;
this can be as important as anything the child does choose to tell in
an initial interview. Giving children opportunities to confirm that what
they've told is the truth, as well as the chance to examine whether
anything they've said is "pretend" or "not really sure" or said for some
reason other than because it's true, can both assist the interviewer's
level of confidence in what has been said and increase the child's
options and feelings of control. It should be done carefully, however,
so that it is perceived as permission to reconsider the validity of all
that has been said in the interview, not as either pressure to recant
earlier statements or doubt about a child's honesty.

Despite the fact that it is frequently necessary to be very specific
in questioning very young children, the specific words used in a ques-

tion and in an interviewer's statements should be deliberate and part of a conscious process of self-awareness on the part of an interviewer. Words of encouragement should be carefully stated. For example, some children need to hear that it is all right with their parents to talk to the interviewer. In such instances, the interviewer might say to a child, "Your mom brought you here because she hopes you will be able to tell me about anything or anybody that's bothering you, and because she knows that you will tell the truth." This is a supportive but noncoercive statement, compared to a statement such as "Your mom brought you here today because she wants you tell me about what Uncle Bill did to you." Aside from being leading, the real problem with the latter statement is that it uses the authority and expectations of the child's mother to suggest what the child should say to the interviewer, and adds the inference that the child will be pleasing the mother by doing so.

Questions should begin by being as open-ended as possible, and should slowly narrow down, depending upon the answers of the child. It is useful not only to give the child a range of alternatives, but to see whether the child says "yes" or "no" to *every* question, especially to those which are not about abuse. If he or she says "no" to every question, it may mean that the interviewer has not considered the reason the child has in mind. Or it may mean that the child is not ready to give an answer (in which case it is very important to watch his or her nonverbal answers to each question). If the child answers "yes" to every question, especially when one "yes" answer contradicts a previous one, the interviewer has an indication that the child may be avoiding the entire issue or is simply trying to please by being agreeable. Deliberately including questions whose responses should be contradictory to other answers ("Was it cold outside? Was it warm?") will help in determining some of these issues.

It is important not to move too quickly from answers that appear to acknowledge abuse to questions that imply specific assumptions about the nature of such abuse. For example, the question "Did Daddy touch you on the pee-pee?" is not a question that should immediately follow a statement by a child that Daddy touched him or her *someplace*. Similarly, the statement "Somebody touched me on the pee-pee," should be followed with an inquiry about who it was, not with a question that includes the name of an alleged or suspected abuser. Questions that ask about a specific person or act should be offered only after children have been given every opportunity to describe for themselves what occurred or what they meant by earlier statements. Such opportunities include asking open-ended questions; asking for clarification ("Maybe you can tell me what you mean?"); providing choices ("Was it your head he touched? . . . Your tummy? . . . Did it feel nice [tickle, feel weird, etc.]?"); asking for an illustration of what happened ("Can you draw the person or put an X on the part that got touched?"); or asking for demonstration ("Can you show me with the dolls how that looked?").

If general inquiries and open-ended questions yield no information, no response, or a symptomatic reaction indicative of something beneath the surface, more direct questions may be indicated. However, if directive questions are answered affirmatively, it is still helpful and important to follow them with additional nondirective questions in order to test their validity. Questions such as "What was that like?", "How did that happen?", or "How did that make you feel?" can help obtain the details that mitigate the need for more directive questions. But, as stated previously, details may not be forthcoming in an initial interview with a frightened child, and the importance of follow-up treatment or extended evaluation of any child who indicates a history of sexual abuse cannot be overemphasized.

It is one thing to ask a question that is "leading" in the sense that it asks for information about a specific act or person ("Was it Daddy who touched your pee-pee?"); it is another matter to ask questions in such a way that they infer or indicate a desired response ("It was Daddy who touched you there, wasn't it?"). Although we have argued that the first type of question is sometimes necessary in order to obtain or rule out certain specific kinds of information that may not be volunteered by a child, the second example represents a type of questioning that may be unduly influential. Therefore, interviewers should be careful about asking young children questions that answer themselves or appear to ask for an affirmative answer, such as "He put his finger inside, didn't he?" Questions that really sound like statements of fact may lead children to believe that an interviewer is asking that they agree with him or her.

Although such questions may sometimes be heard in courtrooms, the interviewer's role is different from that of a trial attorney. An interviewer should not be trying to "prove" that a child was or was not molested; a diagnostic interviewer gathers data in order to try to determine whether or not sexual abuse occurred. Sometimes those data take the form of verbal statements; sometimes the signs are more subtle. In either case, one wants to feel assured that the information is coming from the experience of the child, not from the influence of the interviewer.

Keeping Track of Information

When there is a lot at stake (and there usually is when one is diagnosing child sexual abuse), the initial interview can be a high-pressure time for the interviewer. Trying to remember what to ask as well as how to ask it while simultaneously attending to a child's responses, affect, attention span, and anxiety level can cause even seasoned interviewers to omit critical questions, ask questions that are clumsy or unintentionally leading, or overlook important information provided by the child. It can also be difficult to recall everything later. If an interview is not being audiotaped or videotaped, it is helpful to have another person taking notes of the critical questions and answers. The most inconspicuous way of doing this is via a two-way mirror or through electronic amplification into a speaker in another room. If this is not possible, we have received few protests from children when someone sits in the corner of the playroom on a chair or on the floor taking notes. After a brief explanation of what that person is doing, most children tend to ignore his or her presence.

If none of these options are practical, the interviewer may want to keep a pen and pad handy (on the floor or low table, under the couch, etc.) in order to jot down crucial points. Most children don't seem to mind the brief interruption, although it is a distraction for both child and interviewer, and less exact than a third-party transcript. In any case, if an interview is not simultaneously recorded, it should be written up or dictated promptly after the child or family leaves so that its immediacy is not lost.

In order to help the interviewer remember various facts about a child's circumstances (e.g., the child's names for family members, pets, parts of the body, etc.) or the specific details of a case (e.g., names of adults with access to the child), it helps to jot these things down on a file card and bring them into the interview. An interviewer who is sitting on the floor can sit on the cards or tuck them into the couch for quick reference when the child is preoccupied with something else.

Aside from all of the individual details to remember about each child, it is easy to forget some of the more basic questions when a child begins disclosing or acknowledging sexual abuse. These may not be important to many therapists or necessary in initial interviews, depending on their purpose, but they are usually important for purposes of investigation, and obtaining them can sometimes prevent the need for subsequent, multiple interviews. The following list is fairly elementary, but it can serve as a reference guide to insure that most of the basic information is covered once disclosure begins.

- "Who was there? Were you there? What did you see and hear? Were other kids there?" (Victims? witnesses?) "Did you know them? Were other adults there?" (Perpetrators? witnesses?) "Were they men or women? Did you know them or were they strangers? What did they do? Did they know what was happening to you?"
- "What happened?" (Ask for details about the abuse. Was there penetration, penile or digital; ejaculation; force; a weapon; pornography shown to the child or naked pictures taken; use of drugs on the child or by the adult?)
- "Where did this happen?" (Orient child to familiar places.) "Which house that you used to live in, the green one or the white one?" (Be specific.) "Where in the bathroom?"
- "When did it happen?" (Orient child to time using events, not dates.) "How long ago was the last time? When was the first time? How old were you? Whose class were you in? Was it at night [a school day, a weekend, etc.]?"
- "How often does [did] it happen? How many times?" (A child might say, "sometimes," or "all the time," or "millions of times." The interviewer should try to get more specifics: "*Every* time you visited Daddy [went to Scouts, etc.], or only some of those times?")
- If applicable: "Why didn't you tell before now? Did someone tell you not to tell? Who? What did he [she] say would happen? What did [do] you think will happen? What is the scariest part of this whole thing? Why did you decide to tell about it now? Who did you tell before me? What did they say?" (Depending

on the child's attitude and reactions to other questions, the interviewer may want to avoid questions that begin with "why." Some young children associate "why" questions with getting into trouble, e.g., "Why did you do that," and may assume that the interviewer is blaming them for what happened.)

"Has this happened before? Has anyone else ever done this kind of thing to you?" (Whether a child denies or discloses the abuse in question, this final inquiry toward the end of an interview is important in ascertaining the history and facts of a case, and in letting a child know that the interviewer understands that it can happen more than once or by more than one person.)

REMEMBERING THE CHILD'S VIEW

Brief, often out-of-context statements by children that indicate the possibility of sexual abuse should be responded to in the most calm voice and casual demeanor possible. Even if an interviewer is careful with the actual words used, if he or she suddenly sits up, leans forward, and says in an intense voice, "*Who* touched your pee-pee?", the child is likely to become frightened or cautious over the change of affect, and answer "Nobody" or refuse to answer at all. The interviewer should remember that an underreaction is usually the safest reaction with a scared child. Of course, it isn't always an easy task to keep one's poise in the face of some of the startlingly vivid sexual acts described by severely abused preschoolers. In such instances, or when children say anything that catches an interviewer off guard, the interviewer should consider invoking a standard phrase that is nonjudgmental and "buys" him or her enough time to think of a more appropriate response than the initial gut reaction. That "standby" phrase might be "And *then* what happened?" It's there when one doesn't know what else to say.

In keeping with the need to underreact and appear nonjudgmental in affect, interviewers must be careful that their words do not transmit judgmental attitudes to their child listeners. Because sexually abused children so frequently blame themselves for their abuse (Herman, 1981), they are quick to assign such judgments to others as well. Consequently, it is very important to phrase questions in such a way

as to avoid even the appearance of placing blame or respon,
the child. To do this, it helps to be able to think in the cond
literal way that a child thinks.

Young children have their own way of hearing what we
them. For example, asking children whether they took their c
off, as opposed to whether they *had* to take their clothes off, or whither
someone made them take their clothes off, can make a difference in
whether they answer "yes" or "no." The first phrasing may mean to
them that the interviewer is trying to learn whether or not *they* did
this bad thing, as opposed to what was done *to* them. This difference
is especially applicable when asking about sex acts (oral copulation,
mutual masturbation) that children were told or forced to perform
on an adult. It also applies to children who have been forced or
encouraged to perform sexual acts on other child victims. Children
teach us by their answers the ways that we may inadvertently add to
their feelings of responsibility—and they have much to teach.

There are two direct messages that can be given in the course of
an interview that can help to reduce children's feelings of self-blame
for the situation they find themselves in following disclosure. One is
to be very clear about whose fault it is when grownups do sexual
things with children: It is *always* the grownups' fault, no matter what
the circumstances. Why? The answer might be something like this:
"Because grownups know it's wrong; because they can say no to themselves and to kids; and because grownups aren't allowed to touch kids
in those kinds of ways. They're only allowed to touch other grownups
that way, and only if the other persons want them to. If they touch
kids, then they have a problem—but it's their problem, not the kids'."
The interviewer can begin this conversation by asking the child, "Whose
fault do you think it is that this stuff happened?" It is startling how
many children will say that it was their fault.

The second message that may reduce feelings of responsibility
applies to children who are worried about what will happen to the
persons who abused them, and who feel to blame for potential future
consequences. (The interviewer should remember that children frequently retain positive feelings about their abusers, even though they
have negative feelings about the abuse.) In such cases, the interviewer
should not misrepresent or minimize potential consequences or make
false promises of help if they cannot be assured. The most honest
answer is usually that the interviewer doesn't know exactly what will

happen in the long run. The most important part of the answer is that the decision is not up to "us"—not to the child, his or her parent(s), or the interviewer. It is the job of other people—usually people like police officers, judges and juries—to decide what will happen to that person. The message to the child, phrased in child's language, might be this: "You are not responsible for what happens later; your only job is to tell the truth about what happened before now. If something happens to the person who did this it will be because of what he or she did to you, not because you told about it. Similarly, if nothing happens as a result of telling the truth, it is still important to do so."

Obviously, the situation is more complex than this answer implies (and the answer will have to be more complex if the situation involves parental incest and the child also asks, "What is going to happen to me?"). However, it helps to remember that preschool-age children are very concrete and may not be seeking a complex answer about the workings of the justice or child protective systems. They may really be asking, "If something bad happens to him or her, will it be my fault?" For the child's sake, the answer to that question must be very clear.

CONCLUSION

Conducting professional assessments to determine whether or not young children have been molested is not a task for the faint of heart or for those who seek immediate results and immediate gratification. Competent, sensitive assessment takes time, and systems which demand immediate results must be countered by interviewers who insist upon being given adequate time and friendly environments which are geared to the needs of children, not agencies. On the other hand, we must be cognizant, whatever our professional affiliations, of the various needs for the information that comes out of an interview, and must try to coordinate our efforts in ways that are protective of children's privacy and of their limited tolerance for repeated questioning.

The extent to which we encourage children to disclose abuse must take into consideration their own sense of timing and need to protect themselves and others; their parents' need to know what has happened or not happened to them; and other systems' needs for information or evidence. These sometimes conflicting needs must be carefully weighed against one another, with special emphasis on what is therapeutically necessary for the child at that time. Whatever one's role or primary purpose in interviewing an alleged child victim, it is important to remember that disclosure of abuse and the interview process itself are going to have a psychological impact on that child. That impact can be important to healthy future adjustment, or it can be negative and add to the trauma. If it does add trauma, we may become part of the problem for children who are already in pain.

A final thought for interviewers relates to their role vis-à-vis the legal system. As has been mentioned throughout this chapter, much of what we do and say in diagnostic interviews has potential legal ramifications, which often are inescapable. Therefore, along with being sensitive and skilled with children, interviewers must educate themselves to the many aspects of the legal system that take on significance following a child's disclosure of abuse. These often go far beyond the mandated reporting of sexual abuse, and interviewers can no longer afford to be naive to the process. Unfortunately, few individuals who are expert at communicating with small children are also recognized as expert witnesses in courts of law (Berliner, Canfield-Blick, & Bulkley, 1983). This is usually reflective of a traditional bias, particularly within our legal system, that expertise drives solely from such things as certain kinds of professional degrees, published writings, and national recognition. Unfortunately, few physicians, authors, or national spokespersons are also able or willing to devote large portions of their time to diagnosing and treating child sexual abuse or spending large amounts of time in court. Even more unfortunate is the lack of formal recognition for the expertise and skills of those who do.

As a consequence, those who take on the task of evaluating alleged child victims must also be prepared to become the objects of attack when cases enter the legal system and their conclusions and techniques are challenged. Since it is usually a more palatable defense strategy to attack the credentials, motives, and methods of an interviewer than it is to attack the veracity of a young child, those who diagnose child sexual abuse, whatever their professional affiliations, may be accused of everything from brainwashing and grandiosity to overzealous child advocacy and retaliation for presumed abuse in their own backgrounds. Those who are in fear of the witness stand or who cannot tolerate the vociferous attempts of others to discredit them and their findings should probably seek more gentle career goals. However, for those who can withstand the process in the interest of insuring that the voices of sexually abused children are heard, the risks and the battles are part of the job.

The rewards in the short run often seem obscure, especially in the context of justice systems whose procedures seem so antithetical to the needs of children, and so hostile to those who speak for them. However, the need for competent diagnostic evaluations continues to grow, as does the need for more training in this area. By continuing to arm ourselves with knowledge of the problem and self-confidence in the methods necessary to communicate with young children, we will be better able to meet these needs.

EFFECTS OF SEXUAL ABUSE ON CHILDREN

Rob Lusk
Jill Waterman

A great deal has been written about the short- and long-term effects of child sexual abuse; however, relatively little has been written about effects on preschool children in particular. There is an extraordinary amount of variability in the effects described in the literature (Nakashima & Zakus, 1979; Peters, 1974); in fact, Mrazek and Mrazek (1981) list over 60 effects reported by various authors. Some studies have concluded that the effects can be positive; for example, the sexually abusive relationship may provide the child with at least some caring and concern in "an otherwise depriving environment" (Rosenfeld, Nadelson, Krieger, & Backman, 1977, p. 334; also Westermeyer, 1978). Others have drawn the conclusion that the effects are mixed (Brunold, 1964; Rosenfeld, Nadelson, & Krieger, 1979; Weiner, 1962) or that sexual abuse has little or no effect at all (Bender & Grugett, 1952; Finch, 1967; Powell & Chalkley, 1981; Yorukoglu & Kemph, 1966). however, the great majority of authors have argued that the effects are mainly harmful; it is this literature that is focused upon in the present chapter.

AFFECTIVE EFFECTS

A common finding in the literature has been that there are emotional or affective sequelae to child sexual abuse; for example, in De Francis's (1970) study of 263 victims (mainly older children), two-thirds were judged to be "emotionally damaged." Guilt (or shame) is a common reaction, reported by a host of authors (Boatman, Borkan, & Schetky, 1981; De Francis, 1970; Dixen & Jenkins, 1981; Herman & Hirschman, 1977; Katan, 1973; Kaufman, Peck, & Taguiri, 1954; Kelly, 1982; Knittle & Tuana, 1980; MacFarlane & Korbin, 1983; Meiselman, 1979; Paulson, 1978; Simari & Baskin, 1982; Sloane & Karpinsky, 1942; Tsai & Wagner, 1978). Despite the fact that most of these authors base their findings on informal clinical observation, it seems likely that guilt is a common sequela, because of the large number of cases involved in these reports. Children tend to blame themselves for the abuse, may feel especially guilty if they enjoyed aspects of it, and, in cases of incest, may feel that their disclosure has precipitated the destruction of their families. As Rosenfeld et al. (1979) point out, this guilt often intensifies with time, as children gain a clearer understanding of cultural norms and taboos. Thus, although preschoolers often do not experience this guilt in the short term, it typically becomes a problem for them as they get older. This seems especially true if the abuse is ongoing.

Anxiety is another frequently mentioned result of sexual abuse, both for preschoolers and for older children (Adams-Tucker, 1981, 1982; Brant & Tisza, 1977; Brassard, Tyler, & Kehle, 1983; Browning & Boatman, 1977; De Francis, 1970; Department of Health and Human Services [DHHS], 1981; Goodwin, 1982; Johnston, 1979; Kaufman et al., 1954; Kelly, 1982; Krieger, Rosenfeld, Gordon, & Bennett, 1980; Rist, 1979; Tufts New England Medical Center [Tufts], 1984; Weiss, Rogers, Darwin, & Dutton, 1955; Westermeyer, 1978; Yates, 1982). This anxiety can be quite severe: Adams-Tucker (1981) noted that in her clinic sample (n = 28; a few preschoolers were included, anxiety was often the major presenting problem. The anxiety observed can be manifested in various ways (in both the short and the long term): (1) in relations with the opposite sex (Brassard et al., 1983); (2) via somatic and behavioral symptoms (e.g., enuresis, tics) (DHHS, 1981; Rist, 1979); (3) via phobias and nightmares (Weiss et al., 1955); and (4) in anxiety over separation (Brant & Tisza, 1977).

Concomitant with this anxiety, many authors have noted extreme levels of fear in sexually abused preschoolers and older children (Boekelheide, 1978; Brant & Tisza, 1977; Brassard et al., 1983; Browning & Boatman, 1977; De Francis, 1970; Finch, 1973; Goodwin, 1982; Kelly, 1982; Landis, 1956; Summit, 1983; Tufts, 1984; Vander Mey & Neff, 1982). This fear can arise during the abuse itself (e.g., fear of adults, fear over what will happen in the future), or can be manifested in later life (e.g., as phobias).

Numerous authors believe that depression is a frequent reaction to child sexual abuse at any age (Blumberg, 1981; Boekelheide, 1978; Brooks, 1982; Browning & Boatman, 1977; Heims & Kaufman, 1963; Jiles, 1981; Johnston, 1979; Kaufman *et al.*, 1954; Meiselman, 1979; Molnar & Cameron, 1975; Paulson, 1978; Perlmutter, Engel, & Sager, 1982; Rosenfeld *et al.*, 1977; Sgroi, 1982a; Simari & Baskin, 1982; Tsai & Wagner, 1978; Tufts, 1984; Westermeyer, 1978; Yates, 1982). Blumberg believes that recurrent sexual abuse will "almost invariably result in an ongoing depressive state" (1981, p. 349). In fact, authors have observed depressive symptomatology in sexual abuse victims ranging from preschoolers (Tufts, 1984; Yates, 1982) to adolescents (Heims & Kaufman, 1963) to adults (Meiselman, 1979; Rosenfeld *et al.*, 1977; Tsai & Wagner, 1978). The evidence therefore suggests that depression is another common correlate of sexual abuse.

A final affective reaction noted by several authors is that of anger (Boatman *et al.*, 1981; Browning & Boatman, 1977; Krieger *et al.*, 1980; Simari & Baskin, 1982; Steele & Alexander, 1981; Tufts, 1984). This anger is commonly directed toward both parents (Steele & Alexander, 1981). It has been found in the short term with preschoolers (Tufts, 1984) and older children (Browning & Boatman, 1977), and later on, when the victims become adults (Simari & Baskin, 1982).

PHYSICAL EFFECTS

Although much less frequently reported than affective correlates of child sexual abuse, physical sequelae have been observed. Some of these (e.g., genital injury) are obviously direct effects of the abuse; others are not necessarily causally linked to the abuse itself. In general, it has been noted that although physical effects are probably the most concrete evidence of the harmful nature of abuse, they are relatively rare, and absent in most cases (Stern & Meyer, 1980).

Probably the most common "physical" sequelae reported are somatic complaints, including psychosomatic problems (Adams-Tucker, 1982; Blumberg, 1978, 1981; Boekelheide, 1978; Browning & Boatman, 1977; Burgess & Holmstrom, 1975; Goodwin, 1982; Gross, 1979, 1982; Rist, 1979; Sgroi, 1982a; Westermeyer, 1978; Yates, 1982). Such problems, many noted in preschoolers, include stomachaches, headaches, hypochondriasis, encopresis, enuresis, excessive blinking, and even hysterical seizures.

Pregnancy is another effect of sexual abuse that has been noted (Brunold, 1964; De Francis, 1970; Herman & Hirschman, 1981; Meiselman, 1979; Riggs, 1982). Obviously, this is not a danger to preschoolers. According to De Francis, the pregnant victims he studied (n = 28) showed greater anxiety, fear, shame, and loss of self-esteem than nonpregnant victims.

Although relatively rare, it has been noted that sexual abuse can cause injury, bruises, or bleeding in external genitalia and vaginal and anal areas (Brassard et al., 1983; Brunold, 1964). This damage is often relatively more severe in preschoolers, as these areas are smaller and less well developed than those of older children. Related problems include pain and itching of the genitals (Brassard et al., 1983; Riggs, 1982), unusual genital odors (Riggs, 1982), and problems with walking or sitting (Brassard et al., 1983; Riggs, 1982). Also, sexually transmitted diseases (e.g., venereal disease) have been found in some victims (Brassard et al., 1983; Brunold, 1964; Riggs, 1982; Terrell, 1977).

Finally, authors have observed that changes in appetite (Brassard et al., 1983) and changes in or problems with sleep (Adams-Tucker, 1982; Boekelheide, 1978; Brassard et al., 1983; Burgess & Holmstrom, 1975; Goodwin, 1982; Johnston, 1979; Weiss et al., 1955) can be associated with child sexual abuse. Such problems include changes in sleep patterns (Burgess & Holmstrom, 1975), recurring dreams (Burgess & Holmstrom, 1975), and nightmares (Burgess & Holmstrom, 1975; Goodwin, 1982; Weiss et al., 1955).

COGNITIVE AND SCHOOL-RELATED PROBLEMS

It has been observed that school-aged sexually abused children exhibit cognitive and school-related problems that may be related to the abuse. To date, authors have not addressed how these problems affect preschoolers. However, some of the difficulties discussed may apply to children of any age. For example, Shaw and Meier (1983) and Johnston (1979) have noted that sexually abused children seem to have problems concentrating on tasks; Shaw and Meier believe they tend to have short attention spans. Jiles (1981) writes that these children feel powerless, and perceive a lack of control in many situations; this may be a function of the nature of the abusive situation (in which they are largely helpless). Both Summit (1983) and Knittle and Tuana (1980) have commented that sexually abused children tend to develop a "helpless victim" mentality that affects them in other situations.

BEHAVIORAL SYMPTOMS AND "ACTING OUT"

Not surprisingly, a wide range of behavioral symptoms have been associated with child sexual abuse; again, most of these associations result from observations of older children. The symptoms can be grouped according to whether they involve a form of acting out, withdrawal, or repetition of the abusive relationship.

Behaviors of sexually abused children involving acting out that have been cited in the literature include the following:

1. Hostile–aggressive behavior (Adams-Tucker, 1981; Bess & Janssen, 1982; De Francis, 1970; Tufts, 1984). However, it should be noted that Shaw and Meier (1983) found their sample of six sexually abused children to be *less* aggressive than normal.
2. Antisocial behavior (De Francis, 1970).
3. Delinquency, with school-aged children (Blumberg, 1978; De Francis, 1970; Meiselman, 1979; Vander Mey & Neff, 1982).
4. Stealing, with older children (Weiss *et al.*, 1955).
5. Tantrums (Adams-Tucker, 1981).
6. Substance abuse (including alcohol and drugs), with older children (Herman & Hirschman, 1981; Riggs, 1982; Spencer, 1978; Summit, 1983; Vander Mey & Neff, 1982).

In contrast, authors have also noted a tendency for some sexually abused youngsters to exhibit behaviors indicating withdrawal (Adams-Tucker, 1981; Burgess & Holmstrom, 1975; Jiles, 1981; Riggs, 1982). Such indicators include the following:

1. Withdrawal into fantasy (Riggs, 1982).
2. Staying inside and refusing to leave (Burgess & Holmstrom, 1975).
3. Regressive behaviors (e.g., a return of thumb sucking, fear of

the dark, or fear of strangers) (Adams-Tucker, 1981; Brassard *et al.*, 1983; DHHS, 1981; Herman & Hirschman, 1981; K. L. James, 1977; Riggs, 1982; Spencer, 1978; Weiss *et al.*, 1955).

Finally, a number of authors have observed that many sexually abused children repeat the abusive situation in some fashion later in life (Blumberg, 1978; Brooks, 1982; Cohen, 1981; Freud, 1981; Green, 1982; Katan, 1973; Rosenfeld *et al.*, 1977; Steele & Alexander, 1981; Tsai & Wagner, 1978; Weiss *et al.*, 1955). Authors have noted repetition in relationships with other adults while the children are still young, and after reaching adulthood in relationships with partners and with their own children. For example, Groth and Birnbaum (1978) found that adult perpetrators were frequently abused as children when they were the same age as their victims. Additionally, clinicians are now finding adolescent and even latency-aged victims-turned-perpetrators who are trying to master their own trauma by victimizing younger children.

SELF-DESTRUCTIVE BEHAVIORS

Another set of behaviors that authors have observed to be sequelae of sexual abuse is that of self-destructive behaviors. The self-hate many of these victims feel is translated into self-punishment in a variety of ways (Summit, 1983). One fashion is through self-defeating or self-destructive behavior patterns (Brooks, 1982; DHHS, 1981; J. James & Meyerding, 1978; Yates, 1982); Brooks notes a pervasive "masochistic orientation" to life. This is probably tied in with other behaviors already discussed (e.g., substance abuse, repetition compulsion).

Another behavior that has been observed in child sexual abuse victims is self-mutilation (Adams-Tucker, 1981; Knittle & Tuana, 1980; Simpson & Porter, 1981; Summit, 1983). According to Knittle and Tuana, this may be a manifestation of anger turned inward, like the more commonly found depression. In extreme forms, this inward anger has been observed to lead to suicidal thoughts and suicide attempts in victims, both while they are being abused and much later in adulthood (Adams-Tucker, 1982; Bess & Janssen, 1982; Herman & Hirschman, 1981; Knittle & Tuana, 1980; Meiselman, 1979; Molnar

& Cameron, 1975; Perlmutter *et al.*, 1982; Sgroi, 1982a; Spencer, 1978; Vander Mey & Neff, 1982).

DEGREE OF PSYCHOPATHOLOGY

Child sexual abuse has been associated with a range of psychopathology and diagnostic categories. Several studies have suggested that many victims are psychologically disturbed both in the short term and the long term. For example, Adams-Tucker (1982) studied 28 sexually abused children referred for treatment and found psychopathology in the "moderate to severe" range. These problems were more severe than those of the typical outpatient child at her clinic, but less severe than those of the average inpatient. The Tufts study (1984) found that 17% of the 4- to 6-year-olds studied who were sexually abused demonstrated clinically significant pathology. Additionally, Tsai, Feldman-Summers, and Edgar (1979) compared adult women seeking therapy for problems associated with child sexual abuse to nonmolested controls; they found that the abused women were significantly more disturbed. However, it should be noted that both the Adams-Tucker and Tsai *et al.* samples were selected and therefore may not be representative. Further, there is simply not enough evidence yet to permit firm conclusions to be drawn about the relationship between short and long-term psychopathology associated with child sexual abuse.

The range of psychopathology associated with child sexual abuse is typically anchored on one end by "neurosis," with several authors using this term to describe some victims (Bess & Janssen, 1982; Finch, 1973; Meiselman, 1979; Rist, 1979; Westermeyer, 1978). Authors also believe sexual abuse is associated with the development of character disorders in some victims in the long term (Brooks, 1982; Heims & Kaufman, 1963; Rist, 1979). It has also been noted that a history of sexual abuse is relatively common in individuals with multiple personalities (Saltman & Solomon, 1982; Summit, 1983). Finally, victims have occasionally been observed to develop psychotic features (Adams-Tucker, 1982; Bess & Janssen, 1982; Finch, 1967; Peters, 1973; Summit, 1983; Westermeyer, 1978).

It is unclear how frequently psychopathology results in child victims of sexual abuse; estimates range from about 20% to 50% of victims. However, it appears that gross psychopathology and/or social impairment is the exception rather than the rule as a long-term consequence of sexual abuse. Instead, the long-term effects seem more related to sexual functioning, self-esteem, and establishment of trusting relationships.

EFFECTS RELATED TO SEXUALITY

A number of authors believe that sexual abuse leads to sexualized behaviors in children (Brant & Tisza, 1977; Brassard et al., 1983; DHHS, 1981; Finch, 1973; Freud, 1981; K. L. James, 1977; Kaufman et al., 1954; Krieger et al., 1980; Riggs, 1982; Sgroi, 1982a; Tufts, 1984; Weiss et al., 1955; Yates, 1982; Yorukoglu & Kemph, 1966). It has been hypothesized that this is the result of a lack of inhibition of sexual impulses (DHHS, 1981), or a means of "working through" the abuse (Finch, 1973); in any case, it is one of the most consistent findings reported in the literature for children of all ages (although a subset of children may become extremely sexually inhibited; see Jorne, 1979). A related finding is that molested children (frequently preschoolers) often become preoccupied with sexual matters and exhibit atypical knowledge of sexual acts (Brassard et al., 1983; Riggs, 1982). Also, children may exhibit confusion over and concerns about sexuality and their sexual orientation (Boatman et al., 1981; Brooks, 1982; Jiles, 1981).

In the longer term, as adolescents and adults, victims may become "promiscuous" (Brooks, 1982; Brunold, 1964; Finch, 1967; Herman & Hirschman, 1981; Kaufman et al., 1954; Rosenfeld et al., 1977; Sloane & Karpinsky, 1942; Spencer, 1978; Vander Mey & Neff, 1982; Van Gijseghem, 1975; Weiner, 1962; Weiss et al., 1955). Some authors believe (based mainly on retrospective studies of prostitutes) that child sexual abuse can lead to prostitution (Blumberg, 1978; Spencer, 1978; Vander Mey & Neff, 1982). In adulthood, victims frequently exhibit sexual dysfunctions, typically sexual inhibition and orgasmic dysfunction (Bess & Janssen, 1982; Blumberg, 1978, 1981; Brooks, 1982; Brunold, 1964; DHHS, 1981; Finch, 1967; Freud, 1981; Molnar & Cameron, 1975; Peters, 1973; Rist, 1979; Rosenfeld et al., 1977; Sgroi, 1982; Steele & Alexander, 1981; Tsai et al., 1979; Tsai & Wagner, 1978; Vander Mey & Neff, 1982; Westermeyer, 1978).

EFFECTS OF "THE SYSTEM"[1]

Due to the retrospective nature of virtually all the studies of sexually abused children, it is impossible to separate the effects of the abuse itself from the effects of intervention by the courts and social service agencies. Frequently (in the case of incest), the father is put in jail and the child victim is placed in foster care, obviously disrupting the family's equilibrium (Furniss, 1983b) and often precipitating a crisis (Westermeyer, 1978). A number of authors agree that multiple interviews and legal intervention can affect the child adversely (Alstrom, 1977; Brunold, 1964; Cormier, 1972; De Francis, 1970; Herman, 1981; K. L. James, 1977; Peters, 1973; Walters, 1975). De Francis notes that more than 1000 court appearances were required for the 173 cases he studied that resulted in prosecution. These appearances caused added stress, resentment, and tension for both the children and their parents (in both incest and nonincest cases). It is especially traumatizing for a child to testify against an abuser, who may have been a parent, another relative, or a trusted friend or teacher. Also documented is the harmful effect on young child victim/witnesses of repeated questioning by multiple authorities in the adversarial proceedings involved in criminal court (Katz & Mazur, 1979; MacFarlane & Bulkley, 1982; Parker, 1982).

In England, Gibbens and Prince (1983) conducted the only systematic research on the effects of the court upon sexually molested child witnesses, and found that children were significantly negatively affected by the court process, compared with a control group. However, their results may have been biased, since the cases that actually went to trial were the most severe cases.

Ironically, perhaps the most powerful data are derived from a study surveying judges, rather than children or their families. Bohmer (1974) found tha 84% of the judges surveyed held the opinion that children who testified in court were emotionally traumatized. This opinion is almost universally held by therapists and other mental health professionals who work in the field of child sexual abuse. In fact, some feel that the effects of the social and legal systems may be

1. We are indebted to Ian Russ of Children's Institute International for information on the effects of testifying in court on children.

as damaging or even more damaging in some cases than the sexual abuse itself (K. L. James, 1977; Walters, 1975). As Walters writes, most of the psychological damage "stems not from the abuse but from the interpretation of the abuse and the handling of the situation by parents, medical personnel, law enforcement and school officials, and social workers" (1975, p. 113).

OTHER EFFECTS

As mentioned earlier, a host of possible sequelae to sexual abuse have been reported in the literature. Only those written about by multiple authors or falling naturally into subgroups have been dealt with here; the interested reader is referred to Mrazek and Mrazek (1981) for other possible effects. However, two other types of sequelae have been noted frequently enough that they are discussed here: low self-esteem and problems with interpersonal relationships. These problems have been reported both in children who have just been abused, and in adults years after their victimization.

Several authors believe that sexual abuse causes poor self-esteem (Herman & Hirschman, 1977; Katan, 1973; Steele & Alexander, 1981). Related problems that have been noted include a damaged, inadequate sense of self (Boatman *et al.*, 1981); a poor or negative self-image (Sgroi, 1982a; Tsai & Wagner, 1978); and a poor self-identity (Steele & Alexander, 1981; Van Gijseghem, 1975). With older children, it has been observed that this pervasive self-view is manifested in depreciating self-statements (K. L. James, 1977). However, one empirical study (Tufts, 1984) found no difference in self-esteem between sexually abused 4- to 6-year-olds and their nonabused peers; thus, the relationship between sexual abuse and self-esteem for young children remains unclear.

A number of authors believe that problems with interpersonal relationships are related to child sexual abuse (Brooks, 1982; Peters, 1973; Spencer, 1978; Tsai & Wagner, 1978; Weiss *et al.*, 1955). This has been noted both for short-term relationships with peers (Riggs, 1982; Sgroi, 1982a) and longer-term heterosexual relationships (Boatman *et al.*, 1981). It has been argued by Paulson (1978) that sexually abused children withdraw socially after the abuse; both Sgroi (1982a) and Knittle and Tuana (1980) believe they may have a social skills deficit.

It has been suggested that these interpersonal problems are rooted in a lack of trust, which arises because of the betrayal inherent in the abuse itself (Johnston, 1979; Krieger *et al.*, 1980) or because of poor prior attachment to the mother (Steele & Alexander, 1981). Also seen as contributing are a feeling of being different and distant from others, based on a disassociation from one's own feelings used as a defense during the abuse itself (Herman & Hirschman, 1977); a tendency toward oppositionality (Adams-Tucker, 1982); and a relatively low amount of self-disclosure (Katan, 1973).

MEDIATORS

In discussing the effects of sexual abuse, many authors suggest that there are mediators that contribute to the differential impact of the abuse. One possible mediator is the emotional climate of the child's family prior to the abuse (De Francis, 1970; DHHS, 1981; Emslie & Rosenfeld, 1983; Steele & Alexander, 1981). The victim is believed to be at greater risk for psychological trauma if the pre-existing family system is pathological. For example, Emslie and Rosenfeld (1983) compared 6 nonpsychotic females (aged 9–17) with a history of incest to 10 nonpsychotic girls in the same age range without an incest history. They found no specific effects of incest, and concluded that the psychopathology the girls exhibited was not a simple effect of the incest itself, but rather a consequence of severe family disorganization and resulting psychological impairment.

A second (and related) mediator that has been posited is the child's mental and emotional health prior to the abuse. It is believed that greater prior psychological health is associated with less trauma (Adams-Tucker, 1981; Leaman, 1980; Powell & Chalkley, 1981; Yorukoglu & Kemph, 1966).

A third possible mediator is the relationship between the offender and the child. It is believed that, in general, a closer relationship to the offender means more resultant trauma (Adams-Tucker, 1982; DHHS, 1981; Landis, 1956; Leaman, 1980; Mrazek, 1980; Simari & Baskin, 1982; Steele & Alexander, 1981; Stern & Meyer, 1980). However, it has been pointed out that this is probably not true for sibling incest (Nakashima & Zakus, 1979).

The next mediator frequently mentioned in the literature is the age or relative maturity of the child. It is generally argued that sexual abuse will affect the child differentially, based on his or her age and/ or developmental level (Dixen & Jenkins, 1981; Leaman, 1980; Peters, 1973; Powell & Chalkley, 1981). However, authors disagree on the nature of the relationship between age and effects. Some believe that trauma is greater for younger victims—that is, preschoolers (Adams-Tucker, 1982; Peters, 1974; Steele & Alexander, 1981). Others feel that older victims are more traumatized (DHHS, 1981; Nakashima & Zakus, 1979; Rosenfeld et al., 1979; Ruch & Chandler, 1982; Schachter, 1979; Schechter & Roberge, 1976; Sloane & Karpinsky, 1942; Tsai et al., 1979). Finally, it has been suggested that trauma is curvilinear, peaking at puberty (Stern & Meyer, 1980).

There are at least two possible explanations for this discrepancy in findings. One is that effects are different, depending on age—it has been suggested that preschool victims are more likely to manifest psychosomatic symptoms, for example (Brant & Tisza, 1977)—and authors may draw different conclusions based on idiosyncratic definitions of "trauma" (e.g., if physical complaints are weighted heavily, preschool children may as a result appear more traumatized). Alternatively, it has been suggested that duration of the abuse is a salient factor, with a longer duration increasing trauma (Adams-Tucker, 1982; DHHS, 1981; Tsai et al., 1979). It is more likely that an older victim will have been abused for a longer time, hence compounding the effects; since duration was not controlled for in any of the studies reviewed, it is impossible to separate its effects from those of age.

The nature of the abusive incident(s) is another hypothesized mediator (Leaman, 1980; Powell & Chalkley, 1981; Stern & Meyer, 1980). There is general agreement that genital contact, especially intercourse, worsens the victim's trauma, especially for very young children (Adams-Tucker, 1982; Mrazek, 1980; Tsai et al., 1979). Also viewed as worsening trauma is the use of threats, force, and/or violence by the perpetrator (Blumberg, 1978; Corsini-Munt, 1979; DHHS, 1981; Finch, 1973; Ruch & Chandler, 1982). However, it has been argued that trauma correlates more highly with the climate of the environmental (e.g., system) response to the abuse than with the forcefulness of the encounter (Summit & Kryso, 1978). Also, in the case

of incest (which is typically nonviolent), the presence of other mediators (e.g., family pathology, duration, relationship of perpetrator to
victim) can certainly exacerbate trauma.

Another potential mediator is the amount of guilt the child experiences concerning the abuse; as noted earlier, this is generally
thought to be greater with older children (Schechter & Roberge, 1976).
It is posited that if children experience pleasure during the abuse, or
believe that they precipitated it, they will feel more guilt and shame;
in turn, greater guilt is associated with worse trauma (DHHS, 1981;
MacFarlane & Korbin, 1983; Schechter & Roberge, 1976; Summit &
Kryso, 1978).

Sex of the victim is also thought to be a mediator of the effects
of sexual abuse (Powell & Chalkley, 1981). Vander Mey and Neff
(1982) and Adams-Tucker (1982) conclude that males suffer less trauma
than do females; however, Finch (1973) argues that although boys
suffer less short-term trauma, they show more "long range serious
character problems" (p. 174). There have not been enough direct
comparisons to permit firm conclusions on this point.

A final potential mediator noted in the literature is the parental
response to the child's victimization (Constantine, 1979; Leaman, 1980;
Summit & Kryso, 1978). It is believed that assurance, support, and
emotional security provided by parents right after the abuse is discovered will help offset trauma in both the short and the long term
(De Francis, 1970; Peters, 1974); an unsupportive or overreactive
parental response will result in greater trauma (Adams-Tucker, 1982;
Corsini-Munt, 1979; DHHS, 1981; Stern & Meyer, 1980; Tufts, 1984).

SUMMARY AND CONCLUSION

Table 6-1 summarizes the effects of sexual abuse found in preschoolers. There do not seem to be enough data yet to permit us to conclude
anything definite about the relative frequency or intensity of specific
types of effects in different age groups.

METHODOLOGICAL ISSUES CONCERNING EFFECTS

Although it appears that the majority of studies on child sexual abuse
conclude that its effects are harmful (Star, 1979), there are a host of

TABLE 6-1. *Effects of Sexual Abuse Noted in Preschoolers*

Type of effect	Specific problems noted
Affective effects	Anxiety; depression; anger.
Physical effects	Injury, bruises, and/or bleeding in external genitalia, vagina, anus; problems walking or sitting; sexually transmitted diseases. (Note: physical effects are relatively rare.)
Psychosomatic effects	Stomachaches; headaches; encopresis; enuresis; sleep disturbance.
Cognitive problems	Hypothesized (e.g., problems with concentration).
Behavioral problems	Acting out; withdrawal; regression; repetition with other children and toys such as dolls.
Psychopathology	Manifested in various ways; present in a significant number of cases.
Sexuality	Excessive masturbation; repetition of sexual acts with others (noted above); atypical sexual knowledge; concerns and preoccupation with sexual matters.
Interpersonal problems	Withdrawal (noted above); avoidance; occasionally overfamiliarity.
Long-term effects	Hypothesized: increased guilt; decreased self-esteem; sexual problems; school problems; delinquency; repetition (e.g., entering into masochistic relationships, becoming or marrying a perpetrator).

problems with this research. Definitions of sexual abuse lack precision and comparability, making it difficult to draw conclusions across studies (Powell & Chalkley, 1981). As Mrazek and Mrazek (1981) note, three types of samples have typically been used: children and families referred for treatment soon after the abuse; "deviant" adult populations (e.g., psychiatric patients and prostitutes); and college students. The first type of sample suffers from selection effects and lack of long-term follow-up; "the conclusions that are drawn from the short-range focus may not hold up over time" (Mrazek & Mrazek, 1981, p. 236). Also, it is difficult to separate the effects of the abuse itself from the effects of the previous familial environment, ensuing disruption, and contact with the legal system and social service agencies (Mrazek, 1980; Rosenfeld *et al.*, 1977).

The study of adult "deviant" populations has inherent problems as well: They are selected and retrospective in nature, and causality cannot be inferred from them. As Constantine (1979) writes:

> The absence of adult symptoms traced to early sexual experience cannot be taken simply as evidence for the harmlessness of those experiences. Conversely, psychosocial impairment in adults who were sexually victim-

ized as children cannot be said to demonstrate the dangers of these encounters, for the impairment observed may originate in other experiences, chronic stressors or even be in some measure reflections of constitutional factors. (p. 155)

College students, as Mrazek and Mrazek (1981) point out, "are biased in terms of intelligence, social class, and personal motivation and their data is [sic] also retrospective in nature" (p. 236). Hence, conclusions about this group must be limited as well. Even more limited are the conclusions that can be drawn about case reports, which make up a sizable proportion of the literature; case reports simply do not permit the establishment of general principles about the effects of sexual abuse (Mrazek & Mrazek).

Other problems, also noted by Mrazek and Mrazek (1981), include the lack of standardized outcome measures to evaluate the impact of abuse; unclear and greatly varied criteria for adjustment; inability to infer cause-and-effect relationships; and lack of control and contrast groups. Similar problems have led authors (e.g. Henderson, 1983) to write that, based on the existing literature, very little can be definitely concluded about the effects of sexual abuse. Only one long-term follow-up of sexually abused children has been reported in the literature, and this involved one-time, informal clinical observations of a small sample after a period of 15 years (Bender & Grugett, 1952). Thus, the etiology of long-term sequalae remains unexplored.

OTHER ISSUES AND DIRECTIONS FOR FUTURE RESEARCH

After reviewing the literature on the effects of child sexual abuse, one better understands why a large number of authors conclude their writings in this area with the plea for more and better research. With the current upsurge in interest have come numerous hypotheses, largely untested. As "Edington's Theory" states, "The number of different hypotheses erected to explain a given . . . phenomenon is inversely proportional to the available knowledge" (quoted in Bloch, 1983, p. 48). Child sexual abuse is certainly no exception. For example, it is currently unclear whether sexual abuse results in differential levels of psychopathology in preschoolers versus older children. As noted earlier, authors have drawn very different conclusions about the relationship between age and effects.

Viewed from a psychodynamic standpoint, child sexual abuse is typically seen as being relatively more damaging to preschoolers. For example, Cohen (1981), writing from a psychodynamic perspective, believes that sexual abuse causes psychic trauma. Such trauma during development interferes with the formation of and registration of normal wishes and memory traces; coupled with massive denial, this can cause memory confusion, distortion, deviant mental organization, and psychopathology. From this perspective, sexual abuse is viewed as especially damaging to the preschooler, who is still in the early stages of psychosexual development.

It may also be (as suggested earlier) that differential symptomatology can cause preschoolers to be viewed as more disturbed. Preschoolers appear to demonstrate relatively more overt expression of conflicts (e.g., nightmares, tantrums) arising from sexual abuse, but this may be due to their developmental level (i.e., traumatized preschoolers may tend toward more overt expression, regardless of the type of trauma experienced). Preschoolers do not have the cognitive controls and defensive structures that may cause effects to be displayed in more subtle ways in older children or adults, such as through guilt or fear of intimacy in relationships.

In contrast, it has been argued that preschoolers are *less* traumatized by sexual abuse than older children. Since preschoolers are not likely to understand (at least fully) what is happening to them, it may be that they feel less guilty, and do not really perceive that something "terrible" is happening. For example, a 3-year-old may not know that not all parents rub their daughters' vaginas every night at bedtime. Similarly, sexual abuse that has occurred in the context of a comfortable relationship with a trusted adult may not be seen as negative by the child at the time. From this perspective, it could be argued that (barring physical injury or use of force by the perpetrator) the child's parents' reaction (or the "system's" reaction) may be more harmful than the abuse itself. Thus, consistent research criteria for what constitutes "trauma" must be developed; additionally, comparisons across age groups should be performed.

A second issue deals with the duration and continuity of effects. Currently, we have almost no information on duration of the effects of child sexual abuse; additionally, it is unclear whether effects are continuous from the short to the long term. Do symptoms change at different ages, or are they relatively continuous? Do they "disappear" (e.g., during latency) and reappear later? These questions remain unanswered. It has been suggested that symptoms reappear at "developmentally sensitive" times—for example, puberty, marriage, when victims have their own children, when victims must provide sexual education for their children, and when victims' children reach the age when the victims were abused. Longitudinal studies are needed to address this area.

Third, we do not know how sexually abused preschool children (or older children, for that matter) compare to their nonabused peers. Studies (e.g., Tufts, 1984) are just beginning to include nonabused comparison groups as of this writing. Until such comparisons are widely undertaken, we will not know how severe victims' symptomatology is, since we have little to anchor or compare it to. This is especially true regarding effects on sexuality, since so little is currently known about normative sexual behavior and knowledge in preschoolers and young children. Thus, studies of recent victims with matched controls are badly needed.

Fourth, very little is currently known about the effects of treatment for sexual abuse on preschoolers. Are certain treatment modalities more helpful than others in alleviating current distress or in preventing later disturbance? Is treatment at the time of disclosure enough, or is treatment needed repeatedly as different developmental hurdles are faced? We need more information on how treatment mediates and/or alleviates short- and long-term effects of abuse.

Fifth, it appears that there is a continuum of effects of sexual abuse on preschoolers, ranging from proximal effects (those that are immediate and obviously directly caused by the abuse— e.g., genital injury) to distal effects (those arising months or years later, which may be impossible to link directly to the abuse itself—e.g., problems with intimacy in adulthood). It is important to stress that the term "effects," which has been applied almost exclusively in the literature, can misleadingly imply causality—in other words, that the behaviors noted were caused by the abuse. This may not be true in many cases; for example, pre-existing conditions or intervening factors may have produced the observed effects. As a result, these "effects" may be more properly viewed as sequelae or even correlates. Studies are needed that control for (or at least collect data on) such variables as family pathology, socioeconomic status, time since abuse, and effects of treatment.

Finally, other areas that need to be addressed in more detail are the negative effects of justice system intervention, and what can be done to prevent these effects (a recent advance here has been the admission by some states of testimony by victims on videotape or closed-circuit television to help alleviate trauma); cultural differences in abuse and effects; and societal issues concerning the finding that perpetrators are overwhelmingly male and victims are predominantly female. At present, virtually everyone writing about child sexual abuse concurs that it is a widespread problem; our task now is to understand it so that we can deal with it more effectively.

SOCIAL AND LEGAL CONSIDERATIONS: THE BROADER CONTEXT

CHILD SEXUAL ABUSE ALLEGATIONS IN DIVORCE PROCEEDINGS

Kee MacFarlane

One of the places that is experiencing the most dramatic rise in reported cases of child sexual abuse involving preschool-age children is divorce court. Increasing numbers of contested custody suits involve allegations, usually by the mother, that a young child has been molested by a father or stepfather. It is unclear why reports in this particular category should be increasing at such a rapid rate at this time. What is clear is that such cases are among the most problematic and emotionally charged of any cases with which professionals must deal, and frequently invoke groans of trepidation from those who must investigate the reports.

There are at least two primary factors that make these cases more difficult than those involving intact families or perpetrators outside the home: (1) The child is usually so young (often between 2 and 4 years old) that he or she is not able to provide a clear picture of what, if anything, happened; (2) it is frequently the child's mother or the mother's family who, because of unusual behavior or statements on the part of the child, suspects child sexual abuse. As a consequence, the reporting source is seen as having an ulterior motive for accusing or discrediting the father—that is, the mother's desire for custody, revenge, or limits on the father's visitation. Therefore, her credibility and that of the child are immediately thrown into question. The same motives, of course, are attributed to reporting fathers seeking custody or visitation.

In addition to the dubious motives often attributed to a reporting parent involved in a custody dispute, many cases are further complicated when allegations are raised within a context of financial disputes, such as alimony, child support, and the division of property. Few circumstances are less conducive to evaluating allegations of child sexual abuse than those associated with these cases. Frequently such allegations are dismissed or lightly regarded by the courts as yet another weapon in an ongoing battle over a lost marriage. In some cases, the abuse allegations remain unresolved, while the custody disputes rage on for months and even years at great financial expense to the parents, and often at even greater emotional cost to the children. As one divorce attorney has put it, "There is no better way to throw a monkey wrench into a divorce proceeding than to allege child sexual abuse. Everything immediately screams to a halt and an entirely different light is cast upon the accused parent. The courts are stuck with what to do with these cases. Most of the time they can't prove it happened and they're afraid to gamble that it didn't. This could become the ultimate weapon in the hands of an aggrieved spouse" (Amster, personal communication, 1982).

References in this chapter to children in the female gender and to fathers as the accused parents are made for the purposes of readability of the text. Mothers also are accused and, like fathers, sometimes do molest children of both sexes. Most of the information to be presented in this chapter applies equally to either situation. This chapter does not presume to provide answers to the inherent dilemmas associated with these difficult cases. Rather, it provides a composite view of the many issues to be considered, and a few suggestions for addressing those issues in the most responsible and objective way possible.

REASONS FOR ALLEGATIONS AT THE TIME OF DIVORCE

There are many reasons why allegations of child sexual abuse may surface at certain points in time. The following hypotheses address why child sexual abuse may be revealed (or may begin) at the time of divorce, as well as possible explanations why allegations may be made in the absence of abuse. The latter are examined first, since it is sometimes the motives of the accusing parent, rather than the behavior of the accused, that fall under the most immediate scrutiny.

ALLEGATIONS IN THE APPARENT ABSENCE OF ABUSE

A preface to this section should include a word of caution about making absolute judgments or diagnoses that allegations of child sexual abuse are untrue. It is important to remember that, just because we cannot identify physical, behavioral, or emotional indicators of abuse, this does not mean that abuse did not occur. Children do tell or reveal things to family members that they will not share with strangers. They also get frightened by the consequences of disclosure and become mute or retract their original statements. There have been many cases where evaluators have had to say that they weren't sure of what, if anything, occurred. The following are explanations for the evaluator to consider when there are no observable indicators of sexual abuse, and when the allegations do not seem to "fit" what the child appears to be communicating.

The Avenging Parent

It must be considered that there are some adults who will do and say anything in the course of a bitter divorce in order to retaliate, to punish the other parent, or obtain custody of a child. Although they are rare in our experience, accusations of child sexual abuse involving very young children can be and have been used for those purposes. However, false accusations are rarely ever admitted, and, as with other cases involving preschool children, other methods of assessment must be employed in our attempts to determine the truth. Unfortunately, the "dirtier" the divorce proceeding, and the more accusations (e.g., sexual infidelity, mental and physical cruelty, child neglect, etc.) that have preceded a report of molestation, the more difficult it is to sort out these charges from the others.

Nonetheless, some children are openly exposed to the war between their parents and may find themselves being invited to take sides in the battles. In such situations, where the child's welfare is not the primary concern of one or both of the parents or where a parent feels that any means of obtaining custody is, in fact, in the child's interest, it is possible that a child's statements concerning sexual abuse may actually have come from the parent first. This is a situation sometimes referred to as a "coached child" (i.e., a child who parrots the words of one parent who is attempting to discredit the other). It is usually one of the first explanations for a child's allegations offered by the accused parent and his attorney.

In contrast to this common assumption, the "coached child" constitutes the most infrequent explanation for child sexual abuse allegations that my colleagues and I have seen. When children have been coached or told to make accusatory statements concerning sexual abuse, their words are originally those of an adult and do not represent descriptions of actual situations or the real feelings associated with them. As a consequence, they seem to have several common characteristics: a lack of authenticity, a lack of variation, a lack of convincing detail, and sometimes the use of adult language and adult rationale. For example, in a case involving two young siblings, the children repeated the same statements independently ("Daddy hurt us down there and we hate him"), no matter how differently they were asked to explain. They couldn't even be persuaded to use the first person singular when asked about their own abuse. Further, when asked to describe any other ways that Daddy harmed them, they each were quick to reply that Daddy let them eat junk food and stay up late watching TV. Since neither of the latter transgressions are acts that young children would ordinarily regard as harmful, the interviewer wondered aloud how they knew that such behavior was harmful. They were earnest in their condemnation of pizza and Johnny Carson because Mommy had assured them that these things were bad. Further discussion of other types of harm revealed that Mommy knew and told them that Daddy hurt them and touched them "down there" while they were asleep at night. Neither child could actually remember any such incident, because, of course, they were asleep, but Mommy knew about these things because "we all used to live in the same house." Later discussions about secrets in the family revealed that there were secrets with Mommy regarding what they were and were not supposed to say to interviewers, but that there were no secrets with or about Daddy.

A child's use of adult terminology, such as "Daddy molested me," needs particular scrutiny to try to determine whether she acquired her descriptions from other adults following an initial disclosure in her own words, whether she knew about sexual molestation prior to the alleged incident, or whether she got it from someone who gave her the words and may have convinced her that they were true or appropriate. Although statements such as "Daddy did nasties with me," or "Daddy put his finger [tongue, wiener, etc.] in my goo-goo [muffin, pee-pee, etc.]," usually represent a child's shorthand for what actually happened, it is important for an evaluator to probe for details, especially if coaching is suspected. It should be remembered, however, that "details" for young children may be demonstrated (with dolls, drawings, dollhouses, etc.) more easily than they can be verbalized. Children who make exactly the same statements or use the same words each time to describe the abuse need to be pushed for more descriptive material or seen in additional interviews.

The evaluator has the difficult job of trying to determine whether a child is embarrassed or fearful about telling more, or whether there is no more to tell. The "coached" or "programmed" child may be one who has no more than a few words to describe something of which she has no real knowledge. When a verbal child is encouraged to provide details, the details usually either validate the experience or evolve into imaginative descriptions that give away her lack of understanding of what is being said. The developmental inability of preschoolers to fabricate much factual content about sexual acts with adults should always be kept in mind. Similarly, as anyone who has ever tried to coach or prepare a child to perform in a nursery-school play has learned, preschoolers, unless they are professionally trained actors, have difficulty retaining consistent presentations of things that have little meaning to them in real life.

The issue of authenticity, though less tangible, can also serve as a barometer for evaluators. Authenticity has to do with (1) the way the child's statements "fit" with all the other data collected on a case; (2) the way statements about abuse compare with the child's other feelings and other forms of expression; and (3) the plausibility of the details provided. For example, in the case involving the two siblings described above, getting them to acknowledge that they actually liked pizza and TV, and that it was their mother who regarded these things as harmful, helped them to admit (with some relief) that the only hurt they remembered their father inflicting "down there" was an occasional spanking. With these children, as with many in divorce situations, it was important to let them acknowledge how difficult it is to please two people who don't like each other any more, especially when pleasing one seems to involve having to hate or say bad things about the other. It is important to give such children permission to change their statements, and to emphasize that the truth is the only important thing. In an effort to prevent later retraction, an evaluator might tell them that he or she will be there to explain things to their mother or anyone else, in the event that the facts have gotten confused or out of hand somewhere along the line. They may need to know that they will not get punished or blamed for telling the truth, whatever it is, and that the evaluator is the person who can help them get things straight. (The evaluator must strongly emphasize this with parents as well, so that children will not incur negative consequences from talking with him or her.)

The consequences of what they reveal and of the outcome of the divorce are very important to some children, and can affect what they say or will not say to an evaluator. It is important to try to find out what a child wants to have happen, doesn't want, is afraid of, thinks will happen, and so on, before the evaluator interjects any potential consequences. For example, learning that a child believes she won't ever see her father again if she talks about sexual abuse, may provide more data to help clarify the child's possible motives—whether for talking about it or for refusing to talk.

But the evaluator should beware of simple conclusions. While an allegation of sexual abuse could be used as a way of avoiding contact with a father or stepfather whom a child doesn't like (if that's what she believes will be the outcome), she also may want to avoid contact with him because he actually abuses her. Asking who it was who gave her her ideas about what will happen might provide more data. Similarly, posing the possibility that her assumptions might be wrong and that other outcomes are possible may yield more information in the ensuing discussion.

Having shared these impressions, I must caution the reader that they should only be used as guideposts for information gathering; each, in itself, is rarely sufficient to provide anything conclusive. One other word of caution on the subject of "coaching": Evaluators need to be careful of the question, "Did Mommy [or someone else] tell you to say these things?" Young children tend to be very literal in their thinking, and we have found that an affirmative answer to this question may not always be what it appears. Parents may talk to their children about an upcoming interview in order to reassure them, encourage them, or lessen their anxieties. Sometimes they will say things like "I want you to tell the interviewer [police officer, doctor, counselor, etc.] what you told me about what Daddy did." To some children, that translates as "Yes, she told me to tell you this." It does not mean that the child did not report it to her first, and it is crucially different from coaching. Evaluators need to be sure that children understand their questions, and that they understand children's answers. When the meanings of answers are uncertain, questions should be rephrased or the child should be asked to restate the question in her own words.

The Overanxious Parent

Despite the appearance of an obvious motive, rarely have my colleagues and I seen cases where allegations of child sexual abuse have been totally fabricated. In cases where abuse appears not to have occurred, it is more common to see a situation where a mother has overreacted to something that a child has said or done, or has read meaning into something that a less impassioned observer might not. This may represent a type of heightened vigilance that comes from the fear of sharing a child with or allowing the child to stay with a man who, for whatever reasons, she has decided not to live with any more. It may stem from her personal knowledge of her ex-husband's sexual practices or abuses of power with her, or it might possibly stem from her own memories of molestation as a child.

It should also be remembered that many of the children in this age category are going through what is traditionally thought of as the "Oedipal phase," and are suddenly becoming aware of both physical and sex-role differences between their parents and among other adults. Children at this stage often do become preoccupied with their own and others' genitals, asking numerous questions, increasing masturbatory activity, or becoming coy or petulant with the parent of the opposite sex. (More information on developmental issues is provided in Chapter 2.) Such behavior is sometimes of concern even to parents in healthy, happy households. The ambiguity of children's behavior at such stages is one reason why it is so important to gain their confidence and make them feel at ease enough to be able to talk about what may or may not have happened to them. Observed behaviors are rarely enough to enable an evaluator to confirm or rule out abuse, regardless of the child's developmental stage. The evaluator should be alert for validating details, either verbalized or demonstrated, in order to ascertain why the child has behaved in certain ways. This may take several interviews or ongoing therapy, but it is necessary in order to avoid jumping to conclusions based on preconceived expectations about children's behavior during their preschool years.

To a mother in the midst of a contested divorce whose children may already have visitation rights with a man she may hate or fear, even relatively normal behavior suddenly may appear threatening or suspicious. Whether the motives be self-serving or overprotective, there are cases in which parents hear or see what they believe is evidence of child sexual victimization, where no one else—not even the most conscientious evaluators—can find it.

The preceding section examined some of the reasons why a parent might report or suspect the existence of child sexual abuse when such a diagnosis does not appear to be indicated to others; the following address some of the reasons why children who appear not to have been molested might make statements or exhibit behavior indicating that they were.

The Troubled Child

To begin with, it is obvious that separation and divorce can be as stressful for children as they are for adults. Children, like adults, may behave in ways that they would not under ordinary circumstances. They are subject to a variety of emotional reactions to the dissolution of a marriage, including anger at one or both parents, sorrow or grief over the loss of the home life they have known, guilt or self-blame for what is happening, and a sense of abandonment and emotional insecurity about their own future well-being. With or without the presence of sexual abuse, all these feelings may play themselves out within a child or be outwardly exhibited in a variety of ways. It is possible that a child's anger toward a parent, especially toward the parent who has left the family home, could result in accusations that are unconsciously retaliatory on the part of the young child. However, it is our experience that such charges usually take the form of very concrete accusations—things that the children regard as wrong, such as a claim that a parent didn't feed them, that parents lied to them, or that a parent hit them. Not only are some very young children unaware that there is something wrong with any sexual activity that may be occurring, but often they are unaware of the punitive societal consequences of revealing such acts. Therefore, few even recognize the fact that an allegation of child sexual abuse could serve a retaliatory purpose. The exceptions, of course, are children who have been threatened, but they usually believe that retaliation will be aimed at them.

With all this in mind, it is nonetheless important to conduct the evaluation with an eye to the overall emotional stability and mental health of the child. Early childhood psychosis and other forms of emotional disturbance are important to rule out in cases where suspicion has been cast on the credibility of the child or on her grasp of reality. In some cases, this can be done through simple verbal exchanges (such as those described in other chapters) that are aimed at assessing developmental levels, ability to distinguish truth from fantasy, and reality testing. In other cases, psychological testing may be indicated. In cases where children exhibit distorted thought patterns, or bizarre behavior, the evaluator, if he or she is not a trained child psychologist or psychiatrist, should collaborate with one in order to provide sound diagnoses with regard to such children's overall psychological health.

If children are actively psychotic or otherwise out of touch with reality, the symptoms usually are in evidence in many aspects of the things they say and do. Overtly sexualized behavior or descriptions of bizarre sexual abuse are insufficient diagnostic indicators of disturbance. It is important to remember that distraught, angry, or acting-out children may or may not be mentally ill, and may or may not be exhibiting the sequelae of sexual abuse. The presence of psychosis or other illness in a child does not rule out the possibility of abuse, particularly in young children. In fact, an increasing number of mental health experts are beginning to report that childhood psychosis, splitting, and the development of multiple personalities may develop as a major defense mechanism against early childhood sexual trauma (Kluft, 1985).

The Response Reinforcement Pattern

In a few situations where a child repeats the same accusatory statements over and over, it is possible that the child has said or done something sexual in nature that has been strongly reacted to by her mother or other family members. While some children might be frightened into silence by such reactions, for others they may serve to establish a reinforcing pattern that unconsciously perpetuates the behaviors or statements on the part of the children. For children who are feeling insecure or attention-deprived during the course of separation and divorce, the immediate attention focused on them for whatever they said or did may be enough to continue the behavior for as long as it is reinforced with the attention. Many parents respond to their suspicions of child sexual abuse by drawing even closer to their children and by increasing nurturing behaviors (e.g., talking to and paying more attention to them, holding them more, sitting by their beds until they fall asleep, etc.). All these behaviors may encourage a child to repeat continually what she said or did prior to receiving such attention, sometimes to the extent that it may sound like rote statements or unreliable prattle by the time it is reported to an evaluator. Such response patterns are less likely to be found in older school-age children.

The difficult thing in these instances is to try to determine whether the child's *original* statement or behavior was indicative of sexual abuse or merely sexual in nature. Some parents react with alarm or embarrassment to any sexual behavior by their children. In an attempt to respond appropriately to such reactions, or to please the mother and give her what the child thinks it is she wants to hear, a child may answer affirmatively to such questions as "Did Daddy teach you this?" or "Does Daddy do this with you on visits?" As stated previously, divorce is a very difficult time for young children, and they can be swept into the emotionally charged environment very innocently and inadvertently.

Similarly, young children may initially misunderstand what they are being asked, and a parent may misinterpret a child's answer—thus setting up a response reinforcement pattern based on a misunderstanding. For example, when a 4-year-old asked her mother to "lick her tushee," her mother became very alarmed and demanded to know where the child had done that before. When the child responded "At Daddy's house," the mother became too upset to ask further questions and proceeded to take legal action against the father. Meanwhile, the child kept asking to go to Daddy's house to get her tushee tickled. After considerable furor and outrage on both sides, it was discovered, in the course of the evaluation, that the child *had* been engaging in sex play at her father's house but that the perpetrator was actually his new puppy. Unbelievable as it seemed at first, the child's detailed description of the incidents (once she was finally encouraged to tell the whole story) were confirmed by direct observation of the child playing with the dog.

Despite such examples, it is important to keep in mind that the response reinforcement pattern is *not* an indication that abuse has not occurred—only that young children have responded positively to reinforcement for initial statements or behaviors. The pattern may develop just as quickly when applied to the real thing. It helps to get the responding person to try to remember in exact detail the conversation and circumstances surrounding the child's first statements or behaviors. It is equally important to engage the child in conversation that goes beyond what may have become a pat response to certain questions about abuse.

All of the possible explanations given above point to the fact that, with divorcing families, even more than with children from intact homes, it is very important to explore all the subtle motives that might have given rise to allegations of sexual abuse. This is by no means an easy task, and requires obtaining data from every possible available source. It is the process of systematically eliminating peripheral motives, such as the ones mentioned above, that provides us with a measure of confidence and even-handedness in confirming or disputing allegations of child sexual abuse.

ALLEGATIONS WHERE SEXUAL ABUSE IS INDICATED

Having examined a variety of reasons why a child or a parent may make an allegation of sexual abuse when it may not appear to have occurred, let us examine the evaluation of these charges in cases where sexual abuse *is* indicated. Once the factors described above have been eliminated and the evaluator is fairly confident of the independent credibility of a child, the question becomes this: Why is the child saying or doing these things at this time or at this point in the divorce proceedings?

Why Abuse Is Revealed during Divorce or Separation

It is irrefutable that the timing of some child sexual abuse allegations can look quite suspicious, especially when they are raised for the first time in conjunction with disputes over visitation or property rights, and/or immediately preceding a court hearing. Despite what may at first appear to be an obvious ploy for custody on the part of a parent, it is important that we not jump to conclusions about the existence or nonexistence of child sexual abuse, simply because the charges are made in association with other disputes or charges between parents—even if some of those other charges turn out to be false. Despite what may seem obvious to those who work with divorcing families, there is very little about the hidden problem of child sexual abuse that is ever obvious, even to the well-trained eye.

More important, there are some good reasons why children reveal the existence of sexual abuse at this time. It has been well documented in the literature that intrafamily child sexual abuse often goes on for long periods of time, even years, without a child's revealing its existence or the mother's being consciously aware of it (MacFarlane & Korbin, 1983; Machotka, Pittman, & Flomemhaft, 1967; Summit & Kryso, 1978). Therefore, it should not be viewed as exceptional if some of these children reveal an ongoing history of prior abuse at home. Additionally, aspects of the divorce situation itself may lessen the inhibitions that prevent children from revealing their secrets.

First of all, a child who is physically afraid of an abusive parent or who has been threatened not to reveal abuse may be less afraid of him or his power over her, once he has moved out of the home or is planning to do so. Similarly, a child may have been threatened with dissolution of the family, or told that she or one of her parents would be "sent away" if the secret got out. Realizing that some of these consequences are happening anyway, or possibly associating them with the abuse, may prompt the child to begin to talk about it in order to alleviate feelings of guilt or to try to repair the situation. Also, the general anxiety and insecurity felt by children at the time of divorce may draw them closer to their mothers or other family members and facilitate the sharing of information that they had previously chosen to keep to themselves.

It is also important to remember that young children often do not use words to express their anxieties or to communicate things to adults. Therefore, it is not unlikely for children who have been sexually molested, particularly those who are not aware of the meaning or repercussions of the behavior, to act out in sexual ways during time of extreme stress. It is exactly this reaction to the turmoil at home—manifested through the re-enactment of inappropriate adult—

child sexual activity—that may shock family members and bring the case to the attention of others.

Children themselves have related that one reason why they reveal sexual abuse at the time of divorce proceedings has do with changes or potential changes in their living arrangements. Some children who, for a variety of reasons, have tolerated sexual abuse in their own homes over a period of time, become genuinely terrified at the prospect of having to go and live alone with an abuser. This may be true even when a child's fears bear no relation to reality. We have listened to children fearfully project this outcome, even when they repeatedly have been told that their custody is not an issue in the divorce and that they will continue to live with their mothers. Nonetheless, this feared loss of protection or increased exposure to an abusive parent on a full-time basis may serve as a stimulus for the revelation of past abuse.

The same may hold true for the prospect or instigation of overnight or weekend visitation alone at the home of an abusive or potentially abusive parent. One difference may be that it is not just the fear of potential abuse or even the recurrence of prior abuse that the child is now attempting to convey. What we may be seeing or hearing from some of these children are indications of child sexual abuse that is just beginning to occur during the course of ongoing visitation with an absent parent.

REASONS WHY SEXUAL ABUSE MAY OCCUR DURING DIVORCE

The problem of child sexual abuse whose onset is concurrent with marital separation or pending divorce is one that warrants special consideration by anyone attempting to evaluate such cases. One of the most frequent reactions from families, attorneys, and mental health professionals in response to such suggestions is immediately to discount the allegations as preposterous. The disbelief is often voiced in rhetorical ways that, in effect, pose the following question: Why on earth would anyone who cares about his child and is fighting for either custody, partial custody, or visitation rights ever jeopardize his chances for those things by sexually abusing his child prior to or during the time when such decisions are being determined?

THE AVENGING PARENT

One answer to this question, which is thought to be the reason why some fathers become involved in custody battles at all, may be retaliation against a spouse. His awareness of such underlying motives may be conscious at the time, but is more likely to be unconscious and shrouded by layers of rationale and conflicted emotions. However, as has been observed with regard to false allegations by mothers in these families, although retaliation may at first appear to be an obvious motive, it is a very infrequent one in our experience with these cases.

THE INCESTUOUS PARENT

The question remains as to why anyone with no past history of sexual behavior toward children would suddenly begin molesting a child. The answer, for some perpetrators, may lie within the broader question of why anyone would commit incest with his own child. It is not a question with a single or clear-cut answer at this stage in the conceptual development of this field (Finklehor & Araji, 1983). However, some causative theories may be particularly applicable to divorcing families. They primarily relate to the nature and orientation of the sexual abuser. Unlike traditional concepts of "child molesters," whose primary sexual attraction for children has been a lifelong pattern, there may be a category of sexual abusers who may molest children primarily in response to a variety of situational and emotional variables occurring in their lives at the time (Groth, 1978).

This is not to say that abusers of this type don't carry some sexual predilection for children, nor does it explain why sexual involvement with a child is one of their responses to stress. Rather, it has been observed that some people whose lifelong pattern has involved appropriate sexual relationships with heterosexual peers can and do reach out to children for sexual and emotional gratification under certain circumstances. Dr. Henry Giarretto was one of the first to describe this reaction pattern in his descriptions of incestuous fathers seen in treatment. In his discussion of the situational and emotional variables that affect these families, he describes incestuous abusers as individuals with low self-concepts and generally poor marital relationships; they are persons who are "usually angry, disillusioned and feel they have little to lose" (Giarretto, 1982, p. 19).

The work of Dr. Nicholas Groth also has been highly influential among those attempting to understand the type of sexual abuser described above. He has used the term "regressed pedophile" to describe this particular category of child sexual abuser. He describes the phenomenon as follows:

> Regression is defined as a temporary or permanent appearance of primitive behavior after more mature forms of expression have been obtained, regardless of whether or not the immature behavior is actually manifested earlier in the individual's sexual development. A regressed child offender is a person who originally preferred peers or adult partners for sexual gratification. However when these adult relationships became conflictual in some important respect, the adult became replaced by the child as the focus of this person's sexual interest and desires. Throughout his socio-sexual development, the regressed offender exhibits appropriate interest in age-mates. Yet his development appears to be undermined by a sense of inadequacy that increases as he approaches the responsibilities of adulthood. His self image and sense of identity [are] then further impaired by some challenge to his sexual adequacy or threat to this sense of compentency as a man. The situational crisis may be physical, social, sexual, marital, financial, locational, etc.—or a combination of such factors—but it precipitates the sexual involvement with a child. His offense is an impulsive and desperate act that is symptomatic of a failure to cope adaptively with specific life stresses. Typically this offender is married and a situation develops that threatens this relationship. Feeling overwhelmed by the resulting stresses, this man becomes involved sexually with a child. Quite often he is distressed by this behavior . . . but these feelings occur after the fact. At the time of the sexual activity, this offender is usually in a state of depression, in which he doesn't care, and/or a state of partial dissociation, in which he doesn't think about what he is doing—he suspends his usual values, his controls are weak, and he behaves in a way that is, in some respects, counter to his usual standards and conduct. (Groth, 1978, p. 8[1])

Obviously, such observations do not provide all the answers in cases where sexual abuse is alleged, nor does the presence of situational life stresses constitute concrete evidence that sexual abuse has occurred. Fortunately for children, most parents do not respond to stress in this way. However, for those who are totally unfamiliar with

---

1. From "Patterns of Sexual Assault against Children and Adolescents" by N. Groth in *Sexual Assault of Children and Adolescents* edited by A. Burgess, N. Groth, L. Holmstrom, and S. Sgroi, 1978, Lexington, MA: D. C. Heath and Co. Reprinted by permission.

the etiology of intrafamilial child sexual abuse, these observations may provide some insight into the fact that child sexual abuse *can* occur on the part of individuals who show no prior history of such behavior. It should be mentioned, however, that there is virtually no information about the degree to which this conceptual category applies to those who molest preschool-age children.

Marital separation and divorce are commonly regarded as two of the most severe forms of life stress that adults undergo. Stress itself tends to increase the liklihood of impulsive behavior. Regardless of the circumstances, stressed individuals usually experience feelings of failure, loneliness, and low self-esteem. Parents involved in contested divorces are particularly susceptible to emotional and financial stresses during the process of separation. At such time, they may be particularly vulnerable to the unconditional acceptance and innocent overtures or physical contact offered by a very young child. Although sexual in nature, child sexual abuse is rarely a response to purely sexual needs. More often, it is a sexual response to a misplaced emotional need, which can be transferred from a rejecting adult to a seemingly responsive child. At the time of divorce, the child may represent to the parent the only person left in his world who still depends on him, belongs to him or cares about him.

PREDISPOSING CIRCUMSTANCES

Unfortunately, the financial constraints and limited housing accommodations often brought about by marital separation may sometimes contribute to the vulnerability of the single parent and, therefore, of the child. It may be that there are some parents who, despite their emotional susceptibility at certain crisis points in their lives, would be able to resist their sexual and emotional urges to reach out for children in this way if they were still surrounded by the external inhibiting factors that usually exist within intact families (Finkelhor & Araji, 1983). However, within the context of a weekend visitation in a one-bedroom apartment with a small, adoring child, a parent may find himself unable to resist such urges. And, at those times, he may apply whatever rationalizations he needs in order to justify his actions to himself and to the child. Commonly, he may assume that a young child doesn't understand and won't remember. It is unfortunate for their children how often such parents are wrong.

It is not clear what constitutes the difference between those adults who can take advantage of children in such a situation and those who do not. But it is critically important for those who do evaluations in these kinds of cases to acknowledge the fact that some people do.

NEGOTIATING THE COURT SYSTEM

Some of the problems that arise when child abuse is alleged in the context of a divorce proceeding are related to the legal system itself. First of all, in many if not most states, the part of the court system that hears divorce cases is not the same court that handles cases of child maltreatment. They may be physically located in different places; may operate under very different sets of procedures; and may function with very different sets of players, including judges, attorneys, mediators, court social workers, and groups of mental health experts. In fact, some of these dual systems may be so administratively separate that the key professionals involved in each system (many of whom work with very similar cases) may not even know one another. Not only are some judges and divorce attorneys unfamiliar with the dynamics associated with abusive families or individuals (as well as with the local experts who can help in such evaluations), but they may be inclined to take these cases less seriously than the people who deal with them on a regular basis and see some of their consequences in juvenile or dependency court. Furthermore, since they are accustomed to hearing every kind of allegation or "dirty trick" used in the name of winning a divorce suit, they are likely to view charges of child sexual abuse as simply representing more of the same.

Of equal significance are the differences in the nature of the court systems themselves. The divorce court is adversarial in nature and is accustomed to addressing the rights and needs of conflicting adults. In contrast, the juvenile or dependency court system was designed in response to the limitations and vulnerability of children, and it is replete with special procedures and legal accommodations designed to meet children's needs. (Berliner & Stevens, 1982). Its focus is on child protection and on serving the best interests of children. In addition, the emotionally charged atmosphere of divorce court, where the adversarial stance of attorneys often serves to exacerbate existing conflicts, is not a favorable arena in which to resolve

the difficult dilemmas associated with evaluating charges of child sexual abuse. In contrast, the juvenile court's child-centered focus on the
safety of children, and on the strengthening and treatment of troubled
families, represents an environment where the voices of children are
more likely to be heard.

There are several options for addressing the discrepancies presented by these two systems. The ways in which they are worked out
in relation to these cases will probably depend more on the existing
structure of local judicial systems than on the actions taken by individual family members or their attorneys. In some places, the problems of dual systems are not an issue, because divorce cases and child
abuse cases are handled within the same family court system.

The disadvantages or biases in divorce courts in some jurisdictions
may indicate a need to institute separate proceedings in juvenile court,
once allegations of child abuse are raised in the midst of the divorce
case. While this provides all the advantages previously described, it
should be remembered that it also initiates two separate proceedings
in two different courts, usually involving more players, more hearings,
and additional financial expense. Much of the background work, evaluation, and legal procedures may also be duplicative, due to the fact
that different judges will be involved. In addition, if criminal charges
have been filed, legal proceedings may be pending simultaneously in
three different court systems.

In some states, these cases are serving as the impetus to the consideration or reconsideration of combining dependency and divorce
court, at least in relation to divorce-related child abuse allegations. In
other places, where combined family court systems are deemed to be
impractical or undesirable by the judiciary, these cases have spurred
new levels of coordination between juvenile and divorce courts. Some
judges are holding periodic case conferences with other judges in
order to determine which court is appropriate, and to collaborate with
one another to determine the best handling of individual cases. This
type of coordination—which, for the children's sake, should also be
occurring in conjunction with the criminal courts—provides a good
opportunity to utilize the expertise and the resource of both systems.
Regardless of the structure of existing systems in any given county,
the growing numbers of these cases and the difficulties associated
with adjudicating them demand that the courts re-evaluate the management of these cases in order to insure that their procedures, at-

titudes, resources and decisions are in keeping with the best interests of the children involved.

EVALUATION STRATEGIES

As a preface to this section, the reader is referred back to Section II, "Evaluation of Young Children." This portion of the present chapter is intended to reiterate and/or elaborate upon the information presented in that section, and to provide a few additional points for consideration when evaluating children in divorcing families.

LOGISTICS OF INTERVIEWING

The question of who should evaluate these children can be a sticky one in cases that involve divorce as well as possible child abuse. When one parent or the other takes a child to a private mental health professional to be evaluated with regard to the existence of sexual abuse, the evaluation is invariably subject to the criticism that the professional has been hired by that parent and, therefore, has been influenced by or is working in that parent's interests. This occurs despite therapists' insistence on their own abilities to be objective, and, in some cases, even when a therapist agrees to conduct an evaluation without charge. Further, an evaluation conducted at the request of one parent (particularly if it results in substantiation of the existence of child sexual abuse) frequently results in the child's being taken by the other parent to his own evaluator, usually in hopes of refuting the findings of the first one. If the findings of the second evaluation are substantially different from those of the first, the child may then be forced to undergo a third evaluation at the behest of the parents, the court, or another agency. Aside from the fact that such private evaluations can result in battles over the relative superiority of professional credentials in court, they may not be recognized as "official" or sufficient for use by those agencies mandated to determine the existence of abuse; this can result in the need to duplicate the entire interview process. Along with the unnecessary trauma of making the child repeat her statements over and over, much of the initial, fresh information from the child will be lost or distorted by the process.

In addition to these problems associated with private evaluations, it is often difficult for those who must assess the results of such evaluations to determine the circumstances and expertise that lie behind them. For example, in one case a mother hired a private psychologist to interview and evaluate her 3-year-old, who had made statements to the effect that her father had been putting his tongue in her vagina. The psychologist, who saw the child on several occasions alone, stated in his report that, although he had never heard a child make such a statement before, he felt fairly confident that she was not making it up and that it had some basis in fact. When the father learned of this report, he, in turn, took his daughter to his own psychiatrist. The psychiatrist, who also had no expertise in this area, interviewed the little girl while she sat on her father's lap. Not unsurprisingly, he was unable to elicit any information from the child. Along with a glowing report on the personal attributes of the father, he concluded that the child must have been coached by the mother. In court, a judge struggled with these conflicting reports and finally came to a compromise solution: The father was permitted to continue unmonitored weekend visitation on the weight of the psychiatrist's strong conclusion and medical credentials, while the child and family were ordered to undergo another full evaluation before a final determination regarding custody would be made. Aside from the fact that the child was submitted to eight separate interviews prior to the court-ordered evaluation, the parents had spent approximately $800 on evaluations that did not succeed in substantially resolving the matter on either side.

One of the best ways of avoiding the question of "therapists for hire" is to have the evaluation ordered by the court and conducted by agency or professionals who specialize in child abuse–related evaluations. Evaluations in some counties, particularly when ordered by the dependency court, are paid for by the state. In others, particularly when they are ordered by the divorce court, the evaluations must be paid for by the parents themselves. Either way, when it is the court that orders an evaluation, the question of bias or loss of objectivity is greatly reduced, and the evaluator is ultimately answerable to the court.

The issue of when the child should be interviewed during the process of the divorce is not very different from the issue in relation to other family circumstances described in this book, and the advice remains the same: The child should be evaluated as soon as possible after suspicions or allegations of sexual abuse are raised, preferably before her fears of future consequences have arisen or been realized. If the child has visitation rights with both parents, and abuse is alleged or suspected against only one of them, it is rarely necessary to remove a child and place her in substitute care (such as a foster home or a relative's home), although it sometimes happens in practice. At times when authorities believe that a child is deliberately being coached by a parent or that the alleging parent is psychotic or otherwise mentally unstable, the child may be removed temporarily in order to prevent being used further as a pawn between the parents. If this is to be done, it is of great benefit to the evaluation if the child can be interviewed *before* such action is taken. If there is concern that the child will either be abused further or intimidated into silence during visitation with an alleged abusive parent, the court can order temporary suspension of visitation rights during the process of the evaluation. In such situations, it may be best not tell a young child the reason for the suspension of visits, but simply to explain that they will not be occurring for a while and that it is not her fault. It is important for parents and professionals alike not to discuss the case within earshot of the child or otherwise to convey their own alarm or emotional upset over the situation.

Evaluators who work with divorcing families on these cases need to have a high tolerance for conflict (including projected anger directed at them), and they should have enough clinical experience and familiarity with the dynamics of sexual abuse that they will not easily be taken in, either by the initial claims of one parent against another or by the outwardly rational "best behavior" of any of the parties. Just as each parent will strive to establish a collegial bond or alliance with the evaluator, so may each parent's attorney.

Divorce attorneys can be very persuasive in their attempts to win evaluators over onto their side (as professional peers of the evaluator, often divorce attorneys are better at presenting a case than the parent), and evaluators should limit their conversations to the legal and logistical details necessary to the task at hand. There are enough issues and relationships involved in diagnosing these cases without having to worry about the relationship with a client's attorney.

Another valuable attribute for evaluators of these cases is patience. Evaluations involving divorcing families are simply more complicated than in most other situations, and they often involve a greater time commitment. Although some professionals are used to being able to formulate opinions on the basis of one interview per subject, these cases often require a number of interviews conducted over time— particularly with the children involved. The importance of developing a familiar, trusting relationship with these children cannot be over- emphasized in terms of its contribution to the amount and level of the information ultimately gathered.

Conducting interviews with different combinations of the parties involved can be a useful, if sometimes stressful, way of obtaining a first-hand view of the family dynamics. Starting with the accusing parent, each parent should be seen separately first in order to obtain facts as well as allegations, and to get a sense of the feelings that may underlie the situations described (e.g., anger, hurt, paranoia, revenge, etc.). It may also be helpful to add other involved family members after the initial interview to assess their reactions or influence in the family. If the allegations have been brought by a divorced ex-wife or ex-husband who has visitation or custody, the new spouse, if there is one, should also be interviewed. Depending upon the case, it may be important to keep the separated parents and child(ren) from seeing one another at the time of the interviews. Accidental encounters can add to their stress and influence their frames of mind, particularly for the children. If evaluations cannot be scheduled for different days (or if the evaluator wants everyone present for the purpose of com- bining some of the interviews), arrangements should be made for the parties to enter and wait in separate areas where they will not run into one another.

In any case, the child should be seen alone before any other combinations are tried. A decision about whether or not to interview a child with the accused parent or with both parents together is a judgment call that depends on the circumstances of the case (it may be prohibited by the court) and on how the evaluator thinks it will affect the child. Asking the child's opinion is one important source of data. The evaluator should, when possible, give an accused parent an equal chance at helping the evaluator and the child to get to the truth. However, if a child exhibits strong fear or resistance to being interviewed with an accused parent, or if the evaluator feels that there are already enough data to sustain the allegations, a joint interview should be reconsidered.

Nonetheless, if done with caution and skill, such interviews can yield valuable insights into the nature of the accused parent and child's relationship. In those instances, when a child has exhibited no qualms about being with her father, and the father has welcomed the opportunity to demonstrate their positive relationship, the evaluator might offer the father the opportunity to raise the sexual abuse allegations in front of the child. He can be asked to give his child his genuine permission to tell the evaluator what happened or to explain why she has told those things to other people. The message to the father is, of course, that if there have been no secrets or prior warnings about silence, and if he truly has nothing to hide, then he should have no problem with fully absolving the child of any concerns she might have in talking with the evaluator. Even when structured interviews of this nature are contraindicated, direct observation of children and parents in unstructured settings can provide useful information to the evaluator.

If there are siblings involved in the case, they should be seen separately first, although it can also be useful to see them together as well. Sibling dynamics are particularly important to observe in cases where more than one child is alleging abuse or in cases where half-siblings are contradicting each other's reports. The natural children of an accused parent, though they might seem to be a more reliable barometer of the parent's past behavior, might be more likely to "cover" for the parent out of loyalty and fear than would their stepsiblings. On the other hand, some adults who sexually abuse unrelated children appear to be able to stop short of any sexual involvement with their own children. In some situations, an older sibling may be sexually abusing a younger child, either alone or in addition to a parent. If an accused parent has older children by a former marriage, the evaluator may uncover a history of unreported abuse if he or she can gain access to those children for an interview. Resistance to this is usually strong, and geographic distance can be a problem, but the court will sometimes be of assistance in this effort. In any case, siblings and half-siblings of identified victims should not be overlooked in the evaluative process, and they can often add valuable pieces to the overall family picture.

INTERVIEWING TECHNIQUES

Play therapy techniques should be designed to evoke a child's feelings regarding family members and the present family situation. Getting a view of how the child understands the divorce or separation, why she thinks it is happening, whose fault it is, and what her role may be in the process will help the evaluator to assess how the allegations of sexual abuse may fit into the picture. The sexual material should not be addressed in the first part of the interview unless the child brings it up. Play situations that give the evaluator opportunities to ask for information about the child's living arrangements sometimes provide better information than direct questioning. For example, after asking a child to draw a picture of her house, the evaluator can then ask who lives in the house and get the child to draw all of those people. If one parent is missing, the evaluator can say, "Where is Daddy? Does he live somewhere else?" If the child draws another house with Daddy in it, the evaluator might ask why Daddy doesn't live in the same house with Mommy any more. The answer to that and similar questions will provide a child's-eye view of what the separation might mean to the child. For children who won't draw, similar situations can be created with doll families, doll houses, puppets, or little plastic or felt stick-on people and houses.

When children who the evaluator knows are living with only one parent state that everyone lives together in one happy family, their denial may be a defense against their own feelings of shame, anxiety, or guilt over the separation, or it may reveal an attempt to pretend that everything is fine in hopes that the pretense will make it so. It also may represent a way of testing their credibility with the evaluator. Challenging a child about this or similar statements that the evaluator knows to be untrue may put the child on the defensive, but it may also reduce the evaluator's credibility with the child to let such statements pass unnoticed. Instead, the evaluator might say something like this: "I think that your daddy lives someplace else, because your mommy and daddy told me so. It's okay to talk about it. Lots of kids have parents who live in two separate places. It's not their fault and it's not yours either. It's just the way it is."

In addition to learning how children feel about their family situations, it is important to try to establish their feelings about each of their parents separately. Are they overly fearful, cautious, afraid of evoking parental displeasure for the things they do, or fearful of the consequences of talking to the evaluator about a parent? On the other end of the scale, do they side with or are they overly protective of one parent, are they overeager to please, or do they accept responsibility for the consequences of a parent's behavior? Will they talk about secrets, and do they appear to be keeping any from the evaluator? How do they feel about living with or visiting each of their parents? If they react negatively to either suggestion, is it primarily because they are angry or protective, or is it because they are afraid? Is the issue of sexual or physical abuse brought up by the child in the context of not wanting to live with or visit a parent, or does it surface as a separate issue? The answers to such questions rarely provide definitive conclusions about the existence of abuse, but keeping them in mind may help the evaluator to construct a larger picture. The evaluator needs to probe for what lies behind the statements of children. When they express feelings or make judgmental statements, such as "Daddy is mean" or "Mommy is mad at me," the evaluator should ask them how they know that and who else says so. Feigned confusion and puzzled statements can often elicit details: "I don't understand. Sometimes I can be so dumb. Can you explain it to me more or show me what you mean?"

An evaluator can usually expect some degree of anger from children whose parents are engaged in battle. Often the children won't tell the evaluator it's *their* parents they're angry with, but they will act out their feelings in play with daddy and mommy dolls or puppets. Sometimes their play will get quite violent as they become absorbed in the opportunity to vent their anger by throwing, tearing up, stomping on, or otherwise acting out with dolls or toys. At times their anger may be directed at the evaluator if he or she role-plays someone else in the child's life (or as the source of provocation for all the bad feelings). It is useful to be able to observe the depth of a child's anger, sorrow, or potential for violent acting out, but it also must be maintained within some limits. It may be necessary to physically restrain some children, divert the attention to something else, or get up and walk to another part of the room in apparent lack of interest. When they are calm again, it is important to affirm their feelings (though not necessarily their behavior) with statements such as this: "Boy, you sure have a lot of angry feelings inside of you. Do you think you can talk about the things that make you angry at home?"

When considering the anger in some children from divorcing families, it is important for the evaluator to recognize that it can come from many sources besides abuse. That is why it's so important to probe for the sources of feelings, rather than accepting them at face value or simply relying on one's own interpretations. Young children do not necessarily fear, distrust, or feel anger toward a sexually abusive parent, because they may not have any real understanding of the meaning of this behavior. Depending on the nature of the abuse, they may even view it as a fun game or a special activity that is done in association with other treats and rewards. As one 4-year-old put it, "Daddy touches me here—but I don't get upset like Mommy, because it's okay 'cause it doesn't hurt and I like him." Our work with young children continues to teach us, more than anything else, that their reactions are many and varied. In our evaluations of preschoolers, we must strive to draw conclusions based on our judgments of whether or not abuse has occurred—not solely on children's reactions or on their parents' beliefs and wishes.

INTERVENTION WHEN ABUSE IS ALLEGED OR SUSPECTED

When a parent suspects that a child is being sexually abused by the other parent or by a stepparent, strong feelings such as rage, blame, fear, and guilt are usually evoked. Such feelings can get in the way of rational and constructive action and are often transmitted to the child. The same is true for the parent who is accused of abuse. Advise the parent in either situation to (1) remain calm and underreact to everything said or done by the child while the parent is in the child's presence; (2) find a friend or counselor with whom feelings can be ventilated; and (3) get legal advice from someone who is familiar with divorce law *and* the procedures for handling child abuse cases in a particular community.

One of the first reactions on the part of many mothers who suspect child sexual abuse during the course of separation or divorce may be to refuse to permit further contact between the children and their fathers. A mother's actions may include locking a child in the house, changing her phone number, placing the child with relatives, or fleeing with the child to a hidden place. While these may appear to be natural and protective reactions, it is usually inadvisable to recommend that a mother deny visitation on her own in cases where a father has legal custody or visitation rights, since it will put her in violation of the court order and possibly in contempt of court. It may also cast additional suspicion on the mother's motives and may be regarded as merely an excuse for refusing visitation with the father. There are, however, legal procedures that can be instituted to assure protection when a child is thought to be at risk for abuse. A mother or other suspecting family member will be acting in the child's best interest if she collects all the information she has received from the child and puts it in the hands of someone who is familiar with and capable of dealing with these situations. Whether she calls her own attorney, contacts a new attorney, gets in touch with a therapist, or calls the mandated child abuse reporting agency in her community may depend on the resources available to her. In any case, a formal report of suspected child sexual abuse should be made to the appropriate agency.

There are several emergency actions that can be taken, usually the same day that suspected abuse is reported, in order to protect the child. In cases involving visitation orders, where a prior court order guarantees visitation rights to a suspected abusing parent, a motion can be put before the court requesting a temporary halt to visitation and/or custody, pending an investigation of suspected child sexual abuse. In cases where a suspected abusing parent has ongoing visitation rights, the court may also require that visits be monitored by a third party (either appointed by the courts or agreed to by the parents), pending the outcome of the investigation and a decision by the court. These types of motions can be put before the court by a parent's attorney as *ex parte* motions.

For some sexually abusive parents, public allegations and the fear of losing their children may be enough to extinguish their abusive behavior, temporarily or permanently. But there are no guarantees in this matter, and such a likelihood is diminished by their refusal to acknowledge their behavior and by the inability of the justice system to sustain an allegation or mandate treatment. Still, some safeguards can be added to try to protect a child from further victimization. Regular pediatric examinations by someone familiar with the case history, and ongoing child therapy of the kind described in other chapters of this book, will help to provide some sense of accountability to outside observers. A year or two can make a tremendous difference in a young child's developmental abilities and verbal skills; moreover, through the process of treatment or a follow-up evaluation, the details of the abuse may become clearer. The important things are that children understand what sexual abuse is; that they feel able to resist and to tell someone if it should happen again; and that someone will be there to listen.

CONCLUSION

Conducting evaluations of divorce-related child sexual abuse cases is not for the faint of heart or the short of temper. It is frustrating, often discouraging work; it is not a job for amateurs, whatever their educational credentials. Much of it involves the use of professional judgment, the ability to maintain objectivity in the face of high emotions, and the willingness to make decisions on the basis of data that almost always seem insufficient to the task. The ability to determine the authenticity of the information presented often only comes from experience in evaluating and treating these cases. Although there are often only a few people in any community who specialize in the diagnosis and treatment of this problem, their numbers are growing as the numbers of cases continue to increase.

Unfortunately, there are many cases where diagnoses remain unclear even after evaluation, or where strong suspicions of abuse will never be proved. They are frustrating, and unnerving to all involved, but they are indicative of the nature of this problem and of the young ages of the children involved. Even in cases where an evaluator makes a firm judgment about the existence of sexual abuse, one parent or the other is likely to refute it. It is often not just the accused parent who will denounce a diagnosis if it is not in his favor. Evaluators should not expect expressions of relief from all concerned parents who are told that their children do not appear to have been molested. As noted earlier, whether the motives be self-serving or protective, there are cases in which parents hear or see what they believe is evidence of child sexual victimization, but not even the best evaluators are able to find it.

In such instances, it is particularly important that the children be evaluated by a person or by a team of people who are trained in this subject area and who have broad experience in doing these types of evaluations with both molested and nonmolested children. There are several reasons for this. If evaluators do not find signs of sexual abuse, and their conclusions or recommendations result in continued access to a child by a suspected abuser, then they owe it to that child to have based those recommendations on the most experienced and authoritative assessment that is available. From the opposite point of view, child sexual abuse is an extremely serious and stigmatizing charge, and evaluators owe the same degree of caution and professional expertise to those accused. Similarly, a parent who believes that her child was abused may continue to act in accordance with her own suspicions or feelings, even in the face of contradictory findings by professionals. Evaluators will not always be able to change her opinion or allay her fears. But it behooves them at least to be able to say to her and to all concerned that the final diagnosis or lack of conclusive findings is the result of a comprehensive evaluation conducted by experts.

Finally, it should be emphasized that nothing should be ruled out prior to approaching these cases for evaluation. The fact that a father may be highly educated, deeply religious, or prominent in the professional or business community has little bearing on whether he may or may not have molested his child. Similarly, a mother's educational level, marital history, emotional state, or even depth of anger over the divorce are only variables to be taken into consideration and should not be considered factors that automatically rule in or rule out the existence of abuse or the validity of allegations.

There even appears to be a danger that some parents, particularly mothers, may automatically be regarded as paranoid, hysterical, or perverted in their thinking for simply suspecting their ex-husbands of such a thing as child sexual abuse. It is a reflection of society's long-standing refusal to acknowledge the widespread existence of incest. For divorcing mothers, the assumptions made about their motives can serve as an insurmountable barrier to getting help. This bias may be so strong that their reports to others of what their children have told them can actually jeopardize their own positions as future custodians of their children. This form of double jeopardy will only serve to reinforce the silence that already surrounds this problem, and to endanger children further. Very young children are not prone to fantasizing about molestation and are rarely capable of describing or re-enacting things about which they have no knowledge or experience.

We must guard against our own unconscious motives for participating in this bias. We must recognize that it is much easier and more in accordance with our images of the world to regard a mother as crazy or hysterical than to recognize an otherwise seemingly rational and caring father as capable of the behaviors described. Beyond that, such a view may serve to reinforce our own denial of what we, like most people, would rather not see.

SOCIOCULTURAL CONSIDERATIONS IN CHILD SEXUAL ABUSE

Robert J. Kelly
Merilla McCurry Scott

It is probably a safe assumption that most people dealing with the problem of child sexual abuse neglect the importance of sociocultural factors. Many of us have a tendency to treat all cases of child sexual abuse as though every person came from the same socioeconomic and cultural background. The background that we use as our standard is most often the socioeconomic and cultural background with which we are most familiar, which is usually our own background. This ethnocentric bias causes us to overlook the fact that people with divergent sociocultural backgrounds differ in their sexual beliefs, values, practices, and restrictions.

Anthropologists studying the sexuality of different cultures throughout the world agree that some restrictions, such as the incest taboo, exist to a certain extent in all societies (see Kelly, 1984). However, the degree to which different cultures permit or encourage sexual activity varies greatly. A sexual act that is encouraged in some societies may be considered criminal in others. For instance, the Muria tribe described by Currier (1981) encourage their children to engage in a multitude of sexual activities, including sexual intercourse. Similar behavior in the United States would be interpreted as contributing to the delinquency of a minor. Rosenfeld (1977) describes another example of this cross-cultural diversity:

Authorship of this chapter was a joint effort. Our names are ordered alphabetically.

Finnish families have traditionally taken saunas together so that nudity in the family is both usual and not sexually provocative. An English family doing the same thing with a school aged child or adolescent would probably be overstimulating to the child (and to the adults) since nudity is sexual in that culture. What is acceptable behavior among the Trobriand Islanders would horrify the Amish. (p. 232)

Understanding sociocultural diversity is especially important in the United States because of the multitude of sociocultural groups within it. In a culturally pluralistic society like the United States, many subcultures are embedded within a larger dominant society. These subcultures are differentially affected by the values of the larger society and by social stratification (see DeVos, 1982). Different sociocultural groups interpret, express, and incorporate standards of appropriate sexuality in varying ways. As pointed out by Sanford (1980), people from Afro-American, Asian, Hispanic, Native American, and other backgrounds have unique needs because of the diverse ways in which sexuality is incorporated within each subculture.

Given this sociocultural pluralism, it behooves us to consider the sociocultural issues surrounding the problem of child sexual abuse. The remainder of this chapter examines these sociocultural issues, first from a research perspective and then from a conceptual and clinical perspective.

REVIEW OF THE LITERATURE

There are two sources of research data that are especially relevant to an understanding of sociocultural aspects of child sexual abuse. The first source is research on sociocultural issues that relate to child abuse in general. Lest we reinvent the wheel of sociocultural analysis, we should extrapolate from our empirical and theoretical knowledge of child abuse those issues that pertain specifically to child sexual abuse. The second source includes the few direct studies of sociocultural issues in child sexual abuse. These studies are of special importance because many aspects of child sexual abuse are phenomenologically different from other types of child abuse (cf. Finkelhor, 1982).

Within the literature on sociocultural issues in child abuse in general, four aspects of the research appear particularly noteworthy. The first is a tendency for researchers to overlook or ignore sociocultural data. Garbarino and Ebata (1983) state that ethnic and cultural differences have been treated with "benign neglect" in comparison with other aspects of child maltreatment. A second related problem is that when these ethnic and cultural differences have been studied, results have almost always been confounded by the effects of social class (e.g., Gil, 1970). A third sociocultural obstacle in interpreting child abuse research results from the use of broad racial categories, such as "black" and "white," which obscure the differences between subgroups within each category. For example, the use of the category "white" conceals the differences among white subgroups, perhaps implying that a subgroup such as the Irish does not differ from another white subgroup such as the Jewish. This type of implication is unwarranted without specific data on these subgroups. The fourth noteworthy tendency is for researchers to conclude broadly that child abuse cuts across all social, cultural, and economic lines (Besharov & Besharov, 1977; Steele, 1975). While child abuse has indeed been found within all these groups, such sweeping statements seem to imply that the extent and severity of child abuse are distributed proportionately among the total population. However, Pelton (1978) argues that child abuse is strongly (although not exclusively) related to poverty, and that widespread reports of child abuse as a "classless phenomenon" are unfounded and misleading. He states that the myth of classlessness serves certain professional and political interests, but diverts attention from the actual nature of the problem.

It may be helpful to compare these four research tendencies with the more recent strategies of research in child sexual abuse. To begin with, if the lack of attention to sociocultural aspects of child abuse in general can be described as benign neglect, perhaps the best descriptor for an even greater amount of inattentiveness to these aspects in child sexual abuse is that of gross negligence. This negligence is partially a function of the past tendency to shy away from any research on sexual abuse. This investigative shyness has left the topic of child sexual abuse as a "last frontier" for research and clinical practice. But a second reason for this negligence involves the sensitivity inherent in the topic of sociocultural aspects of child sexual abuse. Researchers who could potentially illustrate differences among people of varying race, ethnicity, or social class may fear accusations of prejudice and discrimination. Moreover, investigators finding subgroup differences may fear that their results will be misinterpreted or misused in a manner which contributes to intergroup disharmony. These fears can be relieved by using broad, nonspecific, and misleading statements, such as those used in the general child abuse literature. Indeed, the use of the sweeping statement that child sexual abuse cuts across all social, cultural, and economic lines can already be found in this sexual abuse literature (Jorne, 1979; Kelly, 1982). While this statement is true, without additional information or caveats, readers of these statements may conclude prematurely that no differences in child sexual abuse exist within or across sociocultural groups. The error comes in concluding that child sexual abuse is a homogeneous problem when, in fact, it is a problem manifested in diverse ways within our heterogeneous society. Failure to acknowledge this diversity impedes the development of group-specific prevention and treatment programs.

The few direct studies of sociocultural aspects of child sexual abuse have also been hindered by the two other obstacles mentioned in relation to the child abuse literature. These studies tend to discuss cultural and ethnic differences without controlling for the confounding effects of social class (e.g., Adams-Tucker, 1981). They also use broad sociocultural categories that obscure intragroup differences (e.g., Lindholm & Willey, 1983).

Without dismissing these four drawbacks, it may still be helpful to examine these few direct studies of sociocultural aspects of child sexual abuse. But first we wish to emphasize why it is important to conduct and examine prevalence studies that separate groups according to the variables of social class, race, and ethnicity. The purpose is certainly not to illustrate intergroup differences in order to point a judgmental finger at the groups with higher prevalence rates. Besides fueling intergroup tensions, this tendency to seek and label groups with high prevalence rates also results in a sort of "self-righteous blindness" within groups with a relatively low (but nonetheless real!) abuse rate. For example, early prevalence studies which emphasized the occurrence of sexual abuse among lower social classes seem to have perpetuated a self-righteous blindness among upper-class members toward the abuse occurring within their own socioeconomic group.

We should not simply focus our attention on the relative quantity of abuse among sociocultural groups. Our ultimate aim is to reduce the absolute prevalence of abuse within each group, independent of the comparative group rankings. For this reason, it is most important to study unique dynamics of each sociocultural group which increase or decrease the likelihood of abuse. This is not to say that comparative studies are without value. Hypothetically, if future research consistently suggests that sexual abuse occurs most frequently among white American families, the variable of race should then be further examined. Researchers could ask which aspects of the white culture promote abuse above and beyond the cross-racial norm. Meanwhile, other research should continue to examine variables which could decrease the absolute prevalence rates within those nonwhite groups. It is this combination of intergroup and intragroup analyses that will be most useful in our efforts to combat sexual abuse.

With this rationale, we now examine the existing literature on sociocultural aspects of child sexual abuse. One question that these studies have attempted to answer is whether the prevalence of child sexual abuse is related to social class. As with studies of child abuse in general, many of the existing data seem to suggest that child sexual abuse is especially problematic in groups with lower socioeconomic status (SES) (Benward & Densen-Gerber, 1975; De Francis, 1971; Gagnon, 1965; Julian, Mohr & Lapp, 1980; Maisch, 1972; Riemer, 1940; Sagarin, 1977; Specktor, 1979; Weinberg, 1955). Righton (1981) asserts that child sexual abuse tends to occur in the poorest and most overcrowded city districts, or in sparsely populated rural areas in which families have restricted access to a wider social network than their own kin. More comprehensive data by Finkelhor (1979b) suggest that the incidence of child sexual abuse is not higher as a function of crowding or rural region per se, although it does seem to be higher among people who were raised on farms. Finkelhor did find that the abuse of girls was more common among lower social classes as measured by father's occupation, family income, and parents' educational attainment. He also found a higher incidence of intrafamilial (but not extrafamilial) sexual abuse among boys whose family income was relatively low.

It is true that lower-SES families are overrepresented in documented cases because they are under the scrutiny of public agencies. And, indeed, researchers have documented cases of child sexual abuse in middle- and upper-income families (Finkelhor, 1979b; Giarretto, 1976a; Kelly & Tarran, 1983; Rosenfeld, 1979). However, there is not enough evidence to conclude that child sexual abuse occurs with equal frequency in all social classes. Finkelhor's (1979b) data, which are consistent with the Kinsey data (Kinsey, Pomeroy, Martin, & Gebhard, 1953), are especially important in this regard because they find a higher incidence among lower-social-class individuals in a sample that is not based on cases reported to authorities. It is still too early to conclude that child sexual abuse is more prevalent in low-SES environments. But while future research tests this hypothesis, researchers should simultaneously investigate which aspects of these low-SES environments tend to cultivate or perpetuate this abuse. Variables to be researched include overcrowding, adequacy of child supervision, and poverty-related stress. Once again, additional research should continue to examine factors related to the absolute prevalence and unique dynamics of abuse within all social classes.

A second sociocultural question asked in studies of child sexual abuse is whether the prevalence of this abuse is related to race. As with research on child abuse in general, the term *ethnicity* in sexual abuse studies usually refers to racial categories rather than intraracial ethnic subgroups (subcultures). Some studies of the prevalence of child sexual abuse do not provide information about racial variables (Kelly & Tarran, 1983; Landis, 1956; Russell, 1983; Sarafino, 1979). The few studies that report prevalence rates as a function of these racial categories have been contradictory. At least one study has reported that black children are less likely to be sexually abused (with respect to their relative representation in the population) than are whites (Adams-Tucker, 1981). On the contrary, at least three studies have suggested that blacks are overrepresented in reported child sexual abuse cases (De Francis, 1971; Finkelhor, 1983; Lindholm, 1984). In a study of 4132 cases of child abuse in Los Angeles County, Lindholm and Willey (1983) found that a smaller proportion of the abuse cases reported by blacks involved sexual abuse (16.6%) (as opposed to other types of abuse) than those reported by whites (26.7%) and Hispanics (28.2%). Nonetheless, blacks (+6.4%) and Hispanics (+3.4%) were still overrepresented, while whites were underrepresented (−5.4%), when comparing proportion of reported sexual abuse cases with racial distribution in the population (Lindholm, 1984). However, when considering only the number of families with reported sexual abuse (as opposed to number of victims), blacks were still overrepresented (+5.1%), whites were slightly overrepresented (+1.1%), and Hispanics were approximately equal (−0.3%) with their racial distribution in the population. Besides being influenced by variables such as social class and the tendency to be under the closer scrutiny of public agencies, these data also illustrate that conclusions about sociocultural factors depend upon how these factors are measured.

Special note should be made of one other recent study by Wyatt (1985) that utilized a sophisticated random sampling procedure with a nonclinical sample. Using a very broad definition of child sexual abuse, Wyatt found a higher, though statistically nonsignificant, rate of abuse among white American women (67%) as compared with Afro-American women (57%). This study is a useful prototype because it attempts to extricate the subtle similarities and differences between groups in the circumstances under which abuse occurs.

Given the contradictory nature of these few studies, it is too soon to make any generalizations about the relationship between racial categories and child sexual abuse prevalence. Even fewer studies have examined intraracial ethnic subgroup variation. One study by Finkelhor (1979b) found a higher incidence of extrafamilial child sexual abuse among Irish-American boys as compared with American boys of Italian, French-Canadian, and English descent. However, we could find no study that attempted to replicate this finding or extend it to other ethnic subgroups. As suggested for research on social class, if consistent differences are found in frequency of sexual abuse within certain racial or ethnic groups, future studies should examine which aspects of these groups make sexual abuse more likely. Such research could focus on the sexual beliefs, values, practices, and restrictions of each subgroup, as well as "nonsexual" variables, such as family dynamics and living conditions.

Clearly, our knowledge of the relationship between sociocultural factors and child sexual abuse is in its infancy. But while researchers are just beginning to outline important issues that need to be investigated in this area, clinicians are encountering clients from a variety of cultural and economic backgrounds on a daily basis. The remainder of this chapter attempts to offer these clinicians suggestions as to how they can adopt a sociocultural perspective on both a conceptual and a clinical level.

CONCEPTUAL ISSUES

The crucial conceptual dilemma involves how sociocultural factors as they relate to the problem of child sexual abuse can be incorporated into a clinical approach without adopting either an ethnocentric bias, which neglects appropriate cultural variability, or a purely culturally relativistic position, which overlooks universal humane standards. On the one hand, if we adopt an ethnocentric standard, we will judge all sexual behavior throughout the world according to its consistency with Western practices. Behaviors ranging from nude public bathing to pubertal initiation rites might be seen as harmful or abusive mainly because they are not practiced and understood in Western cultures. On the other hand, if we assert that all behavior is culturally relative, we run the risk of condoning any behavior that is adhered to by a large enough number of individuals. According to this approach, the practices of the Rene Guyon Society, which is composed of at least 2500 members who have had intercourse with young children (Densen-Gerber & Hutchinson, 1978), might be interpreted as legitimate "cultural" variability.

In attempting to resolve this dilemma, it may be helpful once again to observe how these concerns have been dealt with in relation to child abuse in general. Korbin (1977, 1979, 1980, 1981) has written extensively on the subject of cross-cultural factors in child abuse and neglect. She suggests that clinicians become cognizant of both the individual culture's viewpoint (i.e., an "emic" perspective) and the intercultural viewpoint (i.e., an "etic" perspective). This framework allows for sensitivity to values associated with a particular subgroup, as well as to universal humane standards. Additionally, this framework addresses whether particular values can be applied across different sociocultural groups (Cohn & Garbarino, 1981).

This approach of adopting both an emic and an etic perspective may be useful when dealing with sociocultural factors in child sexual abuse. An emic or intracultural perspective would consider culture-specific norms, values, and practices as they relate to a child's sexuality. This information would shed light on the sociocultural context and meaning of particular sexual behaviors. Moreover, it would help us detect idiosyncratic departures from culturally acceptable standards. For example, we may eventually view penile circumcision within a pubertal initiation rite as an instance of legitimate cultural variability, once we understand the perspective of the culture engaging in this practice. But we would then also understand that further genital mutilation such as castration may be abhorred by that same culture and thus should be considered an instance of abusive, idiosyncratic departure from culturally acceptable standards.

An etic or intercultural perspective would involve a broader, outside frame of reference that would include universal humane standards regarding childhood sexuality. This perspective would encourage the development of sexual norms and values that promote the welfare of the child and safeguard against extreme cultural relativism. One example of this type of norm is the universal taboo against father–daughter sexual intercourse. General guidelines could be devised for evaluating discrepancies in sexual practices between sociocultural groups. In this way, idiosyncratic departures by subgroups, such as the Rene Guyon Society, could be identified as not exemplifying legitimate cultural variability.

In sum, a necessary step in developing a sociocultural perspective on child sexual abuse is the awareness of the intracultural and intercultural contexts in which sexual behavior occurs. As more is learned about these conceptual issues, a greater sensitivity to sociocultural factors will follow.

CLINICAL ISSUES

The final section of this chapter attempts to highlight important issues that a clinician is most likely to confront when working with clients from various sociocultural backgrounds. Prior to discussing these issues, it is imperative to emphasize the need to be aware of one's own feelings and stereotypes about clients from these backgrounds. This will minimize the risk of overpathologizing behavior that is socioculturally appropriate or of minimizing significant events that on the surface may seem socioculturally related but in fact are inappropriate. This process can be facilitated by seeking consultation with a professional who is familiar with the sociocultural background of a client. Additionally, seeking consultation can serve as a means by which a clinician can identify ways to handle some of the following issues appropriately.

ESTABLISHING A RELATIONSHIP

Establishing a strong working relationship is a sine qua non of therapeutic intervention. This process can be disrupted by issues relating both to sociocultural differences and to the fact that the presenting problem involves child sexual abuse. These issues become especially evident when assessing a client's motivation for treatment. Many ethnic minorities are reluctant to seek services outside of the family system because of the lingering stigma attached to mental health services. When the problem involves child sexual abuse, a client may have even less motivation, because he or she has been court-referred or is only seeking treatment while a child custody arrangement is pending. This reluctance is intensified when the particular agency offering services does not have staff members from a variety of ethnic backgrounds. The client may interpret this as a lack of sensitivity to cultural differences on the part of the agency. As a consequence, rapport may be difficult to establish, and initial distrust may persist. In this case, the client needs to know that the clinician is sensitive to these issues and is willing to discuss them if this will help the therapeutic relationship.

OVERCOMING LANGUAGE BARRIERS

Discussing sexual topics is difficult for most people in Western societies. This difficulty is exacerbated when a client from one sociocultural group attempts to discuss sexual issues with a therapist from a different sociocultural group. The therapist should acknowledge that the client may have different words or expressions for sexual terms. This point recently became evident during a group for adolescent sex offenders at Los Angeles County Hospital (see Kelly & Kaser-Boyd, 1984). The therapists used an initial exercise in which group members were instructed to list all words that they had heard that refer to genitalia. This exercise served two purposes. First, it desensitized group members to the use of sexual words in group discussion. But, secondly, it made the therapists aware of differences in sexual language among clients from various sociocultural backgrounds. For example, one Hispanic boy used the word "huevos" (translated as "eggs") to refer to testicles. By becoming aware of these sociocultural differences and accepting them as normal, the therapist can make it easier for the client to discuss the already embarrassing facts that are often inherent in cases of child sexual abuse.

ASSESSING THE CLIENT'S PERCEPTION OF SEXUALITY

Related to the problem of language barriers is the issue of differential perspectives about sexuality among sociocultural groups. Some groups seem to equate sexual ignorance with sexual innocence. They may have a strong sociocultural tradition that values sexual innocence among their female members. This issue recently arose during a group for female adolescent sexual abuse victims at Los Angeles County Hospital. Parents of some of the Hispanic group members were opposed to the incorporation of sex education as a treatment component. Despite the fact that their daughters had already been sexually abused and were confused about what had happened to them sexually, these parents still believed that their daughters' sexual ignorance was more important than the resolution of their confusion through education. This type of sociocultural belief system regarding sexuality needs to be explored early in treatment.

ASSESSING THE CLIENT'S PERCEPTION OF THE PROBLEM

The client's perception of the problem is a crucial aspect of treatment in a case of child sexual abuse. This perception will undoubtedly be influenced by the client's sociocultural background, since different sociocultural groups place emphasis on various aspects of a sexual abuse incident. For example, some groups may be most concerned about religious components such as sin, physical components such as pregnancy, social components such as secrecy, or cultural components such as loss of virginity. Some groups may be less inclined to view the incident as sexual abuse, and instead may label it an overreaction of the system. Moreover, some groups respond differently to the abuse of boys and girls, sometimes viewing an early sexual experience for a boy as an initiation while viewing a similar early experience for a girl as a violation. These group reactions may also be influenced by the same sex versus opposite sex, and the incestuous versus nonincestuous, nature of the abuse (Kelly, 1985; Kelly & Tarran, 1984). One way to approach these questions, is by clarifying how the client perceives his or her culture's view of such behavior. This will also provide information on how assimilated the client is to the majority culture.

CLARIFYING THE CLIENT'S EXPECTATIONS

Given that ethnic minorities continue to underutilize mental health services, many are unclear about the therapeutic process. Clients who are disclosing evidence about child sexual abuse for the first time will almost never expect the often chaotic series of responses from legal, child protective, medical, and psychological agencies that typically follow such disclosure. It is important to educate the client about what is expected of him or her (e.g., keeping regular appointments, getting medical evaluation for the child) and what can be expected from the therapist and other agencies.

Assessing the Family Support Network

One reason why many ethnic minorities have underutilized mental health services is that they often have a strong family support network. There is often more than one primary caregiver, with a number of relatives having intimate access to the child. Clinicians need to be aware of this sociocultural factor and should be willing to include extended family members in therapy sessions. For example, if a sexually abused child begins to act out in oversexualized ways, a therapist may encourage that child's parents to respond to the behavior in some consistent, appropriate manner. However, the child's behavior may not change if the other caregivers are not also acting according to this treatment plan. Allowing extended family members to participate may increase the effectiveness of therapeutic interventions, while also communicating to the client a respect for sociocultural differences.

Assessing the Nature of Stressors in the Client's Life

Often clients from lower-SES backgrounds are faced with a multitude of daily financial difficulties. If a lower-SES woman's child has been sexually abused by her husband, the possibility of losing her husband's income by disclosing information about the abuse causes extra stress, in addition to the stress resulting from the knowledge of the abuse itself. She may also have to endure the ridicule of her sociocultural group, which may perceive her as a failure in her roles as both wife and mother. Clinicians need to be prepared to assist clients with such difficulties by being aware of community resources (e.g., job training courses, Parents United groups, etc.). Such difficulties typically interfere with a client's participation in therapy. What may appear to be resistance on the part of the client may in fact be a variety of reality constraints.

BEING AWARE OF PREJUDICIAL PRACTICES WITHIN THE SYSTEM

Many times, ethnic minorities as well as lower-SES clients face inconsistent delivery of services in the legal system. Wright (1982) reports that in a review of the prison sentences of 12 Afro-American fathers participating in a group for incest perpetrators, 7 of them (58%) were incarcerated. Of the 29 white fathers, on the other hand, only 5 of them (17%) were incarcerated. Thus, clients may have reasons for being angry with the system that are justifiable and need to be explored. By showing a willingness to discuss such issues, a clinician displays a sensitivity to the client's experience that will facilitate a strong working relationship.

Two final suggestions seem appropriate for clinicians attempting to adopt a sociocultural perspective. The most important suggestion is to view clients first as individuals without pigeonholing them according to sociocultural background. Many people do not identify strongly with their sociocultural background and have become assimilated into the larger culture. The second related suggestion is always to be aware of intragroup variability. In this regard, it is especially important to separate socioeconomic factors from cultural factors. For example, the needs of an upper-class white family will be different from the needs of a white family that is on welfare, even if the incidents of sexual abuse within each family are similar.

In conclusion, we hope that clinicians dealing with cases of child sexual abuse will become aware of the importance of sociocultural factors. This awareness on both a conceptual and a clinical level may enable us to serve victims from all sociocultural backgrounds more effectively.

ACKNOWLEDGMENT

This research was supported in part by a postdoctoral grant from the National Institute of Mental Health, Grant IT32 MH17118–02.

VIDEOTAPING OF INTERVIEWS AND COURT TESTIMONY

Kee MacFarlane
with Sandy Krebs

The use of audiotape and videotape recording of interviews and testimony by children for clinical, legal, and investigatory purposes has become increasingly popular over the past few years. The value of making a permanent, first-hand record of initial statements is particularly obvious in a field characterized by the high likelihood of later retraction by child victims. But there are numerous other reasons for tape-recording early interactions with alleged victims of child sexual abuse. There also are numerous pitfalls that can accompany such documentation. The purposes of this chapter are to examine both the advantages and the disadvantages of this form of electronic evaluation; to discuss some of the techniques and strategies associated with taping; and to offer the reader the benefit of considerable experience with both the positive outcomes of utilizing these methods and their potential repercussions. We hope that this chapter will provoke careful consideration and further exploration of those issues.

PURPOSES OF TAPING

Since most of what is said here about videotaping also can be applied to the use of audiotapes, the following discussion, for purposes of brevity, refers to videotape recording. It should be noted that, because sexual abuse is so difficult for children to talk about and acknowledge, it can be a real advantage to visually capture a child's physical reactions, facial expressions, body language, and various expressions of fear, pain, anger, and avoidance—visual reactions that otherwise may never find their way into words. In working with sexually abused children, we quickly realize that we can learn as much from what they are unwilling or unable to say as we do from what they actually tell us.

REDUCING SYSTEMIC TRAUMA

One of the most common and practical reasons why many agencies and individuals have begun taping initial sessions with children stems from the many problems that children face as they are processed through our child protective and criminal justice systems (MacFarlane, & Bulkley, 1982). That is, children are regularly forced to undergo multiple, duplicative interviews by a wide variety of professionals in various systems that have a legitimate interest in their welfare or in the prosecution of alleged crimes. Each successive interview, whether it be for medical, clinical, or legal purposes, necessitates the retelling of experiences and feelings that are usually embarrasing, frightening, guilt-invoking, and anxiety-producing.

In addition, with each telling, children tend to lose the spontenaity and immediacy that is usually apparent in the first disclosure of sexual abuse. In their attempts at self-protection against what they frequently see as unnecessary and repetative intrusions into their lives, they learn to mask the emotional content of their feelings. Some get to the point where they relate their experiences without any emotional affect, with the result that their statements about abuse may appear to have a slick, rehearsed, or matter-of-fact quality to them. This has been particularly observed among children who testify in court following a lengthy investigatory and pretrial process.

There are other disadvantages of multiple information-gathering interviews that can affect case outcomes. Children's own ongoing descriptions may become contaminated by the verbal input and personal reactions of the different adults with whom they interact. They may lose credibility through picking up otherwise unfamiliar terminology from questioning by adults (particularly names for body parts or the word "molested" as a substitute for the word "touched"). Also, the danger of increasing a child's suggestibility or need for compliance might be increased with each interview (although to the authors' knowledge, this has not been demonstrated).

Finally, children do not understand the logic (or illogic) of having to repeat the same information over and over to different adults (Berliner & Roe, 1985). They frequently get angry and frustrated with the entire process. They may take it upon themselves to put an end to such nonsense by completely shutting down all communication on the subject and refusing to answer any questions at a time when it may be most important for the case that they do so. They may retract their stories altogether in order to rid themselves of harassment, which they associate with their having told what happened in the first place.

It is important to realize that preventing multiple information-gathering interviews within a community system requires far more than the purchase of audiotape or videotape equipment. If tape-recorded interviews by one individual or agency are not recognized as valuable or legitimate substitutes for interviews by other individuals within the system, they will do nothing to prevent duplicative and traumatic contact with child victims. This issue, which is crucial to preventing systemic trauma to children, has three distinct aspects: One relates to politics, another to legitimate information needs, and the third to competent interviewing skills.

The first aspect relates to those systems that have jurisdictional interest in a case (i.e., child protective services, police, courts, and district attorneys' offices), as well as those who have health or mental health interest in a case (physicians, psychotherapists, and staff members in specialized child abuse diagnostic centers). Despite many common goals, these agencies and individuals frequently also have non-mutual interests in the kinds of information needed and the process by which it is gathered. More important, they rarely have authority or jurisdiction over one another's activities, and are not individually in a position to direct or coordinate one another's actions except by mutual consent. They must agree to work together to prevent systemic trauma and multiple interrogation of children if it is to occur on a community-wide basis. They may have to give up some things in order to gain others, things that ultimately will be in their interests, because they are in the interests of children who are the objects of their intervention. Videotaped interviews can be very useful in this regard, but only if agreement can be reached as to who will conduct them, what they will be used for, who will have access to them, and what information must necessarily be included in them. Dealing with the politics of mutual consent among systems is one of the biggest hurdles to preventing systemic trauma to child victims.

The second issue pertains to the kinds of information needs that various systems have. This is perhaps the least complex to resolve, if the various systems can get together on (1) how to identify that information and (2) how to obtain it using the fewest number of interviewers possible. This may require cross-staff planning among various community agencies (a good idea in any event), or simply the sharing of interviewing techniques, goal outcomes, and specific types of information needs among a few key individuals within each system.

The third factor, competent interviewing skills, involves training, experience, and comfort-level in communicating with young children about difficult subjects. It should also include knowledge of how to conduct diagnostic evaluations within the legal framework of potential evidence gathering. We found that the latter is easier to teach than the former, which usually requires experience with children and the ability to view the world from a child's perspective.

The objective of considering each of these factors is to obtain the necessary and satisfactory kinds of information from one interview or a set of interviews conducted by the same person or persons, which can then be shared among the agencies with mandated responsibilities or clinical interests in a case. Professionals may initially balk at this idea because of what appear to be mutually incompatible goals of various systems (MacFarlane & Bulkley, 1982). This seems to be particularly true of the differing purposes of law enforcement investigations versus diagnostic assessments by psychotherapists (Topper & Aldridge, 1981). However, it has been our experience that each of these systems has much to learn from the others with regard to the kinds of information that are useful and the ways they can be gathered that are in the interests of the children and the case itself. Obtaining information of an evidence-gathering nature does not have to be antithetical or an impediment to sensitive clinical considerations. However, if systems which need facts and evidence do not coordinate with those which best understand the needs of children, the intended goals, as well as the children, will suffer.

ENHANCING THE THERAPEUTIC RELATIONSHIP

One of the most straightforward reasons for taping an initial interview (particularly for clinical interviewers who will not be providing on-going treatment to a child) is to be able to capture on tape the initial responses, reactions, and statements by children for eventual use in therapy. Not only can it prevent the necessity of asking exactly the same questions in successive interviews, but it captures a child's first responses before they can be influenced by time and other intervening people and events. Also, for a child who is entering treatment with a new therapist following disclosure of sexual abuse to another person, the tape itself can serve as a bridge of information between the child and the therapist; the establishment of rapport, communication, and trust can be facilitated by a prerecorded but shared confidence.

The therapist can tell the child that he or she has seen the tape of the child's talk with the interviewer and then can offer the kind of statement that will help the child to know that he or she needn't be afraid of a disapproving or shocked reaction. Even more helpful can be the opportunity for the child and therapist to sit together and watch the tape. This provides an opportunity for the therapist to observe the child's reactions to viewing the initial interview. It also provides a means by which children can communicate some of the things that have happened to them without having to repeat them to another new person. Additional information is sometimes offered by a child if the therapist stops or "freeze-frames" the tape at significant intervals—for example, when the child discloses something on the tape that was particularly difficult to say, or demonstrates a strong reaction to something the interviewer said or did. The therapist may want to maximize that moment for several purposes: (1) to obtain more information about what the child was feeling during that particular moment; (2) to get more clarification or more detailed information about something the child was describing; acknowledging, or denying; (3) to give the child the opportunity to reconsider, take back, or rephrase anything he or she may not have meant to say or imply; or (4) to be supportive or reassuring of something the child did or said at that point on the tape.

The appropriate time in the therapeutic process for using a tape for this purpose should be considered. As already suggested, it might be used as an introductory tool that allows a child to tell his or her secrets to a new person without really having to relate them again so soon; on the other hand, it may need to wait until much later in the therapy of a child who requires a long time to develop enough trust to share such secrets (Rush, 1983). It is important (1) to the treatment of sexually abused children that they be able, at some time, to confront and, it is hoped, master the trauma associated with their victimization; and (2) to court cases that children be able to talk about what happened to them, and interview tapes can be used at varying points in time to facilitate these goals (Melton, 1981).

Preventing Retractions

The likelihood that sexually abused children will take back their disclosures of abuse is beginning to be well documented in this field (Summit, 1983). One of the most therapeutic uses of videotaped interviews that we have found is as a deterrent to such initial retractions. Although sometimes children retract their disclosures because of what actually happens in their lives as a result of system interventions following disclosure, often such retractions stem from their own projections and anticipation of the reactions of those who are close to them, particularly their parents or caretakers (Berliner, Canfield-Blick, & Bulkley, 1983).

One of the greatest advantages of showing a videotaped interview in the presence of the child to nonabusive parents or other important adults in the child's life is that the child is able, in a slowly unfolding way to actually see the nonpunitive reaction of the adults to the disclosure and feel validated by this reaction. Of course, this does not happen automatically. The adults, if they were not fully aware of the abuse beforehand, must be carefully prepared by the interviewer for what they are about to see and hear on the tape. Nothing should be minimized, and reactions (such as consistent avoidance to certain cues) that are typical or indicative of particular feelings should be explained beforehand. Notes taken during the interview by the camera operator or another person are particularly helpful during this process. Since many nonabusing caretakers are in some stage of shock after hearing about the initial disclosures, it is important to give them time and support to ventilate their feelings while someone else stays with the child in another room. Then, it is important to help prepare them for how they will react while actually viewing the tape with the child.

Most of all, the adults must be low-key and supportive of the child, no matter how distraught they may feel inside. Some parents may need to be convinced that they can and will be what their child needs them to be, but most do well with proper preparation. Going over some of their actual responses in advance also may give them more confidence. They should be cautioned against expressions of shock, surprise, outrage, and disbelief. Neutral statements, such as "It must be hard to tell that secret but I know that it wasn't your fault," or "I hope you know that you can tell me anything from now on," will not only set a tone of support, but will give the child permission from important adults in his or her life to continue the dialogue following the initial interview. Parents must control any impulses to bombard the child with additional questions during the tape viewing (the child may interpret such questions as expressions of disbelief on their part, and may not be ready to provide more information so soon) or to express their disappointment that the child did not confide in them first. Similarly, it is not advisable for parents or interviewers to overly reinforce or reward a child following a first disclosure of abuse or to express such strong feelings that the child feels overwhelmed or confused.

Since some adults' body language or inability to physically relate to a child during this time of personal crisis can serve to transmit their own anxiety, it helps to create a setting for tape viewing that promotes physical closeness. Bean bag chairs or a soft couch or rug where everyone sits together, can help induce a feeling of security for children and can encourage parents/caretakers to reach out and show their support. Quiet toys, such as puzzles, or coloring books should be available for very young children or for those whose own anxiety cannot endure uninterrupted focus on the contents of the tape. Children who do everything possible to distract their parents from watching the tape often do so because they fear their reaction. In most cases parents watch the tape while children watch their parents. It is an important time for children and can be a determining factor in whether they get over their fear of the consequences of disclosure or retract their statements and return to their previous worlds of silence.

CONFRONTING DISBELIEF AND DENIAL

Disbelief

One step beyond the use of videotapes to allay children's fears of disbelief by parental figures is the use of tapes to confront disbelief or denial where it actually exists. Some nonabusive parents and caretakers (particularly those in incestuous situations) are so disinclined to believe an interviewer's impressions or conclusions, and so unwilling to accept even the possibility of abuse, that it may be useful to show them the videotape (if it is shown at all) out of the presence of the child.

Again, the tape can be "freeze-framed" at significant points, such as when a child disclosed details of a situation that revealed personal knowledge of abuse or when a child demonstrated a sexual act with anatomical dolls. This pause gives the interviewer an opportunity to discuss with parents their fears and expectations about the consequences to themselves and their families of the allegations, should they be true. It also gives the interviewer a chance to discuss the child's actions and reactions and how they may compare to the characteristic reactions of sexually victimized children.

Showing disbelieving adults a tape of an interview that has convinced the interviewer that a child was abused can be far more effective than an interviewer's attempts to convince them alone. The tapes also can be shown to therapists or other professionals of the adults' own choosing as a secondary way of validating the interviewer's findings and confronting their own resistance to what their child is saying.

Denial

Audiotapes of children discribing their abuse have been used for years by some police departments in attempts to obtain confessions from alleged perpetrators. Such tapes, usually recorded during police interviews and sometimes containing the sounds of children crying or becoming emotionally upset, have been effective primarily in obtaining confessions from incestuous fathers who do not want to put their children through any further trauma, and who usually profess not to have realized how traumatic the abuse itself has been to the child. However, it is hard to predict the exact reactions of any alleged per-

petrators to the viewing of videotaped initial interviews, particularly
if most communication is done through an attorney.

In one case where the prosecution was attempting to introduce
a videotaped interview as evidence to support a motion before the
court, the defense attorney angrily demanded the right to view the
tape with his client. In the hallway outside the courtroom, he promised
the interviewer that, by the time he was finished, she would regret
ever having documented her interview on tape. However, in a move
that surprised everyone (including defense counsel), the defendant,
a neighborhood "babysitter," broke down after watching the tape of
a particularly frightened little girl and pled guilty as charged.

Other, ramifications of making videotapes available to the defense are discussed later in this chapter.

The legal issues concerning access to alleged perpetrators once
they have retained counsel are complex. As most incest treatment
programs have demonstrated, the issue of obtaining guilty pleas in
child sexual abuse cases is as much related to the availability of real
options and alternatives to long-term incarceration as it is to many of
the emotional issues associated with this crime. Nonetheless, the emotional attachments between abusers and victims can play an important
role in what happens during the early crisis phase of a case. The
opportunity for abusers (or their attorneys) to see the poignant presentations of children on videotape and to recognize the strength of
such potential testimony can exert considerable influence on whether
the abuse is acknowledged or whether the truth of the allegation must
ultimately be determined on the basis of an adversarial process.

Certainly, it is not appropriate or desirable in many cases to show
a videotaped interview of a child to an alleged perpetrator. It may
also be a violation of the child's and family's confidentiality, depending
upon the nature of prior agreements, who made the tape, and what
legal actions are pending in court. However, in cases where the defendant has strong emotional or protective feelings for the alleged
victim, the ability to see and hear the child's perspective on and reactions to the abuse may influence the defendant's willingness to subject the child to further anguish as a result of his or her continuing
denial. Similar uses of videotapes of child interviews have been applied
in numerous child sexual abuse treatment programs. Showing such
tapes in therapy groups for perpetrators has been found to be useful
in the development of empathy responses. Even in cases where the

perpetrator's emotional attachment to the child is not an issue, the showing of one powerful interview may aid in the motivation to plead the case. On occasion, when defense counsel can see how well a child is able to describe his or her abuse and the circumstances surrounding it, and can see that the child may do exceptionally well in court, counsel may advise the client to consider pleading guilty to at least some of the charges against him or her.

The success of videotapes in obtaining acknowledgments of responsibility in child sexual abuse cases is, in part, determined by the strength of the taped interview itself. But it should also be recognized that such discussions with accused perpetrators are delicate and necessarily require the skills of someone with a great deal of experience in this area.

USES OF VIDEOTAPES IN COURT

Increasingly, videotapes are being viewed as a vehicle for aiding or supporting the prosecution of criminal cases of child sexual assault or juvenile court actions to protect dependent children (Bulkley & Davidson, 1980). Currently there is much discussion in clinical, legal, and legislative circles around the country with regard to the legality, admissibility, and use of tapes as evidence in legal actions. Along with this discussion has come considerable misunderstanding, particularly among the media, of the uses and proposed uses of videotapes in court.

The most common misconception is that videotapes of initial interviews with children can be used as substitutes for the children, themselves (Melton, 1983). That is, it is believed that the statements of children about their abuse may be introduced at trial in place of child witnesses when they are either unwilling or unable to testify in person, due to their youth, psychological states, or inability to qualify as competent witnesses. Few such options exist because traditional diagnostic evaluations with single interviewers (regardless of whether they are from law enforcement or from a clinical discipline) do not afford the opportunity for cross-examination or any means of confrontation of the accused by the accuser, as provided for in the Sixth Amendment of the U.S. Constitution (although videotaped interviews have been used in place of child witnesses in some grand jury proceedings and some states have legislative provisions for their use in trial under specified circumstances).

Nonetheless, a variety of innovative uses of videotapes involving child victims are being proposed and enacted in several state legislatures (Rogers, 1982). To date, many of them have never been tested in court, due to the concerns of many prosecutors, attorneys, and judges that their use will result in a lengthy appeal process or in the making of bad case law. In the next few years, the appellate and supreme courts of a number of states will undoubtedly bring forth decisions that will determine the legality and efficacy of using videotapes as avenues for the prevention of additional trauma to child witnesses. Within the parameters of due process, courts and legislatures around the country are exploring ways in which video equipment can be utilized to aid judicial procedures involving children. The following are descriptions of some of those existing and potential uses.

CORROBORATION OF EXPERT TESTIMONY

Despite the limited use of videotapes as evidence per se, it has been possible to introduce, in some courts, a prerecorded interview as corroboration for a clinical or expert opinion rendered and challenged in court. That is, if the prosecution's expert witness and/or the testimony of the initial interviewer is challenged in court by the defense, it may be possible for the prosecution to introduce the videotape as a way of laying the foundation to support the particular opinion offered. The tape serves as a vehicle for "dispute resolution" by providing a way to objectively counter the possible bias of the opinion of the witness. This process may require the consent of both attorneys and will probably require that the defense be permitted to view the tape prior to its introduction in court.

CORROBORATION OF MOTIONS FOR SPECIAL COURTROOM PRECAUTIONS

Prerecorded interviews may also be introduced as part of expert testimony with regard to the need for the court to take special precautions to prevent additional trauma to children (e.g., closing the courtroom to spectators and the press, conducting in-chamber sessions, and/or utilizing closed-circuit television during children's testimony).

The image of a frightened, avoidant, or extremely embarrassed child during a videotaped interview may support the argument for the creation of special courtroom circumstances better than the words and observations of any expert could. On the other hand, such tapes can be misleading, in that the environment of a diagnostic evaluation is a far different one from the intimidating environment of a courtroom. If the evaluator is skilled and sensitive and puts the child at ease, the reactions of the child may not accurately reflect the child's underlying fear of the perpetrator or anxiety about the courtroom setting. In that case, the tape would not be supportive of the argument being put forth in court or representative of the child's ultimate reaction to the courtroom setting.

In any case, the use of videotapes as corroborative data to the testimony of professionals is increasingly being explored in a number of courts. Their potential utility is likely to be far more applicable in juvenile or dependency court settings, where the burden of proof is less than that of the criminal court and where there is a greater tradition of procedural exceptions that are geared to the vulnerabilities and developmental needs of children (Berliner & Stevens, 1980).

USE OF PRERECORDED INTERVIEWS IN COURT

In many states the prosecution is not permitted to introduce prerecorded interviews of children as evidence in trials, even when the children are also available to testify, due to the absence of an opportunity to cross-examine the child during the recorded interview.

However, some states, such as Texas and Kentucky, have recently enacted legislation that permits prior videotaping of child victims' statements for trial purposes in criminal prosecutions involving victims of sexual assault who are 12 years of age or younger. The recording of an oral statement by a child witness made before the criminal proceeding begins is usually only admissible into evidence under certain circumstances and with certain stipulations. These generally include the following: (1) The child must still be available to testify, if necessary, and either party may call the child to testify and be cross-examined; (2) the person who conducted the taped interview must be present at the proceeding and available to testify; (3) no attorney for either party was present when the videotaped statement was recorded; and (4) the child's statements must not have been made in response to questions that were calculated to lead the child to make a particular statement.

Some of these new statutes also allow the actual testimony of the child to be taken outside the courtroom, and either televised live by closed-circuit equipment to the proceeding, or recorded for showing in the courtroom before the court. The only persons permitted to be present in the room with the child during such testimony are the attorneys for both sides, a person "whose presence would contribute to the welfare and well-being of the child," and persons necessary to operate the camera equipment (who must be out of sight of the child) (Kentucky Prosecutors' Manual, 1984).

To many prosecutors and child advocates, these types of provisions represent bold new steps on behalf of young children and of the state's ability to bring these cases before the court. Others are very skeptical of their "staying power" in higher courts, and many believe that they will be found to be unconstitutional under the Sixth Amendment, once there has been time to test them on appeal. One thing is clear: Within the next few years, all of the issues involving the use of videotaped statements of children by legal systems will be before appellate and state supreme court jurists in states across the country.

IMPEACHMENT OF RETRACTING CHILD WITNESSES

Because of the high rate of retraction by victims of child sexual abuse, taped interviews are being viewed as a means of impeaching the testimony of child witnesses who contradict all of their previous statements about abuse, and on the witness stand say that nothing happened to them. In other words, the reliability of the initial interview statements under nonthreatening circumstances may be used to refute later retractions made by the same child in court. It is argued that the intimidating environment of the courtroom, the physical proximity to the defendant, and the succession of negatively valenced events that frequently follow disclosure tend to predispose some child victims to take back initial statements by the time they get to court (Berliner *et al.*, 1983). The prosecution's arguments that courtroom retractions are consistent with both the battered child syndrome and the child sexual abuse accommodation syndrome (Summit, 1983) might be strengthened by the introduction of a videotape contradicting the child's current denial that abuse occurred.

Although impeachment of their own witnesses is not a process that most prosecutors relish, documentation of earlier statements can be an influential factor in determining which of the child's statements are the truth. The child's unwillingness to testify to abuse in criminal court may cause a criminal case to be dismissed; but the strength of earlier recorded statements may be enough to result in a positive adjudication in juvenile court which provides for continuing protection of the child.

MONITORING, LICENSING, AND POSTADJUDICATION ISSUES

Whether or not a child later retracts initial disclosures of abuse, statements and allegations recorded on videotape may be useful in legal proceedings which are aimed at protecting other children from an alleged abuser. These include the monitoring by state licensing boards or investigatory bodies of public and private day care facilities as well as the determination by state licensing boards of examiners whether or not individuals may be permitted to retain licenses to teach, practice, or engage in other licensed activities. These legal or quasi-legal investigations may not involve prosecution or criminal court sanctions but they may lead to administrative hearings, where videotaped interviews are deemed admissible, particularly for the purpose of determining whether administrative action is possible without the potential of traumatizing children with further testimony.

USE OF CLOSED-CIRCUIT TELEVISION IN COURT

As noted above, increasing numbers of states have begun to pass new laws or utilize existing ones that make it possible to be innovative regarding the circumstances under which children can testify in court (Goodman, 1983). One of the most promising of these approaches involves allowing the testimony of children to be transmitted live via video cameras to television monitors in other locations. This technique, although it uses the same equipment, is unrelated to whether or not there are prerecorded interviews of a child. Rather, it permits a child to testify in a location other than the courtroom, while the child and his or her testimony are seen and heard on monitors situated in the courtroom. It can also allow others outside the courtroom to view the child's testimony if the child remains in the courtroom.

There are a number of logistical options for conducting this type of testimony. The one most frequently discussed and utilized in some states is the "isolated child" model. In this model, the child is isolated from all other participants in a preliminary hearing or trial and is situated in a room next to or near the courtroom, sometimes accompanied by a supportive adult. Video cameras trained on the child project his or her image onto monitors located in the courtroom. These are viewed by certain individuals (i.e., the judge, the jury, the defendant, and counsel) or, in a case where the courtroom may not be closed to the public, the image might be projected onto a large screen. The child in turn might have one or a number of television monitors in front of him or her, which, at a minimum, project the image and voice of the prosecutor or defense counsel questioning the child. Other monitors may be placed in front of the child, which might include the images of the defendant, the opposing counsel, the judge, etc.

Whether or not a child must observe the accused on a monitor is usually determined by either a stipulation on the part of the defendant or specific legislative provisions that address this issue. Special provisions aside, the child is usually required to "confront" the defendant via an electronic monitor if closed-circuit television testimony is permitted. The advantages include the following: (1) The child does not have to face an open courtroom full of spectators; (2) the child is less likely to be intimidated by the physical presence of the defendant in the courtroom; and (3) the child is less likely to be frightened or distracted by other participants in the courtroom, such as bailiffs, the court reporter, and other legal personnel. Another advantage is that objections, arguments, and motions by counsel can be "tuned out" of a child's awareness simply by turning off the monitor during such interruptions in questioning.

Disadvantages to the isolated child model might include (1) increasing a child's feelings of isolation through separation from those with whom he or she is communicating and from the room where everything else is going on; (2) potential distraction or intimidation of the child by the presence of the camera and other necessary electronic equipment (unless it and the camera operator are hidden); and (3) the child's potential difficulty in concentrating on a face and a voice speaking to him or her from a television over a prolonged period of time.

A variation on this model is the "child-centered courtroom" or "children's court" (Libai, 1969). The principle behind this concept is to create a courtroom environment that is comfortable and nonthreatening to a child, but that could include a minimum number of participants involved in each case. This might include as few people as the judge, the prosecutor, the defense counsel, and a support person for the child, or it might also include the court reporter and other necessary personnel. In this model, the defendant might be situated in another room watching the child's testimony via a monitor. If the proceeding is open to the public but special efforts are deemed necessary to insulate the child, the "miniproceeding" involving the child's testimony could be conducted in the judge's chambers and the entire thing could be beamed back into the courtroom for viewing on monitors.

Consideration has even been given to building a large glass enclosure within which the child might testify (Libai, 1969). The enclosure, which could be located within the courtroom, could be constructed out of two-way mirrors, so that persons outside could see into it but the child witness on the inside would not be able to see out. Inside the glass cube, there might still be television monitors that would permit the child to see whomever the court deemed necessary for the child to have in his or her view. Although, to our knowledge, no such arrangement has been instituted, it has been contemplated in response to some defense lawyers' arguments that their clients' right to confrontation includes the physical presence of both parties in the same room.

Many of these innovations are still in experimental stages and involve ongoing struggles with logistical and legal issues alike. For example, while child advocates point out that many children want and expect the judge to be in the same room with them when they testify, advocates also seek to limit the number of attorneys and other people who are usually present during testimony. If those who must communicate with one another during the course of the child's testimony (i.e., the judge and lawyers, or defense counsel and defendant) are not in the same room, then it might be necessary to provide two-way head sets to permit them to communicate with one another from their various locations. While this would spare the child from hearing objections and arguments, it would clearly make communication between and among the adult parties more difficult.

As more states create test circumstances for higher court rulings, child advocates and sympathetic prosecutors are taking increasingly active roles in protecting children from trauma and traditional prosecutorial attitudes are giving way to the need to accommodate the limitations of child witnesses in criminal actions. The physical presence of a threatening figure (or even a sympathetic figure, in the child's mind) who is charged with harming that child, along with the stigmatizing and guilt-provoking presence of the general public, can constitute the primary impediment to a child's ability to testify. It can, in some cases, be the sole determinant of whether or not a case can be successfully brought to trial. The use of closed-circuit television as a means to facilitate a child's testimony represents innovative and optimistic reform in child sexual abuse cases.

TAPING PRELIMINARY HEARINGS

Some states, including California, have begun to videotape the court testimony of young children during preliminary hearings and grand jury proceedings. A primary purpose of taping a child's statements on the witness stand is for potential use at the trial should the child, for any reason, be unable to testify again. Some young children become so traumatized as a result of intense questioning or their fear of having to face the defendant that they become distraught or even physically ill at the suggestion that they must testify again—even when many months have passed between hearings. Some become electively mute as the trial date approaches, or burst into tears when going back to court is mentioned.

Even when it is physically possible to produce a child witness for testimony at trial, it may be the strong opinion of the child's therapist or an expert evaluator that the child would be psychologically damaged by having to testify a second time (Melton, 1983). Such opinions may be based on the child's reaction during or following his or her previous testimony, on his or her subsequent regression in therapy, or on his or her psychological response to the prospect of testifying again. If the court found the child physically or psychologically "unavailable" to testify, the prosecution, where permitted, would present a motion asking that the child's videotaped testimony from the previous hearing be introduced in place of the child.

In California, the request to videotape children's testimony at a preliminary hearing must, by law, be granted by the court, regardless of whether its use will be permitted at the time of the trial. In other states, the cost to the state of videotaping and logistical considerations may become factors in whether or not taping is permitted. Although videotaped testimony can serve as an important aid in preventing additional trauma to young children, and can actually permit a trial to continue in the absence of the complaining witness, a child's testimony on tape is rarely as convincing as the real thing. In any case, prosecutors usually prefer live testimony to prerecorded testimony, unless they and others are convinced that the child will suffer harm and/or the case will collapse without the substitution of prerecorded testimony. This use of videotape can serve to prevent both.

TECHNICAL CONSIDERATIONS IN TAPING INTERVIEWS

The following are some suggestions regarding the actual equipment and facilities used for videotaping diagnostic interviews. They are not definitive, nor do they come from specialists in the operation and use of video equipment. Rather, they come from the trial-and-error experiences of those who have purchased and operated video cameras in therapeutic and investigatory settings: therapists, administrative assistants, police, and volunteer camera operators. The suggestions represent the adaptations that have came about through combining cameras, television monitors, and interview rooms with the adults and children necessary to conduct videotaped interviews. More sophisticated technology is often desirable, and professional consultation is encouraged. However, the following observations are likely to be applicable to the limited resources available in many agencies where alleged child victims are interviewed.

SETTING

A video interview room should be set up so that most of the activity is designed to take place in one area—in a corner, around a couch or low table, or the like. The rest of the room should be relatively barren, in order to discourage children from running all over while the camera tries to follow their every move. Art materials, anatomical dolls, and other communication aids should be within easy access of the interviewer. Other toys and materials used in special circumstances or when children need an emotional time out from the interview are best kept in a locked toy box.

Whether the camera and cameraperson are in the same room as the interview, behind a two-way mirror, in a "projection room," or separated via remote control from another room usually depends on the resources and facilities available to an agency or interviewer. Effective tapes of interviews have been made without a camera operator, using a stationary camera mounted inside a closet behind a 12-inch-square one-way mirror. This type of setup may be the only option for a single therapist in private practice.

While there are obvious advantages of using concealed camera equipment and out-of-sight camera operators, such arrangements are not always feasible, and sometimes even limit flexibility and the range of camera angles (e.g., those that are only possible at a close distance or by moving the camera). Most of our experience has been, by necessity, with a camera operator and camera in the interview room. While some children do become self-consciously "camera-shy" or preoccupied with the process of taping, it has been our experience with hundreds of young children that most of them quickly lose interest in the camera and proceed with the interview as if it wasn't there.

Even more surprising, in our early days of videotaping, were the beneficial aspects of the relationship that can develop between the camera operator and the child. The fostering of that rapport evolved into a team approach to interviewing that became incorporated into our basic interview protocol. The camera operator, rather than being a distracting detriment to the process of winning a child's trust, can actually become an asset that is not available with hidden cameras. Of course, this requires a camera operator who is a special person and who sees his or her job as more than a technical service.

EQUIPMENT

It is advisable to purchase good-quality but not necessarily sophisticated equipment. Quality is important in order to obtain a good picture under what is usually less than optimal lighting. Similarly, highly sensitive sound equipment is necessary for picking up some of the barely audible sounds and statements of children. Durability is also important where equipment is used on a daily basis or where it is occasionally subject to being toppled by curious and energetic children. It is helpful, though not essential, to have a numerical counter appear on the tape to guard against any suggestion that portions could be erased. This can also be accomplished by placing a large clock within view of the camera lens. (The camera operator should be sure to pull the plastic tab on the videotape cassette to safeguard against accidental tapeovers.) Other camera additions, such as visible timers or titles printed on the actual tape, are not only unnecessary, but may render the equipment too difficult to operate on short notice for some of the people recruited for the job of cameraperson. A permanent, paid video operator is a luxury that few agencies can afford, and the emergency nature of some evaluations may necessitate training someone very quickly in the technical operation of the equipment.

A zoom lens is an important aspect of this type of taping, because it is so helpful to capture, at close range, the expressions and behaviors of children during interviews. For example, when a child uses anatomical dolls to demonstrate what has happened, it is important to be able to see his or her every move and nuance; many of the most significant demonstrated "statements" can be missed from the distance it takes to incorporate both child and interviewer in the picture. Such demonstrations often happen quickly and may never be repeated. A zoom lens with an easily accessible trigger button is one way to avoid missing such moments. A zoom lens with a self-adjusting focus is strongly recommended in order to allow the camera operator full concentration on the child and to avoid blurred segments of tape between manual adjustments.

The more sensitive the camera equipment is, the less attention must be paid to lighting. Indirect wall or ceiling lighting is usually best, although shaded lamps are generally more reliable than natural sunlight. Window shades or curtains are advisable, because if a child moves in front of a bright window (or a bright lamp), the camera lens will react in a similar way to the pupil of an eye and will shut out the glare. The result will be a suddenly dark or very murky picture when the tape is played back.

Since the sound is as important as the picture in taped interviews, we recommend using high-quality stereo microphones, a paddle microphone, or other sound equipment designed for sensitivity to low-volume sound levels. A stereo microphone appears to make a considerable difference in sensitivity of pickup, and can compensate for a lower-quality television monitor at the time of playback. Using a microphone that is mounted on the side of the camera is strongly discouraged, because it is too far away from the child to be effective and because the loudest sound heard upon playback is usually the sound the camera makes. Few experiences are more frustrating than playing back an important tape of a child's disclosure of abuse and not being able to hear or understand the child's words. We recommend that the microphone be concealed, hung from the ceiling (it can be concealed in a hanging plant), or securely fastened to something near the child. (Preschoolers, however, tend to run all over the room.) If the microphone is within sight of young children, they will invariably play with it. This isn't necessarily harmful, but it creates a tremendous amount of feedback when the tape is played.

We do not recommend lavalier microphones, either worn on the interviewer's body or clipped to something near the child. Aside from making the interviewer's voice boom out much louder than the child's, children find them too fascinating to resist and usually end up turning them into toys, which they play with throughout the interview. Finding the right place for a microphone usually takes a lot of trial and error, and even then will still be a problem with some children. Careful research and technical consultation concerning the best sound equipment for the proposed setting is well worth the time invested.

THE ROLE OF THE CAMERA OPERATOR

Although camera operators usually are thought of primarily as video technicians, the cameraperson can become part evaluator, part playmate, and part documentor of the interview process when viewed as part of an interviewing team. It is relatively simple to teach someone how to operate a video camera, but, as with the task of interviewing, it is a different matter to try to teach someone how to interact therapeutically and appropriately with young children. Therefore, if the cameraperson is going to be in the interview room, it is important that he or she, like the interviewer, be someone who is comfortable with small children.

The cameraperson and the interviewer might want to meet the child at the same time. Then, while the parents or caretakers meet with the interviewer to obtain the child's history, the cameraperson and the child can play together in the interview setting. This is the time to help the child feel comfortable with the surroundings and to give an explanation of the video equipment if the child asks for one. During this initial playtime, the cameraperson can get a sense of how the child interacts with others. Is the child shy, verbal, bright? Can he or she read, write, play games with simple instructions? Is the child able to identify colors and/or his or her birthday? This initial play should be non-interview-related, but can provide a sense of what the pace of the interview may need to be. The information can be relayed to the interviewer in a positive and nonthreatening way—for example, "Suzie is so good at the memory game; she won two out of three games," or "Johnny found our shyest puppets."

The transition from the role of playmate to the role of cameraperson should be made smoothly and with as little attention as possible. Upon entering the room, the interviewer should immediately be made a part of the existing play situation. When the child's focus moves to the interviewer, the cameraperson can move behind the camera and begin to tape. A good rule to remember as the operator of the camera is always to keep the child in view. It is important to try to anticipate the child's moves. If a child is demonstrating something with dolls, the camera operator should keep a steady fix on the child and the dolls. When a child is discussing his or her feelings about an incident, the operator should use the zoom to get facial expression. Children may not repeat many of the things they say and do, so constant attention to them is important.

Another helpful function of the cameraperson is to keep a written record of what is on the tape. It takes practice to take notes while operating a videocamera, but it is entirely possible to do both. The notes should represent the interview as closely as possible. Reasons for writing down information during the interview include the following: (1) The notes, if correlated with the numbers on the video recorder's counter will provide a guide to viewing specific portions of the videotape; (2) they serve as a reminder to the interviewer of what was said and done so that he or she can adequately prepare parents or others for what they are about to view; and (3) they may be the only initial written documentation of what occurred in the interview.

In deciding what is noteworthy during the course of the interview, it is important to follow closely the interactions between the interviewer and the child. It is not practical or useful to try to write down everything that is said, and attempts to do so will surely be at the expense of something that occurred out of view of the camera. The most important piece of documentation is the videotape itself, so careful camera work should be the first priority. Anything that is recorded in notes is helpful, but not essential, because it can always be transcribed onto paper at a later time.

Some children will be very inquisitive and sensitive about the videotape equipment, and they need to be reassured about why it is there and how it will be used. Many children today are familiar with video equipment, but, for those who are not, it is important to explain that the monitor is like a private TV set that only works on that screen, and that their picture will not appear on anyone else's regular TV. We have found that describing the videotape equipment as a "secret machine" is a nonthreatening and acceptable answer to the question "What is that stuff here for?" In further explanation of the "secret machine's" function, we describe it as something that hears and sees everything we do and stores it in a box (the tape in the video recorder) for us to look at later on the special TV screen. Our "secret machine" specializes in eating up secrets—good secrets and "yucky" secrets— because, once they're stored in the box, they aren't secrets anymore.

Although we once thought that giving children a preview of themselves on tape would be a good way to acclimate children to the idea of videotaping, it has been our experience that showing children what they look like on television before or during the interview can be distracting and disruptive to the interview. They tend to become preoccupied with the camera and repeatedly ask when they can see themselves again. Showing them the tape on the fast-forward speed during playback can have a similarly disruptive effect on the process of watching the videotape. Children are fascinated at seeing themselves move like cartoon figures; in addition, it provides a potential way for them to avoid what was said during the interview. Using the fast-forward speed at the end of viewing the videotape, however, is a light and nonthreatening way to end an interview session.

LEGAL–ETHICAL ISSUES: THE OTHER SIDE OF TAPING

Many interviewers of alleged victims of sexual abuse initially regarded videotaping as a relatively simple means of recording disclosure while helping to prevent additional trauma and retractions. In some instances, more forethought is given to anticipated logistical problems (setting up a tape room, storing the tapes, etc.) than to those involving law, ethics, and conflicting rights of various parties. What has occurred in and out of courtrooms, and the many controversial issues that have surrounded the use of videotaped evaluations in the brief span of time since they have been utilized, have caused some interviewers to discontinue their use and many others to seriously question whether they cause more trouble than they are worth. Why has such a seemingly simple and important concept for children been so quickly abandoned by many of the very pioneers who advocated its development?

Many of the problems center around three issues: informed consent, the protection of confidentiality, and the use of the videotapes by attorneys. Most problems relate to the last of these. When a child becomes a complainant in a criminal court case, the defendant and his or her lawyer have the right to see (and sometimes to obtain copies of) all existing evidence in the case, including videotaped interviews. This is particularly true if such evidence has already been shared with the police or prosecutor.

The issue of what constitutes privileged communication varies from state to state, according to which categories of professionals are designated by law to hold patient–therapist privilege. In some states, the privilege is extended only to licensed psychiatrists; rarely does it extend to social workers, who constitute the largest category of professionals working with sexually abused children. Even in situations where the privilege exists, it may not apply in some types of criminal and even dependency court proceedings. Unfortunately, an interviewer often does not know at the time of an initial interview whether or not a case will result in a criminal court trial. Therefore, interviewers should be aware when they videotape initial interviews with alleged victims of child sexual abuse that their tape may be disclosed at a later date. Even if law enforcement authorities have no intention of filing charges on behalf of a particular child because of his or her age or other reasons, the videotaped interview may be subject to release under subpoena or other court order, if that child is one of many alleged victims in a multiple-victim case.

There are several consequences to what, in legal terminology, is called the "discovery" of videotaped interviews or therapy sessions. The first involves the issue of privacy and confidentiality, which many parents or caretakers assume will be held sacred if they bring their children to a private clinician for an evaluation. Even when a child is interviewed by a police officer or a child protective services worker, the parents probably do not envision at that time that the videotape may be viewed by the alleged perpetrator, defense attorneys, judges, juries, and any number of other individuals hired by the defense as well as the public and press sitting in a courtroom. When parents sign a waiver allowing only law enforcement authorities to view their child's tape in order to prevent further interviews, they may (unknowingly) be waiving their right to confidentiality and their ability to keep that tape from the defense and others—even if the child is not a complaining witness. Such was the ruling in a 1984 multiple-victim case in California, where the judge ruled that the defense be given access to *all* interview tapes and their accompanying files where parents had signed such waivers (*People v. Buckey et al., 1984*).

Another potential consequence of the release of interview tapes as part of a highly publicized trial is that, in the process of duplication and transfer of tapes to the defense, copies of tapes might fall into the hands of the media (as happened with the national televising of the John DeLorean tape). Similarly, when interview tapes are played in an open courtroom during a preliminary hearing or a trial (as has recently occurred in California), the identity of the child is fully visible and the child's and the interviewer's statements may be widely quoted in the media (*People v. Buckey et al., 1985*). Such a consequence can have a devastating impact on children and families, given the intensely personal nature of many initial disclosures, and it is a source of tremendous concern for parents once they become aware of the issue. An even more painful consequence for child victims whose initial disclosure interviews were videotaped has also recently occurred in a case in California. Segments of videotapes showing children's initial denial of abuse have been played back to children on the witness stand in order to impeach their testimony and attack their credibility. The viewing of a taped segment may be followed by such defense questions as: "At first you said that nothing happened, now you say it did. When were you lying, then or now? Do you lie a lot? Why did you lie to the interviewer? How do we know that you're still not lying? Do you know what happens to children who lie like you do?" etc. Such questions are clearly guilt provoking and intimidating for young children. Having to watch their initial interview, especially in the midst of a courtroom of people, can bring back all of their memories of initial disclosure and the fears that went with it. The replayed videotape adds to the vividness of such an experience.

Obviously, the potential repercussions of making videotapes must be carefully considered; consent forms must be well researched legally; and parents or caretakers should be fully informed of all foreseeable consequences in order to make informed decisions. Unfortunately, they may find themselves in an uncomfortable double bind: In order for them and their children's therapists to see the interview, and in the hope of preventing additional trauma through multiple interviews, they take the risk of giving up some of their own rights to privacy and confidentiality.

Even when parents are able and willing to give their informed consent, there remains the issue of children's consent. This chapter does not proport to provide more than questions to ponder on this subject. Since the inability of a child to provide informed consent or to foresee the future consequences of sexual contact with adults are primary arguments in regard to what is wrong with child sexual abuse, it is worth at least contemplating them in relation to the issue of videotaping children. It would be difficult, if not impossible, to explain the potential ramifications of legal discovery to a preschooler, but should an interviewer explain (prior to taping) that the child's parents (if they are supportive) will be viewing the tape? If so, the interviewer risks inhibiting the child dramatically; if not, the child may object later or feel tricked. If the interviewer proposes the idea at the end of the interview and the child adamantly objects, which rights are paramount: the child's, the parents', or the considerations of the case as a whole?

There are no easy answers to such questions. Certainly, parents and other adults make many decisions affecting children about which the children are not informed and to which they cannot or do not consent. Some decisions are in the best interest of children, some are not. Short of giving children *Miranda* warnings (". . . anything you say can and will be held against you . . ."), it is difficult to truly inform them of the consequences of taping. In our own interviews, as stated previously, we do tell children that we are making a tape, explain the process to them, and show them the tapes. Fortunately, most of the children we interview voluntarily agree to allow their parents or a supportive adult, if a parent is suspected of abuse, to view the tape with them following an interview. In the few instances where children have become visibly upset at the idea, the parents have agreed not to view the tape at that time, but to wait until the children were ready to share that experience.

The issue of subpoenaed tapes being viewed by alleged perpetrators is more complicated and can be more difficult for children — especially if an alleged abuser is a family member and has threatened a child not to tell the secret. Since interviewers often do not know at the time of interviewing whether a tape will be released to the defense (or even if there will be a defense), it is an issue that may arise months after the interview. Some children never know if and when it does occur, and may never need to know, since they will never be alone with their alleged abusers again. For others, particularly older children, it comes as a betrayal, a breach of trust by the interviewer and by the system. Some interviewers choose to forewarn children of this possibility before taping (although few things are more inhibiting to an abused child), and some try to prepare them for it following the interview. To others (including parents) who are in continuing contact with the children falls the difficult task of explaining why none of them have the power to prevent the release of tapes to defendants and their attorneys.

Another major consequence of videotaping initial interviews involves their use by the defense if the case results in legal action. In addition to being used to discredit child witnesses, tapes are often used to discredit the interviewer, the techniques used, and the prosecution's case. This primarily has to do with the approaches and methods necessary to permit frightened, embarrassed, or avoidant children to feel safe and comfortable enough to reveal sexual abuse if it has occurred (Bulkley & Davidson, 1980). Few children voluntarily divulge information of this nature unless they have already disclosed it to someone else. Asking children to share forbidden secrets is not like asking them what they had for lunch. They need to know that the interviewer is comfortable and familiar with this subject and that they won't be blamed or rejected for talking about it. Interviewers who remain neutral, nonprobing, and detached, and who conduct evaluations as though they were in a courtroom or other legal arena, will have difficulty breaking through to small, frightened children.

On the other hand, those who utilize nontraditional interview methods and who ask directed or leading questions in order to get children talking about what might or might not have happened— may be in for a hard time in court. Their techniques and professionalism will be challenged by the defense and by experts hired by the defense to view the videotapes and proffer critical opinions. The most common tactic usually involves trying to show that the interviewer led, coached, or played upon the suggestibility of the child, who then alleged child sexual abuse in order to please the questioning adults. Interviewers also have been accused of "brainwashing" children during interviews into ever after believing that they had been sexually abused.

Of course, the absence of videotapes does not preclude such accusations in court. In fact, when carefully conducted with children who readily disclose abuse, videotapes can be used to counter allegations that a child was led by an interviewer. Nonetheless, the videotapes can provide ammunition (whether or not they are ever viewed in court) for defense arguments. Regardless of how convincing a child's disclosures or demonstrations with anatomical dolls may be, initial interviews with young, molested children are usually also full of inconsistencies, disclaimers, and retractions. If leading questions or reinforcement techniques are also part of an interview, they will be used to discredit the interview and to invalidate the child's allegations.

This is not to imply that such defense tactics always work or that the power of some videotapes do not outweigh their liabilities. Nonetheless, the consequences to individual interviewers and to the outcomes of some cases have led more than one interviewer to discontinue the routine practice of videotaping.

CONCLUSION

If this chapter has left the reader in a quandary as to whether the benefits of videotaping initial interviews with children outweigh their disadvantages, then it has succeeded in reflecting the ambivalence of those with experience in this area, and in accurately depicting one of the current dilemmas in this field. It represents an advancement of the electronic age that holds great promise and great pitfalls. On the legal battlefield, videotapes can help us win important battles for children, but they can also contribute to losing some wars.

One thing is clear: A decision to videotape an alleged victim of child sexual abuse should not be made on the grounds that the equipment is waiting in the closet and someone is available to operate the tape. Issues associated with its use, such as: who can/must consent to the taping and to the viewing of tapes, and what should be on the consent form; who owns the tapes, who may have copies and how they will be protected and used should be carefully researched and decisions should be made with full knowledge of the potential consequences as they relate to each situation.

Perhaps, as more experience is gained in this area, more options (as well as more safeguards) will be developed for utilizing videotapes more effectively. To those who might have concluded that the seemingly obvious way to prevent potential "misuse" of videotapes (however defined) is to erase them following showing them to selected parties, a word of caution is in order. Some of our colleagues in the legal profession take a very dim view of such actions. In fact, if a diagnostic interview is conducted as part of an investigation expected to result in legal action, especially criminal prosecution, erasure of a taped interview may be regarded as destruction of evidence—an act that can carry legal penalties. Therefore (as with written information taken under the same conditions), under such circumstances, it is safest not to destroy, give away, or tape over the videotape.

Other options are undergoing consideration and experimentation by interviewers. One option is not to tape initial interviews when children have not previously disclosed abuse, where they are initially very frightened, or where there is a likelihood of more than one child victim in a case. Some interviewers have considered taping the third or fourth session, after children have had some time to overcome their initial fears or embarrassment, are less contradictory and prone to denial, and do not require as much support or encouragement in order to describe the abuse. While this idea is far more appealing than repeatedly having to explain or justify the contradictory and avoidant ways that children initially disclose sexual abuse, it may still incur legal problems and potential accusations concerning what went on during the first sessions and why they were not taped. Other options for preventing multiple interviews and sharing diagnostic information with others include viewing interviews through two-way mirrors or sending a live picture onto a monitor in another room using camera equipment without an actual tape in the video recorder. None of these options provides the flexibility of videotaping, but they also won't come back to haunt the interviewer or the child. Increasingly, agencies and individuals who videotape clinical sessions are developing formal, written policies regarding what they will videotape, how tapes will be used, and when tapes will be erased.

Perhaps the most basic issue at the core of these dilemmas relates back to the purposes of videotaping. Therapeutic goals and legal goals are not always the same, just as that which is in the best interests of child victims is frequently not in the best interests of a court case. Nonetheless, at a time when there is increased recognition of the value of interdisciplinary teamwork on these cases, growing realization of the need to reduce systemic trauma to children, and greater availability of video equipment, it is discouraging to see interviewers turn away from this technique in self-defense and in order to protect their clients' privacy.

Much more needs to be tested and worked out in interview rooms and in courtrooms before many of these issues can be resolved. Few would disagree that interviewers should be accountable for what goes on behind closed doors in conversations with young children. We should be accountable to the children and families we serve, subject to scrutiny by our professional peers, and accountable to those whose lives will be affected by charges and other legal actions which may arise from disclosures made during interviews. Certainly, accused persons and their attorneys desire and demand such accountability. However, the potential benefits of this form of accountability is currently in jeopardy as more and more interviewers see their videotapes being used to discredit them and the statements of children, and to undermine the court cases that have resulted from them. Videotaping has so many potential benefits for children that we can only hope that many of these problems can be resolved in ways that are favorable to children. Much of that, like so many issues in this complex field, may depend on the responsiveness of our legal systems.

TREATMENT OF YOUNG CHILDREN AND FAMILIES

OVERVIEW OF TREATMENT ISSUES

Jill Waterman

While interest in and concern about sexual molestation of preschool children have been increasing, treatment plans and therapeutic issues for young sexually abused children have rarely been addressed. Generally, references have been made in passing to the use of play or arts therapy in treating young, cognitively unsophisticated victims (Naitove, 1982; Stember, 1980). The literature on treatment of child sexual abuse victims of any age is currently sparse, and almost all of our knowledge is based on clinical anecdotes and case studies (MacVicar, 1979; Rosenfeld, 1976; Schoettle, 1980), rather than on careful empirical investigations with meaningful outcome measures. Sgroi's *Handbook of Clinical Intervention in Child Sexual Abuse* (1982) represents one notable effort to deal with data from a full, ongoing specialized program for in-depth treatment of child sexual abuse, including at least rough measures of therapeutic outcome. However, even in Sgroi's extensive exploration, issues in treatment of very young victims are not delineated clearly or specifically addressed. Actual treatment protocols or detailed therapy plans for preschool-age sexually abused children are mostly nonexistent.

TREATMENT MODALITIES

In reviewing what literature is available on treatment of child sexual abuse, it appears that most writers espouse some sort of family systems approach to treatment planning (Eist & Mandel, 1968; Jorne, 1979; Kroth, 1979; Pittman, 1976; Rosenfeld, Nadelson, Krieger, & Backman, 1977; Walters, 1975). In a review of treatment strategies, Dixen and Jenkins (1981) concluded that a combination of behavior therapy (to change the perpetrator's arousal to children), marital therapy, and family therapy has considerable potential. While some psychoanalytically oriented therapists advocate individual therapy that is generally long-term (Krieger, Rosenfeld, Gordon, & Bennett, 1980; Rosenfeld, 1976; Schoettle, 1980), recommendations from comprehensive treatment programs are for use of a variety of therapeutic modalities. For example, Henry Giarretto, in describing the pioneering Child Sexual Abuse Treatment Program in Santa Clara County, California, advocates the following order of treatment for father–daughter incest: (1) individual counseling for the child, mother, and father; (2) mother–daughter counseling; (3) marital counseling; (4) father–daughter counseling; (5) family counseling; and (6) group counseling, including Parents United and Daughters and Sons United self-help groups (Giarretto, 1976a).

Similarly, Suzanne Sgroi of Connecticut's Sexual Trauma Treatment Program uses a multiple-modality, multiple-therapist approach to families involved in child sexual abuse (Sgroi, 1982b). In her program, the first step is to assign each family member a separate individual therapist. Dyadic therapy for mother and daughter may follow, and may occur simultaneously with group therapy. Sgroi feels that group therapy is the preferred eventual treatment modality for most adolescent victims (Porter, Blick, & Sgroi, 1982). Arts therapy is seen as helpful for younger children who may not have reached a level of cognitive development where they are able to resolve problems verbally. Like Giarretto's group, the Connecticut group feels that family therapy must be preceded by individual therapy, and in some cases group therapy, for all involved members. Family therapy is seen as only appropriate in incest cases when the parents are willing to take total responsibility for the sexual abuse of the child (Porter et al., 1982).

Most information available about individual therapy with child sexual abuse victims comes from case reports, involving either a single case (Rosenfeld, 1976; Schoettle, 1980) or several cases treated over a period of time (MacVicar, 1979; Krieger, Rosenfeld, Gordon, & Bennett, 1980). The children described were school-age or adolescent, and some treatment successes were reported using psychoanalytically oriented long-term therapy (Rosenfeld, 1976; Schoettle, 1980). The common therapeutic issue that seems to come up repeatedly in individual treatment is the initial sexualized behavior of the child victim, and the need to set appropriate limits on these behaviors (Krieger *et al.*, 1980; MacVicar, 1979; Rosenfeld, 1976; Schoettle, 1980). While the discussion in the literature has centered around older children, the same phenomena of sexualized responding in the initial phases of treatment is also found in many preschool-age sexually abused children.

Group therapy of various sorts has been advocated for adolescent victims of sexual abuse (Blick & Porter, 1982; Porter *et al.*, 1982), and many programs refer adolescent and preadolescent abused children to Daughters and Sons United, a self-help group. In contrast, Jorne (1979) feels that children whose major problems relate to sexual abuse are not appropriate candidates for group therapy and should be seen individually. Group therapy for younger sexually abused children has also been described (Beezley, 1977; Delson & Clark, 1981), although less frequently than individual or group therapy with older children. There are no published reports detailing group therapy treatment with younger children, and only one unpublished report of use of a group modality with children under 4 years of age.

Delson and Clark (1981) instituted a weekly play therapy group for children under 12 years of age that involved art therapy, role playing, and drama; the children's group became an integral part of the ongoing treatment program. In a group for 4- to 7-year-olds described by Beezley (1977), each weekly session included a talking and sharing time, a structured activity to initiate further fantasy and discussion, free play, and a snack. While the bulk of the content of these groups was not sexual, Beezley felt that the girls came to be able to acknowledge the sexual trauma that had occurred and to discuss their feelings. The therapists reported that the group experience was beneficial to all the children; more objective outcome measures were not obtained.

In a preschool play therapy setting, Haase, Magaz, Lazoritz, and Chiaro (1982) describe a treatment program for sexually abused children under the age of 5 years. Through structured and unstructured play, the program attempts to provide a safe, nurturing, and consistent environment for children three mornings per week; developmental and psychological outcome data are currently being collected, and the therapists report very beneficial effects of the program.

As mentioned earlier, while a family systems approach to treatment planning is generally accepted, practitioners disagree somewhat on when actual conjoint family therapy is indicated. While some advocate immediate use of family treatment in cases of incest, in order to restore appropriate role relationships (Pittman, 1976), others feel that families are not ready for conjoint meetings until after a period of individual therapy for all members (Giarretto, 1976a; Porter *et al.*, 1982). Similarly, Furniss (1983a) uses a family systems approach, but feels that initial work must be confined to individuals and dyads. In family treatment, the perpetrator must admit responsibility, apologize to the child, and offer reassurances that the sexual abuse will not be repeated, and the nonoffending parent must take responsibility for not protecting the child (Porter *et al.*, 1982). In most cases, it is clear that much work on denial and responsibility would need to be done individually with the parents before this sort of family therapy would be possible.

For younger children, art or play therapy has been frequently advocated (Jorne, 1979; Naitove, 1982; Stember, 1980) but specific ideas of how these might be used with molested toddlers and preschoolers have been difficult to obtain. While addressing treatment with a range of age groups, Burgess, Holmstrom, and McCausland (1978) discuss techniques for encouraging a child to verbalize, using art media and age-related toys in structured and unstructured play to decrease the child's anxiety and to engender trust. Examples of puppet play, building with blocks, drawing, and use of anatomically correct dolls with victims of child abuse are given.

LENGTH OF TREATMENT

Another treatment parameter in child sexual abuse is length of treatment: Should it be short-term or long-term? Leaman (1980) asserts that a crisis intervention model can be very helpful in immediately helping the family to gain an intellectual understanding of the incident, helping family members bring their feelings into the open, exploring coping mechanisms, and making plans to reduce further trauma to the child. During the crisis stage, families may require "total life support," involving a combination of concrete social services and very intensive support and guidance (Porter, *et al.*, 1982). Short-term treatment (generally 2–6 months) has been seen as sufficient in various circumstances: (1) for younger victims not involved with violence (Beezley, 1977); (2) for victims of one-time sexual abuse by a stranger (MacVicar, 1979); (3) for victims who have not experienced severe physical and emotional trauma, who receive much emotional support from significant others, and who do not live with the perpetrator (Porter *et al.*, 1982).

In contrast, longer-term treatment appears most necessary when (1) there has been significant physical and emotional damage; (2) a social support network is not readily available for the child in the community (Porter *et al.*, 1982); (3) there is a continuing question of whether the child is safe from further molestation; and (4) the abuse has been going on for a period of time with a known adult (MacVicar, 1979).

TREATMENT ISSUES

Specific issues to be addressed in treatment have been reported in isolated fashion by a variety of clinicians. Recently, Porter *et al.* (1982) have listed and elaborated on treatment implications of 10 issues for victims of child sexual abuse; the first 5 are purported to affect all sexually abused children, while the last 5 are more likely to be issues for victims of intrafamily child sexual abuse. These issues are (1) the "damaged goods" syndrome; (2) guilt; (3) fear; (4) depression; (5) low self-esteem and poor social skills; (6) repressed anger and hostility; (7) impaired ability to trust; (8) blurred role boundaries and role confusion; (9) pseudomaturity, coupled with failure to accomplish developmental tasks; and (10) self-mastery and control. Feelings of the child that must be explored include positive and negative feelings toward the perpetrator and the nonoffending parent (in cases of incest), feelings about reactions of siblings and peers; and feelings about boy–girl relationships (Porter *et al.*, 1982). Additionally, sex education, birth control and assertive techniques to control exploitation must be addressed (National Center on Child Abuse and Neglect, 1978). Clearly, some of the issues specified are more applicable to work with preschool victims than others.

Major issues for therapists treating sexually abused children concern their own feelings and reactions, both to the abuse itself and to the frequent sexualized behavior of children in treatment. Therapists working with incest victims often experience such outrage at the breaking of the taboo that their clinical judgment may be affected. Sometimes therapists find the children's sexualized behavior arousing; this causes discomfort and guilt, and may lead to avoidance of the sexual material (Krieger *et al.*, 1980). In addition, how best to handle the children's sexuality is an issue for therapists in the field of sexual abuse (MacVicar, 1979; Schoettle, 1980); these children understandably confuse sexuality with affection, and it is extremely important to be predictable and consistent, placing limits on the children's attempts to manipulate. If a therapist responds to a child in a sexual manner or fails to set appropriate limits, then he or she may be viewed as similar to the child's parents (Krieger *et al.*, 1980).

TREATMENT OUTCOME

Evaluating the outcome of treatment with sexually abused children has been woefully inadequate so far. Most results have been presented in terms of the therapists' opinion about improvement. Giarretto (1976a) did present treatment results in terms of objective criteria; he reported no instances of reabuse in more than 250 incestuous families receiving a minimum of 10 hours of treatment who formally terminated with mutual consent of the program and the family. These cases, however, involved families where the parents were willing to admit responsibility for the sexual abuse. In Giarretto's sample, 90% of the marriages were saved. The Connecticut Sexual Abuse Program also tried to look at more specific measures of outcome. Therapy had the greatest effect on the referring problem of being safe from reabuse by the perpetrator (62% of the cases), and improvement was also noted in social relationships (58%) and intrapersonal difficulties (53%). In 46% of the cases, the perpetrator admitted guilt and accepted responsibility. Of couples involving perpetrators, 42% were separated or divorced during involvement with the program (Bander, Fein, & Bishop, 1982b). While some improvements were clearly made, the cost-effectiveness of such a program, utilizing several therapists intensively with each family, must be examined in light of the somewhat disappointing outcome results.

The best predictors of positive outcome for the child seem to involve the degree of parental concern for the child (Leaman, 1980) and the degree of parental involvement and responsibility in treatment (Giarretto, 1976a). However, as Porter *et al.* (1982) point out, the child victim still needs treatment and can receive some benefit even if the parents deny the sexual abuse and will not cooperate. Treating only the child seems to be more feasible when the victim is an adolescent or preadolescent. At the preschool level, parental involvement seems mandatory in order to achieve a positive outcome. It seems necessary to develop treatment programs and protocols for sexually abused preschool children and their parents; to do careful evaluation of treatment outcomes; and to follow some children longitudinally, in order to assess the long-term effects both of sexual abuse during preschool years and of special treatment programs for them and their families.

FAMILY DYNAMICS OF INCEST WITH YOUNG CHILDREN

Jill Waterman

While there is a great deal of information published about family dynamics in cases of sexual abuse of children, there is little or nothing written about the family dynamics that occur when a child victim is of preschool age. The overwhelming majority of case studies and published reports deal with dynamics occurring in incestuous families in which the children are either of late elementary school age, pre-adolescent, or adolescent. In other reports, the age of the children is not specified, but the implication is that the children are "sexually attractive" to the parent or are budding sexually; such definitions are not generally applicable to preschool children.

The approach taken in this chapter is to review the theoretical notions and research findings about family dynamics occurring with incestuous families where the victim is older than preschool age, and then to look at which of these findings apply to preschoolers as well. Next, some ideas about how the family dynamics may differ in families where the victims of sexual abuse are preschool children are presented.

FAMILY DYNAMICS WITH OLDER CHILDREN

There are three major theoretical formulations about the dynamics that lead to sexual abuse of a child within the family setting: sociological, psychodynamic, and family systems. These represent three different foci for explanation of the abuse, and some combination of these factors is probably involved in most cases of incest.

SOCIOLOGICAL FORMULATIONS

In sociological explanations of incestuous behavior, factors such as low socioeconomic class, poverty, overcrowded living conditions, and social or geographical isolation are implicated. In early reports of incestuous cases, the preponderance of families came from lower socioeconomic backgrounds (Gagnon, 1965; Weinberg, 1955), though later investigators pointed out that incestuous behavior cut across social classes (Giarretto, 1976b; Rosenfeld, 1979). As data on larger and larger groups of incestuous families have become available, it appears that lower socioeconomic groups may be overrepresented, but it is clear that this family pattern occurs in all social classes (Finkelhor, 1979a). Other aspects of social deprivation, such as overcrowded living quarters, have been implicated in incest (Maisch, 1973); however, some might argue that overcrowding could mitigate against sexual abuse by not providing the opportunity for parents and children to be alone or keep secrets (Frude, 1982).

That sexually abusive families tend to be socially, psychologically, or physically isolated is quite well documented (Mrazek, 1981; Vander Mey & Neff, 1982); for example, Finkelhor (1979a) discovered that an unusually high percentage of his college-age respondents were raised on farms. Similarly, some studies have noted that high stress increases the risk for abuse. For example, Maisch (1973), Meiselman (1978), and Justice and Justice (1979) all found that stressful events in the father's life, such as loss of a job, work problems, or loss of a significant person, frequently preceded the onset of abuse. While some have asserted that incest is usually perpetrated by the biological father in an intact family (Justice & Justice, 1979; Vander Mey & Neff, 1982), others have suggested that molestation by stepfathers may be less taboo and proportionately more frequent (Frude, 1982; Perlmutter, Engel, & Sager, 1982; Russell, 1983). Finkelhor (1980a) found that the strongest correlate of victimization in his sample was having a stepfather.

PSYCHODYNAMIC FORMULATIONS

Psychodynamic formulations have generally been made regarding particular traits, historical events, or underlying personality dynamics that characterize the various participants in the incestuous relationship. A myriad of speculations have been proposed with regard to what the father, the mother, and the child are like in an incestuous family. With the burgeoning of interest in sexual abuse, there are enough overlapping findings to give support to some earlier psycho-dynamic speculations, as well as to call into question some widely accepted assertions about the incestuous family. While the earlier literature focused heavily on father–daughter incest, other family constellations are now being reported and investigated; perpetrators of incest are not only fathers, but mothers, older siblings, uncles, and grandfathers, and males are victims of sexual abuse much more fre-quently than had ever been suspected.

Most of the older studies have looked at preadolescent or ado-lescent girl victims, and perhaps the most common finding about the incestuous father from this group of studies is the domineering, au-thoritarian style in which he relates to his family (Herman & Hirsch-man, 1977; Kaufman, Peck & Tagiuri, 1954; Maisch, 1973; Weinberg, 1955). He is seen as rigid and moralistic, and demands complete obedience. His impulse control is seen as impaired, particularly in family matters, and some report that he may exhibit "restricted psy-chopathy" in connection with the incestuous behavior while function-ing in a well-adjusted manner in the community (Wells, 1981). A variety of psychiatric diagnoses have been given to the fathers, but there is little agreement about them. Recently, the possibility that the offender exhibits borderline personality organization has been raised by several authors (e.g., Brooks, 1982); additionally, more varied pat-terns of paternal behavior have been noted in current investigations, and these are discussed in the section on family dynamics with pre-school children.

Alcoholism or overuse of alcohol frequently characterizes the father (Browning & Boatman, 1977; Finkelhor, 1979a; Martin & Wal-ters, 1982; Virkkunen, 1974); this probably not only is a usual style of coping with anxiety, but also tends to disinhibit the father's behavior and facilitate sexual abuse. Gebhard, Gagnon, Pomeroy, and Chris-tenson (1965) found that many fathers had been drinking at the time of the first incestuous experience, although they were not alcoholics. There is disagreement about the fathers' sexuality; some have re-ported that they are "oversexed" (Lukianowicz, 1972; Weiner, 1962), are open to a variety of deviant sexual activities, and have high sexual needs (Frude, 1982), but others have disputed these contentions (Geb-hard et al., 1965; Maisch, 1973).

Mothers in incestuous families where the father is the perpetrator have been the subject of much speculation, yet this group has actually been studied much less than either the perpetrators or the victims. While a profile is presented here, it should be noted that with the increase in awareness and reporting of sexual abuse as well as in treatment programs, this is only one common profile of many different ones that exist. A variety of sources have reported that the mother in incestuous families is frequently emotionally or physically ill, disabled, or absent (Finkelhor, 1979a; Herman & Hirschman, 1981; Lustig, Dresser, Spellman, & Murray, 1966; Maisch, 1973; Mrazek, 1981). In terms of personality, many have found that she tends to be dependent and passive in general, feeling powerless in most aspects of her life. Very frequently, the mother was sexually abused herself as a child (Mrazek, 1981; Wells, 1981), and has been characterized as frigid, nonsexual, or repressive in her feelings and attitudes about sex (Cormier, Kennedy, & Sangowicz, 1962; Finkelhor, 1979a; Maisch, 1973).

Because of her passive–dependent stance, the mother may not move to protect the child and may side with the father if the incest is disclosed, for fear of losing his support and protection (Meiselman, 1978; Perlmutter et al., 1982). Some even feel that the mother may consciously or unconsciously "set up" the incest in order to free herself from her husband's sexual demands (Justice & Justice, 1979; Weinberg, 1955).

The child's psychodynamics in incestuous families have received cursory attention until recently. This reflects the general feeling that the child is a victim who, previous to the incest, did not differ from other children in basic physical or intellectual capacities (Martin & Walters 1982), although in a very early study, the victims were referred to as having "unusually attractive and charming personalities" (Bender & Blau, 1937). The oldest daughter has frequently been found to be at greatest risk for abuse (Browning & Boatman, 1977). One study (Finkelhor, 1979a) found that girls with fewer friends were more likely to be abused, although it is hard to interpret the direction of this finding. A girl who is involved in an incestuous relationship may be less free to make outside relationships because of the father's demands, and may be inhibited in her friendships by the very heavy secret that she carries. Some feel that girls who are involved in sexual abuse may be more passive and dependent than their peers (and in this way may resemble their mothers), and therefore comply with the demands of the sexualized relationship with the father. In authoritarian, patriarchal homes, however, this passive compliance may have more to do with the father than with personality characteristics of the child (Gebhard *et al.*, 1965).

FAMILY SYSTEMS FORMULATIONS

The family systems perspective on incestuous families has been explicated in two different ways. Descriptions of common relationship dynamics found in incestuous families have been given, and family patterns in incestuous families have also been extrapolated from theoretical formulations in the family therapy literature. Both of these approaches are discussed here.

The two main areas in which the marital relationships in incestuous families have been found to be consistently dysfunctional are power and sexual relationships. The common finding is that power is distributed very unequally in sexually abusive families. While much of the evidence points to a dominant, authoritarian father with a passive, dependent, and ineffectual mother (Herman & Hirschman, 1981; Perlmutter *et al.*, 1982), the opposite pattern has also been reported, where the mother is domineering and the passive father can only feel powerful in relationship to his child (Cavallin, 1966; Cormier *et al.*, 1962). In either case, the power imbalance is significant.

Some authors have reported that domineering fathers may be violent at times toward family members to ensure power (Weinberg, 1955); the sexually abused daughter sometimes enjoys a special position of immunity in relation to physical abuse (Herman & Hirschman, 1981). Walters (1975) has suggested that sexual abuse of a child is the father's ultimate act of anger toward the wife. However, certainly not all incestuous fathers are violent, and rarely is actual force used in the sexual activities (Frude, 1982), although subtle coercion through fear of consequences and sometimes through concrete bribes is common (Justice & Justice, 1979; Maisch, 1973).

Sexually, the marital relationship is almost always quite troubled. A common pattern is that the wife is not interested in sex and rejects the husband sexually (Maisch, 1973). There are several possible explanations for this dynamic. One is that the husband may be unusually sexually demanding. Another is that the wife may be ill, disabled, or absent. A third is that the woman, frequently sexually abused herself as a child, may never have felt sex to be a pleasurable, loving experience. In any case, the husband is frequently sexually frustrated.

In sexually abusive families, as mentioned earlier, there seems to be a great deal of social isolation. Not only does this mean that the parents relate to very few other people, increasing the frustration of their poor relationship; it also decreases the chances of the husband's using more common means of dealing with sexual frustration, such as visiting a prostitute or developing an extramarital affair (Gebhard *et al.*, 1965; Meiselman, 1978). Instead, he develops a "family affair." There is also some evidence that incestuous fathers may have rigid moral values, and therefore are less likely to use masturbation (which may be conceived of as sinful) as an outlet for sexual frustration (Frude, 1982). Both the power imbalance and the sexual frustration contribute to the underlying tension evident in the marital relationships of incestuous families.

The mother–daughter relationship in cases of father–daughter incest has been consistently found to be characterized by role reversal (Kaufman *et al.*, 1954; Lustig *et al.*, 1966; Perlmutter *et al.*, 1982; Weinberg, 1955). For example, Herman and Hirschman (1981) found that 45% of incest victims reported taking on a maternal role in the family, in contrast to 5% of the comparison group who had seductive but nonincestuous fathers. The mother frequently either overtly or covertly turns over some of the household tasks to a girl, usually the oldest daughter. This may include domestic chores such as cooking, cleaning, and caring for younger children. Even 4- and 5-year-olds have been reported to prepare meals or be responsible for keeping the house clean. The daughter frequently does not feel close to her mother or see her as a source of nurturance. Once the family roles are blurred, it becomes more understandable how the daughter may ultimately take over other activities of the mother's role, such as providing comfort and sex for the father. The daughter feels that she cannot depend on the mother to take care of her or protect her, and may develop hostile or condescending feelings toward the mother, whom she in essence mothers (Brooks, 1982).

The father–daughter relationship in incestuous families is mainly distinguished by its sexualized nature. There is evidence that incestuous fathers have a great deal of difficulty with affectionate touch and generally avoid it (Finkelhor, 1979a; Mrazek, 1981). As a consequence, the daughter may be starving for affection, since her father avoids touch and she is the caretaker in the mother–daughter relationship. The only time she is likely to feel cared about, loved, or nurtured in her relationship with her father is during sexualized activities. She may be likely to relate to others in the sexualized fashion that evokes affection and attention from her father, because this is frequently the only style that has successfully elicited any type of nurturance in the past.

In addition to exploring the relationship dynamics discussed above, several authors (Brooks, 1982; Mrazek & Bentovim, 1981) have utilized concepts from family systems theory and attempted to view incest as the symptom of generalized family distress. The family systems approach that seems to provide the most useful concepts for understanding the dynamics of the incestuous family is structural family therapy (Minuchin, 1974). The most relevant concepts from this approach are "boundaries," "subsystems," and "functional roles."

Generally, in families, there is a marital subsystem that is related to but separate from the parental subsystem, and a sibling subsystem. In well-functioning families, there are clear role definitions for the marital subsystem (e.g., sexual activities are appropriate only here; there are certain details of finances and the marital relationship that are only shared between husband and wife), the parental subsystem (e.g., disciplining, rearing, and nurturing the children) and the sibling subsystem (e.g., learning to interact with peers, pulling the wool over the parents' eyes in certain situations).

Between the subsystems, and between the whole family and the outside world, there are boundaries that have certain characteristics. For example, if all the family members are very close, but they feel strongly that they should not let in outsiders, there are likely to be diffuse boundaries between family members and a rigid boundary around the family that protects them from the outside world; such a family is toward the "enmeshed" end of the boundary continuum. In contrast, if the family members rarely see each other, do not share common interests or activities, and are each almost exclusively involved for social contact with peers or associates outside the family and the home, then the boundaries between family members would be rigid, and there would be diffuse boundaries between the family and the outside world.

In a healthy family, there are clear boundaries between the marital and sibling subsystems and between the parental and the sibling subsystems; there is contact across boundaries, but it is appropriate to the role definitions of the subsystems. Additionally, there is some discrimination between family and outsiders, but not so much that family members cannot interact comfortably with people outside the family and develop meaningful relationships that eventually facilitate the children's growing up and moving out, leaving parents who have developed some other interests as well as the children.

In examining the dynamics in the incestuous family from a systems perspective, it appears quite evident that such families are likely to exhibit general patterns of enmeshment within the family system (Brooks, 1982) and disengagement from the outside world. Let us examine in detail the patterns that might exist in a family where there is father–daughter incest. The marital subsystem is dysfunctional, in that it is composed of the daughter and the father; this indicates rigid boundaries between the mother and father, and diffuse boundaries between the parents and the children. Similarly, there is intergenerational boundary confusion in the parental subsystem also; in incestuous families, the frequently ill, passive, or dependent mother is often replaced in child-rearing activities by the oldest daughter, who is being molested by the father. She in effect becomes the "parental child" (Minuchin, 1974); she and the father compose the parental subsystem, and she leaves the sibling subsystem, where she more appropriately belongs.

In this family systems analysis, the incestuous behavior can be seen to follow from dysfunctional role definitions and boundaries in the family. The rigid boundaries between the incestuous family and the outside world further exacerbate the problem; it is the family "secret," and is not available for scrutiny or feedback from others outside the family system.

FAMILY DYNAMICS WITH PRESCHOOL CHILDREN

SOCIAL FACTORS

If we examine which factors involved in sexual molestation of older children apply also to incestuous relationships with preschoolers, it appears that certain categories of factors cut across age groups, while others may be quite different with molested preschool children. The social factors that facilitate incest seem similar for families with preschool children and with older children. The presence of stress in the family, social isolation of the family, opportunity for sexual contact, and a sexualized climate in the home found with older incest victims frequently also characterize incestuous families in which a preschool child is the victim.

In fact, three of these factors—social isolation, stress in the family, and opportunity for sexual contact—may be stronger in families with preschoolers. The social isolation of the family may be more pronounced because, although older children must attend school, the parents are not obligated to send a preschooler to school, where a natural setting for interaction with nonfamily members is provided. Incest-prone families, experiencing much separation anxiety and a rigid boundary between themselves and the outside world, may be less likely to send their children to preschool than other families. For children who do attend nursery school, sexual abuse is frequently uncovered in this setting when the children exhibit inappropriate play behaviors, such as "humping" other children, touching others' genitals, or excessive masturbation.

There are also certain stress factors that are likely to play a major role in families during the preschool years. The adjustment to parenthood is certainly a very significant stress in any family. The father and any other children may feel very rejected by the mother's attention to a new baby, and the family's lifestyle is likely to change in many ways when a child is added to a couple. The dependency of the very young child most definitely influences the parents' relationship, and normal developmental periods such as the "terrible twos" are also highly stressful.

The fathers of preschool children may also have greater opportunity for sexual contact than fathers of older children as a result of the children's developmental level. High-risk times for sexual abuse of preschoolers include bathing, cleaning up, and changing clothes; these activities are carried out by children alone at an older age, without the need for parents to be involved. Similarly, a father may frequently spend time in his preschool child's room at bedtime and may even cuddle the child until he or she falls asleep without any suspicion of impropriety. In contrast, a father who lies down on the bed with his 13-year-old daughter would probably be viewed as overstepping a sexual boundary. The opportunity is even more available for a mother perpetrator, since mothers are expected to provide these caretaking activities for children and would almost never be questioned about doing so.

MARITAL RELATIONSHIPS

The marital relationship also seems to be similar along some relevant dimensions in families of preschoolers and families of older children, although there are possible significant differences, which are discussed later. The two major characteristics of the marital relationship in incestuous families—little communication or intimacy, and an imbalance in the power status of husband and wife—are frequently found in the families of sexually molested preschoolers. Sexual relations may decrease dramatically after the birth of a child, and in quite a few cases of preschool incest, sex between the parents may never have resumed or may occur very infrequently. Alternately, the parents may be having sex, but finding it quite unsatisfying. Some workers in the field speculate that perpetrators of incest with preschool victims may engage in unusual sexual practices, bizarre fantasies, and fetishes in preference to intercourse.

The power imbalance described earlier in incestuous families seems to apply as well to those with preschoolers. However, as elucidated later, there may be a somewhat larger proportion of cases involving a dominant mother and a dependant father among families with preschoolers than among those with older molested children.

THE ROLE OF THE CHILD

The role of the child is in some ways similar, regardless of the age of the child; however, here some differences between dynamics involving a preschool child and an older child are striking as a result of the child's and the family's developmental stage. As with older children, the preschool victim is usually the oldest daughter in the family, and she is generally compliant with the father's wishes. There may or may not be signs of role reversal occurring in the mother–daughter dyad when the child is a preschooler; certainly, role reversal at this age is much less developed than among older girls.

There are at least three major differences between the preschool victim and the older victim of incestuous relationships that are important to note. First, the preschooler bears less resemblance to an appropriate adult sexual object than does the older child, who may be physically mature or at least budding. It is hard to conceptualize sexual activities with a preschool child as a leaning backward from the age of consent, and it is difficult to utilize a model of the older man attracted to the younger woman when the "woman" is 3 or 4 years old.

Second, the preschool child generally has very little knowledge about sexual activities, is not cognitively able to understand moral rules, and is most often unaware of the taboos and stigmas attached to incestuous behavior. As a result, the preschooler is likely to experience less shame and sense of responsibility than an older counterpart might, especially prior to discovery of the incest and the fuss that ensues. However, if the child is told that he or she is bad, that what is happening is bad, or that bad things will happen if he or she tells anyone, the result may be even more traumatic for a preschooler because of the child's developmental state and egocentric thinking.

A third major difference between preschoolers and older children in the dynamics of incest relates to the developmental levels and tasks of these different age levels. With preschool children, normal developmental trends may be interpreted by the parent or parent substitute as indicating an adult sexual come-on. For example, it is a normal phenomenon for a 4-year-old girl to flirt with her father and tell him, "I want to marry you, Daddy." She may finagle to have him all to herself at times, and may not very politely suggest that her mother go out or find something else to do. These manifestations of the Oedipal phase of psychosexual development occur frequently in the preschool years and are generally handled by parental setting of loving but firm and clear limits. However, to a vulnerable, emotionally deprived, and sexually needy father, these expressions of affection may be viewed as if they come from a woman who would be an appropriate sexual object.

A similar dynamic may appear in response to the preschool girl's natural curiosity about the difference between the sexes; she may ask questions about anatomy, comment with glee if she sees her father's genitals, and show off her own. This may be sexually stimulating to the needy father, and if a climate of loosened sexual boundaries exists in the home, or disinhibiting factors such as alcohol are present, the child may be approached and abused sexually.

PARENTAL DYNAMICS

So far, we have seen that the social factors and the marital relationships bear considerable similarity among the incestuous families of pre- schoolers and older children, while the child victims may be quite different as a result of different levels of physical, emotional, cogni- tive, and psychosexual development. What about the dynamics of the fathers and the mothers in families with preschoolers? Are they similar to those discussed above, or do they differ significantly? Do their dynamics interact to form different sorts of relationships from those found in families with older abused children?

While there is no published or written information on special dynamics that may be present in the parents of preschool children, clinicians who work in the area speculate that these fathers and moth- ers may be quite different from the parents in families in which sexual abuse begins or comes to light when the children are preadolescent or adolescent. It may be that fathers who abuse preschool children are not always the tyrannical, domineering men who abuse their older daughters. Instead, the men may more often be dependent, passive people with low self-esteem who do not feel personally valued or sexually validated. They may need soothing and comforting, and may feel especially safe with preschool children: "I felt safe with her . . . I didn't have to perform. She was so little that I knew she wouldn't and couldn't hurt me."

As noted earlier, blurred boundaries are common; the parents may not set limits in sexual as well as nonsexual areas of child rearing. If, as Groth and Birnbaum (1978) have noted, perpetrators very fre- quently have been abused themselves at the same age as their victims, the abusing fathers of molested preschool children may very well have been molested themselves at a very early age.

When we examine our clinical knowledge about preschool incest victims and their families, we become aware of how little we know about the perpetrators in these cases. While our knowledge of dy- namics in preschool children and in their mothers is very limited, our understanding of the perpetrators is almost nil. This appears to be due to the fact that these parents and parent substitutes rarely admit to the abuse, and cannot generally be prosecuted because the children are unable to give legally credible testimony. As a consequence, the perpetrators most commonly do not enter treatment programs where their dynamics and patterns can be determined and dealt with therapeutically. This lack of knowledge certainly points to the need for more innovative and responsive legal processes, as well as better evidence gathering during evaluations of preschool-age victims.

While we have seen earlier that issues of enmeshment versus autonomy and dominance versus submission are both present in most incestuous families, it may be that the balance is different when the children are preschoolers than when they are of school age or older. Those who abuse preschoolers may be relatively more concerned about the issues of nurturance, abandonment, and separation, while the prime concerns of those who abuse older children may center more frequently on power and dominance. Additionally, those who abuse very young children may be more likely to view children as their primary sexual objects than those who abuse older children who more closely resemble adult sexual objects. There are certain characteristics of the fathers that seem common to a majority of incestuous families, regardless of the age of the children; these include poor impulse control (at least in certain situations), sexual concerns, and alcohol or drug use.

There also may be significant differences between the mothers of preschoolers involved in father–child incest and their counterparts with older children. Two major possible differences are these: (1) Mothers of preschoolers may tend to be less threatened at a deep self-esteem level by the incestuous behavior than do mothers of older children; and (2) mothers of preschoolers may tend to be less dependent in their marital relationships than those with older children.

Because the mother is less likely to view her preschool child as a rival, she may not be personally threatened by the incestuous behavior in the same way that the mother of an older, sexually budding child is. It is hard to conceptualize a 3-year-old as serious sexual competition. Additionally, the mother may be less likely to attribute blame to the preschooler for the incestuous incidents because the child is not aware of the implications of the sexual activity, although certainly some very young victims are blamed by their mothers nonetheless. Thirdly, the role reversal so prominent in families of older molested children is present in a less evolved form with preschoolers, if at all. Preschool children lack the emotional maturity, the cognitive sophistication, and the necessary competencies to adequately fulfill the roles of wife and mother, so that the mother generally does not feel that she has been replaced in family functions that are her responsibility.

Mothers of preschoolers who have been sexually abused by the fathers may tend to be less dependent in their marital relationships. Instead of the passive, dependent, ill, or disabled mothers frequently found in families where the victims are older, clinicians have found that mothers of abused preschool children exhibit quite different dynamics in many cases. Since they have been married for a shorter period of time, the mothers do not seem as tied to the perpetrators as do mothers who have been in their marriages for 10 to 15 years. When a preschool child is involved, the mother is less likely to view the child as having ulterior motives, in part because it is difficult to imagine what other source of sexual knowledge a preschool child might have. On the other hand, she may discount the child's story entirely because of the child's age, or may not be able to make sense out of the child's account of the sexual molestation.

In our experience, it appears that mothers of preschoolers are considerably more likely to separate or divorce in response to the discovery of the incestuous behavior than are mothers of older children. There are several possible explanations for this phenomenon. First, the system forces the father or father substitute to deny the abuse; he will probably be arrested if he admits he did it, while the system cannot and generally will not attempt to pursue him if he denies the allegations. Second, once the mother believes the child, she tends to be more outraged about the abuse because of the young age and vulnerable developmental status of the child. Third, the father or father substitute may be ordered to leave the home, and may never resume contact with the family. Fourth, the mother of a preschooler may be more willing to leave the father than the mother of an older victim because she is involved in a less long-term and dependent relationship or marriage. It should be noted in this context that allegations of sexual abuse as part of divorce proceedings are significantly more common when children are of preschool age than when they are older (see Chapter 7).

While we still know very little about the dynamics between the adults in incestuous families with preschool victims, it appears that there is a broad range of sexual attitudes involved, with no one pattern completely predominant. While some mothers are reported to be repressed sexually, others are felt to have loose sexual boundaries. In a family with a single parent, a child may be at greater risk for sexual abuse if the parent has serial heterosexual relationships, with the partners having unmonitored access to the child in the home. Additionally, parents with preschool children are likely to be younger and more sexually interested and active than are parents with teenaged children.

In view of the different dynamics explored above concerning families of molested preschool children, several competing hypotheses can be generated. First, it may be that there are patterns of dynamics to be found in families in which incest occurs with preschool children, as opposed to those in families in which incest occurs with preadolescent or adolescent children. Generally, the family in which a preschooler is abused frequently may be characterized by a dominant mother and a dependent father, while the family in which the child is abused at a later age may be more likely to have a dominant father and a dependent mother. If this hypothesis is true, these family types should be essentially nonoverlapping and should represent two distinct family constellations.

A second hypothesis is that there really are no significant differences in family dynamics when the child is under school age and when the child is older. It may be that all patterns of imbalanced power may be found with all ages of victims. Dominant-mother–passive-father and passive-mother–dominant-father parenting pairs may occur equally frequently in families when incest victims are younger and when they are older. Other factors, such as situational stress, may be more important determinants of incest than specific family dynamics.

The third hypothesis is that the differences may be related to the developmental stages of families, instead of different family patterns. It is possible that the large majority of cases of incest start with fondling and affection between fathers and their preschool children that gradually slide into sexual abuse. The crucial factor in determining outcome may be the response of a child's mother. If the mother is dependent, passive, and frightened of losing the security and protection provided by her husband, or was herself a victim of sexual abuse, she may not recognize the abuse that is occurring with her preschool child. As a result, the incest may not be disclosed until the daughter is an adolescent who is trying to become independent; more likely, it will never be disclosed, but will remain the family's secret.

In contrast, if the mother is not threatened personally by the incest and is not overly dependent in her marital relationship, she is more likely to recognize that incestuous behavior is occurring with her preschool child and to make appropriately assertive moves to end the sexualized relationship and protect her child. It should of course also be noted that some mothers really *are* unaware of what is happening between fathers and preschool children, with no known psychodynamic interference.

CONCLUSION

In summary, the most accurate statement about the dynamics in the family with a preschool incest victim is that the knowledge remains to be discovered and validated. While my coauthors and I are beginning to see some possible patterns of interaction emerge in our clinical work, our assertions are still at a speculative stage, and no conclusions are warranted at this time. We may hope that, with current awareness of and interest in abuse of very young children, better legal procedures and expanded treatment programs will provide us with more knowledge about these family dynamics. Because of the greatly increased numbers of cases, it may soon be possible to distinguish the dynamics in families where the child is abused as a preschooler and disclosure occurs immediately from those in families where the abuse begins in the preschool years but is not disclosed until much later, as well as from those in families where the abuse begins in the school years or adolescence. Such a knowledge base would help us to sort out the confounding effects of duration of the abuse and time of disclosure. As a consequence, we should be able to develop better ideas of how to treat and prevent incest among families with preschool children.

GUIDELINES FOR TREATING YOUNG CHILDREN

Suzanne Long

Mental health professionals preparing to treat young sexually abused children are confronted with a dearth of literature on specific treatment methods; this is especially frustrating and dismaying, in view of the growing numbers of such cases now being uncovered. Those involved in this field want to hear and see what other clinicians are doing with young victims of sexual abuse, how they are doing it, and what their own thoughts and reactions are in this work. Many struggle and feel isolated in their attempts to treat this particular child population.

This chapter, then, focuses on the treatment of the young sexually abused child and is organized in the following fashion. First, mention is given to the need for case management and teaming, followed by a discussion of an overall treatment approach including the different treatment phases. The treatment approach described in this chapter focuses on individual modified play therapy for children between the ages of 2 and 9, combined with an emphasis on mother–daughter rebonding. Next, the focus is on the general treatment issues involved, moving into a more specific discussion of treatment issues indicated by my findings. The chapter concludes with a brief discussion of indicators for termination of treatment.

The material presented in this chapter is drawn from 25 long-term cases seen between 1979 and 1983; length of treatment varied from 7 months to 2 years. Only one boy was treated (he was sexually abused by an uncle). The present discussion therefore relates pri-

TABLE 12-1. *Statistics for Children Treated*

Variable	Number of victims
Age group	
2–3	2
4–5	11
6–9	12
Molester	
Father/stepfather	14
Mother's boyfriend	4
Neighbor	3
Grandparent	2
Uncle	2

marily to the girls, accordingly, the female pronoun is used in this chapter to refer to a victim of sexual abuse.

Case referrals were obtained through self-referral or from county child protective services, mental health clinics, hospital social service staff, police, a victim/witness assistance program, and private practitioners. At the time of intake, only three mothers were living with perpetrators; separation, for whatever reasons, had already occurred in the other cases where perpetrators were fathers or stepfathers. During the course of treatment, those three women divorced the perpetrators. There were no reconstructed families in this sample, in contrast to incestuous families of older children. The statistics of the children treated are given in Table 12-1.

IMPORTANCE OF CASE MANAGEMENT AND TEAMING

Child sexual abuse cases require reporting to the local child abuse registry and interfacing with the various social and legal systems involved. In order to assess the situation effectively and to develop a sound treatment plan, it is important to draw from the experience and understanding of the many other professionals involved in the case. Dr. Roland Summit (1978) stresses that a therapist cannot effectively work alone in this kind of treatment. The cases are too complicated and involve too many facets. Nor can a therapist wait for others to initiate collaborative contacts. A therapist who accepts cases of child sexual abuse must be prepared for the extra amount of time to be spent in crisis intervention, gathering data, and conferring with colleagues.

TREATMENT APPROACH

The treatment approach presented in this chapter can best be described as modified play therapy by an active therapist using traditional play therapy toys, as well as the sand tray, arts and crafts, storytelling, creative dramatics, role playing, music, and body movements. Other intervention techniques include education, some behavior modification techniques such as behavior charting and time out, and the user of audiotape and videotape equipment.

In this modified play therapy, it is essential to demonstrate three basic attitudes, both verbally and nonverbally: respect, acceptance, and faith. "Respect" in this sense means respecting the child for who she is at that particular moment in time, with the right to feel whatever she feels—not attempting to take that feeling away. "Acceptance" means to accept the child with her problems and her feelings. "Faith" means to believe and have faith in the child's own ability to solve problems and to grow. The overall goal is to provide for this young child a safe, warm, accepting climate that enables her to explore her feelings and problems, and ultimately to see new options for handling them. The young child needs that environment in order to learn to be more trusting and secure.

The therapist first works toward getting acquainted in order to establish a relationship of trust and confidence. Less threatening material that is comfortable for the child is introduced first before delving into more difficult material. Violet Oaklander, in her book *Windows to Our Children* (1978), asserts that a foundation of shared pleasant experiences builds a base of trust that enables the child to be more open to talking about the harder things.

More than likely, the first drawing tasks will be a self-portrait, the child's favorite activity, or the child's family—long before the child is asked to draw feelings about her parents. When I have asked a child to draw a picture with sad feelings about Dad or Mom on one side and happy feelings about Dad or Mom on the other side, the child has often found it difficult to share the sad feelings until she has shared the happier, safer feelings. Sometimes, however, children need to let out the hurt and anger before the good feelings can come through.

The child is given a choice to tell about her molestation experience whenever she wants within the first three appointments. Open acknowledgment of the molestation by the therapist helps. The time limit helps. The choice helps. These children have experienced blurred boundaries and few choices. Not one child I have seen (including teenagers) has refused to cooperate in sharing the details and emotional side effects of the molestation within this three-appointment time frame. The goal is to assess the child's perception of the event, her emotional reaction to it, and her current guilt, fear, and anxiety about the molestation.

Tremendous energy must be expended in listening intently to the children's stories, drawings, play-acting, dreams, and the like. Sexually abused children are rarely listened to, much less understood. A child can tell if someone listens to what she has to say. Art Kraft, in his book *Are You Listening to Your Child?* (1973), clearly addresses this issue. "I remember when you said this or told me that story" will frequently bring a surprised look and then a grateful smile.

It is especially important in dealing with a young child to keep interpretations to a minimum. Children need shared, positive experiences, not insight. The preschooler tends to use denial to deal with upsetting experiences, to try to make them go away. Oaklander (1978) and others have pointed out that often the very act of drawing without therapist intervention is a powerful expression that helps a child to establish self-identity and provides a way of expressing feelings. Often the sheer enjoyment of the activity and the nonverbal release of the feeling through a painting or "scribble" may open the child up and facilitate the sharing of some deep feelings. With the young preschooler, sometimes it is a major accomplishment to express feelings through a picture or a story; she expresses in her own way what she needs or wants to communicate at a given time.

At other times, a child may be engaged in dialogue through telling and discussing a story. For example, in discussing the story of a bunny looking for her mother, the therapist might say, "Does that ever happen to you?", in an attempt to make a connection between the character in the story and the child's own experiences. However, the process of making those connections occurs slowly over time and with caution. This awareness opens the door gradually to examining options and choices available, and may mean dealing with the fear the child has tried to keep hidden.

It is important for the therapist to move at the child's pace and know when to speak and when to keep silent. Similarly, the therapist must appreciate the child's natural activity level, and must vary treatment interventions and techniques accordingly. It is vital to get to know the child and to use this knowledge to move from structured task to free play as it seems appropriate. Each therapist must find his or her own style in maintaining the delicate balance between following the child's lead on the one hand, and directing and guiding on the other.

Two rituals are helpful in this endless and creative process. One is giving prizes. Children love a small container with prizes such as stickers, gum, candy, and other small items. In order to get the prize, the child must "work hard," which means talking about things that are hard to talk about; such topics may include the molestation, the child's sadness and hurt, and so on. The prize can also be a reward for the child's struggle in sticking to a subject or completing a task.

The other ritual is making notations on a chart during each appointment, helping the child to see that what happens to her is important enough to be noted. The mother is invited in at the beginning of the session. The child and mother are asked about the latest news or important events, either successes or problems. Sometimes snacks are given to the needier and more emotionally deprived children. This further nurturance is consistently given, regardless of behavior. The children need to have some fun when they come in to work, yet must also know they are expected to work on their issues. If the therapist has the expectation that the child will grow, the child rarely disappoints.

TREATMENT PHASES

The treatment of a child sexual abuse victim can be divided into three main phases:

1. *Crisis intervention.* Even if no symptons may be observable, all small children who have been molested need a minimum checkup of three to six appointments to assess for disruption and dysfunction. For the symptomatic child and those facing unusual life stresses, classical crisis intervention is beneficial. A therapist must offer immediate

support to the client in coping with medical exams, investigative interviews, attorneys, court appearances, separation from home, and so on. For some children, crisis intervention is enough, while others need short-term treatment.

2. *Short-term therapy* (up to 6 months). Short-term therapy generally follows the crisis intervention phase and suffices for some children. The greater the support for the child in her own family circle or community is, the more likely it is that short-term therapy will be sufficient.

3. *Long-term therapy.* The critical goal is to establish a trusting relationship. Sgroi (1982) says that a child who has felt powerless, insecure, and afraid to trust others for some time must develop trust in the therapist before other issues can be resolved. Trust develops with time; it comes partly from the therapist's emotional support and stated belief that the child is, in fact, telling the truth, and that sexual abuse did occur. Other children likely to need long-term treatment include the following: children in foster home placement; children of punitive, resistant, and/or uncooperative parents; children whose parents deny that the abuse occurred; children who reside with the perpetrator; children involved in custody–visitation disputes; and children of parents who are unsupportive or are themselves feeling deeply injured, insecure, and in need of parenting. Also, the initial bonding or rebonding process between mother and child requires long-term therapy.

GOALS

In treatment, not just the sexual intrusion or violation is addressed. Psychodynamically, the major thrust of treatment involves strengthening the child's ego—helping the child to improve her self-image, to establish a better sense of self with boundaries, to learn to trust others, to begin to feel more secure, and to experience having choices. This is a tall order, yet these are the ideal goals of therapy.

GENERAL TREATMENT ISSUES

A book edited by Suzanne Sgroi and published in 1982(b) synthesizes 10 treatment issues for victims of child sexual abuse. The last 5 of these issues are much more likely to affect intrafamily child sexual abuse victims. My own findings, based on 25 long-term cases, support Sgroi's style of organizing the issues.

1. "Damaged goods" syndrome. The sense of being "damaged goods" may have to do with the possibility of real injury or fear of physical damage and retaliation. Another important aspect is the community's response in viewing the child as "used"; this may trigger intense curiosity, pity, hostility, and disgust toward her. Two girls among my 25 long-term cases were remolested by neighbors who were aware of the girls' previous molestation. Sometimes parents begin to dress a child poorly because she is seen as damaged.

2. Guilt. Most little children do not feel much guilt about their behavior before disclosure. After disclosure, some guilt feelings may emerge, depending upon the responses of significant others and the victim's age and developmental level. Sgroi sees guilt on three levels:

a. Responsibility for the sexual behavior. Little children typically feel it is somehow their fault when anything negative happens. The perpetrator frequently denies the molestation. Who then will believe a young child who sometimes makes up stories? It is my own experience and that of the others in the field that children rarely lie about sexual molestation. However, in the court system, molesters of children aged 3–9 are often believed innocent. The district attorney generally asks with skepticism what kind of a believable witness a 3-, 4-, or 6-year-old child will be in trial. Since many cases of father–child abuse do not get to criminal court, they may be handled in civil court in connection with custody–visitation matters. The father denies molestation and is deemed innocent according to the judicial system, yet wants visitation with his daughter. It is a very difficult treatment position to be in. A major issue is clarifying who was responsible. The victim needs to know that she is believed, that she is not a "bad girl," and that the perpetrator *is* responsible. After all, he is the adult.

b. Responsibility for disclosure. Young children may purposefully or accidentally tell a friend, neighbor, or teacher about the "games" she and Daddy play, for example. The perpetrator is generally angry and scared at the "secret" being blown, and the child is blamed.

c. Responsibility for disruption. The separations and suffering that may occur intensify the child's feeling responsible for the sexual behavior, the disclosure, and ultimately the disruption in the family. One child in the sample was repeatedly punished for minor mistakes

by her mother, who was angry at being separated from the perpetrator. Another child's brothers and sisters were abusive to her; these
siblings were confused and furious about their father being taken
away from them and blamed their sister for the loss.

3. *Fear.* Fears vary from child to child. The primary fear young
children experience is of separation and abandonment, although there
may also be fears of physical damage. In one case, a neighbor threatened to cut up a child using tiny pieces of glass and sharp knives if
she told what he had done to her. Sleep disturbances and nightmares
may abound as a result of such fears. Other regressive behaviors
frequently seen in response to fear are thumb sucking, bedwetting,
and eating problems.

4. *Depression.* Many child victims exhibit symptons or signs of
depression. Young children react to the losses, confusion, changes,
and disappointments; they may appear sad, subdued, or withdrawn.
There are many ways children may mask depression. They may act
as if nothing significant happened. They may feel unusually fatigued
or tired. They may have physical illnesses. They may deny all their
feelings. After being placed in a foster home, one young child sat on
her bed staring into space, refusing to eat her favorite foods, and
holding a prized toy listlessly. When her mother came to visit, the
child's behavior perked up, but she maintained a depressive quality
in reaction to the sudden unexplained disruption in her family. In
this case, the mother was more closely allied with the father/perpe-
trator, choosing to believe him rather than her young child.

5. *Low self-esteem and poor social skills.* Small children may feel
helpless and unable to be assertive on their own behalf. They may
feel unworthy and undeserving. The family is generally isolated, with
few outside contacts or opportunities to learn more appropriate social
skills. I have adapted from Schutz (1967) one of many ways of looking
at social skills individually or in a group by seeing the interaction in
terms of "joining" (how does one join in?), "control" (how does one
lead or follow?), and "affection" (this includes giving and receiving).
One child in the sample had been left alone for inordinate amounts
of time in charge of her toddler brother. At other times she was
molested by her mother's visiting boyfriend. This child learned to
survive by grabbing food from others. As she grew older, in playing
with peers, she continued to aggressively take what she wanted. Play-
ground squabbles and classroom theft were common. This child "joined"

by barging in. She "controlled" with bossy and aggressive activity. She desperately wanted and needed "affection," yet did not succeed in receiving much because of the inappropriateness of her efforts. In this case, considerable time was spent in close collaboration with the foster mother, working toward improving the child's social skills. The goal was that she be given enough by her foster mother to enable her gradually to become less demanding in relationships with others. She particularly liked the dramatics of role-playing the different ways of getting her needs met in peer play situations.

I have found that most of these children enjoy acting out or roleplaying specific situations to improve problem areas. Several 8-year-olds enjoyed the following self-esteem exercise: "Design a trophy you would like to receive. Make an acceptance speech into the tape recorder. What did you like about what you did?"

6. *Repressed anger and hostility.* Some young children are so sym-biotically linked to the perpetrator that they do not experience aware-ness of anger. Others experience the anger, but repress it rather than talking about it or acting it out. Some children become outwardly angry, after passing through an initial stage of confusion.

Over time, one child moved from repetitive and vigorous smash-ing of Play-Doh to beating up a large plastic inflated Superman for "not doing his job." She explained, "He wasn't up there watching and helping people. . . . He's a big dummy. . . . He doesn't do his job." At her initiation, with time she moved toward direct displays of anger at the perpetrator. She would throw a doll replica of the offender across the room, jam it in a play doll closet, and call it jail. The most difficult anger to express was the anger with her mother. The child was very confused, disappointed, and angry at her mother for not protecting her and stopping the sexual abuse.

7. *Inability to trust.* The degree of impairment in a child's ability to trust depends on a number of variables: the length of time mo-lested; the identity of the perpetrator; the type of relationship with him; the degree of pain, discomfort, or disadvantages experienced as a result of sexual abuse; the type of relationship with the mother; the amount of disruption following disclosure; and responses of others to the disruption.

One 5-year-old child's ability to trust was not altered significantly by a minor molestation, partly due to the mother's immediate and consistent belief and support. In contrast, with another 5-year-old, only the babysitter the child originally disclosed to believed her. The intense family disruption and chaos that followed contributed to her confusion in regard to questions that many such children examine: Who can you trust? Who will believe? What kind of a difference will it make? Is it worth it?

8. *Blurred role boundaries and role confusion.* In cases of incest, blurring of boundaries occurs between mother and child, father and child, and generally mother and father. What is expected of a child? Is a 4-year-old subtly encouraged to take care of Daddy? The familiar father has put on the strange mask of lover. The mother may give up large parts of her role as parent, spouse, and caretaker to her daughter. An ultimate treatment goal is for the mother to take on a stronger parenting role and to provide routine, structure, and boundaries. The young child in particular needs this.

It was at least a year into treatment before one 6-year-old began to demonstrate progress in this problem. In her sand play, she started going to her mother for help, as opposed to having the mother in bed asleep or out of the play altogether. In a following session, she played the role of the mother calling the police to get the perpetrator to leave the house on an unannounced visit; still in character, she then asked the child to stop taking care of her younger brothers and sisters because that was the mother's job.

9. *Pseudomaturity and failure to complete developmental tasks.* The sexual stimulation and preoccupation with the sexual relationship disrupts the accomplishment of age-appropriate tasks of emotional development. One 7-year-old girl acted more like a 16-year-old, in that she walked, dressed, wore makeup, and flirted like a teenager. This pseudomaturity is typical of sexually abused children and is almost always evident in the young children. Many of these children have been robbed of the typical childhood experiences by having other responsibilities foisted upon them. A standard treatment goal is to work toward a child's returning to age 5 going on 6 versus 5 going on 14. The caretaker is encouraged to introduce and support activities that are age-appropriate, and to lovingly divert pseudomature behavior. For example, mudplay, jacks, making cookies, swim team, Brownies, and so on are appropriate for younger children. This is difficult, as it involves the mother's seeing the child as a person with needs to be met, and may require the mother to give up the gratification of the daughter's "older," coping, helpful behavior to her.

Thus, the mother's resistance is to be expected and dealt with as part of her ongoing treatment.

10. Self-mastery and control. The child has experienced a violation of her body, privacy, and rights. The young child typically feels that she had no choices, no other options, no power, in regard to the molestation. A large, powerful adult dictated what was to be. The child may continue to act like a victim awaiting rescue. This theme recurs often in stories children tell. Using Gardner's (1975) "mutual story-telling technique," the therapist tells a story after the client finishes her story. The therapist's story offers a solution, an option. It is important to instill a sense of hope—to teach the child that options do exist, that there can be some mastery.

One 5-year-old who was being checked physically for molestation lay on the examining table with a smile on her face, appearing to be "too cooperative." The child had been programmed to see herself as an extension of the perpetrator, to be used at will. This belief prohibits a child from seeing herself as separate or having any control over anything, especially her body.

In summary, then, the feelings presented by the 25 children included abandonment, bewilderment and confusion, lack of protection, betrayal, and feelings of isolation. Although children such as these may feel reluctant to do so, they need to express many questions about their mothers and their fathers (or other perpetrators) and ask lots of "why" questions. "Why did he do that? Why didn't Mom stop him? Has this really happened to others? Should I tell my friends? Why can't I live with Mom?" These questions can be handled in various ways; for example, reflection of feelings and education can be utilized in contacts with mothers and/or perpetrators. Therapists must remember that children need to deal with pushed-aside feelings and issues, which over time cannot be ignored.

Most young children focus on wanting a relationship with their mothers. They want to be closer to them, to spend more time with them, to be "forgiven" by them, and in general to bond with their mothers in a way not previously accomplished. One 6-year-old demonstrated this clearly as she lovingly cared for her doll baby and agreed with the therapist that this was how close she wanted to be to her own mother.

SPECIFIC TREATMENT ISSUES

I have found five additional areas to be especially important in working with the younger child. Some of this material is applicable to
working with troubled children in general, but seems particularly
relevant to these child molestation cases. These areas are as follows:

1. Importance of teaming with the child's mother.
2. Inappropriate attachment behavior.
3. Infant regressive behavior.
4. Need for body contact and body awareness.
5. Need for education on feelings.

IMPORTANCE OF TEAMING WITH THE CHILD'S MOTHER

Work with a child's mother is an integral part of treatment. To begin
with, the therapist tries to help the mother see that the two of them
must work together; the therapist cannot "fix" the child alone. The
therapist thus approaches the mother: "We are in this together. Perhaps, if we all work hard together, you can have a happier family. I
need your help. I need to see you at a minimum of twice a month,
and preferably each appointment for a few minutes. You can share
with me how your daughter has been this week, what she's been into,
and so on."

The mother needs to see the therapist as aligned with her and
not as someone who is trying to usurp her position. This requires an
appreciation of systems theory. It is the interaction between mother
and child that is functional or dysfunctional, and treatment should
work toward improving that interaction. Giarretto (1982) states that
one of the cornerstones in the treatment of the incestuous family is
the rebuilding of the mother–child relationship.

After disclosure of the molestation, the mother herself is in crisis.
She needs a great deal of support and nurturance. She generally needs
a therapist for herself. She needs to express her pain and anger at
family disruption and perhaps forced independent living. She may
be one of the many mothers who were molested themselves as children, and her own issues as a victim may have been reignited.

It is equally important to team with the foster or substitute mother, if there is one. She may be angry at the birth mother for not protecting the child. She may try to deny the molestation. Some of the therapist's work may include dealing with complicated feelings between the foster mother and the birth mother over visitation.

The child is seen alone the majority of the time, particularly in the beginning. The child's needs warrant this. As the child grows, emphasis shifts to working with mother and child to rebond, build, or rebuild the relationship. In the meantime, the mother and the child each need to deal with their own injuries separately. The therapist's goal is to be a role model to the mother, to educate her, and to gradually shift the focus back to the primary relationship between mother and child. Thus, therapy may begin by seeing the mother and daughter together for 10 minutes and then the child alone for 40–45 minutes. Not every case is the same. For example, the mother may need more time, so the hour may be split to see each half the time. As treatment progresses, the therapist may work toward seeing the mother and daughter together for half the hour and the child alone the other half. Toward the end of the contacts, the majority of the hour is with the mother and daughter together. Always, a few minutes are saved for the daughter alone, since she remains strongly connected to the therapist.

Mothers frequently have not bonded with their children, and have difficulty empathizing with them. Mothers may typically say, "I can't explain it. I just don't feel close to her. She felt different from the beginning." One mother said, "It's like there is a force field between us and always has been." Having the mother as an ally and developing the spirit of teaming provides entry into discussing these issues of bonding. In order to prevent future molestation or problems, it is important to assist the mother and daughter to develop a closer relationship with better communication and trust. The timing is crucial. Some examples of exercises used in the rebonding process include having the mother cuddle and sing to her daughter, put lotion on her hands and arms, brush her hair, play peek-a-boo, play catch with a nerf ball, find hidden raisins, count freckles or teeth, tell the daughter's fortune by reading her palm, teach her something new, play games together, or draw pictures together.

The mother may be shocked or touched when she sees a family picture drawn by the daughter, with cartoon headings and words expressing what each member *needs* to say to each other and/or what

FIGURE 12-1.   *A child's pictorial expression of her relationship with her mother and the mother's boyfriend.*

each member *wants* to say to each other. In one of my cases, a $5\frac{1}{2}$-year-old girl, Sally, drew a picture of herself, her mother, and the mother's boyfriend Ron (see Figure 12-1). Upon completion of the drawing, I asked Sally what she wanted the figures to say. Sally wanted to tell her mother that she loved her and that she didn't want to clean up her room. The mother said to Sally, "You have to!", and to her boyfriend she said, "I see you making dinner." Sally wanted Ron to say, "I love you, Sally," and in return she wanted to say, "I want you to be my Daddy."

In discussing the drawing with the mother, I focused on three issues:

1. Sally was reaching out to Ron and wanting a relationship with him, and how would the mother handle this differently from the relationship with the molesting father?
2. Sally was expressing her love to her mother, and at the same time testing to see whether the mother would follow through on discipline.
3. The mother was glad to have boyfriends to help with the household duties; at the same time, she had no arms and hands, which accurately reflected her sense of feeling overwhelmed and inadequate in most situations.

The mother was shocked by her daughter's clear image of their family

situation, and I myself was impressed with Sally's 5½-year-old wisdom
in spelling out the immediate treatment goals.

In other situations, the mother's support is necessary in order to
work toward less pseudomaturity on the daugher's part and more
age-appropriate activity. Once a child has been sexually molested over
a period of time, the light switch of eroticism has been turned on.
How should this eroticized behavior be handled? One of the most
sensitive and difficult areas for the mother to handle is the child's
continued sexualized behavior. This may take the form of sex play
with peers, exaggerated physical greetings to men, or masturbation.
The mother needs to confront her own views on sexuality and masturbation, and to decide what is acceptable for her daughter. The
therapist frequently has to help the mother accept that masturbation
may be appropriate if not excessive and if not done in public. In
almost every case, time is spent on these issues: How can your daughter be sexual? Can she not be sexual? Can she masturbate? Why not?
Where? For example, in one family, the mother was able to decide it
was permissible for her daughter to masturbate in the privacy of her
bedroom, but not in the family room under a blanket while watching
TV. In another case, an 8-year-old girl who had too much free time
ended up fantasizing and masturbating excessively. I helped the mother
determine an activity that would be interesting to her daughter, encourage some sublimation, be good exercise, and be more age-appropriate. The mother picked a swim team with almost daily workouts.
It is essential to have the mother's cooperation and assistance in solving
such a problem, whether the solution be swim team, Brownies, Girls
Club, soccer, or the like.

It is difficult for the mother when the daughter begins to grow
and change. She may ask for more time and attention from the mother,
while the mother may be resentful or jealous of the daughter's success
or beginning individuation. Most of these mothers want to be good
parents; they simply don't know how. If they receive nurturance in
therapy, they in turn have something to give their daughters. Teaming
with mothers and networking with their therapists create avenues for
handling these issues.

INAPPROPRIATE ATTACHMENT BEHAVIOR

There is such emotional neediness in these children that after a cursory appraisal, there is typically an immediate, dramatic attachment

to the therapists. The emotional desperation evident in many of the incestuous family members is quite obvious in the child. As contact continues, it is clear that this is frequently more than just identification with the therapist, but, rather, a wish on the child's part to merge with the therapist. This indicates either a current developmental stage or regression back to the need to be "one with mother."

A six-year-old client and I were drawing sailboats, an activity initiated by the child (see Figure 12-2). The sailboats were separate on the page. Once the boats were named, the child could not tolerate the separation and moved her boat to merge with mine. Lauri went on to say, "This is how it's supposed to be," followed up by her loud, proud declaration—"I am Suzanne Long." I sat close to her and acknowledged how Lauri wanted to be very close to me, be cared for and protected by me, and be like me in some ways. Lauri nodded her head vigorously. I then stated that we would be close every week for a long time until Lauri felt safe and stronger.

The sexually abused child has been in a silent world of hopelessness and confusion. Now the therapist is imbued with magical

FIGURE 12-2.   *A child's pictorial expression of her need to merge with her therapist.*

powers and wishes. "Here I get to do what I need and want. Can I live with you? Will you live with me and Mom?" Frequent "I love you" drawings and notes are given. This can be very flattering to the therapist, but also encourages "responsible-for" feelings in countertransference. It is very important to be tuned in to the child's developmental phase and to set limits while being appropriately nurturing. It is important to establish clear boundaries for the child. For example, the therapist cannot live with the child, and usually cannot come to dinner. They will see each other weekly. It can be helpful to point out that the therapist's honest feelings of liking the child are not dependent on gifts of any kind. The intense attachment gradually tapers off to a more appropriate level as the child begins to need the therapist less, and to feel more secure in her own competence and safety.

There is frequently jealousy and some possessiveness when siblings are included at certain points in the treatment. Siblings of victims have their own anger, confusion, and hurt. I make a point of addressing at least some of these issues in the family system, so as to make the victim's life easier by eliciting more support for her. The importance of including siblings in some part of the treatment plan was most dramatic with a 7-year-old victim and her 5-year-old sister. It was thought that the 5-year-old had escaped molestation and had been only occasionally physically abused. In a joint session, out came detail after detail of extreme physical abuse, such as being totally buried in dirt and sand. Lurid details emerged of enemas and forced defecation on the perpetrator. The 5-year-old then recounted her natural father's physical abuse of her when she refused to silently watch her sister's molestation or to participate with the father in her own molestation. Clearly, this child had an individual need for treatment, which might never have been uncovered without sensitive collateral sibling contact.

INFANT REGRESSIVE BEHAVIOR

The sexually abuse child needs to regress and complete her unfinished developmental tasks. When these needs are met, she is better prepared to spring forward to the next issue. Almost every little girl, for example, chooses the baby bottle from among the play therapy toys. She asks verbally or nonverbally to be fed, burped, rocked, cuddled, and sung to. The glazed look in her eyes while sucking on the bottle and the comfort shown at being nuzzled reveals the need to recreate the mother–infant interaction. Many children need to repeat this activity over and over.

Two things happen next. The child either gradually drops the regressed activity, returning to it periodically, or may act out growing into the preschool and older ages. For example, the child may act out playing with rattles, drinking from a cup, crawling, learning to walk, and finally learning to talk. None of my own child clients had grown developmentally to their actual chronological ages. This growing activity may be played out repeatedly until no longer needed or initiated by the child in play therapy.

Theraplay, a book by Jernberg (1979), although not written for traumatized children, describes a technique that addresses the need in treatment to recreate the natural mother–infant pattern of interaction. This technique includes intruding, nurturing, structuring, and challenging the child. These concepts are quite useful in dealing with sexually abused children, even though their application in these cases is quite different from *Theraplay* methods. Although it is important to respect the child's overall pace and style of interacting, a therapist should intrude and ask to be related to when appropriate. Nurturing is vital and may take many different forms. For example, the child may be rocked or her physical hurts attended to. The therapist must challenge the child with new thoughts, questions, and tasks. Gradually, the mother is assisted to engage in these kinds of activities with the child. The therapist may model this for the mother in their sessions together. These are the kinds of bonding activities that did not take place for the child in a significant way in her early months and years.

Most children are embarrassed at their mothers' knowing about their using, or seeing them use, the bottle. This is a "secret" they would like to keep. The therapist asks some of the mothers to participate in feeding, burping, and rocking. It becomes apparent that many exhibit strong distaste and resentment. These mothers do not want a return to babyhood, make fun of the bottle, and tend to demand more mature behavior. Their comfort level increases when this activity is structured to occur either in the therapy session or within the 30-minute special time encouraged at home. Mothers are asked to give high-quality focused interaction to their children as often as possible; it remains a difficult thing for many mothers to do.

NEED FOR BODY CONTACT AND BODY AWARENESS

The sexually abused child needs to have a better sense of her boundaries. Body awareness is basic to a strong sense of self and is an
important aspect of self-acceptance. Many children with low self-esteem are not only unfamiliar with their bodies; they also do not like
how they look or how they think they look. It is helpful for a child
to talk to her image in the mirror, make self-portraits, look at baby
pictures, draw a large-sheet body portrait, and talk about the body
parts.

In incestuous families there has been little normal affection or
support, due in part to the role confusion and blurred boundaries.
The children are sexualized at an early age, and many have an eroticized way of seeing the world. These children tend to be evasive or
overly affectionate with men and sometimes with women. However,
they do need a lot of body contact. The emotional neediness, previous
stimulation, and habit may lead the children to climb on laps, sit as
close as possible and be very physical. There appears to be minimal
if any awareness of body space, where to touch and where not to
touch, or how to hug and how not to hug. I spend a lot time helping
these children look at their bodies in new ways.

The children need to experience their bodies as capable of giving
them pleasure without fear, violence, embarrassment, dirtiness, or
sexual arousal. It is important to see the body as wholesome and
beautiful. Deep breathing and relaxation exercises are activities the
children enjoy. They help the children to become more in touch with
their bodies—for example, in how to settle down from hyperenergy,
stress, and discomfort.

A necessary ingredient is sex education and prevention. Permission should be asked of the parents. Frequently, they will read the
book or material first. Many of the mothers have a lot to learn in this
area themselves. Later, the mother and the therapist together go over
the teachings a second or third time with the child if there is interest.

Role playing to help the child gain options for prevention of
further sexual abuse is helpful. Writing out descriptions of situations
on index cards and asking the child to respond is usually fun for the
child. There are many other similar activities to help the child handle
prevention more appropriately. Specific examples of role-play scenarios are given in Chapter 13.

Need for Education on Feelings

First, it is essential to assess a mother's ability to respond appropriately to her daughter. It sets up a child for further depression if she is encouraged to ask for something from the mother that the mother is unable to give.

Many of these young victims have not had "quality time" with their mothers. Their needs have not been recognized, nor have they known how to ask appropriately for what they need. While the children are usually very confused and internally upset in reaction to the sexual abuse disclosure and subsequent disruption, they may not have the words to explain all this. Beyond providing the opportunity to play it out in therapy, providing some education on feelings helps sort out the confusion. Education helps the child to feel better about herself and to develop coping skills, and the mother can assist in this process. Mother and child are helped to identify feelings, to talk about them, to experience acceptance for having them, to learn self-acceptance, and finally to see that there are choices in the ways they can be expressed. Some helpful exercises from *The Second Centering Book*, by Hendricks and Roberts (1977), include the following: "What does a feeling look like? Draw it. Act it out. Where do you feel it in your body? Try to use all your senses in discovering feelings."

Here is a list of feelings I have drawn from. The therapist and client can also make up their own list.

> happy, sad, good, proud, angry, afraid, hurt, upset, disappointed, frustrated, pain, lonely, alone, love, like, jealous, envy, special, private, bad, joy, delight, sick, anxious, worried, glad, calm, nervous, gloomy, silly, blank, guilty, sorry, shame, disgust, cheerful, sure, strong, weak, pity, empathy, grief, understanding, understood, admiration, tired. (Oaklander, 1978, p. 122)

It may be useful to have a "Bag of Words" sack (Gardner, 1975), from which a child draws a card, sometimes telling a story about that word or feeling. The "squiggle technique" originated by Winnicott (1971) may be used, with first the child and then the therapist either picking one word or feeling to describe the squiggle, or telling a story about the squiggle. Also, a therapist can use large pictures from magazines glued to manila folders; the child can be asked to pick her favorite, the scariest, one that reminds her of Mom or Dad, one that looks like what she worries about, and so on. It is amazing how helpful these are in drawing out a discussion of the child's feelings or perceptions. These are a few of the activities that have been helpful in educating sexually molested children about feelings.

INDICATORS FOR TERMINATION

As therapy nears termination, it is important to evaluate the progress that has been made toward meeting long-term treatment goals.

The child:
- Has she dealt sufficiently with her feelings of guilt, fear, anger, confusion, and depression?
- Has she dealt sufficiently with the specific nature of the molestation, the methods of coercion, negative and positive feelings about it, possible secondary gains?
- Does she feel less responsible for the sexual behavior, the storminess following disclosure, and the disruption to her family?
- Has she dealt with her anger and hostility at both her mother and the perpetrator for the molestation and the lack of protection from it?
- Does she demonstrate trust in her mother and see her as a protector (or have another trusting relationship with another significant adult)?
- Is she aware of earlier confusion between sex and affection?
- Is she able to set limits on sexual advances?
- Is she able to seek help in the event that she is approached again?
- Has she developed an increase in overall social skills?
- Has she developed outside social contacts and activities?
- Is she more age-appropriate in activity?
- Have her ego boundaries been strengthened?
- Does she feel better about herself?
- Is she more trustful?

The mother:
- Is she able to protect her daughter and herself from abuse?
- Has she overcome holding her daughter accountable for the molestation and aftereffects?

- Has she told her daughter it was the perpetrator's fault, not hers?
- Is she more adult-like and responsible with the child?
- Does she have expectations of the child that are age-appropriate?
- Is she able to set appropriate limits?
- Is she able to empathize and see her daughter as separate from herself, having needs to be met?
- Is she better able to meet those needs?
- Does she enjoy her daughter?
- Has the overall relationship between the mother and daughter been sufficiently improved?
- Can she allow her daughter to receive emotional "goodies" from people outside the family?
- Is the mother more separate, independent, and assertive in her relationship to the perpetrator or current man in her life?

Preparing a child for termination is crucial. Termination needs to be done gradually and carefully. Children often convey readiness in additional ways beyond changes in the problem behaviors. The shared material that comes through in sessions may indicate sufficient improvement. Often the child has done enough work so that she can continue on her own, especially with the improved support of her mother and others. The child may have reached a plateau (not a stumbling block) in therapy, and this can be a stopping point. As Oaklander (1978) states,

> Sometimes the child needs an opportunity to integrate and assimilate with her own natural maturation and growth, the changes taking place as a result of the therapy. Sometimes this plateau is a sign of resistance that needs to be respected. It's as if the child knows she cannot handle breaking through this particular wall at this time. She needs more time, more strength; she may need to open up to this particular place when she is older. (p. 199)

As part of termination, it is important to give permission and encouragement to the mother and child to return to treatment if and when needed. When the child grows into puberty, dating and later sexual activity may stir up the old issues so that they need to be reexamined and put into perspective.

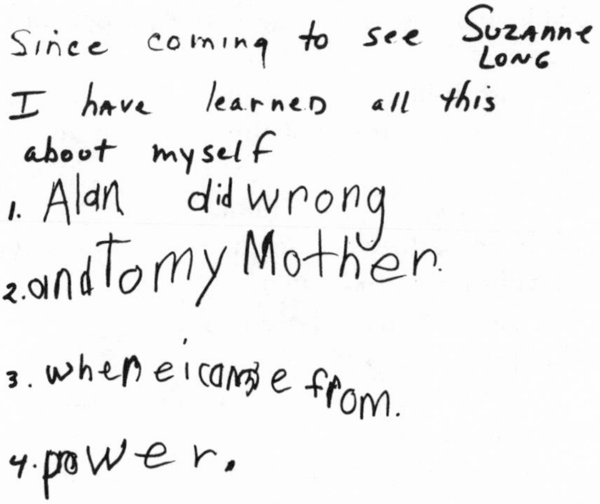

Since coming to see Suzanne
Long
I have learned all this
about myself
1. Alan did wrong
2. and To my Mother.

3. when ei came from.

4. power.

FIGURE 12-3.   *A child's summary of her progress in therapy.*

In one case, I used a book completion exercise in the session as one way to say goodbye. One page of that book is shown in Figure 12-3. Patti and her mother had been in treatment 2 years when she summarized her progress. She explained:

1. "Alan did wrong." This meant that it wasn't her fault that the offender did wrong and shouldn't have.
2. "and to my mother." This meant that she needed to mind her mother, rather than being bossy and taking over managing the family. Her mother could do just fine and needed her to be the child.
3. "where i came from." this referred to sex education and all the time devoted to that subject.
4. "power." This meant that Patti saw herself at age 7 as having choices, options, safety, and security. All of this was wrapped into her use of one important word.

SUMMARY

The findings and observations summarized here resulted from 25 long-term treatment cases involving child sexual abuse. This chapter attempts to fill a severe gap in the sexual abuse literature in the treatment of children. It is written in the hope that it will be helpful in providing some general guidelines for treatment, as well as providing specific treatment issues and techniques. It is hoped that more practitioners will see the value of sharing and writing about their experiences in this pioneering field.

PARALLEL GROUP TREATMENT OF CHILDREN AND THEIR MOTHERS

Linda Damon
Jill Waterman

The treatment or supervision of a number of families in which the mothers and/or their young children were sexually abused has revealed that the mothers and children share many common issues and conflicts. The emergence of these common themes has suggested that they might be more systematically addressed if a curriculum were developed for treatment of mothers and children in a parallel fashion. A series of modules for treatment of children and their mothers, developed in parallel mother–child therapy groups, is described in this chapter. These modules may be used in group or individual treatment of sexually abused families. The structured nature of the treatment format lends itself very well to situations where resources are limited or where short-term intervention is needed. Although the modules have been developed specifically for treatment of children aged 8 and under (the average age is about 5 years), they may be utilized for older children, with modifications as needed for a child's age or developmental stage.

The parallel treatment of mothers and their children seems the most useful model for the following reasons:

1. It has been found that many mothers of sexually abused children (particularly in cases of incest or prolonged sexual abuse) have themselves been sexually abused as children (Mrazek, 1981; Wells,

1981), and they tend to deal with their children's sexual abuse in much the same way that they were handled. As a consequence, the mothers are likely to be unable to help the children unless they are assisted to work through their feelings and thoughts about their own sexual trauma.

2. The structured and directive therapeutic format utilized with the children is very powerful and produces immediate results. The mothers are apprised of the issues that the children's group has covered on a weekly basis, and, therefore, they can respond more appropriately to any material the children bring up at home. Mothers who are not so informed would be more likely to suppress their children's expressions of feelings in an attempt to maintain the family homeostasis and the denial of sexual trauma. Parallel use of these materials in a group therapy setting provides an environment in which children and their mothers are able to stimulate each other, thereby enriching the therapeutic experience for both.

3. Discussion with the mothers of the children's weekly structured activities in great detail facilitates the mothers' ability to explore feelings and thoughts about their own early sexual abuse. Through these discussions, contact is made with the traumatized child who resides within each mother.

GENERAL DESCRIPTION

The group therapy setting allows for the inclusion of six to eight families. It is not necessary that all of the children be victims of sexual abuse; if the mothers themselves were sexually traumatized as children, their children may be at risk for sexual abuse (Meiselman, 1978; Sgroi, 1982b), and may participate in the children's group with the goal of preventing future sexual abuse. Modules from the sexual abuse curriculum can be introduced when relevant in long-term parallel parent–child therapy groups, or the curriculum may be used in short-term parallel parent–child therapy groups over a 20 to 30 week period. Individual and family therapy may be introduced as needed with families who are involved in the structured group therapy setting. This method of treatment is not advised for borderline psychotic or psychotic mothers, who are apt to become overwhelmed by their own rage, and who therefore may act out in a self-injurious or aggressive manner.

The groups with which these structured modules are utilized meet weekly for $1\frac{1}{2}$ hours. The mothers meet in a group room, while the children meet in a larger group room equipped with a full stock of play therapy equipment. There is at least one therapist for every two children in the group. A supervising child therapist from the professional staff oversees the work of the other therapists, who are either students in a mental health field or psychologically minded volunteers who have received training through seminars at the clinic.

The groups are conducted in the following manner each week. At the beginning of each group, one of the child therapists comes into the mothers' group and receives a very brief weekly report as to each child's problems and progress, as well as any relevant responses a child might have had to the structured group exercises the preceding week. If, for example, the child therapists know that a child has witnessed a violent scene between the mother and a boyfriend, they are better able to understand aggressive, fearful, or counterphobic behavior on the part of the child.

After talking about events of the week, the children are then introduced to that weeks' structured module, which takes from 30 minutes to 1 hour to implement, depending upon the levels of anxiety and attention spans of the children. Afterwards, the children may engage in free play if time allows until 10 minutes before the group ends, when snacks are served. In the meantime, the mothers are discussing the children's activity as well as other items in the mothers' sexual abuse curriculum. The mothers also have time to talk about their own special concerns or crises. Ten minutes before the therapy group ends, the adult leader takes the mothers into the children's therapy room for feedback from the child therapists. In this way, the mothers can be apprised as to how their children have responded to the structured module, so that they can follow through more appropriately at home. Whenever the child therapists are unsure about the impact of the feedback on the mothers and children, they seek consultation from the supervising child therapist before giving feedback to the parents.

After each group therapy session ends, the adult and child therapists meet together as a treatment team in order to discuss the reactions of all group members to the curriculum and to coordinate treatment plans for the families. The 1-hour team meeting provides for supervision of the child therapists; individual and family dynamics are discussed, and feelings and anxieties of the therapists are also explored. Additionally, a weekly 30-minute meeting before the group starts allows the therapists to discuss and rehearse various aspects of that week's curriculum.

GOALS OF TREATMENT

The goals of treatment for the children are as follows:

1. To validate the expression of their various feelings surrounding the sexual abuse.
2. To help children think about the sexual abuse in ways that are less destructive to their self-image by assisting them to reduce their sense of responsibility and guilt, and to develop labels for their feelings and past experiences.
3. To teach children to be more assertive in sexual, as well as in nonsexual, situations.
4. To set limits on children's sexualized responses and to help them explore appropriate ways of expressing their needs.
5. To help children integrate their conflicted feelings toward the perpetrator.

The goals of treatment for the mothers are these:

1. To assist denying mothers to accept that the sexual abuse really did happen.
2. To sensitize mothers to what constitutes sexual abuse, and to help them be more alert and vigilant to possible abusive interactions that may occur with their children.
3. To help mothers protect their children from reabuse.
4. To assist mothers in working through their own feelings regarding their early sexual trauma, thereby enabling them to assist their own children more effectively.
5. To help mothers to become more nurturing, less guilt-inducing, and more positive with their children.

6. To help mothers work through and integrate their feelings toward the perpetrators.

THE CURRICULUM: THIRTEEN MODULES DEALING WITH COMMONLY OCCURRING THEMES

Thirteen modules dealing with the most commonly occurring themes for sexually abused children are presented below. These modules may be presented in the suggested order, or the order may be determined by the therapist using them. If clinical experience suggests that the module be spread over more than one session, this is indicated in the discussion. Not all modules may be relevant for a particular child or group and may be dropped if warranted by the case.

The following outline is used in presenting each module: (1) goals to be accomplished through use of this module; (2) techniques used with the children, their reactions to the exercises, and the feedback given to the mothers; (3) techniques used with the mothers, and their reactions to the structured activities.

The issues dealt with are as follows:

1. The Right to Say "No"
2. What Happens When You Say "No"?
3. Private Parts
4. Who Can You Tell?
5. Anger and Punishment
6. What Happens When You Tell?
7. What Happened to You?
8. Fault and Responsibility
9. Separation
10. What Happens to the Perpetrators?
11. Integration of Positive and Negative Feelings toward the Perpetrator
12. What If the Denial Is Maintained?
13. Sex Education

MODULE 1: THE RIGHT TO SAY "NO"

The theme addressed in this module is whether or not a person has the right to set limits. Mothers and children will not be able to stop unwanted advances if they do not feel that they have this right. The goals of this module are these:

1. To help children become more aware of various situations in which they have the right to say "no" to adult figures.
2. To assist mothers in exploring their right to say "no" to authority figures who make unreasonable demands upon them.
3. To allow for gradual introduction of the topic of inappropriate sexual advances in both children's and mothers' groups.

This module generally requires two or more sessions.

Techniques Used with Children

The topic of "The Right to Say 'No'" is introduced by one of the child therapists, who presents rather innocuous, nonsexual situations at first. The therapist talks with the children about what they should do if a babysitter asks them to do something that they don't think is right. The children are asked, for example, what they would do if:

> Your babysitter says "Don't tell your mom that I talked to my boyfriend on the phone tonight."
> Your babysitter says "I will let you stay up later if you play a game with me and take off your clothes."

The children are asked to respond to each hypothetical situation, and examples of similar situations that have happened to them are elicited. Questions such as the following can stimulate the children to think further about their right to assert themselves:

> Do you have the right to ask your big brother or sister to knock on the bedroom door before they enter the room?
> Can you tell your mom or dad that they can't come into the bathroom if you don't want them in there?

The exercise ends with the child therapist explaining to the children that they are going to play a game in which the children are supposed to tell them when they begin to sit too close to them (Adams & Fay, 1981). The children are told, "Everybody has different ideas about how close they want people to be to them. It is okay to tell somebody to move away or to move away yourself if you feel that a person is too close to you." As the therapist get closer and closer, the children are continually reminded that they can stop the advances of the therapist at any point.

Reactions of Children

The children, especially those who have been abused over a long period of time, tend to become anxious and regressive in their play during presentation of this topic, and may leave the structured therapeutic situation. The therapist may need to hold and comfort them while they listen to the various hypothetical situations. The most severely abused children tend to have the most difficulty in putting limits on the physical closeness of the therapist, and some try to shrink their bodies up so that they take up less space in order to accommodate to the closeness of the child therapist.

Feedback Given to Mothers

The mothers are given feedback about their children's ability to assert themselves and set limits. Thus, some of the mothers are alerted that their children have great difficulty in setting limits with intrusive adults.

Techniques Used with Mothers

The mothers first receive a brief explanation of the goals of overall treatment for themselves and their children. They are then asked to think of various examples of how they feel coerced in their own lives, and whether or not they feel compelled to give in to authority figures. As with the children, hypothetical examples of coercion, such as the following, are introduced to facilitate discussion:

> Suppose your boss asks you to cover for him and tell a lie. For example, suppose he tells you that if his wife calls, you should tell her that he was working late that night.

Most mothers would agree that they would be risking their jobs if they did not comply with their boss's request. The parallel is drawn to young children's inability to resist adult coercion for fear of the consequences. The mothers are then asked to think of other examples in which they have felt coerced by authority figures or other prominent people in their current lives and in their childhoods. They are encouraged to remember and write down examples during the week so that they can bring them in to share the following week.

Reactions of Mothers

While the mothers tend to deny having experienced sexual coercion, and may feel that they are too unattractive to merit any sexual advances by authority figures, they are able to relate many other examples of feeling coerced nonsexually in their everyday lives. This exercise heightens the mothers' sensitivity to their children's dilemma; many bring up instances in which they had not properly protected their children from another adult's coercion. For example, one mother realized she had been unresponsive to her daughter's repeated protestations about sleeping in the same bed with the babysitter. Many mothers mention incidents when their children had resisted going unescorted to relatives' or friends' houses, and they wonder whether or not they should have forced their children in these situations. They realize that like their children, they themselves do not feel the freedom to say "no," and that they therefore have difficulty teaching their children this same right.

Module 2: What Happens When You Say "No"?

Given that a person has the right to say "no," how does one do this in a safe and nonhurtful manner? The children and their mothers not only lack the belief that they have the right to put limits on others, but they also lack the social skills necessary for successfully limiting coercive interactions. The goals for this particular module are as follows:

1. To help parents and children continue to increase their awareness that they do have the right to say "no."
2. To give parents and children practice in saying "no" and in anticipating perpetrators' or coercive persons' responses.
3. To assist mothers in increasing their understanding of why it is so hard for their children to say "no" to adult figures, thereby encouraging them to be more protective with their children.

Techniques Used with Children

The children are presented with examples involving coercion by an adult figure and are asked how they might say "no" and what the consequences might be. The following hypothetical situation can be presented to the children:

> Uncle Bruce was playing with Billy, and he loved to tease Billy and scare him by hiding behind couches and jumping out at him. He also liked to chase Billy around the house and make loud noises like he was a big monster. The trouble is that Billy got really scared when his uncle did this with him, and he wanted to tell his uncle to stop. But he was worried

that his uncle would get mad at him if he said, "Don't do that." What do you think that Billy can say to Uncle Bruce? Is there anything that Billy can say that won't make his uncle mad?

The children are then asked to respond as if they were in this situation. If they have difficulty, a child therapist can model various ways of responding, such as "Please don't scare me." After each response to the uncle, the children are then asked to talk about what the uncle might feel or say back: For example, would the uncle get mad at them?

Other similar situations can be presented to the children; they are role-played first by the therapists and then by the children. In one such situation involving an uncle and a child, the therapists can act out a scenario in which Uncle Larry keeps insisting that he wants his niece to sit on his lap so he can tickle her. She keeps trying to resist Uncle Larry's advances. This scene can be very powerful when the therapist playing the little girl acts tremendously confused and ambivalent about whether or not she should let Uncle Larry tickle her. In the scenario, the little girl eventually is able to say "no" to him. Then he says, "If you don't do this, you will get in trouble with your mom." The little girl then struggles with whether or not to comply, saying, "Maybe I should do this because I don't want to get in trouble with my mom. But then I know that Uncle Larry will tickle me too hard, and I hate that!" The little girl continues exploring her dilemma by saying, "Well, maybe I'll say 'no' to him even though I'm scared I'll get in trouble with my mother." The children are asked whether the girl should have said "no" to her uncle, and are given the opportunity to act out the parts of Uncle Larry and/or the little girl.

In the next role play, a stranger in a car approaches a child who is walking home from school and asks if the child wants a ride. One therapist plays the stranger, and another plays the little child. Afterwards, the children are usually eager to assume the roles that the child therapists have just played and to act out ways in which this child could have responded.

An important situation to present is one in which the sexual advances or inappropriate coercive behaviors are occurring in the presence of the mother or caretaker, who may be insensitive to or unaware of the child's negative reaction. The parent's failure to intervene would leave the child confused and unassertive, since the mother is seen as condoning the perpetrator's behavior. The children are told a story in which a child is sitting on a neighbor's lap and he is rocking the child back and forth while the mother is in the same room. He then starts to rub the child up and down over his crotch as he rocks in the chair and the child begins to feel funny about what the neighbor is doing. She doesn't like being rubbed up and down the neighbor's leg, but since her mother is in the same room, she figures that it must be okay. Therefore, she doesn't say anything to the neighbor, nor does her mother intervene. The children are asked whether they think the mother really knows that the neighbor is doing anything wrong. They then take turns practicing what they might say to their mother or to their neighbor in this particular situation. If they are having difficulty coming up with responses, the therapists model a few suggested responses for the children (e.g., getting down off the person's lap, or saying, "Mom, let's go home").

This module needs to be spread out over at least two sessions. It is most effective to intersperse several other sessions in between each repetition, thereby giving the children an opportunity to talk about their own attempts to assert themselves. In addition, the concept of assertion is not an easy one for small children to acquire, and they need a lot of practice.

Reactions of Children

Sexually abused children tend either to withdraw from the assertive task or to react in a very angry fashion. In role playing, some of the children threaten to hit the adults, while others either run away or comply. The inappropriateness of the use of physical force is discussed. Some of the children are able to offer appropriate responses, such as "Please stop tickling me. You are making me sick to my stomach." One sexually abused girl became quite anxious and asked to go to the bathroom, where she then began to masturbate.

Feedback Given to Mothers

The mothers are told briefly about their children's responses to the hypothetical stories. They are also warned that their children might begin to respond to them in a more assertive manner. The mothers are told that the angrier they become in response to their children, then the more successful their children have been in being assertive. They are encouraged to think about their children's appropriately assertive behavior in a more positive manner and to be less punitive in response.

Techniques Used with Mothers

First, the scenarios used in the children's group are described to the mothers, and they discuss whether a child really has the right to challenge adult authority. They need to struggle with the issue of how to maintain their authority while still allowing their children to express disagreement with them. Second, the mothers then report on some examples of coercion in their own childhoods that they have recorded over the past week. Third, a situation is presented where each mother is asked to imagine that she is at work and the boss comes in at three o'clock. He tells her that he has a special project that has to get out that evening, and therefore he needs her to work overtime. Ordinarily, this mother might have complied. However, today is her child's birthday and she has promised to take the child out for a special birthday dinner with some of her friends. The group explores possible responses to this situation. In addition, mothers are encouraged to bring in other examples of a similar nature, to allow practice in assertion skills.

Reactions of Mothers

The mothers seriously question whether or not their children will be able to successfully avoid the advances of sexual perpetrators, since they themselves are struggling with their own helplessness and inability to place limits on other people. They fear that their children will be hurt if they place limits on a perpetrator, and they frequently explore their own childhood memories of fearfulness in similar situations. While some mothers still may have grave doubts that their children could actually resist a perpetrator, most realize that they might have been more successful in resisting sexual abuse in their childhoods if they had received parental support.

MODULE 3: PRIVATE PARTS

This module should be introduced early in the curriculum, so that parents, children, and child therapists will all utilize the same labels in the succeeding play therapy exercises. The goals of this module are these:

1. To help parents and children arrive at mutual definitions and labels for sexual body parts so that they might more easily discuss these at home.
2. To assist children and parents to develop conceptions of appropriate and inappropriate touch between people.
3. To reinforce previous learning about how to assert oneself, utilizing appropriate labels for parts of the body.

This module is best spread across at least two sessions; this allows the children to integrate the material better.

Techniques Used with Children

Children are introduced to the topic of private parts through a discussion of "good touch and bad touch." The children are told that there are many kinds of good touch and that they can tell when touch is good because they feel nice and warm, and it does not worry or bother them. The following examples of good and bad touch are given.

> Holding hands is usually an example of good touch. However, holding hands can be bad touch if your hand gets hurt or pressed too hard by the other person.
> Being patted gently on the fanny by somebody who is close to you sometimes can feel good and sometimes [can] feel bad. If someone pats you too long on the fanny, then that is bad touch.
> Getting a kiss on your face or mouth feels good. However, a kiss can be bad touch if it comes from somebody that you don't like or if the kiss lasts too long.
> Being tickled too hard is one example of bad touch; however, if you get tickled real gently and it feels good, then that is an example of good touch, as long as you don't get tickled on your private parts.
> Whenever anybody touches your private parts, this is also an example of bad touch. [The few exceptions to this rule are described later on in this module.]

Each child receives two pictures (see Figure 13-1 through 13-3) of cartoon figures wearing bathing suits. While listening to the child therapist describe private parts, the children color these pictures, which they may later take home. They are told that their private parts are those parts of their bodies that are covered by a bathing suit, and that nobody has the right to touch them on their private parts, except sometimes parents or doctors. They are asked to point out "private

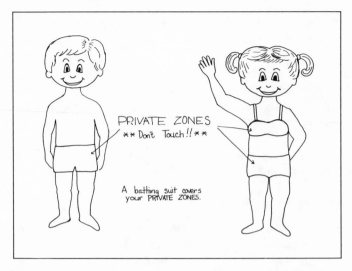

FIGURE 13-1. *Picture for children, illustrating "private zones."*

FIGURE 13-2. *Picture for helping boys describe "bad touch."*

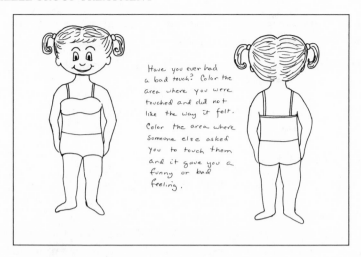

Inside figure image, handwritten text reads: Have you ever had a bad touch? Color the area where you were touched and did not like the way it felt. Color the area where someone else asked you to touch them and it gave you a funny or bad feeling.

FIGURE 13-3. *Picture for helping girls describe "bad touch."*

parts" with anatomically correct dolls and with felt figures in order to make sure that they have acquired this concept.

Hypothetical situations about good touch and bad touch are presented:

> What if your father or mother is washing you with the wash cloth on your private parts and keeps his or her hand there for a long time? Would this make you uncomfortable? Is this an example of good touch or bad touch?
>
> Is it okay for your mom or dad to pat you on the fanny? Is it okay for a neighbor to pat you on the fanny? When is it okay and when isn't it okay?

The children are reminded that good touch feels good and doesn't make them feel funny inside, and that sometimes they can feel both good and bad about a touch. It is stressed that it is all right for them to tell someone to stop if they get bad feelings.

> Is it okay for somebody to touch your private parts if your clothes are on?
>
> Is it okay if the doctor touches you on your private parts? (The therapists mention that sometimes children may not like being touched on their private parts, but that doctors are allowed to do that in order to complete an examination.)

The children are again assisted to talk about how they would respond to the following situations:

> Your grandmother is giving you a hug that feels good.
> Your dad is kissing you for too long.
> An uncle won't let go of you when you want to get off his lap.

The children's ability to use the special word "no" if needed is stressed repeatedly.

Reactions of Children

The children tend to react very positively to this material, as long as the child therapists provide sufficient structure and are sensitive to the children's increased expression of anxiety. As the children become more anxious, the therapists' reflection of their difficulty in listening to the presentation usually helps the children to become more focused. The children especially enjoy coloring their pictures and utilizing the dolls and the felt figures. Each should be able to use the phrase "private parts" and to talk abut good and bad touch by the time this module has been completed. Some of the children are able to begin monitoring one another's sexual behavior within the group setting. For example, one child told another girl to put her dress down and cover up her panties. The mothers report that their children start limiting other people's touching them and are able to verbalize the words "private parts" at home, as well as in other appropriate situations.

During this particular module, a few of the children may talk about sexual abuse that has occurred to them, some of which may be previously unknown to the parents and the therapists. For example, one girl disclosed that an uncle had sexually abused her, while a little boy revealed that his grandmother had touched his private parts. After this module, children seem to be much more trusting and open. Not only do they seem to be more comfortable with the continued introduction of the concept of sexuality, but they also begin to utilize the labels given to them in describing their experiences to the therapists. In addition, the children seem to stimulate one another to disclose more freely within the group setting.

Feedback Given to Mothers

The mothers are warned that their children might attempt to utilize their newly acquired skills by telling their mothers not to touch their private parts; this warning can help mothers to avoid punishing their children's new assertion techniques. Indeed, a few of the mothers may actually attempt to touch their children's private parts in order to determine whether their children will put limits on them. One mother reported that she put her foot on her child's penis while he was taking a bath and he told her not to touch him on his private parts; another related that she put her hands on her child's chest, and her daughter then told her to take her hands off her private parts. Another mother was surprised to have her child tell her that he didn't want her to bathe his private parts in the bathtub.

Techniques Used with Mothers

This module is introduced to the mothers in the same way as it is to the children; the mothers are shown the pictures used in the children's group and are told about the step-by-step examples that are given to the children regarding good touch and bad touch. This facilitates the mothers' discussion of inappropriate sexual advances that might have been made toward them when they were children. The topic of nurturance is raised, and the mother's ability to obtain nurturance from significant people in their own childhoods is discussed. Many women reveal that their sexual abusers were their only source of nurturance; as a result, they may still feel guilty about enjoying or seeking out sexualized nurturance with others. Previously denied or repressed memories of sexualized contact begin to emerge. Some of the women then begin to wonder if it is possible to trust males, and express concerns about further exploitation.

The term "sexual abuse" is then defined for the mothers as inappropriate verbal or physical sexualized contact with children, usually without penetration. An attempt is made to normalize the sexualized behaviors that can occur, in order to assist those mothers who deny the occurrence of sexual abuse to become more accepting of the possibility that it might indeed have occurred.

Reactions of Mothers

Before the exercise on private parts is presented to the children, the mothers are asked whether they want the child therapists to introduce terminology for the genitals in their discussion of private parts. Most mothers appear to be uncomfortable about this and do not want their children to learn the technical names for sexual parts of the body.

They anxiously express concern that their children will utilize these terms inappropriately with other people; this apparently reflects a wish to minimize their own, as well as their children's, sexuality. The consequence of mothers' typically punitive reactions to their children's masturbation are explored. The mothers gradually seem to become more aware of their own sexuality and more open to exploring their children's sexuality as well. Some of the mothers have raised questions about their own nudity around their children and about bathing with their children.

MODULE 4: WHO CAN YOU TELL?

Neither the mothers nor the children generally share their difficulties with other people. While they may entertain fantasies that others will help them deal with their hurt, they rarely take active steps toward obtaining assistance. This difficulty is compounded by the parents' desire to deny sexual abuse and maintain the family secret. At a very young age, children realize that they too must keep the secret. The goals of this module are as follows:

1. To help parents and children learn that they do not need to deal with painful feelings all by themselves.
2. To reinforce with both parents and children that sexual abuse and inappropriate sexual advances are not okay and must be stopped.
3. To help mothers and children acquire the belief that abuse can be stopped by approaching authority figures who can assist them.

Parts of the module need to be repeated over two or three different sessions.

Techniques Used with Children

The story of Uncle Larry, who wants to tickle his niece (used in Module 2), can be repeated. The children are encouraged to think about who might listen to a problem like this without getting mad or disbelieving their story. They then role-play the experience of telling the trusted adult about Uncle Larry's advances.

The theme of "Who Can You Tell?" also can be explored through the use of felt figures on a board, dolls, or puppets that represent nurses, doctors, police officers, teachers, mothers, and so on. After the child therapists model the use of puppets or dolls, the children use these play materials, familiarizing themselves with authority figures who are trained to respond to reports of child sexual abuse. With these play materials, a variety of scenarios of possible sexual abuse can be covered.

Once some children have talked about their sexually abusive experiences, they may become quite indiscriminate in sharing the abuse with casual acquaintances and neighbors. Children can be assisted through use of a story, illustrated by a picture out of a magazine, or a collage depicting a variety of adults and children. The little girl in the story has a touching problem, which she shares with all the people in the pictures. However, not all of them can help her, and some kids even make fun of her. Then pictures of the authority figures to whom one should turn, such as doctors, police, social workers, nurses, and the like, are shown, and the children are told that these are the people who try to help little children who have a touching problem. Nonsexual examples, such as worries about Mom being sick or the cat being lost, further illustrate the importance of talking to someone who will understand without making fun of a child. If a child continues to approach others indiscriminately after this exercise is completed, then the child's motivation and concerns about being a bad person because of the sexual abuse should be more thoroughly explored.

Reactions of Children

The children almost always report that they would not want to tell their mothers if somebody touched them in the wrong way. Most are concerned that their mothers would be angry with them. In one case, a girl who had previously been quite secretive about her incestuous experience finally told one of the teachers at school about what had happened to her, utilizing the terminology she had learned in the group. The school responded with thorough questioning of the girl, her sister, and their mother, until it was confirmed that the sexual abuse had already been reported. Unfortunately, the girl's report at school elicited a punitive response from the mother, who feared that her children would again be removed from her.

Feedback Given to Mothers

The mothers are advised that, following this module, their children may tell others about their sexual abuse, they are cautioned that they may feel angry or even betrayed if this happens. It is stressed that the children must learn how to approach other helpful authority figures in addition to their mothers, so that they have somebody to turn to whenever their mothers are not available to them.

Techniques Used with Mothers

The module begins with a presentation about how children tell their parents about sexual abuse, inappropriate touching, and nonsexual worries through their behavior and development of symptoms. The aim is to sensitize the mothers to the message behind some of their children's problematic behaviors. The following symptoms, which may indicate sexual abuse, are discussed in detail:

- Sleep problems
- Separation problems
- Irritability
- School or concentration problems
- Eating problems (undereating or overeating)
- Fearfulness at various times during the day or night
- Regressive behaviors
- Sexual play with other children ("humping," French kissing, etc.)
- Excessive masturbation

After this introduction, the mothers role-play a story entitled "Helping Susan" (see Appendix 13-1), involving a mother and child. The script describes two different reactions by a mother to her child's disclosure of sexual abuse to a neighbor—one an angry, destructive reaction, and the second a supportive exploration of the child's experiences and feelings. The mothers are helped to understand that their tendency to respond in a punitive manner is related to the way in which they were treated as children, and their disappointment in not obtaining support from authority figures during childhood is explored. Through role-playing, the mothers have the opportunity to concretely practice a way in which they might explore their own children's feelings about a traumatic event; they may take copies of the script home so that they can study and practice appropriate ways of responding to their children.

Next, "Jimmy's Bedtime Story" (see Appendix 13-2) is introduced to increase the mothers' skills and comfort in discussing sexual abuse with their children. The mothers take turns role-playing the parts of Jimmy and his mother, and receive a copy of the script to take home.

If the mothers still express anxiety about discussing sexual abuse with their children, they can receive further practice by responding to some of the following statements, typed onto cue cards:

> Grandpa sure looks funny without any clothes on.
> Why does Uncle Larry like to take a bath with me?
> I don't like getting undressed with my aunt.

Reactions of Mothers

This module—especially "Jimmy's Bedtime Story"—stimulates the mothers' anxiety, rage, and helplessness about their own sexual abuse. After exploring these feelings, they become increasingly comfortable in their attempts to approach the topic of resisting sexual abuse with their children. In the instance described previously, where one of the children shared her sexual abuse at school, the mother attempted to drop out of the group. It was important to empathize with her anger at the therapists for having suggested the possibility of approaching other authority figures and with her fear that her children might be removed from her.

MODULE 5: ANGER AND PUNISHMENT

A disclosure of sexual abuse is often greeted with intense anger by the parent. While one hopes that the anger is directed only toward the perpetrator, it is often directed toward the child also, either overtly or subtly. The goals of this module are these:

1. To help children understand that they might not always be the source of their parents' anger.
2. To encourage expression of the children's feelings of fearfulness and anger in response to their parents' anger, and to help them acquire the skills needed to talk with their parents about their feelings.
3. To help mothers be aware of how they show anger toward their children and what the impact of their anger is.
4. To assist mothers in learning how to channel their anger and gain more control over the expression of rage with their children.

Techniques Used with Children

The children are shown a picture or cartoon drawing of an angry person. The picture is identified as an angry face, and the children are asked what things they do that make parents mad. The child therapist gives several examples, such as "wetting my bed," "telling my mother I'm scared to go to sleep at night," "not minding my mother," and "telling my parents things that they don't want to hear about, such as somebody touching me on my private parts." Children's reactions to their parents' anger are explored.

The group then thinks about new methods that could be tried by children to help them deal with their parents' anger. A child therapist may say, "When my mom gets angry, then I get frightened, so I sit down and I draw a picture of my secret feelings." He or she can then demonstrate by drawing a picture. The children are given paper and asked to draw their feelings in the same way. The child therapists also raise the possibility of writing a note to the parent about their feelings, and assist any children who want to do so by doing the actual writing while the children dictate.

Additionally, the more direct route of talking with their parents about how they feel is demonstrated. A dialogue is role-played between two child therapists:

CHILD: Mommy, I'm really scared because you are so mad at me. Do you hate me?
MOTHER: I'm sorry I scared you, I'm just mad because this happened to you and everybody is upset with us. I don't hate you at all!

The children are encouraged to take turns playing the parts of child and mother, while the therapists give them feedback; asking a parent in an appropriate manner that minimizes the parent's anger and defensiveness is stressed.

Next, a child therapist playing a little girl tells the following story:

> I'm really worried that my uncle touched me on my private parts. I told my mother and now I'm worried about what is going to happen to him. My mother was so mad that she said she was going to kill him or beat him up. I'm really scared. I am so worried I can't sleep at night and I'm even wetting my bed. I can't stop from running around, and my mom gets mad at me because I keep moving all of the time. My stomach hurts and I can hardly eat. I wish I could tell my mother not to hurt my uncle. Do you think I can tell my mother not to hurt him?

The children are asked to give ideas about how they would try to tell their mother about their fears if they were this little girl. The child therapists can assist through role playing;

CHILD: I'm so scared because you are so mad at my uncle. Are you going to kill him like you said?
MOTHER: Oh, no, I am not going to kill him. I'm just so mad at him that I feel like killing him, but I'm not going to.

The children can then be engaged in a conversation about killing and violence, how they feel about what happens on TV, and whether they think such things happen in real life.

Reactions of Children

Even children with good reality contact respond with a great deal of anxiety in the beginning of this module, but tend to deal better with the topic as the child therapists provide more structure. More disturbed children may relate disjointed, aggressive fantasies and descriptions of violent incidents that happened to them or to others around them. Some express their anxiety motorically—for example, crashing cars into one another; the child therapists help them put their feelings into words. Others react with vivid fantasies in which they role-play destroying one of their parents or the abuser. The children may worry that the mothers can "feel" their anger or will be destroyed by it, and need reassurance that neither will happen.

Feedback Given to Mothers

The mothers are warned that their children may try to practice talking to them about feelings they might have in response to the mothers' anger, and possible ways of responding are covered in the mothers' meeting. If a child appears overinvolved with violent fantasies, the mother is encouraged to monitor actual and televised violence at home.

Techniques Used with Mothers

The first exercise involves early memories of how the mothers' parents and other significant people expressed anger, including whether threats of violence or actual violence were used in their own families. The mothers are encouraged to reflect on the impact that threats and violence had upon them as children. They then engage in a discussion of how they each currently express anger toward or in the presence of their children. Alternate ways of managing anger are explored, using anger management techniques (e.g., removing themselves from their children when they feel explosive, counting to 10, going to their own room and beating up a pillow, writing down their own angry feelings, etc.). The link between parental expression of anger and children's resulting expression of anger, fearfulness, and negativism is emphasized.

In explaining the children's exercises to the mothers, the therapist inquires about how they might feel if their children shared their fears in a manner similar to what was role-played by the child therapists. The mothers then take turns playing the part of the mother and the child in carrying out the same role play that the children experienced. This prepares the mothers for possible approaches their children might use when they feel upset by their mothers' expressions of anger.

Reactions of Mothers

The mothers are able to explore their early memories of violence and anger. Some are surprised to see that their children might be as frightened of them as they were of their parents when they were growing up. It is typical for mothers to report in later sessions that they are trying to monitor their violence and threats of violence in front of their children. Some mothers also later report that their children are telling them when they feel frightened by them, and they are able to respond appropriately.

MODULE 6: WHAT HAPPENS WHEN YOU TELL?

Children's disclosures of sexual abuse do not always bring sympathetic understanding from adults. Very often, the first response is disbelief, denial, or anger at the children. Even when parents initially accept the reported sexual abuse, they may later collude and minimize or attempt to alter their children's stories in order to keep their families intact or smooth things over. In these cases, the children certainly do not experience the act of telling adults as helpful. Therefore, it seems important to inform children about the possible consequences of their disclosure, allowing the therapists to maintain credibility and preserve the trust of the children. This module may be presented two or three times. The goals of this module are as follows:

1. To prepare both mothers and children for the consequences of disclosing incidents of sexual abuse.

2. To offer empathy to both mothers and children and to validate their anger and disappointment for the lack of support from other important figures in their lives.
3. To assist parents and children to explore their feelings and reactions to any previous disclosures of sexual abuse.
4. To help mothers and children understand why there is often confusion and contradiction in children's accounts of the sexual abuse.

Techniques Used with Children

The module begins with a child therapist reading or acting out the story of Susie, a little girl who tells about her secret of sexual abuse at school. The story is as follows:

> I live in a house with my mother, my dad, my grandfather, and my dog. My grandfather started to come into the bathroom and look at me taking a bath. I thought maybe that was okay since he was older than me and he was trying to look after me. First he touched my arm, but then he started to touch my private parts. He told me not to tell my parents or else he would have to leave the house. I didn't want him to go, so I didn't tell Mom or Dad. But I told a teacher at school one day that my grandfather was touching my private parts. And then a social worker came to our house and we had to go to court after that. Now my grandfather can't stay with us any more, and I can't see him alone any more because that's what the judge said. My mom and dad got really upset that I had told the secret and they were very mad that a social worker came to our house. I think they were also mad because they had to go to court. My parents still get mad at me sometimes, and I worry that they don't love me as much as they used to. Sometimes I want to hurt myself to see if they really care about me. Do you think I should have told the teacher at school about what Grandpa did to me? What should I do about my mommy and daddy being so mad at me? Why did the judge say I can't be alone with Grandpa?

When anxiety about the parents' anger with Susie arises, the children's feelings are responded to empathically, and the child therapists role-play a conversation between Susie and her mother to model how a child might respond in this situation:

SUSIE: Do you still love me after I told the teacher about Grandpa?
MOTHER: You shouldn't have told the teacher about what happened. Why didn't you just tell me about it?
SUSIE: But I didn't think you would believe me if I told you, and

Grandpa said I shouldn't tell you. He told me that if I told you, he would have to go away.

MOTHER: Well, I sure miss Grandpa and I'm mad that you didn't tell me. But I love you anyway.

The children are then asked whether anything like what happened in the story has ever happened to them. After they bring up examples from their own lives, they are given the opportunity to take turns role-playing the angry parent and the child who has disclosed. The child therapists can act as "alter egos" if the children need help in playing out the roles. It is communicated that even though parents may initially respond with anger or disbelief, the anger may eventually go away, and does not mean the parents have stopped loving the children. The importance of telling the secret to somebody who can help them is stressed, even though it is painful to do so.

The second story is about a little boy named Jimmy and deals with a common reaction of children who receive negative consequences for disclosing; they may retract their story and deny that the sexual abuse occurred. A child therapist role-plays Jimmy and says:

> I told the principal about my uncle touching me on my private parts. Everybody at school got real upset and asked me lots of questions. So finally I told the principal that it didn't really happen.

At this point, the children are asked whether or not they think that Jimmy was touched on his private parts by his uncle, and why they think he changed his story. Jimmy continues:

> I am really mixed up because I don't want to get my uncle in trouble, but my therapist told me I am supposed to tell grownups when someone touches my private parts. I like my uncle, and I don't want to get him in trouble.

The children are now asked what Jimmy feels; fear about getting somebody in trouble and confusion in Jimmy's feelings are discussed. Jimmy resumes:

> I was afraid to tell my mom about what my uncle did because I was sure she would get mad at me, and that she wouldn't believe me, but now she is going to find out anyway. So now I am really worried. I did what I was supposed to do and told someone about my uncle touching my private parts, but now I am worried about it.

The children are asked whether they think Jimmy should have told the principal about his uncle touching his private parts. They generally respond, "No, because he is going to get in trouble." It is emphasized that it is not Jimmy's fault, even if it felt good to Jimmy when his uncle touched him. The child therapists reflect understanding of the children's dilemma about disclosure and may need to reiterate the reasons for telling a grownup who can help protect them about the sexual abuse. It should be mentioned that whenever children tell about someone touching their private parts, adults will ask them a lot of questions in order to find out all of the information; however, this does not mean that they are not believed.

Reactions of Children

The children's concern about their parents' anger at them is greatly attenuated after this module and the preceding one have been completed. One girl, who had been a long-term victim of incest with continuing family denial, began to test out the child therapists by asking them to tell her secrets about themselves or by telling them secrets about herself. In her play, she became angry with a child therapist who would not disclose some confidential information to her, despite her insistence; her confusion about whether or not to disclose her secrets was then discussed.

Feedback Given to Mothers

The mothers are advised that the children might begin sharing more information about any sexual abuse that has occurred to them in the past or may be occurring in the present. The possibility that the children may be very concerned about the parents' getting angry is also discussed.

Techniques Used with Mothers

The mothers are asked whether or not they disclosed their own sexual abuse to their parents or other authority figures, and why they might have withheld disclosure. The mothers discuss in detail their fears that if they had disclosed the secret, then the perpetrators would have left home (if they were fathers or other relatives) or would have harmed them. Other fears center on being blamed for the abuse or feeling responsible for it. Mothers recount mixed messages they may have received from their parents. For women who were the victims of father–daughter incest, their own mothers' difficulty with the abuse is related to jealousy and competition with their children, and their concerns about their own adequacy as women and as sexual partners. The mothers are also asked what might have helped them deal better with their secret.

They then discuss whether or not they would believe their children if future disclosures of sexual abuse were made, and how they think they would cope with such disclosures. It is stressed that young children are unable to manufacture fantasies about sexual abuse unless they have some kind of experience as a basis, so that it is very important to take such stories seriously.

Reactions of Mothers

Almost universally, the mothers agree that it would have been most helpful if they could have had someone to talk to about their secret. They share their fantasies that some helpful adult would have noticed their distress and seen that they needed assistance. They frequently feel that, as children, they communicated their pain through silence and withdrawal, and they remember being unable to understand why adults did not respond to their silent suffering. It apparently would have helped the mothers if they had received sex education at home, and they frequently request assistance from the therapists in learning how to talk with their children about sex. Their request signals a growing acceptance of their own sexuality and a willingness to educate their own children about sex.

One mother stated that although her own mother accused her of lying about her father's sexual abuse of her, her mother began locking her daughter's bedroom door at night.

Module 7: What Happened to You?

This module allows the children to address their feelings of anger, hurt, and even enjoyment of the sexual acts in which they have engaged as they demonstrate and tell one another about their experiences, using anatomically correct dolls. The goals of this module are these:

1. To facilitate sharing among the children, thus reducing their sense of isolation and shame.
2. To assist them in expressing various feelings accompanying their sexual abuse.

3. To allow the children to receive appropriate comfort, nurturance, and validation of their experiences from therapists and other children.
4. To reinforce the children for just being able to "live through" the experience.

This module generally takes several sessions.

Techniques Used with Children

Young children have a very difficult time describing their experiences, because of their lack of verbal skills, their inability to determine exactly what behaviors were inappropriate, their repression, and their high level of anxiety about disclosure. Therefore, it is very helpful to use role playing and doll play to "show" rather than tell. In order to facilitate disclosure, it is usually necessary for a therapist to begin the module with a role play. The following dialogue can be acted out by two therapists, one playing an empathic therapist and the other a molested child ashamed to disclose:

THERAPIST: Why don't you try to show me how your private parts were played with by using these dolls? Were the dolls' clothes on or off?

CHILD: I can't tell you. I hate these dolls. (*She throws the dolls across the room.*) I promised not to tell.

THERAPIST: I know you promised not to tell, but why don't you show me what happened?

CHILD: Okay. (*She then begins to show fondling, etc., with dolls.*)

After the role play, the children are given the opportunity to act out how a girl or boy was molested. They may need to distance themselves from the abuse by telling a "story" about a child who was abused. Similarly, it may be necessary for them to place puppets on their hands before picking up the dolls, or to use a pointer to facilitate their explanation. Children will usually respond to instructions to demonstrate the events, although they may need to stop the demonstration periodically as their anxiety level mounts. The therapist can allow a little digression and then bring the children back to the demonstration of abuse. Each child may need 30 to 45 minutes to complete the demonstration. The child is encouraged to express any feelings, positive or negative, toward the molester as the demonstration proceeds. The process allows the other children to voice how they might have felt if they were in the shoes of the little boy or girl portrayed.

Reactions of Children

Children are usually very enthusiastic about having their turn to demonstrate, once the therapist has started the process. Some children become quite tangential and need to be refocused or told that they will have another opportunity in the future to show what happened if they are too anxious. Some children are able to identify additional perpetrators or additional sexual acts. Children seem to benefit from being able to express anger toward the perpetrator doll, and they often seem to experience a sense of mastery by fantasizing that they were rescued from the perpetrator by a hero or that they were able to get free.

Some children express only loving feelings and acceptance toward the perpetrator doll, stating that there is nothing wrong with what was done to them. These children are obviously at very high risk for remolestation, and their special needs are addressed in Module 8, "Fault and Responsibility."

Feedback Given to Mothers

Mothers are told if their children gave additional, previously unknown information about their abuse. In addition, mothers are warned that their children may be especially angry or regressive if they have nonverbally disclosed more information through the doll play and therefore are now dealing with previously unacceptable and repressed material. Once the children allow themselves to experience anger toward the perpetrators, then they may continue to be quite angry with their mothers, siblings, peers, and authority figures for 2 to 3 weeks. Mothers are encouraged to validate the anger while maintaining consistent limits.

Techniques Used with Mothers

Mothers are told that their children will be demonstrating their abuse for several weeks, and the goals of the module are explained to them. During the time period of this module, details disclosed by their children the previous week are shared with the mothers, as mentioned above. This allows them to experience additional rage or guilt related to their children's abuse.

The mothers' role in relationship to the nonprotection of the children is explored, with emphasis on what they have learned and what they would do differently in the future. Mothers are warned that children will probably be angry with them for not providing better protection. They are also told that since the perpetrators are usually inaccessible to the children, they may then displace anger toward the perpetrators onto the mothers.

Reactions of Mothers

Mothers experience additional pain and anger as their children go through this module. Some of the mothers realize that they have not shared their anger toward the perpetrators with their children, and they are encouraged to do so in an appropriate manner. After the mothers have shared their anger, the children's anger with their mothers usually is dissipated, because they feel both aligned with and protected by them.

One mother with unresolved conflicts about her own history of molestation became very distressed upon hearing about some of the other children's abuse, and insisted on pulling her child out of the group because she feared that her child would become overly sexualized. They were placed in individual therapy because the mother appeared to be too distressed and stimulated by the children's activities to continue in the group.

MODULE 8: FAULT AND RESPONSIBILITY

The issue of who is responsible for the sexual abuse and its consequences is addressed in this module with the children and their mothers. Cognitively, children under the age of 7 are egocentric; they tend to see themselves as the cause of most actions, including those over which they in fact have no control. Therefore, they are apt to assume responsibility for their sexual abuse. Young children's tendency to assume responsibility is further heightened by the scapegoating and blaming of them that frequently occurs. Removal of a child from the home may reinforce the sense of blame. Some aspects of the sexual abuse may have felt good to a child, and the child may actively have sought nurturance from the perpetrator at times. Additionally, the mother may attribute sexualized motivations to the child's behavior, and may respond harshly to innocent attempts to seek out nurturance from other adults. Furthermore, research done by Terr (1983) suggests that older children and adults tend to assume responsibility for traumatic events over which they had no control in order to avoid feeling helpless. The goals of this module are as follows:

1. To reiterate clearly and emphatically to both mothers and children that it is adults who are responsible for sexual abuse, and not children; even if a child seeks out sexual contact and/or enjoys aspects of it, it is still the adult's responsibility to stop inappropriate touching and sexualized contact.
2. To clarify that it is adults' responsibility to protect children from future sexual abuse.
3. To help both mothers and children develop a clearer understanding of the boundaries between sex and affection, and to assist the children in learning appropriate alternative techniques to attain nurturance from others.
4. To help both mothers and children let go of the responsibility and guilt they have assumed for the sexual abuse, and give up self-punitive behaviors developed as a consequence.

Techniques Used with Children

The module begins with the following role play by two child therapists. The first one plays Bobby:

> My aunt touched my private parts for a long time. I am afraid to tell my mommy that she put her hands on my private parts, because I am worried that she will think it was my fault. Besides, it did feel kind of good, and so I am sure it must be my fault. I know my mom will get upset if I tell her about it, and I know she will blame me for it. Do you think it was my fault that this happened?

After the children respond to Bobby's question, the second child therapist also responds:

> This was not Bobby's fault, because he is just a little boy and he didn't even start it. It was his aunt who started touching his private parts. But even if Bobby did start it and put his aunt's hand on his private parts, it's still not Bobby's fault because it is up to his aunt or to the adult to stop touching his private parts. Adults are not supposed to act this way with children. Do you think his mom would get mad at Bobby?

The second scenario in this module, about a little girl named Rosie, is especially helpful for children who have been removed from the home after sexual abuse has occurred:

> My name is Rosie and I feel really sad. My daddy touched me on my private parts, and finally one day I told a nurse at school. She called the police, who came and picked me up and took me away from home. They made me go stay with some other people in a foster home. They tell me I have to stay there so that my daddy can't touch my private parts again. I know it must be my fault that my daddy touched me on my private parts because they took me away from my mommy and my daddy. They punished me by taking me away, and so I know it was my fault.

A child therapist responds:

> Rosie, I know that you feel like it is your fault that this happened, and I know it makes you feel very sad, and you are even mad at yourself because you think you made this happen. And I feel very sad also, but you know it's really not your fault at all. Your daddy never should have touched your private parts, and you had to tell somebody about it. The sad thing is that they took you away from your home, and that made you feel even more like it was your fault. But you know they didn't take you away from your home because you were bad or because it was your fault. The reason that they took you away from your home was to protect you so that your daddy won't do this again to you.

Some children are able to mouth the words that the sexual abuse was not their fault, without convincing affect. It can be counter-therapeutic for these children if the therapist continues to talk them out of their feelings of responsibility, because the child may feel un-heard and unvalidated.[1] In fact, these children may be identifying with the aggressor to a certain extent, because they too have attempted to engage or are still engaging in sexual acts with other children or adults, or because they enjoyed the sexual acts. These children need to struggle with and confront their feelings of responsibility and the accompanying feelings of shame for behaviors labeled "wrong." If they are unable to confront their shame over their real or imagined transgression, then they will continue to be fearful of abandonment for their behavior.[2] For these children, it is important to explore whatever happened that leads them to believe that they are still re-

1. We are indebted to Rachel Downing, LCSW, for these insights.
2. We gratefully acknowledge Saul Neidorf, MD, for material about the concept of shame.

sponsible. The following role play, using therapists, dolls, or puppets, may help validate and deal with some children's continuing sense of responsibility:

THERAPIST: You know, Rosie, I think you still feel responsible for the way your daddy touched you. You don't seem to believe that it's not your fault that your daddy touched your private parts.

ROSIE: It was my fault.

THERAPIST: What makes you feel that it was your fault?

ROSIE: I can't tell.

THERAPIST: Maybe you're afraid that I won't like you if you tell me. You know, there's nothing you could do that would make me dislike you, and I guess it's hard for you to believe that.

ROSIE: You would hate me if I told you.

THERAPIST: I wouldn't. I could forgive you for anything you did.

ROSIE: (*Said with distress*) Well, I sucked my brother's pee-pee and I'm as bad as my father. I made my brother take his pants off.

THERAPIST: Now I understand why you feel so ashamed. It must feel terrible to you to know that you tricked your brother the same way that your father tricked you.

ROSIE: (*Sobbing*) I have been so ashamed and afraid people would hate me if they knew.

THERAPIST: I don't hate you. I forgive you. Do you believe me?

ROSIE: I'm not sure.

The therapist asks the other children if they forgive Rosie too. The other children are then asked to role-play a child who feels ashamed of his or her behavior. They can choose to whisper to one therapist, if necessary, before sharing with the whole group.

Throughout the group sessions, whenever children attempt to engage adults or children through sexualized behaviors, the therapists interpret the meaning of the behavior and suggest alternative ways for them to get their needs met. For example, one girl jumped onto the arm of a male child therapist and started rubbing her vagina across his arm. He informed her that it was not okay to act this way with adults or with children; however, if she wanted, she could come and sit on his lap or sit next to him while he read a story to her. The child therapists are frequently bewildered and threatened by the sexual provocations of the children and may respond in an inappropriately rejecting and harsh manner, rather than simply setting clear limits. Child therapists must be given the opportunity to discuss the strong and possibly frightening feelings elicited by role-playing a perpetrator or being approached sexually by young children. Ongoing supervision is essential for the child therapists.

Reactions of Children

It is very difficult for the children to acknowledge that the sexual abuse was not their fault, and they benefit from repeated opportunities to engage in the role-playing situations. Some of the children are eventually able to assert that they were not responsible. The children's self-punitive and sexualized behaviors begin to diminish as a result of interpretations and suggestions of alternative behaviors that the children could utilize to engage others. Some children also stop other children's sexualized interactions.

Feedback Given to Mothers

The mothers are told that the children are being taught that they should not take responsibility and blame for all events that happen to them, especially with regard to sexual abuse by adults. They are cautioned that their children might attempt to test out this new attribution by proclaiming that certain things are not their fault. If the children are *not* responsible, it is suggested that the mothers offer positive reinforcement for these assertions.

Techniques Used with Mothers

The mothers are first told about the vignettes used with the children, and are then asked to recall their own feelings of fault and responsibility for their sexual abuse as children. They must begin to realize that as young children, they were unable to avoid the sexual abuse, yet still assumed full responsibility for it. The discussion then centers on what kinds of messages the mothers received from their own families about who was responsible.

Reactions of Mothers

As the mothers explore their reactions to their sexual abuse, they become more aware of they might be blaming their own children. For instance, one mother revealed that she felt so guilty about her enjoyment of a sexual relationship wtih a family friend that she had never been able to previously disclose it. After sharing her feelings, this mother was able to become much more protective toward her own girls. Some mothers express anger or concern about their daughters' seeking out even unsexualized nurturance from other adult figures, fearing that they might resort to promiscuous sexuality in order to get attention from men in the future. One mother, whose daughters were sexually abused by her husband, was able to begin to acknowledge her feelings of competitiveness and the underlying sexual inadequacies she felt as a result of her perception that her husband preferred her daughters sexually.

MODULE 9: SEPARATION

After a disclosure of sexual abuse by a father or stepfather, typically either the child or the offender is removed from the home. Thus, not only the child, but also the mother and other siblings undergo the often overwhelming pain of separation. Unfortunately, the pain of the actual separation may get lost in the chaos, anxiety, and anger that follows disclosure of sexual abuse. A child's attempts to talk about where Daddy is or missing Daddy may be greeted with an angry attack on the part of the mother, who is defending against her own sadness. Thus, the child quickly learns that it may not be safe to talk about sadness and anger about the loss of the perpetrator with the mother. The goals of this module are these:

1. To assist family members in expressing their sadness and anger with regard to separation.
2. To help mothers acknowledge that their own pain is heightened by that of their children, thereby sometimes causing them to respond angrily rather than supportively.

Techniques Used with Children

The child therapists begin by role playing:

> I really miss my grandpa. He is the only one who really had the time to hold me. He must have really loved me, and I really loved him too. But now he is gone and sometimes I feel really sad at night. Sometimes my tummy hurts and I cry and then I feel better, but my mommy doesn't

like to see me cry because it makes her sad too. Have you ever gotten sad about somebody who has left you?

The children are encouraged to talk about loved ones who are no longer in their lives, including grandparents, relatives, their mothers' old boyfriends, pets, and so forth. They are asked if they ever cry about these loved ones, get angry that they are gone, or wonder how to find them.

The departure of a child or of a therapist from the group can give children the opportunity, once again, to deal with their feelings of separation and loss. Puppet play may be utilized by the child therapists to engage the children in discussing the planned departure of a child or a therapist. For example, wearing a hand puppet, a therapist may say:

> You know Johnny's moving away today and I feel real sad. I cried and cried for days and then I got real angry. So, now that Johnny's leaving, I feel real sad again, and it reminds me of all the other times that I felt sad when people have left me.

Additionally, children are presented with a Xeroxed picture from a storybook of a sad-looking child. As the children color their pictures, each tells a story about the child in the picture; the therapists then copy the stories down on the children's pictures and talk about their feelings with them.

Reactions of Children

In spite of their anxiety about separation issues, most children become involved in the activities. Some are able to talk quite openly about their sadness and anger with the persons they miss. One little girl returned the following week and laid her head in a child therapist's lap, crying for a long period of time about the departure of her father. Another girl said that she wasn't able to talk to her mother about missing her father because her mom would get mad at her; a session involving both the mother and the girl was arranged to facilitate their discussion of feelings about the absent father.

The therapists may need to deal with multiple expressions of children's feelings surrounding a separation. For example, the father of one girl moved out of the home during the group. Their dog had a litter of puppies shortly thereafter, and the mother eventually gave the puppies away because they were wetting all over the house. Right after the father left, the little girl began wetting her bed, and her symptoms increased when the mother gave away the puppies. She revealed that she was frightened that she too would be sent away, like her father and the puppies. The mother was able to reassure her daughter once she understood the dynamics behind the symptom.

Feedback Given to Mothers

The mothers are advised that the children might begin to express some anger and sadness regarding the loss of significant others from their lives, as well as to ask more questions about the absent persons.

Techniques Used with Mothers

The mothers are asked to recall childhood memories of separations from loved ones, and to share their feelings about those experiences. They try to remember why they thought the separations occurred and whether or not they assumed any responsibility for them. They explore the coping mechanisms they used to deal with their anger, sadness and guilt surrounding the separation experiences.

The question of how one helps a person who is sad about a separation is explored. Typical but ineffective methods of trying to help people are discussed, such as "Don't be sad," or "Stop crying— let's see you put a big smile on your face." They are encouraged to experiment at home with more effective ways of helping their children deal with sad feelings, such as reflection of feelings, allowing the children's appropriate emotional expressions, and responding with nurturance. Mothers then discuss which significant people have left the children, in order to optimize their handling of their children's feelings.

Reactions of Mothers

Mothers are able to recall some meaningful, previously unavailable material about why they thought some significant people had left their lives. For example, one mother remembered that on the day her parents separated, her father gave her a cup of tea to drink, which angered her mother; she thought that this was the reason her mother asked her father to leave. Another mother recalled that her father left one day when she was sick, and therefore she thought that her illness drove him away.

MODULE 10: WHAT HAPPENS TO THE PERPETRATOR?

Guilt, worry, and concern about the perpetrator may weigh very heavily on the mother, the abused child, and other family members as
well. It is sometimes difficult to comprehend the consequences of
sexual abuse for the perpetrator, and it is frequently hard for family
members to accept that the consequences may be justified, especially
if the perpetrator has to go to prison. In addition, the court and
investigation processes are very confusing and scary to family members, since the possible consequences are unclear, potentially severe,
and extremely unpredictable. The goals of this module are as follows:

1. To provide children and mothers with information about the
   workings of the criminal and dependency court systems, and
   to confirm that the process is indeed confusing, frequently
   arbitrary, and occasionally unjust.
2. To help families understand that sometimes prison or monitored visitation may be the best way, or the only way, to prevent
   further damage to the children.

Techniques Used with Children

A child therapist retells one of the previous stories about a perpetrator
(such as "Uncle Larry" from Module 2 or "Susie" from Module 6)
and then asks what the children think will happen to the perpetrator
in the story. Their reactions to the various options, such as monitored
visitation, seeing a psychotherapist, or going to jail, are explored.
However, it is unlikely that a perpetrator involved with a child under
3 or 4 years of age will go to prison, because children under this age
generally cannot qualify to give testimony that will be acceptable in
criminal court.

The following explanation can be given by a child therapist, who
asks questions and encourages discussion where indicated:

> It is against the law for a grownup to touch a child's private parts. So
> an adult may go to jail for touching your private parts, because that's
> against the law. When people break the law, they need to be punished,
> or sometimes they need to get counseling because they have a problem.
> It's not your fault if somebody you know went to jail; it's the fault of the
> grownup who touched your private parts.
>   Sometimes the person who touches a little child's private parts does
> not go to jail because people don't believe the child. Do you think people
> believed you? Even if they did believe you, the police need to have proof

that it happened in order to punish the grownup person. Now the problem is that usually little children have not yet learned how to tell time and know about dates. They can't do that until they are a lot older, usually 8 or 9 years old. Did any of you have to talk about dates and times when you talked to policemen or social workers or lawyers or judges?

Reactions of Children

The children are generally quite concerned about the possibility that loved ones may have to go to prison. They easily understand that it is against the law for the perpetrators to sexually abuse them, and it makes sense to them that the sexual abuse may be punished by a prison sentence because a law is broken. Viewing the abuse as against the law as well as against themselves may be helpful for them. Nonetheless, as discussed in the preceding module, separation may still be very painful for everybody.

Feedback Given to Mothers

The mothers are told that the children may raise questions about what will happen to the perpetrators, as well as about appropriate punishment for themselves or other people, since they are struggling with the idea of just punishment for offenses.

Techniques Used with Mothers

The same information given to the children about what might happen to the perpetrators is also shared with the mothers. In addition, their confusion and anger about the criminal court system is explored thoroughly, if this is needed.

Reactions of Mothers

The mothers express a great deal of hostility about the arbitrariness of the criminal court system. They also feel angry that they seem to bear the brunt of the punishment as well as the blame for their children's sexual abuse, even in cases where they reported the sexual abuse to the police. The anger of mothers who acknowledge that sexual abuse occurred is especially acute in cases where the perpetrators did not go before a criminal court or where they were not ever charged with sexual abuse because the children were too young to testify.

MODULE 11: INTEGRATION OF POSITIVE AND NEGATIVE FEELINGS TOWARD THE PERPETRATOR

Both mothers and children have a great deal of difficulty integrating their positive and negative feelings toward perpetrators. Since sex offenders are highly frowned upon in our society, it is very shocking and traumatic for a mother in an incestuous family to realize that she has been involved with somebody as "perverted" as a child molester. At the same time, the mother may still care very much about the perpetrator and be unwilling to relinquish him totally. From the child's point of view, even though he or she may have been hurt during the abuse, the offender has also frequently provided a great deal of nurturance. The goals of this module are these:

1. To assist children and mothers to better integrate their positive and negative feelings about the perpetrators.
2. To help mothers gain a clearer understanding of the dynamics of the sexual offender (Groth, 1982), allowing them to accept more easily that they have cared about persons who have also sexually abused their children.

Techniques Used with Children

A child therapist role-plays Jenny, a sexually abused child, and addresses a series of questions to the children and remaining child therapists. If the children do not respond, other child therapists reassure Jenny, commenting on both the positive and negative aspects of feelings expressed.

> I'm really confused about my grandfather. My mother says that he is sick and he has something wrong with him because he touched my private parts. But I really love him. He used to hold me all the time. But if he is bad, is it okay for me to love him?
>
> If my grandfather is bad because he touched my private parts, does that mean that I am bad too?
>
> I'm mad because my grandfather left me and because of what he did to me. Could he really love me and still do those kinds of things to me?
>
> My grandfather never calls me or writes me any more. Does that mean he doesn't love me? Are other grandparents like my grandfather?

The technique may be broadened to allow work on integrating

positive and negative feelings about significant people with other confusing problems. Here is one example:

> I'm really confused about my daddy because he is not around any more. He had to leave because he uses drugs. Does that mean that he is a bad person because he uses drugs? Am I bad because I love him? Will I grow up to be a bum like him?

Reactions of Children

Some children respond with sadness to the vignettes given. However, the techniques seem effective in helping the children begin to clarify and integrate their positive and negative feelings about the perpetrators.

Feedback Given to Mothers

It is suggested to the mothers that their children may talk about their conflicting feelings toward the perpetrators.

Techniques Used with Mothers

After discussing the children's material, the mothers are encouraged to talk about their own conflicting feelings toward the perpetrators. It is a very important step when some mothers are able to admit that, in spite of their anger, they still love the perpetrators and often think about going back to them, even if court-ordered to avoid them. The mothers examine their attraction to the perpetrators, explore their feelings of self-doubt, and begin to see their increased self-destructive behaviors as ways of punishing themselves for involvement with sexually abusive persons.

Reactions of Mothers

The mothers are able to share both their strong positive feelings about and their rage with the perpetrators. They also express a good deal of anger toward themselves for having become involved with such persons. Exploring these feelings seems to foster greater self-acceptance.

MODULE 12: WHAT IF THE DENIAL IS MAINTAINED?

Unfortunately, even after an investigation, a child sometimes is returned to the same environment in which the perpetrator resides or frequently visits because of a retraction or inadequate information. The family may continue to deny that the sexual abuse occurred, or they may express overt or covert hostility toward the child for betraying the family secret. Children's needs to maintain the denial must be respected and handled sensitively by the therapeutic staff. Additionally, the children may have concerns about their own reality testing and whether or not they actually imagined the sexual abuse. The goals of this module are as follows:

1. To communicate understanding and empathy to the children concerning the confusion over what the truth is and concerning the need to keep the secret.
2. To confront mothers with the potentially destructive consequences of denying the abuse, so that they may at least be more protective of their children, even if they cannot openly admit that the abuse has occurred.
3. To reinforce with both mothers and children the importance of maintaining appropriate sexual and generational boundaries.
4. To stress to children that if the sexual abuse continues, they need to tell a therapist or other helping authority.

Techniques Used with Children

The following dialogue is role-played by two child therapists:

JANIE: Once I told my mom about how my dad had touched my private parts and she got mad at me and didn't believe me. Then I had to go to court and talk to the judge about it, but I don't think anybody believed me. So now I don't tell anybody about my secret. I never talk to my mother about him touching my private parts because I don't want her to get mad at me. Besides, I want my daddy to still stay with me, so I keep quiet about it.

CHILD THERAPIST: It must be really hard for you to keep the secret.

JANIE: I have to. If I don't, my parents will get mad at me and I'll get in more trouble. Besides, they don't believe me.

CHILD THERAPIST: You must have to be awfully careful if you can't tell anybody about your secret. It must make you feel really sad and lonely sometimes.

JANIE: Yes, sometimes I wonder if I am the only kid who has to keep a secret like this.

CHILD THERAPIST: Oh, no. Lots of kids keep secrets because they think they have to protect their family, too. Sometimes kids will keep a secret from their mommy or daddy because they have been told to, and all of these kids feel very alone because they have to keep the secret. And they all think that they are the only person who has to keep a secret too. But you know what? Sometimes these kids find a grownup or another kid to tell about their secret, and then they feel a little bit better. But you must never tell your secret to somebody whom you don't really trust.

JANIE: I wish I could talk to some of those kids so that I won't feel so lonely.

CHILD THERAPIST: Well, you can talk to the people at the clinic about having a secret and about how hard it is for you to keep the secret, but you don't have to tell us what the secret is.

JANIE: You mean if I tell my therapist, then my therapist will promise not to tell my mother?

CHILD THERAPIST: The only time the therapist would talk to your mother or to the police or the social worker is if bad things are still happening to you, or if we're afraid that it might happen again, or if a new person touched your private parts. If somebody is still touching your private parts, then we have to tell the police or the social worker because it's against the law for that to happen. We would try to protect you again; even if no one believed you or did anything about it before, we will try it again so that we can make sure we protect you.

JANIE: Well, my dad still comes into my room at night when I'm sleeping, but he doesn't touch me anymore. But it still worries me.

CHILD THERAPIST: Can you ask him not to come into your room? Or can you ask your mother for a lock so that you can lock your door at night?

The child therapist then turns to the other children and asks them, "What else could Janie do to protect herself from her father?" After the children have responded and their answers have been discussed, Janie continues:

Sometimes it really bothers me that nobody believes me about what my daddy did to me. Sometimes I wonder if it really did happen. I get confused because they tell me that it didn't happen and then I start to wonder if I just imagined it, or maybe I dreamed it. Do you think I dreamed or made up the story that my daddy touched my private parts?

The children are encouraged to give feedback to Janie, and to share any similar feelings and thoughts that they have had.

Reactions of Children

Some of the children who are attempting to maintain the family secret of incest may acknowledge that the same thing happened to them as happened to Janie. A great sense of relief at not being alone in carrying such a secret is experienced.

Feedback Given to Mothers

Feedback may or may not be given after this module. A child's best interests are the primary determinants of whether or not information is disclosed. If it appears that sexual abuse is still continuing, if new information emerges, if a new, unreported perpetrator is implicated, or if the child contradicts a previous retraction, of course another child abuse report must be made. It is up to the discretion of the therapist whether the new information is shared with the mother before or after the report is made.

Techniques Used with Mothers

In order to explore the topic of keeping secrets, a variety of family secrets are examined, including drug abuse, adultery, physical abuse, and sexual abuse. The negative impact on the stability of the family if these secrets should be disclosed is discussed, and a hypothetical situation in which a woman learns that her husband has been committing adultery is presented. Some mothers acknowledge that they might deny the adultery to avoid the breakup of the family. An analogous situation is then discussed in which a mother may decide, probably unconsciously, that it is worth it for her daughter to be fondled by her husband in order to keep the family together. These situations facilitate the mothers' understanding of their need to deny the sexual abuse or other family secrets. A collection of poignant stories and poems written by adult women who were sexually abused as children (MacFarlane, 1980) is also utilized to raise awareness of the long-term effects of undisclosed sexual abuse.

Reactions of Mothers

Some mothers become more appropriately protective of their children, while continuing to overtly deny that sexual abuse has occurred. Mothers are touched by and able to relate to the biographical sketches of adult sexual abuse survivors in the book cited above. One mother who was suspected of maintaining an incest secret attempted to leave the group. Since this module is highly threatening to such families, it can be mentioned at the beginning that some mothers attempt to drop out of the group at this point because they feel so threatened by the material; this paradoxical maneuver may help some mothers to remain in the group.

MODULE 13: SEX EDUCATION

As the mothers become more comfortable with discussing sexual issues, they typically begin to ask for assistance in talking to their own children about the facts of life. Most of the sexually abused mothers were raised in a restrictive sexual atmosphere, feel ignorant about sex, and are ashamed and unaccepting of their own sexuality (Finkelhor, 1979b; Frude, 1982). Since the mothers are also likely to be sexually restrictive with their own children, there is a greater possibility of continuing sexual abuse, because the children are unlikely to discuss any sexuality related topic with them. This module generally occupies three sessions. The goals of this module are these:

1. To provide an opportunity for mothers to correct any erroneous ideas they may hold regarding sexuality and conception, thereby lessening their shame about sex.
2. To help mothers learn how to teach their children about sexuality.
3. To give mothers some guidelines about how children think and process information about sex at different ages, so that they can gear the sex education to their children's developmental level.

Techniques Used with Children

Both children and mothers can be present for the initial part of the sessions as the therapist reads a children's sex education book, *Making Babies* (Stein, 1974), to the combined groups. While the book is being read, questions directed toward the children, such as "Where do babies come from?", "Where do they grow?", and "How do they get out of their mommy?", are interspersed. Mothers thereby have the opportunity to hear about their children's knowledge of sexuality, and to desensitize themselves further to discussions of the topic. After 15 to 30 minutes of reading and discussion, the children and their therapists adjourn to their own group room, where their knowledge is further assessed and reinforced in the structured play therapy activities.

Felt board figures are an excellent way to stimulate further learning. For example, a figure of a pregnant woman can be placed on the board while the children are asked questions about where the baby is, how it comes out, and so on. Anatomically correct dolls are undressed, discussed, and used in play to reinforce the children's learning.

Reactions of Children

The children are quite interested in the story and material from the sex education book, and most appear relatively comfortable with the information. They are attentive and enthusiastic about sharing their knowledge. Most of the children are excited about pursuing the homework assignment with their mothers discussed below; only one has been resistant to further exploration of the topics in the book.

Feedback Given to Mothers

Mothers are told about how their children are integrating the information after each week's session to help them facilitate further discussion at home.

Techniques Used with Mothers

Prior to the joint sessions, the mothers share what they were told as children about sex and having babies. Ideas are elicited about how they have discussed or would discuss where babies come from with their own children. The therapist aids the discussion by showing the mothers various books on sex education for preschool children.

To facilitate the mothers' learning and teaching, it is very helpful for them to understand how children conceptualize sex and conception at different ages. An article entitled "How Children Learn about Sex and Birth" (Bernstein, 1976) is extremely useful; it is discussed in the group, and copies are given to the mothers for future reference.

Since the mothers may be uncomfortable at first about reading a sex education book with their children at home, the therapist begins the process by reading a book to the entire combined group, as described above. The mothers are then asked to go over sections of the book already covered in the group with their children each week at home, providing opportunities for questions and discussion, and increasing comfort in talking about sexual issues.

Reactions of Mothers

Many mothers are unable to remember being told anything about the facts of life by their parents. They are very anxious during the first joint session with the children, and may be surprised about their children's knowledge or confusion concerning sex. The children's relative comfort and openness with the material is quite reassuring to them.

SUMMARY AND CONCLUSIONS

The general aims of the group treatment model described here are to help mothers and children to express and resolve their feelings regarding sexual molestation; to assist them in being more assertive in both sexual and nonsexual situations; to help mothers become more aware of their children's need for protection from coercion, and to assist them in providing appropriate protection; and to help mothers and children to obtain nurturance in less sexualized and more appropriate ways.

There are several unique aspects to this program. First, the structured curriculum provides for exploration of common issues in sexual abuse for both mothers and children in a parallel fashion. Second, specific, focused play therapy techniques are utilized to facilitate the children's examination of their feelings and fears. Third, the use of role playing allows children to experiment with alternate ways of expressing themselves through an engaging and nonthreatening medium. Fourth, the parallel group allows mothers to handle their children's sexual trauma more effectively as a result of receiving help in dealing with their own abuse simultaneously.

Verbal reports and behavioral observations of participating children and their mothers have suggested that they benefited greatly from their structured group experience. Both mothers and children were increasingly able to express and explore the complex feelings elicited by sexual abuse. Some of the mothers were able to recall previously repressed traumatic memories of their own sexual abuse, and begin to deal with feelings generated by the memories. The children demonstrated that they had cognitively restructured the events to a large extent, and were able to place responsibility on the perpetrators in most cases. Many mothers reported that they could more easily comprehend that they were not responsible for their own abuse as children when they were exposed to other families struggling with issues of responsibility and blame; they were then able to provide more proper protection for their children.

Some striking changes occurred in the children's actual behaviors. Children showed increased assertion skills in the group exercises, suggesting that they would be better able to protect themselves in future threatening situations. They interacted in less sexualized ways and were able to express their needs for nurturance in more appropriate ways. Although many of the mothers continued to have difficulty nurturing their children, their attitudes toward their children appeared to be more positive; perhaps this was due to the nurturance they themselves received during their treatment.

The mothers also appeared to gain relief in discovering that their positive feelings toward the perpetrators were understandable and acceptable to the other group members. All but one of the mothers showed less denial of the sexual abuse. This mother acknowledged that her daughters had been sexually abused by an uncle, but refused to believe that they had also been molested by their father, with whom she wished to reunite; these girls understandably showed the least progress.

Although the modules described may be presented in approximately 20–30 therapy sessions, it appears that more extensive therapy is frequently necessary for these seriously disturbed families to show significant, lasting gains. The minimum treatment period is probably 1 year if the sexual abuse was intrafamilial. In addition, children going through criminal court procedures need to be in treatment until completion of the process, because the issues of responsibility and blame remain activated as long as a child must go before a judge. Treatment time must also be extended for those children who are not believed and/or are scapegoated for the disclosure of the secret. Individual therapy seems indicated for most mothers, in addition to group therapy.

It may be necessary to repeat some of the key concepts periodically as a child continues to progress cognitively. When children were reassessed 6 months after their groups sessions had ended, a few appeared to have "lost" some of the knowledge that they had previously acquired. Not only may information need to be reinforced at different stages of development, but it seems likely that the onset of adolescence will reawaken some of the old issues, so that short-term treatment may be needed at that critical time.

Only mothers were included in the initial parent group on whose experiences we base our descriptions. In future groups, custodial fathers whose children were molested by the noncustodial mothers' boyfriends will be included. In addition, future groups will include children molested by their mothers or other female relatives. The curriculum will also be utilized with older school-age children after appropriate modifications. Older boys and girls (aged 8 to 11) will be placed in separate groups because clinical experience indicates that their level of anxiety would be too high if they were placed together.

Obviously, research into the effectiveness of this type of treatment will be illuminating. Parents and children in future groups will be assessed along a number of different dimensions before and after parallel group therapy to obtain more objective measures of potential therapeutic gains. The children's assertion skills will be assessed before and after treatment; their locus of control will be measured, to test the hypothesis that the children will perceive themselves as having more control over positive events in their lives as a result of treatment; and developmental testing will provide an assessment of anticipated gains in intellectual growth as a result of healthier emotional functioning.

Mothers' protectiveness of their children will be assessed before and after treatment. A measure of maternal attitudes toward the child will also be given to learn whether mothers really do view their children more positively as a result of treatment. Follow-up data also need to be collected at 6- to 12-month intervals to ascertain whether children retain the information and maintain treatment gains after termination. Eventually, matched groups of children and mothers receiving other types of treatment should be compared with those participating in the parallel group treatment program. The parallel group treatment approach appears quite promising; collection of meaningful outcome data seems to be the next step.

SEXUAL ABUSE RESOURCES

CHILDREN'S BOOKS ON SEXUAL ABUSE PREVENTION

Bassett, K. (1981). *My very own special body book*. Redding, CA: Hawthorne Press. (Ages 3–8.)

Stowell, J., & Dietzel, M. (1982). *My very own book about me*. (Available from Super Kids, Lutheran Social Service, N. 1226 Howard, Spokane, WA 99201. $3.75. Ages 3–7.)

White, L. A., & Spencer, S. L. (1983). *Take care of yourself: A young person's guide to understanding, preventing and healing from the hurts of child abuse.* (Available from Take Care of Yourself, 905 Maxine, Flint, MI 48503. $5.95. Ages 5–10.)

Williams, J. (1983). *Red flag, green flag*. (Available from Rape and Crisis Center of Fargo–Moorhead, P.O. Box 1655, Fargo, ND 58107. $4.00. Ages 3–8.)

Wochter, O. (1983). *No more secrets for me*. Boston: Little, Brown. (Ages 3–11.)

CHILDREN'S GAMES AND SONGS FOR PREVENTION AND TREATMENT

Alsop, P. My body. Song on the album *Who d'you want to do?* (Available from Peter Alsop, P.O. Box 960, Topanga, CA 90290. Ages 4–Adult.)

Play it safe with Sasa. (Available from SASA & Company, 2008 LaBrea Terrace, Los Angeles, CA 90046. $78.50. Ages 4–11.)

The talking and telling about touching game. (Available from Victim Assistance Games, P.O. Box 444, Akron, OH 44309. $3.00. Ages 4–12.)

The touching song. (Available from Children's Self-Help Project, 170 Fell St., Room 32, San Francisco, CA 94102. Ages 3–11.)

VIDEO MATERIALS FOR PREVENTION

Better safe than sorry II [Videotape]. (Available from Film Fair Communications, 10900 Ventura Blvd., P.O. Box 728, Studio City, CA 91604. $290.00. Elementary school ages.)

Strong kids, safe kids [Video cassette]. (Available at most video cassette retail outlets or Paramount Pictures, 5555 Melrose Ave., Hollywood, CA 90038. $29.95. Ages 3–12.)

Touch [Videotape]. (Available from MTI Teleprograms, 3710 Commercial Ave., Northbrook, IL 60062. $395.00. Ages 4–16.)

CHILDREN'S BOOKS FOR TREATMENT

Kissell, C., & Tibbits, E. (1979). *Daddy's girl.* (Available from Parents Center, 530 Saguel Ave., Santa Cruz, CA 95062. $3.10. Ages 7–16.)

McGovern, K. B. (1985). *Alice doesn't babysit anymore.* (Available from McGovern & Mulbacker Books, P.O. Box 25537, Portland, OR 97225. $7.95. Ages 3–11.)

Sweet, P. (1981). *Something happened to me.* Racine, WI: Mother Courage Press. (Ages 4–12.)

APPENDIX
13-1

HELPING SUSAN

PART I: THE DESTRUCTIVE REACTION

(*Mother is on the phone in the kitchen.*)

MOTHER: No, I'm glad you told me. Thanks. (*Hangs up phone.*) Oh, my God! (*Slumps forward, hand to face. Then begins to compose herself and is interrupted by Susan.*)

(*Enter Susan.*)

SUSAN: Who was that on the phone, Mom?

MOM: It was Sharon. She told me what you've done.

SUSAN: What, Mom?

MOM: You know what I'm talking about. You and that man.

SUSAN: Mom, I couldn't help it. He made me do it.

MOM: He made you, huh? God, this is just what I needed right now. This really makes my day. If you're innocent in all this, why didn't you tell me? Why did you tell our neighbor? She is the biggest gossip in the world. Now, everyone's going to know. Are you sure you're telling the truth?

SUSAN: Mom, please. I was scared to tell you. I thought you'd be mad.

MOM: I don't believe it. Why would you be afraid to tell me? Haven't I always told you to tell me everything?

From *The Touching Problem* by S. L. Klevin and J. Krebill, 1981, Bellingham, WA: Soap Box Productions. Reprinted by permission of the Coalition for Child Advocacy.

SUSAN: But, Mom . . .

MOM: (*Shaking her head.*) How could you do this to me? How could you let something like this happen? Now, you better tell me everything and NO lies!!

PART II: THE POSITIVE REACTION

(*Mother is on phone in kitchen.*)

MOTHER: No, I'm glad you told me. Thanks. (*Hangs up phone.*) Oh, my God! (*Slumps forward, hand to face. Then begins to compose herself. Walks to stove, pours a cup of coffee. Places it on the table, sits down.*)

(*Enter Susan.*)

SUSAN: Who was that on the phone, Mom?

MOM: It was Sharon.

SUSAN: Oh.

MOM: (*Takes deep breath, then:*) She told me, Susan. She told me about the problem with Frank Grassman.

SUSAN: Oh, no. (*She sits down at table.*) She promised she wouldn't tell you. Why did she have to tell?

MOM: Sharon wants to make sure that you're going to be safe. So she had to tell me. I'm real glad she did, Susan.

SUSAN: You're not mad.

MOM: Susan, I feel bad that you didn't tell me, but I understand how hard it is to tell something like this to someone you care about. You were real smart telling Sharon. I'm real glad you told *someone*. That's the important thing. Can we talk for awhile about what happened?

SUSAN: I can't. You'll hate me if I tell you and I'll get sent away.

MOM: I know it's hard to talk about. So we'll take it real slow, Honey. Nothing would ever make me hate you. I wouldn't ever send you away from me. Where did you get an idea like that?

SUSAN: He said you would. Oh, Mom, I just can't talk about it.

MOM: Come on. Start at the beginning.

SUSAN: Well, I was gonna help Mr. Grassman weed the garden. He said he'd pay me $5.00, remember? So I said okay. And I was weeding the garden. Then he said, "Come in the garage and help me find a special shovel." A spade, I think.

MOM: So you were in the garage with Mr. Grassman and then what happened next?

SUSAN: He said he knew a touch game. He asked if I wanted to play. He was being real nice and I would get tickled in some place and wherever it was, I was supposed to tickle him there. That's how it worked. I was laughing. Then, he wanted me to sit on his lap and I didn't want to. I started to feel icky. I didn't know what to do. And, Mom, I was bad and you'll hate me. (*Sobs, head down on table.*)

MOM: Come on, Honey, it'll be okay. I won't hate you, no matter what. So you felt confused because he wanted you to sit on his lap.

SUSAN: (*Tearfully*) Well, I wanted to stop and then he said he'd give me some more money. Well, I wanted more money 'cause I'm savin' for the bike. So I sat on his lap so I could have the money. (*Cries.*)

MOM: What happened then?

SUSAN: I just can't say it, Mom.

MOM: Did he touch you?

SUSAN: (*Nods.*)

MOM: Where?

SUSAN: (*Head down, shakes her head indicating that she doesn't want to answer.*)

MOM: Did he touch your crotch?

SUSAN: (*Nods.*)

MOM: Did he put his hand inside your pants?

SUSAN: Mom, he was tryin' to and he held me real tight. I was so scared then. I couldn't get away. Then, he let go of me. And I ran.

MOM: Did you get away from him?

SUSAN: Yeah, and I was coming home to tell you. Then I got scared. He told me I better not tell. He said no one would believe me. Then, I started to think it never happened. Then I thought maybe it didn't and if I forgot about it—it would be just like it didn't happen. I stayed away from him. I was so ashamed. I never even took the money. But then today he talked to me on the street. He said to come help him again. I said that I was busy. And then he told me that I had to go see him or he would tell that I had done nasty things for money. I said I never took any money. He said that that doesn't matter and if anyone found out I would be sent away. He said only a bad, bad girl would do things like I did. So I had to go with him.

MOM: What did he do?

SUSAN: Oh, Mama, it was so awful. When I went with him he wanted me to take my clothes off. He kept scaring me about the trouble I'd get in if I told. But I couldn't do what he said. I didn't care. I ran. Then Sharon saw me crying, she said "What's the matter?", and I accidentally told her. I didn't mean to and I never wanted you to know how bad I was.

MOM: (*Takes Susan on her lap.*) Honey, you weren't bad. Mr. Grassman was lying to you. It wasn't your fault. You felt guilty because you told him you wanted the money—but you didn't know what he was going to do. He told you lies about what would happen and used your guilty feelings to trap you. I'm so glad you told someone. That was real smart.

SUSAN: He's a real mean man.

MOM: Mr. Grassman has a serious problem. You made a mistake and you got tricked. It wasn't your fault. Lots of kids make worse mistakes than the one you made. Now, come on, Honey. Everything's going to be okay.

SUSAN: What are we gonna do, Mom?

MOM: We're gonna call the people who protect children. Then together you and I are going to tell them what happened.

SUSAN: What'll they do to him, Mom?

MOM: They'll get him help so that he doesn't trick any more little girls. You know, Susan, you probably aren't the first girl he's done this to. We're going to stop him. You and me. Okay?

SUSAN: Okay.

MOM: How do you feel now, Susan?

SUSAN: Better. Oh, Mom, I feel lots better.

APPENDIX
13-2

JIMMY'S BEDTIME STORY

MOM: This is a play about touching problems. In this play I'm the mother.

JIMMY: And I play her boy. I'm about . . . 7. My name's Jimmy.

MOM: I am really embarrassed to talk about this problem, but Jimmy is very special and important to me, so I'm going to do the best I can. Jimmy, one of my favorite things to do is tickle your tummy (*She does it*) and give you a hug (*She does it*) and pretend to bite your ear.

JIMMY: (*Laughing*) Stop it. Stop it.

MOM: Okay. Okay. When you say stop I always do. Right?

JIMMY: Yeah, but I'm kidding. Do it again.

MOM: Not now 'cause I want to talk about touching problems.

JIMMY: What's a touching problem?

MOM: Well . . . if I kept tickling you and tickling you after you were out of breath and I wouldn't stop no matter what you said, *that* would be a touching problem.

JIMMY: Oh, that would be a mean thing to do.

MOM: Yeah, it's mean to force somebody to do things. And there are other kinds of touching problems.

JIMMY: Like when girls kiss me. Yuck!!

From *The Touching Problem* by S. L. Klevin and J. Krebill, 1981, Bellingham, WA: Soap Box Productions. Reprinted by permission of the Coalition for Child Advocacy. "Jimmy's Bedtime Story" is available as *Touching*, an illustrated story book, and can be obtained from the Coalition for Child Advocacy, P.O. Box 159, Bellingham, WA 98227.

MOM: Yeah, or when a bully gets you down, sits on you, and won't let you go home.

JIMMY: That happened to me once.

MOM: How did it make you feel?

JIMMY: Mad! I was so mad. And I couldn't get him back. Boy, was I mad!

MOM: Have you ever been tricked?

JIMMY: Like when someone says, "Open your mouth and close your eyes and you will get a big surprise." And the surprise is a worm!

MOM: Yeah, that's what I mean. Or like this: Once there was a little girl.

JIMMY: Did I know her?

MOM: No, but she is a real-life person. This girl was in her own neighborhood and one of her neighbors said, "Come in my house to see the new kittens." This person was a grownup so the girl went right in to see the new kittens. But she didn't see any. Then the man said, "I'll show them to you if you sit on my lap." Then the girl felt funny. She didn't know why but she could tell it was a trick. Then the man tried to put his hand down her panties.

JIMMY: He did!

MOM: Yes, and she ran out of there as fast as she could!

JIMMY: Did she get away?

MOM: Yes, and she told her mom.

JIMMY: What did they do to the man?

MOM: He got in trouble for what he did and then they got him help for his problem. Later she said that even before he tried to do it she felt that warning feeling. This is exactly what she said, "I just knew and besides there weren't any kittens."

JIMMY: I bet she was *so* mad!

MOM: Yeah, she was. And I think a kid does get a warning feeling when something funny is going on and I think you need to learn to trust it. Some kids say it's a funny feeling in your stomach or an uncomfortable feeling, and when you get it—you better get out.

JIMMY: Is it like you're gonna throw up?

MOM: Maybe. But Jimmy, if anyone tries to touch private parts of your body like your bottom or penis, you don't have to let them no matter what they say, even if you don't get a warning feeling.

JIMMY: I wouldn't let anyone do that.

HELPING PARENTS COPE WITH EXTRAFAMILIAL MOLESTATION

Kee MacFarlane

INTRODUCTION

Extrafamilial child sexual abuse (i.e., that perpetrated by a stranger, a teacher, a babysitter, a neighbor, etc.) poses a somewhat different set of challenges to the clinician than those associated with incestuous families. Investigatory procedures and evaluation techniques should be quite similar, although an emphasis on criminal prosecution and the involvement of the police may be more frequent in these cases. On the one hand, such a family may experience fewer torn loyalties because the abuser is not seen as one of them (although that should not automatically be assumed, since many abusers are very close to the children or the parents), but, on the other hand, there are fewer therapeutic resources available to the family. Departments of public social services may not be mandated to investigate or treat extrafamilial abuse; most child sexual abuse treatment programs focus their efforts on incestuous families; and many mental health centers and private therapists are untrained and inexperienced in helping families with this problem. The common tendency of many parents to try to ignore or forget all about the abuse as quickly as possible is often reinforced by well-meaning clinicians who are unfamiliar with the dynamics and aftermath of molestation of young children.

This chapter is written for those who work with families in which a child has been extrafamilially molested, and for parents who must help themselves and their children deal with the abuse. It is addressed directly to parents who may not have access to professional help at the time they are in crisis. Copies are also available in booklet form.[1]

In addressing the issue of parental reactions to abuse, the primary thing to recognize is the significance of parental reactions to the child's future ability to integrate and recover from the abuse. Negative, blaming, or inappropriate responses sometimes can do as much damage as the abuse itself. Parents need and deserve a great deal of help with this process. Many are so overwhelmed with their own feelings of guilt, blame, or denial that it is very difficult for them not to project them onto their children. Some find themselves being blamed by other family members, such as grandparents, who also need help in getting control of their feelings. Some even initially overreact by physically lashing out at their children for not telling them sooner or for not providing details of the abuse.

This chapter is intended as a practical guide to identifying and managing many of the difficult emotions associated with the discovery of extrafamilial child sexual abuse. It recommends professional counseling for children and their parents. It is hoped that this guide may assist and inspire clinicians to be available to these families and to provide this badly needed service.

COPING WITH SEXUAL ABUSE OF YOUR PRESCHOOL CHILD: A GUIDE FOR PARENTS

YOUR CHILD HAS BEEN MOLESTED

There is nothing you can do to change the fact that your child has been sexually abused. There probably was little you could have done to prevent it. But there is much you can do to lessen the effects of sexual abuse on your child and to help yourself cope with its aftermath. You and your child are not alone. As many as 4 out of 10 children become victims of some form of sexual abuse by the time they reach grade school. The majority of cases go undetected because the children are afraid to tell anyone. So, as hard as it is to hear what

---

1. For booklet, contact Children's Institute International, 711 S. New Hampshire Avenue, Los Angeles, CA 90005.

your child has to tell you about the abuse, be glad that he or she is willing to talk about it—it is an important step toward emotional recovery. And it gives us all a chance to help. This guide has been written to help you help your child to integrate this experience in ways that will not have lasting negative consequences.

What Does It Involve?

Child sexual abuse or sexual molestation can include any kind of sexual act between a child and an adult or significantly older person. Sexual acts may include the following: touching of the other's genitals by either the adult or the child; exposure of the adult's or child's genitals, including photographing the child's genitals; adult masturbation in front of or by rubbing against a child; oral sex performed on a child or by a child on an adult; and any type of penetration of a child's vagina or anus, however slight, by a penis, finger, or other object. Such descriptions conjure up frightening images in a parent's mind—images that are almost too painful to contemplate. But we must be able to consider the possibility of their existence if we are to be able to help a child who has been subjected to such acts.

Sexual activity between children who are peers may be upsetting to parents and others, but it is not usually considered to be abuse unless there is some element of force, coercion, or intimidation involved. However, real force is rarely necessary because, in the vast majority of cases, the abuser is someone whom the child knows and trusts. A child's compliance (and silence) is usually acquired through trickery, bribes, or threats of consequences. This aspect is particularly confusing to children and must be dealt with very carefully by parents and other adults.

Emotional Reactions to Abuse

The reactions of children vary greatly, depending on the child, the experience, and what is done about it. They range from withdrawal to aggression to seeming lack of interest. Try not to expect a particular reaction—be supportive of your child's feelings, even if they are very different from your own.

Confusion is one of the most common reactions of very young

children. It is we adults who often pass on the sense of seriousness and crisis that can cause children to panic and withdraw. Children must be allowed to work through whatever feelings they have.

Your child's emotional reactions to sexual abuse may include the following:

- Fear, insecurity
- Guilt, shame, embarrassment
- Uncertainty about how to feel
- Feelings of being dirty, spoiled, disgraced
- Fear of consequences from abuser, parents, system
- Guilt because some things may have been pleasurable
- Anger, hostility, blame
- Acute anxiety
- Self-blame, self-doubt
- Fear of internal damage
- Betrayal—by abuser or by parent protector
- Confusion about what happened that was wrong

MEDICAL INDICATORS

Often there are no obvious medical indications that a child has been sexually abused. This is because there is usually a delay between the time of the abuse and its discovery, and because many sexual acts leave no clear signs. A lack of medical evidence does not mean the absence of abuse, however, and a child's statements should never be discounted simply because a doctor cannot prove them medically. Most doctors (even your own pediatrician) have not been trained in this type of examination and may not recognize many of the subtle signs of child sexual abuse. For this reason, children should be examined by physicians who are trained and experienced in diagnosing sexual abuse. As confident as you may be in your family doctor, you may get better answers if you discuss your fears with a specialist.

There may have been medical indications of sexual abuse in the recent or distant past, which, at the time, you did not associate with this problem. That is quite natural; few people ever assume that this could happen to their children. However, if someone is being investigated or prosecuted for abusing your child, your memories of any unusual symptoms exhibited by your child could help provide a link between the abuse and a particular person's access to your child.

After reading this guide, it might be very helpful to the police or prosecutor handling your case to write down any medical, behavioral, or emotional indicators that you remember noticing, as well as the approximate dates when they occurred. Following are some of the possible medical problems that your child might have experienced as a result of sexual abuse.

- Pain in the genital or anal areas, including pain while going to the bathroom or when held or picked up
- Redness, rash, swelling, or tears in genital or anal area
- Blood, discharge, or unusual odor from vagina or anus
- Unusual anxiety, embarrassment, or distress from any medication applied to treat the above conditions
- Other medical problems that could be associated with anxiety or possible sexual abuse, such as stomach pains, headaches, leg pains, throat infections, asthma

Many parents are reluctant to take their children to a doctor for an examination of this kind. They are afraid that the examination will only add to the children's trauma. This is a natural reaction and an important factor to consider. However, a gentle, sensitive diagnostic examination for sexual abuse need not be any more upsetting to a child than any other visit to the doctor. Children often worry about whether or not they have been damaged or might have something wrong with their bodies. Aside from determining whether your child has sustained any physical injury that may require treatment, a doctor's magical authority to a child can provide the needed reassurance that the child's body is still in perfect condition and that he or she will be just fine. Again, it takes a doctor with special training and experiences with these cases—don't be afraid to ask.

POSSIBLE BEHAVIORAL CHANGES

There are many kinds of behaviors that children may display following molestation. Young children tend to act out some of their reactions because the abuse is so hard to express verbally. Be observant of behavior changes, but try not to look too hard for what may not be there. Some common behavioral reactions during and after molestation are these:

- Sleep disturbances, nightmares, fear of "monsters," bedwetting

- Loss of appetite, problems with eating or swallowing
- Fear of certain people or places
- School phobia: sudden dislike, refusal to attend, fear of a teacher, upset upon return
- Social withdrawal, stranger anxiety
- Wetting pants, thumb sucking, rocking
- Unprovoked crying
- Unexplained anger, irritability, or crankiness
- Clinginess, fear of separation, fear of other caretakers
- Sexualized behavior: excessive masturbation, new terms for genitals, pseudomaturity
- Secretive behavior: having a secret, questions about them, answering, "I can't tell you"
- Re-enactment of abuse using dolls, drawings, or friends
- Regression: behaving younger
- Sudden talk of an adult, imaginary, or secret friend
- Threatened behavior: fear of violence, games with threats
- Anxiety-related illness

All of these are signs of anxiety and common reactions by preschoolers to molestation. Your child may develop some of these problems or none at all. They usually last from several weeks to many months following disclosure of the abuse. Try not to react strongly to them, especially any sexual behavior. Be comforting and supportive of your child's nonverbal messages, and encourage him or her to put those feelings into words. The duration of your child's reactions depends, in part, on how you and others respond.

RESPONDING TO YOUR CHILD

It is natural for you to feel shock, outrage, and disbelief over what has happened, but the most important thing you can do for your child is to get control of your feelings. You may be screaming inside, but you must make every effort to be calm with your child. It may be the hardest role you've ever had to play—and the most important. It is best that your child not see you express your anger or pain. It may increase your child's guilt about the abuse and about telling. Moreover, your child may feel that he or she has somehow harmed you, and may not confide in you again.

Most children don't tell about sexual abuse because they are afraid they will be blamed, disbelieved, or rejected. When preschoolers do disclose abuse, many do so in stages—saving the "worst parts" until they see how you react to what they tell you first. Rarely do young children ever fabricate an accusation of sexual abuse; they do not have extensive sexual fantasies involving adults. It is more common for them to deny victimization when it has occurred or to minimize its severity. They do this to protect themselves and others, including, sometimes, the abuser. Some children repress an incident to the extent that they are emotionally incapable of remembering it. In cases involving multiple victims, it is not uncommon for them to describe each other's abuse while denying their own. Since children already come to us bearing this kind of anxiety, we must do all we can to lessen it.

The following are some suggestions on how to respond:

• Underreact: The more matter-of-fact you can be, the more your child will be willing to share with you.

• Assure your child that you believe what he or she has told you, and that you are glad that he or she is able to talk to you. Give permission to clarify any misunderstandings or false information.

• Be careful never to give the impression that you are blaming the child for what has happened. Even without meaning to, some questions sound blaming (e.g., "Why did you let him?", "What were you doing in the closet anyway?", "Why didn't you tell me this before now?").

• Emphasize that, no matter what your child said, did, or felt, it was not his or her fault, and that he or she did not cause it or deserve to have this happen. Children need to know that when there is sexual behavior between an adult and a child, the adult is *always* responsible.

• Consult with professionals who are trained, sensitive, and experienced with child sexual abuse cases, regarding the need for diagnostic examination and treatment. Reassure your child that he or she is physically fine and that there is no lasting harm to worry about.

• Stay close to the child immediately following disclosure and provide an extra sense of physical security. If the child or your family was threatened with harm by the abuser, reassure your child that he or she is safe with you. Explain that the threats were only a trick to keep the child from telling, and that there is no real danger.

• Do not make efforts to bury the incident, "forget all about it," or put it behind you immediately. Even children with a strong desire to block out the abuse are unlikely to forget that it happened. Children need to be given the opportunity and the permission to express their feelings as they come up. They need to be helped to put the abuse in its proper perspective so that it won't smolder in them as a forbidden secret for life. When we consciously or unconsciously silence child victims by our actions or our attitudes, it is usually out of our own need not to hear or think about the abuse, not theirs.

• At the same time, try not to "talk the abuse into going away." Be a good listener, but try not to pry beyond what is necessary to understand what happened. Enough other professionals probably will have to ask your child for the details of the abuse. Continual probing questions from you may only add to your child's embarrassment or sense of shame, and may even become a means of getting attention. It is also important to respect your child's privacy by not telling a lot of people about it or repeating the story to others in the presence of the child.

• Permit your child to have positive as well as negative feelings if that's what he or she expresses. People who sexually abuse young children often are very good at working with children and at winning their confidence and friendship. As a result, your child might have some good feelings about the abuser, who may be regarded as his or her friend, even though he or she did some confusing and uncomfortable things or even hurt the child. It is usually very hard for a parent to hear this from a child victim without reacting very negatively. However, if you can allow your child to express whatever he or she is feeling without getting an adverse reaction from you, the child won't have to feel additionally guilty about these thoughts.

• Try not to become overprotective or restrictive of your child's usual activities following the disclosure. Make every effort to follow normal routines and to help your family return to its normal lifestyle. If your child concludes that the abuse has caused disruption of his or her entire family pattern, it may take on even larger traumatic proportions.

• Maintain your normal expressions of affection and physical interactions with your child. Some parents, particularly fathers, tend to withdraw from physical contact with molested children because of their own emotional reactions or because they assume that it will be upsetting to the children. Instead, it may make your child feel that there is something wrong with him or her, that he or she is being punished, or that molestation and family expressions of affection are similar and related behaviors. Your child may not want to be held or kissed at first, but that will usually pass quickly. Try to interact with your child as you have always done, and take your clues from him or her as to what feels comfortable.

• Use this opportunity to educate all your children about what sexual abuse is and what they can do to help protect themselves. Teach them that there is good touch and bad touch, and that parts of their bodies are private and belong only to them. Give them permission to say "no" to some adults, to run away from people who scare them, and to ask for help. Emphasize that most adults are not like the abuser and will help them if they are in danger.

• Don't ignore your other children during the crisis or try to pretend that nothing has occurred. They need reassurance and attention during this time, too. Tell the brothers and sisters in a general way what has happened to the child victim, but that he or she is okay now and they are all safe. It is best not to go into any real details of the abuse. If the victim tells them later, that is his or her choice, but you might caution against scaring the others. If they know the abuser, they may have ambivalent feelings toward him or her, or they may feel guilty for not being able to protect their sibling. Stress that the victim is telling the truth and that no one in the family is to blame, especially the victim. Point out that this can happen to any child and has happened to lots of other children.

HOW TO EXPLAIN WHAT HAS HAPPENED

It is very difficult to find the words to help your child understand what has happened. Some children know it was bad because it hurt, they were uncomfortable, or they were threatened not to tell. Others sense that it was wrong, but they aren't sure why. Some who aren't hurt or scared and who may have experienced physical stimulation may want to know what was bad about their "game" or their "friend." It is difficult to know what to say to a child who has had little prior knowledge about sex. Saying that a person is "sick" or "sick in the head" can be confusing to young children, who generally equate those words with physical illness. They may worry that they or you may catch this sickness or that someone is going to die from it. On the other hand, we don't want children to grow up thinking that all sex is dirty and wrong.

One way to approach it is to say that there are some things that grownups can do that children don't do (e.g., children don't drive cars, they don't have jobs, they don't drink alcohol, they don't stay up late, etc). The things that the abuser did to them are like those things—they're not okay because they were between an adult and a child and because they are against the law. They're against the law because the child didn't really have a choice and because those things aren't good for you until you're grown up.

You might explain that the abuser has a problem—he or she does sexual things with children instead of grownups. Your emphasis should be on the behavior, not the abuser, since the child may have some positive feelings about him or her. If you can communicate the idea that a person's behavior can be bad or wrong without the person's necessarily being bad, it also will help children to understand that they aren't bad just because they participated in or were exposed to it.

LONG-TERM EFFECTS

It is difficult to make a blanket statement about the future consequences of sexual abuse, except to say that they vary from child to child and depend upon a number of factors. Some of the most significant of these factors are these:

- The nature of the abusive acts
- The relationship between the victim and the abuser
- The duration of the abusive behavior
- The presence of violence, threats, and physical harm
- The child's age and developmental level
- The child's individual personality and strengths
- The process of intervention and reactions of others

Space does not permit a discussion of all these variables or how they interrelate with one another. It is a complex issue, and the reasons why children react differently are not fully known. However, this problem has been referred to as a "psychological time bomb" because, for some children, its effects may not show up until years after the abuse. This is why it is so important to help your child express and master his or her feelings at the time they occur. Many former victims who suffer from long-term effects in adulthood never had the opportunity to work through the trauma when they were young.

It might help to know that recent studies indicate that as much as one-third to one-half of the population has experienced some form of sexual abuse before the age of 18. Considering how widespread this problem is, it would appear that most children do recover from the effects of molestation and grow up to function adequately. What is clear is that a child's ultimate reactions are strongly affected by the way the situation is handled by the significant adults in the child's life. If your child is dealt with directly and sensitively during disclosure and afterward, he or she need not suffer permanently from the abuse.

What about Homosexuality or Possible Sexual Problems

There are absolutely no data to suggest that children become more prone to homosexuality as a result of child sexual abuse. Rape victims do not become attracted to rapists following an assault, yet many parents of boys molested by men worry about this unnecessarily. Similarly, promiscuity, frigidity, or sexual abusiveness by themselves have not been causatively linked to childhood sexual abuse. However, even preschool-age children often are aware of antihomosexual attitudes in our society, and are afraid that they will be labeled as such when they are molested by someone of the same sex. It is believed to be a primary reason why boys rarely ever report sexual abuse. Consequently, it is important to let your son know that he did not cause the abuse to happen by anything he did or said—he was just there. It is just as important not to transmit any anxieties about homosexuality to your son through such actions as grabbing his sister's dolls away from him, overreacting to masturbation or sex play with other children, or curtailing activities that he engaged in before the abuse occurred. The same applies to abuse of girls by women.

Again, it appears to be insensitive reactions, mismanagement of cases, and lack of disclosure that lead to many later difficulties. Helping your child to relearn what constitutes appropriate behavior sometimes takes patience, but need not be an upsetting process for either of you.

DIAGNOSIS AND TREATMENT FOLLOWING ABUSE

Many parents assume that, because they have a close relationship with their children, the children will tell them if abuse occurred and describe what happened. What they often don't realize is that children usually are warned or threatened by the abuser not to tell their parents. The threats can be very frightening: "I will come back and hurt you or hurt your parents," or, even worse, "Your parents won't love you any more if they find out." As a consequence, children may be more resistant to telling parents than anyone else.

A diagnostic evaluation by a trained, experienced child therapist or interviewer can help your child unburden his or her secret and help you to learn what happened to your child. Similarly, it is important to provide therapy for your child to help him or her work through the many confusing feelings brought on by sexual abuse. You may feel that your child is too young for therapy, but a good child therapist can create a safe environment for dealing with hidden fears and anger. Therapy need not necessarily be long-term, but it can be more helpful now than later in life.

TAKING CARE OF YOU

When preschoolers are molested, the anguish of their parents often is more visible and more deeply felt than that of their children. You need help and support at least as much as your child does, so that you will be able to provide support to your child. Some of the things you may be experiencing at this time are as follows:

• *Rage, the urge for retaliation.* These are common reactions—but don't let yourself react on impulse or attempt to settle the score. You will only hurt your child more. Do constructive things with your anger: Ventilate it, cooperate with authorities, file a suit on behalf of your child, develop prevention programs, or work to improve the response system.

• *Guilt or self-blame.* Also common, but totally useless to your child and unproductive for you. Lamenting on why you didn't prepare your child better or adequately investigate who your child was with will only divert your energy and attention from your child's needs. Leave your anger and blame where they belong—on the abuser—and move on.

• *Fear for your child.* Reactions resulting in overprotectiveness are very natural but not very useful. Children need to regain their self-confidence and the feeling that they can still be trusted. Treating a child as you did when he or she was younger also may reinforce regressive behavior. Your fears may undermine the child's need to re-establish self-sufficiency and could actually increase his or her vulnerability to others.

• *Embarrassment, secrecy.* Some parents need to suppress the abuse because it causes them to feel embarrassed or personally responsible, or it brings back memories of their own childhood traumas. Dealing with the sexual abuse of your child will be particularly difficult and painful if you were molested as a child, because it usually triggers many unresolved feelings of your own. You may need help in handling those feelings, and there are increasing numbers of therapists and self-help groups available to help you do that. Try not to project your own old fears or denial onto your child. Your need for secrecy will not help your child.

• *Exacerbation of recent marital problems.* Child sexual abuse puts a strain on any marriage, but it is particularly difficult on one that already is shaky. Some parents secretly or openly blame each other for failure to protect their child. Sometimes one partner will have difficulty having sexual relations during this crisis. Sometimes one parent will deny that this could have happened, leaving the other feeling unsupported or forced to choose between a child and a partner. Some degree of family crisis is to be expected when parents discover that their child has been molested by someone outside the home. But if that crisis does not subside over time, if it precipitates other crises, or begins to affect the foundation of your marriage, seek help for both of you.

Whatever your feelings, find someone to talk to whom you can trust and with whom you can talk about your feelings. That may be a friend, a relative, or a therapist. If your problems around those issues escalate, or your child's behavioral and emotional reactions to the abuse do not subside, get professional help. It works and you deserve it.

CONCLUSIONS AND IMPLICATIONS

CHALLENGES FOR
THE FUTURE

Jill Waterman
Kee MacFarlane
Shawn Conerly
Linda Damon
Michael Durfee
Suzanne Long

Following is a summary of many of the major issues addressed in this book. They are presented under functional categories, according to issue or role, and they include recommendations for research and improved intervention strategies. Many of these issues and recommendations are not new. Many apply to older children as well as to preschoolers, and many have been addressed in previous publications. However, they warrant reiteration, because of the greater difficulty in communicating with very young children; the greater complexity of sorting out facts, motives, and circumstances surrounding these cases; and the present inability of our legal systems to respond adequately to young victims.

No discipline, whether medical, legal, or clinical in orientation, holds sole responsibility for what should be done with cases involving preschool-age victims; no discipline has all the resources or all the answers. However, professionals in all disciplines who interview, diagnose, or treat alleged young victims of sexual abuse should have two things in common: (1) familiarity and experience in communicating with young children, and (2) expertise in and knowledge of the problem of child sexual abuse. Children suspected of being abused and those suspected of abusing them deserve no less, though they frequently receive it. The suggestions that follow are presented with the hope that one day they will receive the specialized attention they deserve.

ASSESSMENT

The increased use of innovative tools and techniques for diagnostic assessment is indicative of our growing awareness that face-to-face verbalization is only one of many avenues of communication with very young children. The use of puppets, anatomical dolls, art materials, and so forth not only provides children with familiar options with which to communicate; it also provides a measure of distance from subjects that may be too threatening to deal with initially in a direct manner. Those who employ these tools and techniques should be trained in their use and in interpreting the meanings of how they are utilized by children.

In the initial stage of identification, a series of interviews with the same interviewer is usually indicated in order to build rapport, establish trust, and give the interviewer a clear sense of what (if anything) has happened to the child. This may not be necessary with every child, and it may also depend on the purpose of the interview. The child's developmental level must be kept in mind with regard to what can and cannot be expected from a particular age group or stage of development. The young child may reveal little in one short assessment interview in a stranger's office, but, given time and trust, may re-enact the abuse for a caring person who has established a relationship.

Sexually abused children are frequently afraid to disclose the abuse, due to threats made by their abusers or their own fears of what will happen if they tell. Therefore, it is important to address those fears and potential consequences early in an interview, so that a child can begin to feel safe enough to describe what happened. It is equally important to recognize the children's use of defense mechanisms against disclosure, such as denial and projection, and to differentiate those protective devices from the statements of children who honestly tell us that nothing abusive occurred.

Retractions of initial disclosure of sexual abuse are common among young children and should not be assumed to be indicative that abuse did not occur. In general, the longer the period of legal intervention involving the prospect of testifying, and the more family disruption involving hostility and denial by significant adults in the child's life, the more likely the young child will be to recant. This likelihood can frequently be reduced by careful preparation and involvement of nonabusive parents or parent figures in the initial interview process. When adults have been prepared to respond in a supportive manner, it allows children to see right away that they are not being blamed, and that significant adults in their lives are emotionally able to handle the disclosure. This result can be achieved through use of a videotape of the interview or of a two-way mirror, or by conducting a carefully prepared session with the child and adult(s), where the disclosure interview is sensitively and thoroughly discussed. Laying this foundation for adults' acceptance of children's disclosures, and realistically preparing children for the types of intervention that may follow, can do a great deal to alleviate the fears and stress that lead to children's retractions.

Questions that are focused, in the sense that they inquire about specific events, acts, or individuals, are often a necessary part of the assessment process with young children. The questioning phase of an interview should begin with general, open-ended questions, which give the child an opportunity to volunteer pertinent information that can then be probed further. However, sexually abused children usually have been warned not to disclose the abuse and are unlikely to do so voluntarily, particularly when they are unsure of how the interviewer will respond. Therefore, if questions about sexual abuse are not specific, the information, whether it indicates positive or negative findings of abuse, is likely to be missed. On the other hand, questions that are leading to the point where they clearly anticipate or ask for certain responses are problematic with young children, because of concerns about exerting undue pressure on children, and because they may lead to accusations of coercion later on in the legal process.

Videotaping initial interviews can be a powerful therapeutic tool in the assessment process. The use of videotape provides a way of sharing a secret, a means of preventing retractions and confronting disbelieving parties, and a way of preventing multiple interviews by different evaluators. However, initial interviews of young children are frequently riddled with denials and disclosure information that may prove to be inconsistent with details or with additional disclosures that the children may make once they have overcome their initial fears. In such instances, videotapes can create additional problems in court if they are used to impeach children's and interviewers' credibility. In criminal cases involving multiple young victims, multiple charged perpetrators, and multiple defense attorneys, videotaping of initial disclosure interviews should be carefully considered because of the increased likelihood of their use to discredit children, and because of the difficulty of protecting individual privacy once they are released to defense counsel.

Recommendations for Assessment

• Specialized diagnostic centers and specialized units in existing agencies should be available in every community, so that suspected victims of child sexual abuse can receive thorough, sensitive assessments by experienced professionals.

• Wherever possible, medical, psychosocial, and law enforcement evaluations should be coordinated and jointly conducted in one place in order to prevent duplication and minimize investigatory trauma to children.

• Professionals, regardless of their discipline, who conduct diagnostic assessments of alleged victims should be trained in the legal aspects of cases and in how to conduct a legally supportable interview, and should be properly prepared to write reports and testify in court.

• Research is needed that compares sexually abused children to nonabused children, utilizing standardized interview protocols that address such issues as susceptibility to suggestion; reinforcement and leading questions; degree of sexual knowledge by age group; reactions to anatomically correct dolls; and normative developmental understanding of sexuality, touch, and so forth.

• Continued use and research on new medical tools of identification, such as the colposcope, is important in order to further our ability to corroborate the statements of young children, whose testimony frequently does not hold up in court. Forensic research, such as documented autopsy findings of sexual abuse victims, also is necessary to increase medical knowledge of this problem.

• Increased legal research is needed to further explore ways in which videotaped interviews, depositions, and out-of-court statements by children can be utilized to minimize their involvement in the adversary legal process.

TREATMENT

All children who have had a sexually abusive experience should have the opportunity to obtain treatment, even if the abuse was short-lived or has been denied by a child. The many issues that need to be resolved for a child include feelings of shame, concerns about trust and betrayal, fear, sexualized behavior, and protection from further abuse, as well as others that are specific to the particular child and situation. Many incestuous families will not voluntarily enter treatment, and the leverage of a court order is often necessary to ensure that the child and family receive needed therapy. It is also likely that young children will need to return for therapy at later stages of development as they begin to process their experiences and to express them in different ways.

Treatment should involve a variety of modalities in which the needs of each individual and of the whole family are considered. With preschool children, play therapy of some sort is usually the most useful modality; this can be structured or unstructured, and may take place in group or individual settings. A variety of play materials can be used, including anatomically correct dolls, drawings, puppets, and games. However, it is important to evaluate the effectiveness of play therapy with the young preverbal and barely verbal child. If the child is very young or developmentally delayed, therapists should consider making the parents or caretakers the primary recipients of therapy to help them with issues such as bonding, guilt, and the like. The child would then receive adjunctive play therapy for catharsis in a supportive environment, with the focus on validating experiences and feelings.

Part of the therapist's job is to assist the child through the contacts with the medical, legal, and law enforcement systems that will occur, as well as through frequently traumatic court testimony. Additionally, the therapist may need to manage the case and serve as liaison among a variety of relevant parties. Even if therapy is discontinued before court proceedings ensue, the therapist should arrange to see the child for a period of time immediately preceding and following testimony, in order to provide support and address new issues that may be triggered by the court process.

Unfortunately, since court proceedings are usually quite removed from the time of the original abuse, young children's recall of details may become somewhat distorted over time. This is why knowledge of developmental issues is necessary in gathering evidence during the therapeutic process and in preparing a child for court appearances. A child's confusion about the details of an event does not invalidate the fact that the event occurred, and should not be regarded as evidence that a child has fabricated an incident of abuse. In addition, children's responses in therapy and in court may be confusing or contradictory at times, because they do not understand the concept or intent of the questions. It can be helpful for the therapist to seek consultation with a child development specialist in preparing a child for court, and either to share the information with the attorneys involved or to suggest that they also seek such consultation.

Therapists working with sexually molested preschool children must also be in touch with the variety of personal feelings generated in themselves by this type of work. Many feel tremendous rage that someone could so mistreat a 2- or 3-year-old, and may find it hard to concentrate on what is best for the child's therapy in the midst of their own feelings of anger or sympathy for the child. Therapists are also likely to feel uncomfortable with the sexual material generated. Watching very young children play out explicit sexual acts with dolls or puppets is often very difficult. Even harder is dealing with children whose sexualized behavior is directed toward the therapist or toward themselves in the form of overt masturbatory behavior during therapy.

Recommendations for Treatment

• Since the treatment of very young children is a relatively new phenomenon, very little research exists that evaluates the impact of treatment on children at different ages and stages. Well-controlled research that compares the effects of various types of treatment of young sexually molested children and their families is very much needed. Similarly, much information is needed on short-term and long-term effects on behaviors and feelings of children who have received therapy versus those who do not receive treatment.

• Long-term follow-up studies are also needed to examine whether specific new issues come up for victims of sexual molestation at various developmental points, and whether further treatment is necessary at these times.

• Also warranting investigation is the issue of when treatment occurs: Is it less useful to have treatment months or years after the abuse when it is finally disclosed than immediately after it has occurred, and is this difference meaningful?

• Another issue needing consideration is whether disclosure is a necessary aspect of treatment when sexual abuse is strongly suspected but is not acknowledged by the child. Similarly, is recall of the sexual molestation necessary for children if they are able to master their trauma through the use of metaphor in play therapy?

It is hoped that research projects will begin to address these questions, as significant numbers of molested preschool children are now entering treatment programs.

SYSTEMS RESPONSE

Despite recent advances in clinical assessment, medical evaluation, police interviewing techniques, and treatment strategies for preschool-age victims, the biggest problems for children and professionals in this field occur after a child has been identified as sexually abused. What must be taken into greater consideration in cases involving small children are the ways in which they perceive the world and how they interpret and internalize the things that happen in their lives. For many preschoolers, sexually abusive acts, though confusing and upsetting, may be viewed as far less traumatic life events than the consequences of disclosing the abuse, such as being forcefully removed from their families, questioned repeatedly by unknown adults, and sent to live with strangers. Even very young children are quick to associate cause and effect when the result of telling about something that happened to them is that everything in their world that means security is taken away. They are equally quick to take back what they said, or to become electively mute in the hope that their lives will go back to normal. More importantly, their commonly egocentric view that they are responsible for the things that happen in their lives is strongly reinforced when subsequent actions leave them feeling punished and isolated from those they love and depend upon.

While child protective services and juvenile and family courts at least were designed to be responsible to the environmental, privacy, and developmental needs of minors, our adversarial-based criminal

justice system was designed to foster confrontation between competent adults and to provide a forum for the presentation of corroborative or exculpatory evidence—components that are frequently not
available in child sexual abuse cases. Many of the basic concepts on
which criminal cases are built, such as competency, credibility, face-
to-face confrontation, and witnesses' ability to convincingly communicate memories and perceptions of past events, are tremendously
problematic when the central witness is a child. It is doubtful that the
architects of this system envisioned that they would be pitting the
congnitive resources of sophisticated adults and trained attorneys against
those of young, frightened children. As a consequence, most criminal
courts are toxic environments for children.

The issues that confront prosecutors, clinicians, and families alike
often become distilled into one central dilemma of least—worst alternatives: Is it worse to put a young child through the ordeal of a
criminal trial, with uncertain prospects of successful prosecution and
unknown pyschological consequences for the child, or is it worse to
take no action to try to stop those who prey upon the most vulnerable?
The merits and consequences of such choices are hard to weigh. More
often, there is no real choice to be made. The vast majority of cases
involving preschool-age victims never result in criminal prosecution,
because the children are too young to qualify as competent witnesses,
because they are too frightened to repeat their disclosures in a courtroom, or because the lack of anything to corroborate the children's
statements creates a high likelihood of an acquittal.

Numerous efforts are under way to rethink the way in which
child sexual abuse cases are handled by our legal systems. Some of
them involve legislative and procedural changes to make testifying
easier on children and to allow the presentation of a wider variety of
evidence and testimony that might corroborate children's statements.
Some involve improved coordination of community systems and increased advocacy for the needs of child victims, such as the many
innovative efforts undertaken in Seattle, Washington, over the past
decade. Some of these changes are strictly legal; some are attitudinal;
and some require the ability to step back from what has always been
done and to think creatively about how to protect children, society,
and the rights of the accused without traumatizing child victims in
the process.

The prospects for improved system responses are very encouraging in many communities, especially for children who, with support, are emotionally and developmentally able to navigate the legal system. However, for many if not most preschool-age victims of sexual abuse, our criminal justice systems is not working and is not healthy. When traditional responses to familiar problems are applied to extraordinary circumstances or problems, they are rarely adequate to meet the unanticipated needs that accompany those circumstances. The realization that large numbers of small children are being sexually assaulted is an exception to everything we want to believe about our society, and it is a problem that demands exceptional solutions. The task before us is not to defend tradition, but to find better solutions.

Recommendations for Systems Response

• It is especially important to minimize trauma and disruption when alleged victims of sexual abuse are under 5 years of age. Initial interviews should be conducted by those most qualified and experienced in working with preschool-age victims, in settings that are nonthreatening and child-oriented. Other professionals who need access to the same information should obtain it via two-way mirror observation, videotapes, or written and oral communication with the interviewer.

• Whenever possible, very young children should be left in their own homes with a supportive adult, and the alleged perpetrator should be persuaded or required by law to leave the premises until a thorough preliminary investigation is concluded. When no supportive or capable parent is available, every effort should be made to locate familiar, protective relatives who are willing to take on a temporary custodial role on behalf of the child, including careful monitoring of any family contacts permitted by the court.

• Coordination between law enforcement personnel working on a case and clinicians who are involved in diagnosis or treatment of the children involved is particularly important with regard to decisions concerning such issues as arrests, filing of charges, children's competency and degree of fearfulness, and the anticipated effects of the court process.

• Coordination is also extremely critical when cases involving young children are being heard simultaneously in criminal, juvenile, and/or family courts. Traditionally, these separate legal systems have had very little to do with one another. As is being done in some communities, greater efforts must be undertaken to resolve protective, custodial, and criminal issues within the context of one system or set of proceedings, or to physically coordinate all judicial proceedings that involve the same child or children.

• Young children should not have to go through the ordeal of testifying in a criminal case more than once, and they should not be subjected to traditional depositions prior to trial. These goals are being achieved in a number of states where preliminary hearings and grand juries are not required or are conducted without the testimony of young children. Similarly, videotaped interviews are being substituted for testimony on some preliminary proceedings (and in trials in a very few states), and testimony in preliminary proceedings is being video-taped for possible use in later trials. Efforts such as these are important steps toward reducing systemic trauma to child witnesses.

• Other legislative and procedural changes aimed at minimizing trauma are necessary if young victims are to participate successfully in the criminal justice process. Some of these include testimony via closed-circuit television or out-of-court depositions; expansion of the hearsay rule to include statements to credible others; availability of support persons in court; the presence of child development specialists to monitor proceedings; and the possibility of "child interpreters" to formulate and ask questions for attorneys on both sides.

• Finally, every step possible should be taken to keep young children out of court and away from personal interaction with the justice system. We must seek case resolutions that are not solely reliant on what we learn from children, and legal proceedings that are not solely dependent upon their testimony. The fact-finding and investigatory skills of law enforcement, physicians, and clinical personnel evaluating alleged perpetrators must be highly developed if we are to take the burden of proof off the statements of young children. Ultimately, child sexual abuse cases should not have conviction through prosecution as their goal, but the admission of guilt. Only through this outcome do children and society (and, sometimes, perpetrators) all benefit in ways that are not at the probable expense of the victim.

TRAINING

There is currently no degree that reflects specialty training in the area of child sexual abuse, and such training is only rarely a part of professional degree programs. Nonetheless, those who deal with child sexual abuse come from a wide range of diverse professions. Judges, physicians, lawyers, social workers, nurses, police personnel, educators, psychologists, and child care personnel all need to have a basic understanding of the phenomenon of child sexual abuse, and many should have an in-depth understanding of the issues and dynamics involved. Ideally, this should be a part of the curricula of their professional training. All professionals who might come in contact with child sexual abuse cases need to know (1) what clues to look for to recognize the problem; (2) what they are required by law to report, and how to make a child abuse report; (3) what specialized services they need to request; and (4) how to make a referral to a competent and specially trained therapist or agency.

Those who will be closely involved with many cases of child sexual abuse need specialty training. This education should be of three varieties. First, they should receive skills training regarding their professional role in cases of child sexual abuse. For example, law enforcement personnel and child protective service workers who respond to the first reports of child sexual abuse should develop specialized interviewing and investigating skills. Similarly, pediatricians working with many child sexual abuse cases must know how to do a sensitive and thorough history-gathering and diagnostic examination with children of all ages. Legal authorities need to know the goals and intake criteria of social services and treatment systems, as well as the effects on children of various placement options.

Second, those professionals specializing in child sexual abuse need to know what they can expect from other professionals with whom they are involved. For example, child protective services workers and attorneys do not need to know how to do a medical examination, nor do therapists need to understand the entire child protective services system; however, they all need to be able to evaluate whether a client's needs are being effectively met in terms of diagnosis, appropriate placement, protection from further abuse, and so on. It is important that each professional be an educated consumer who can recognize whether or not a child and family are being well served.

Third, professionals must have a basic body of knowledge about child sexual abuse. They must understand some of the basics of child development and family systems, and must have a sense of what elements are necessary for healthy growth and development of a child. Also needed is general knowledge of the social service, child protective, and legal systems in their communities.

There currently is a proliferation of workshops on child sexual abuse, aimed at a variety of audiences. These sessions are augmented by a growing mass of books, pamphlets, films, and articles in the popular media. While such workshops and information are useful and appropriate for continuing education for professionals not specializing in the area (or as specialty skills training in specific subjects for those who are), they are not a substitute for specialized formal education and training in the various professional schools. Additionally, the field does not yet have either minimum standards for what training is needed to function successfully in various roles, nor does it have well-validated data about the dynamics and effects of child sexual abuse. These points need to be stressed in such workshops, so that simple formulas and easy answers are not given out in the face of inadequate validation.

Recommendations for Training

• Basic training in child sexual abuse needs to be included in curricula in professional programs for all those who deal with abused children or their families.

• Specialty training, perhaps leading to certification, is necessary for those whose work centers on child abuse (e.g., police officers, child protective service personnel, family court judges, and attorneys). The training should include discipline-specific as well as cross-discipline education and experience.

• Research on the effectiveness of training programs in the area of child sexual abuse is needed; this should be based on data such as number of successful prosecutions, efficacy of particular treatments, and so on.

• All professionals in positions where they routinely interact with preschool-age victims of abuse should have experience working with young children and specialized training in child development. Such training should be a prerequisite to working in these positions.

PREVENTION

Parents and providers of care for children are clearly much better educated about the symptoms of sexual abuse than was the case a decade ago. More importantly, because the symptoms are frequently so subtle, children are finally being educated about the problem. The recent proliferation of sexual abuse prevention programs for children is a first step in developing such programs as part of the standard curriculum for young children in preschools, day care centers, and elementary schools. However, the current focus of many programs on teaching preschool children to prevent abuse by saying "no" must be augmented with other important messages and skills training. Because of their respect for authority figures and the ease with which they can be overpowered and intimidated, it must be expected that many young children will be unable to say "no," even if they would like to and know it is the "right" thing to do.

Therefore, an additional major focus of prevention programs for children must be on the fact that sometimes children get abused no matter what they try to do, and on encouraging them to tell someone if that happens. Concepts such as "It's not your fault," "Never keep a bad or scary secret," and "Always tell your parents about this, especially if someone says you shouldn't tell them," are emphasized in most existing programs. In addition, it is important to alert children to the kinds of threats they might receive in order to keep them from revealing the abuse. Knowing that they will be believed and won't get in trouble, that they or their families won't be harmed or killed, and that their parents would never stop loving them will help them resist believing such threats if they should ever hear them from someone who has molested them.

The recent upsurge of sexual abuse in child care settings suggests that these children and their families are in special need of preventive education. Presentations to young children are most likely to be understood and retained when they are given over a period of several short sessions, using language and tools that will help them to process the difficult concepts presented.

Because young children are so vulnerable to molestation, better societal controls over child care facilities are also essential. There is a great need for more licensed day care facilities in this country. There is also a need for better screening of, monitoring of, and accountability from the employees in these settings. In addition to educating parents, it is also necessary to educate preschool and day care center administrators and teachers about how to recognize symptoms of sexual abuse in play and classroom settings, what must be reported, and how to make a report of suspected abuse.

Currently, there is a crisis in many child care settings over the fear of unfounded allegations of sexual abuse. This fear may drive some qualified child care providers out of the profession, while others are becoming afraid to touch children or even to be alone with them. Others avoid such common acts as changing a child's diaper or wiping a child's bottom because they fear being falsely accused of molestation.

The backlash that is now occurring in some preschools threatens to deprive children of the nourishment and affection that is so important to healthy development and so rewarding to children as well as teachers. Workshops assisting parents and teachers to explore these issues in a safe environment might help adults to confront some of these very sensitive issues. Optimally, prevention programs should focus as much attention on encouraging affection and healthy physical contact as they do on emphasizing how to identify sexual abuse.

Another prevention goal must be to reduce the systemic abuse that many children endure after an abuse report is made. As resources begin to be channeled into prevention programs, they should also be going toward the improvement of our systemic responses to the abuse. It will not be helpful to generate a significant increase in reports of molestation of young children if there are not appropriate agencies and facilities to handle the cases sensitively and effectively.

Ultimately, it is necessary to identify and effectively treat perpetrators in order to prevent sexual abuse of young children. Currently, very little is known about the dynamics of those who molest infants and preschool-age children, although some professionals believe that they constitute a population that is very different from other sexual abusers. It is necessary for future prevention of abuse to determine how these perpetrators differ from those who molest older children, in order to develop appropriate and meaningful prevention and treatment programs. The question of whether perpetrators who molest very young children can be treated effectively in ways that will prevent further victimizing behavior is particularly crucial, given the current difficulty in obtaining convictions and the relatively short duration of most prison sentences. Finally, treatment programs for youthful perpetrators is very important, given the cyclical nature of this problem and the research indicating that most victimizing behavior begins at a very early age. Our best hope for preventing sexual abuse may lie in stopping it when it first begins, and in better understanding its relationship to prior victimization.

Research is needed to determine what children learn from prevention workshops. Are the children only able to mouth the concepts presented, or are they able to use them effectively to prevent harm? It is also important to determine whether further prevention workshops must be given at different developmental stages. In summary, there are several significant directions to be taken toward the prevention of sexual abuse of young children.

Recommendations for Prevention

• The effectiveness of prevention education that also emphasizes immediate disclosure of abuse must be evaluated.

• Prevention programs need to include encouragement of appropriate touching and nurturance.

• Preparent education and training of child care providers needs to be available on issues of child sexual abuse, sexuality as it relates to developmental stages of children, and confronting molestation in one's own past.

• Effective treatment programs for perpetrators must be developed, as well as counseling centers where individuals who recognize that they may have problems relating sexually to children can go for help before abuse occurs.

• Extended treatment programs are needed for child victims who show signs of identification with their abusers or any indications of potential abusiveness.

CONCLUSION

Important advances have been made in the past 5 years with regard to the identification, evaluation, and treatment of young sexually abused children. Perhaps the most important of these has been the rapidly increasing public and professional recognition of the existence of this problem, together with the realization that most of the children affected by it are either too young to describe it, too immature to understand it, or too frightened to report it. Our society finally appears to be willing to take a stronger position of child advocacy and child protection concerning a problem from which, historically, it has turned away in disgust and disbelief.

More than 80 years of denial and suppression of the existence of child sexual abuse by the Freudian establishment (Masson, 1984) have finally given way to a new surge of research, publication in the professional literature, and national attention in the media. The prevalence of child sexual abuse is surely an instance where we have had to relinquish blind illusions in favor of unpleasant realities. Increased public awareness that preschool-age children can be objects of violence, exploitation, and sexual perversion has put pressure on those systems responsible for responding to this problem. Advances in medicine, law enforcement, and clinical services, such as the use of colposcopy and some of the evaluation techniques described in this book, have no doubt been accelerated by media attention and the rapidly increasing number of reported cases.

Along with technical advances have come a series of common realizations or themes that now reverberate throughout the field and within most communities struggling to respond to this problem. The most significant of these includes the recognition that (1) no single agency or discipline can or should be totally responsible for management of child sexual abuse cases; (2) cooperation between local agencies (particularly between law enforcement and clinical services) not only serves the best interests of children, but enhances cases outcomes as well; and (3) as with most difficult medical, legal, and social problems, those affected are best served by specialists in that field. An additional theme is our newfound awareness that sexual abuse is something that must be openly discussed with young children and their families—both before it occurs, in the forms of sensitive prevention programs, and afterward, in the form of therapy.

However, the good news on how far we have come in our awareness in this area is still overshadowed by the bad news concerning how far we have to go. Although we are getting better at detecting child sexual abuse, we still fall short in terms of what we do with it once we have found it. Most communities still count themselves as fortunate if they have one or two professionals in each discipline who are experienced and qualified to handle these cases. Few physicians in either pediatrics or gynecology are experienced in what to look for when examining an alleged child victim. Few police officers and attorneys have any specialized training on how to communicate with young, traumatized children, just as few mental health professionals have been trained about the legal aspects of these cases. There are virtually no graduate or professional schools in any discipline that offer specific tracks or programs leading to a specialty in this area, and even specialized courses in the subject are rare. Most experts in this field have not gained their expertise through traditional avenues or formal education.

Similarly, specialized treatment programs that coordinate legal and clinical aspects of cases still number only in the hundreds nationwide, and most struggle continually to remain financially viable without the benefit of sustained public funding. Federal and state funding for child sexual abuse has been focused primarily on demonstration projects, which are time-limited and frequently shorter in duration than the time required to treat an individual child or family.

Given the fact that child sexual abuse may affect more than one-third of our population, our current resources and expertise are sorely inadequate to address the problem, especially among very young children. We are at a crossroads in this field. Public awareness and improved clinical techniques have done much to bring this issue to the forefront, but already there is a public backlash of disbelief, including accusations of hysteria and witch hunting. As in the days when Freud first uncovered and then discounted the existence of the problem, many professionals and society as a whole may be inclined to quickly push this problem back into its closet. Whether we prevent that from happening, and whether we improve our ability to respond to its presence, may largely be determined over the next few years.

Some improvements will come with increased education and training; some may come with increased funding and specialized programs; and some will only come with an increased willingness to rethink traditional approaches and try new methods of intervention and treatment. Our legal systems have a large role to play in determining the outcomes of cases in the upcoming years. There is increasing interest at this time in legal reforms on behalf of child victims. However, the question of whether our cumbersome and tradition-bound legal system can stretch and conform itself to the developmental and psychological needs of children remains to be seen. If not, then surely the youngest victims of this problem will continue to be either unprotected as a result of our disregard or retraumatized as a result of our attention.

The crossroads we face is one of trust, as well as one of choice. We are asking children to trust us with their secrets and with their futures. All over the country, new programs are being instituted that encourage children to tell us if they are or have been sexually abused. Will their disclosures be met with sensitivity, support, and competent intervention that feels like help, or will they learn that it is not only individual adults they can't trust, but our protective, therapeutic, and legal systems as well?

REFERENCES

Adams, C., & Fay, J. (1981). *No more secrets: Protecting your child from sexual assault.* San Luis Obispo, CA: Impact.

Adams-Tucker, C. (1981). A socioclinical overview of 28 sex-abused children. *Child Abuse and Neglect, 5,* 361–367.

Adams-Tucker, C. (1982). Proximate effects of sexual abuse in childhood: A report on 28 children. *American Journal of Psychiatry, 139,* 1252–1256.

Alstrom, C. (1977). A study of incest with special regard to the Swedish penal code. *Acta Psychiatrica Scandinavia, 56,* 357–372.

Altchek, A. (1981). Vulvovaginitis, vulvar skin disease, and pelvic inflammatory disease. *Pediatric Clinics of North America, 28,* 397–432.

Anderson, S. C., & Berliner, L. (1983). *Evaluation of the child sexual assault in the health care setting* (American Training Manual). Seattle: Sexual Assault Center.

Bander, K. W., Fein, E., & Bishop, G. (1982a). Child sex abuse treatment: Some barriers to program operation. *Child Abuse and Neglect, 6,* 185–191.

Bander, K. W., Fein, E., & Bishop, G. (1982b). Evaluation of child-sexual-abuse programs. In S. M. Sgroi (Ed.), *Handbook of clinical intervention in child sexual abuse.* Lexington, MA: Lexington Books.

Beezley, P. (1977). *Sexual mistreatment of young children: An intervention model.* Paper presented at the conference of the National Center for the Prevention and Treatment of Child Abuse and Neglect, Denver, CO.

Bender, L., & Blau, A. (1937). The reaction of children to sexual relations with adults. *American Journal of Orthopsychiatry, 7,* 500–518.

Bender, L., & Grugett, A. E. (1952). A follow-up report on children who had atypical sex experience. *American Journal of Orthopsychiatry, 22,* 825–837.

Benward, J., & Densen-Gerber, J. (1975). *Incest as a causative factor in antisocial behavior: An exploratory study.* Paper presented at the meeting of the American Academy of Forensic Sciences.

Berliner, L., Canfield-Blick, L., & Bulkley, J. (1983). Expert testimony on the dynamics of intra-family child sexual abuse and principles of child development. In J. Bulkley (Ed.), *Child sexual abuse and the law* (4th ed.). Washington, DC: National Legal Resource Center for Child Advocacy and Protection, American Bar Association.

Berliner, L., & Roe, R. (1985, March). *The child witness: The progress and emerging limitations.* Paper presented to the American Bar Association, National

Policy Conference on Legal Reforms in Child Sexual Abuse Cases, Washington, DC.

Berliner, L., & Stevens, D. (1980). Advocating for sexually abused children in the criminal justice system. In K. MacFarlane, B. M. Jones, & L. L. Jenstrom (Eds.), *Sexual abuse of children: Selected readings* (DHHS Publication No. OHDS 78-30161). Washington, DC: U.S. Government Printing Office.

Bernstein, A. C. (1976, January). How children learn about sex and birth. *Psychology Today*, pp. 31–35, 66.

Besharov, D. (1981). Toward better research on child abuse and neglect: Making definitional issues an explicit methodological concern. *Child Abuse and Neglect, 5*, 383–390.

Besharov, D., & Besharov, S. (1977, Winter). Why do parents harm their children? *National Council of Jewish Women*, pp. 6–8.

Bess, B. E., & Janssen, Y. (1982). Incest: A pilot study. *Hillside Journal of Clinical Psychiatry, 4*, 39–52.

Bixler, R. H. (1981). The incest controversy. *Psychological Reports, 49*, 267–283.

Blick, L. C., & Porter, F. S. (1982). Group therapy with female adolescent incest victims. In S. M. Sgroi (Ed.), *Handbook of clinical intervention in child sexual abuse*. Lexington, MA: Lexington Books.

Bloch, A. (1983). *Murphy's law and other reasons why things go wrong*. Los Angeles: Price/Stern/Sloan.

Blumberg, M. L. (1978). Child sexual abuse: Ultimate in maltreatment syndrome. *New York State Journal of Medicine, 78*, 612–616.

Blumberg, M. L. (1981). Depression in abused and neglected children. *American Journal of Psychotherapy, 35*, 342–355.

Boatman, B., Borkan, E. L., & Schetky, D. H. (1981). Treatment of child victims of incest. *American Journal of Family Therapy, 9*, 43–51.

Boekelheide, P. D. (1978). Incest and the family physician. *Journal of Family Practice, 6*, 87–90.

Bohmer, C. (1974). Judicial attitudes toward rape victims. *Judicature, 57*, 303–307.

Brant, R., & Tisza, V. (1977). The sexually misused child. *American Journal of Orthopsychiatry, 47*, 80–90.

Brassard, M. R., Tyler, A., & Kehle, T. J. (1983). Sexually abused children: Identification and suggestions for intervention. *School Psychology Review, 12*, 93–97.

Broderick, C. B. (1969). Normal sociosexual development. In C. B. Broderick & J. Bernard (Eds.), *The individual, sex and society*. Baltimore: Johns Hopkins University Press.

Brooks, B. (1982). Familial influence on father–daughter incest. *Journal of Psychiatric Treatment and Evaluation, 4*, 117–124.

Browning, D. H., & Boatman, B. (1977). Incest: Children at risk. *American Journal of Psychiatry, 134*, 69–72.

Brunold, H. (1964, January/February). Observations after sexual traumata suffered in childhood. *Excerpta Criminologica*, pp. 60–66.

Bulkley, J. & Davidson, H. A. (1980). *Child sexual abuse: Legal issues and approaches*. Washington, DC: National Legal Resource Center for Child Advocacy and Protection, American Bar Association.

Burgess, A. W., & Holmstrom, L. L. (1975). Sexual trauma of children and adolescents. *Nursing Clinics of North America*, *10*, 551–563.

Burgess, A. W., & Holmstrom, L. L. (1978). Interviewing young victims. In A. W. Burgess, A. N. Groth, L. L. Holmstrom, & S. M. Sgroi (Eds.), *Sexual assault of children and adolescents*. Lexington, MA: Lexington Books.

Burgess, A. W., Holmstrom, L. L., & McCausland, M. P. (1978). Counseling young victims and their parents. In A. W. Burgess, A. N. Groth, L. L. Holmstrom, & S. M. Sgroi (Eds.), *Sexual assault of children and adolescents*. Lexington, MA: Lexington Books.

Cantwell, H. (1981). Vaginal inspection as it relates to child sexual abuse in girls under thirteen. *Child Abuse and Neglect*, *7*, 171–176.

Cavallin, H. (1966). Incestuous fathers: A clinical report. *American Journal of Psychiatry*, *122*, 1132–1138.

Cohen, B., & Parker, S. (1977). Sex information among nursery-school children. In E. K. Oremland & J. D. Oremland (Eds.), *The sexual and gender development of young children: The role of the educator*. Cambridge, MA: Ballinger.

Cohen, J. A. (1981). Theories of narcissism and trauma. *American Journal of Psychiatry*, *35*, 83–100.

Cohn, A. H., & Garbarino, J. (1981). *Towards a refined approach to preventing child abuse*. Paper presented at the meeting of the National Committee for Prevention of Child Abuse.

Constantine, L. L. (1979). The impact of early sexual experiences. In J. M. Samson (Ed.), *Childhood and sexuality*. Montreal: Editions Études Vivantes.

Cormier, B. M. (1972). The dilemma of psychiatric diagnosis. In H. L. P. Resnick & M. E. Wolfgang (Eds.), *Sexual behaviors: Social, clinical and legal aspects*. Boston: Little, Brown.

Cormier, B. M., Kennedy, M., & Sangowicz, J. (1962). Psychodynamics of father–daughter incest. *Canadian Psychiatric Association Journal*, *7*, 203–217.

Corsini-Munt, L. (1979). Sexual abuse of children and adolescents. In J. M. Samson (Ed.), *Childhood and sexuality*. Montreal: Editions Études Vivantes.

Cowell, C. (1981). The gynecologic examination of infants, children, and young adolescents. *Pediatric Clinics of North America*, *28*, 247–266.

Currier, R. L. (1981). Juvenile sexuality in global perspective. In L. L. Constantine & F. M. Martinson (Eds.), *Children and sex: New findings, new perspectives*. Boston: Little, Brown.

De Francis, V. (1970). *Protecting the child victim of sex crimes committed by adults*. Denver: American Humane Association.

De Francis, V. (1971). Protecting the child victim of sex crimes committed by adults. *Federal Probation*, *35*, 15–20.

Delson, N., & Clark, M. (1981). Group therapy with sexually molested children. *Child Welfare*, *60*, 175–182.

Densen-Gerber, J., & Hutchinson, F. F. (1978). Medical–legal and societal problems involving children—child prostitution, child pornography, and drug-related abuse; recommended legislation. In S. M. Smith (Ed.), *The maltreatment of children*. Lancaster, England: MTP Press.

Department of Health and Human Services. (1981). *Child sexual abuse: Incest, assault and sexual exploitation*. (DHHS Publication No. 81-30166). Washington, DC: U.S. Government Printing Office.

DeVos, G. A. (1982). Adaptive strategies in United States minorities. In E. E. Jones & S. Korchin (Eds.), *Minority mental health*. New York: Praeger Press.

Dixen, J., & Jenkins, J. O. (1981). Incestuous child sexual abuse: A review of treatment strategies. *Clinical Psychology Review*, *1*, 211–222.

Eist, H. I., & Mandel, A. U. (1968). Family treatment of ongoing incest behavior. *Family Process*, *7*, 216–232.

Emslie, G. J., & Rosenfeld, A. (1983). Incest reported by children and adolescents hospitalized for severe psychiatric problems. *American Journal of Psychiatry*, *140*, 708–711.

Fay, J. (1979). *He told me not to tell*. Renton, WA: King County Rape Relief.

Finch, S. (1967). Sexual activity of children with other children and adults. *Clinical Pediatrics*, *6*, 102.

Finch, S. (1973). Adult seduction of the child: Effects on the child. *Medical Aspects of Human Sexuality*, *7*, 170–187.

Finkelhor, D. (1979a). Sexual socialization in America: High risk for sexual abuse. In J. M. Samson (Ed.), *Childhood and sexuality*. Montreal: Editions Études Vivantes.

Finkelhor, D. (1979b). *Sexually victimized children*. New York: Free Press.

Finkelhor, D. (1980a). Risk factors in the sexual victimization of children. *Child Abuse and Neglect*, *4*, 265–273.

Finkelhor, D. (1980b). Sex among siblings: A survey on prevalence, variety and effects. *Archives of Sexual Behavior*, *9*, 171–194.

Finkelhor, D. (1982). Sexual abuse: A sociological perspective. *Child Abuse and Neglect*, *6*, 95–102.

Finkelhor, D. (1983). Removing the child—prosecuting the offender in cases of sexual abuse. *Child Abuse and Neglect*, *7*, 195–205.

Finkelhor, D., & Araji, S. (1983). *Explanations of pedophilia: A four factor model*. Durham, NH: University of New Hampshire Press.

Fraser, B. G. (1981). Sexual child abuse: The legislation and the law in the United States. In P. B. Mrazek & C. H. Kempe (Eds.), *Sexually abused children and their families*. New York: Pergamon Press.

Freud, A. (1965). *The writings of Anna Freud: Vol. 6. Normality and pathology in childhood*. New York: International Universities Press.

Freud, A. (1981). A psychoanalyst's view of sexual abuse by parents. In P. B.

Mrazek & C. H. Kempe (Eds.), *Sexuality abused children and their families.* New York: Pergamon Press.

Frude, N. (1982). The sexual nature of sexual abuse: A review of the literature. *Child Abuse and Neglect, 6,* 211–223.

Furniss, T. (1983a). Family process in the treatment of intrafamilial child sexual abuse. *Journal of Family Therapy, 5,* 263–278.

Furniss, T. (1983b). Mutual influence and interlocking professional–family process in the treatment of child sexual abuse and incest. *Child Abuse and Neglect, 7,* 207–223.

Gagnon, J. (1965). Female child victims of sex offenses. *Social Problems, 13,* 176–192.

Garbarino, J., & Ebata, A. (1983). The significance of ethnic and cultural differences in child maltreatment. *Journal of Marriage and the Family, 45,* 773–783.

Gardner, R. (1975). *Psychotherapeutic approaches to the resistant child.* New York: Jason Aronson.

Gebhard, P. H. (1977). The acquisition of basic sex information. *Journal of Sex Research, 13,* 148–169.

Gebhard, P., Gagnon, J., Pomeroy, W., & Christenson, C. (1965). *Sex offenders: An analysis of types.* New York: Harper & Row.

Giarretto, H. (1976a). Humanistic treatment of father–daughter incest. In R. E. Helfer & C. H. Kempe (Eds.), *Child abuse and neglect: The family and the community.* Cambridge, MA: Ballinger.

Giarretto, H. (1976b). The treatment of father–daughter incest: A psychological approach. *Children Today, 5,* 2–5.

Giarretto, H. (1982). *Integrated treatment of child sexual abuse: A treatment and training manual.* Palo Alto, CA: Science and Behavior Books.

Gibbens, T. C., & Prince, J. (1983). *Child victims of sex offenses.* London: Institute for the Study and Treatment of Delinquency.

Gil, D. G. (1970). *Violence against children: Physical abuse in the United States.* Cambridge, MA: Harvard University Press.

Goodman, G. S. (1983). The child witness: Conclusions and future directions for research and legal practice. *Journal of Social Issues, 40,* 169.

Goodwin, J. (1982). The use of drawings in incest cases. In J. Goodwin (Ed.), *Sexual abuse: Incest victims and their families.* Littleton, MA: John Wright.

Green, C. M. (1982). Filicidal impulses as an anniversary reaction to childhood incest. *American Journal of Psychotherapy, 36,* 264–271.

Gross, M. (1979). Incestuous rape: A cause for hysterical seizures in four adolescent girls. *American Journal of Orthopsychiatry, 49,* 704–708.

Gross, M. (1982). Incest and hysterical seizures. *Medical Hypnoanalysis, 3,* 146–152.

Groth, A. N. (1978). Patterns of sexual assault against children and adolescents. In A. Burgess, A. N. Groth, L. Holmstrom, & S. Sgroi (Eds.), *Sexual assault of children and adolescents.* Lexington, MA: Lexington Books.

Groth, A. N. (1979). *Men who rape: The psychology of the offender.* New York: Plenum.

Groth, A. N. (1982). The incest offender. In S. M. Sgroi (Ed.), *Handbook of clinical intervention in child sexual abuse*. Lexington, MA: Lexington Books.

Groth, A. N., & Birnbaum, H. J. (1978). Adult sexual orientation and attraction to underage persons. *Archives of Sexual Behavior, 7,* 175–181.

Groth, A. N., Longo, R. E., & McFadin, J. B. (1982). Undetected recidivism among rapists and child molesters. *Crime and Delinquency, 28,* 450–458.

Gundersen, B. H., Melas, P. S., & Skar, J. E. (1981). Sexual behavior of preschool children: Teacher's observations. In L. L. Constantine & F. M. Martinson (Eds.), *Children and sex: New findings, new perspectives.* Boston: Little, Brown.

Haase, C., Magaz, C., Lazoritz, M., & Chiaro, J. (1982). *Clinical experiences of the therapeutic group program for sexually abused preschool children.* Unpublished manuscript, Child Protection Team, Orlando Regional Medical Center, Orlando.

Heims, L., & Kaufman, I. (1963). Variations on a theme of incest. *American Journal of Orthopsychiatry, 33,* 311–312.

Henderson, J. (1983). Is incest harmful? *Canadian Journal of Psychiatry, 28,* 34–40.

Hendricks, G., & Roberts, T. (1977). *The second centering book.* Englewood Cliffs, NJ: Prentice-Hall.

Herjanic, B., & Wilbois, R. B. (1978). Sexual abuse of children. *Journal of the American Medical Association, 239,* 331–333.

Herman, J. (1981). Father–daughter incest. *Professional Psychologist, 12,* 76–80.

Herman, J. (1982). *Father–daughter incest.* Cambridge, MA: Harvard University Press.

Herman, J., & Hirschman, L. (1977). Father–daughter incest. *Signs, 2,* 735–756.

Herman, J., & Hirschman, L. (1981). Families at risk for father–daughter incest. *American Journal of Psychiatry, 138,* 967–970.

James, J., & Meyerding, J. (1978). Early sexual experience as a factor in prostitution. *Archives of Sexual Behavior, 7,* 31–42.

James, J., Womack, W. M., & Strauss, F. (1978). Physician reporting of sexual abuse of children. *Journal of the American Medical Association, 240,* 1145–1146.

James, K. L. (1977). Incest: The teenager's perspective. *Psychotherapy: Theory, Research and Practice, 14,* 146–155.

Janus, S. S., & Bess, B. E. (1981). Latency: Fact or fiction? In L. L. Constantine & F. M. Martinson (Eds.), *Children and sex: New findings, new perspectives.* Boston: Little, Brown.

Jason, J. (1982). Epidemiologic differences between sexual and physical child abuse. *Journal of the American Medical Association, 247,* 3344–3348.

Jernberg, A. (1979). *Theraplay.* San Francisco: Jossey-Bass.

Jiles, D. (1981). Problems in the assessment of sexual abuse referrals. In W. Holder (Ed.), *Sexual abuse of children.* New York: Pergamon Press.

Johnston, M. S. K. (1979). *Nonincestuous sexual abuse of children and its rela-*

tionship to family dysfunction. Paper presented at the Fourth National Conference on Child Abuse and Neglect, Los Angeles.

Jorne, P. S. (1979). Treating sexually abused children. *Child Abuse and Neglect, 3,* 285–290.

Julian, V., Mohr, C., & Lapp, J. (1980). Father–daughter incest: A descriptive analysis. In W. M. Holder (Ed.), *Sexual abuse of children: Implications for treatment.* Denver, CO: American Humane Association, Child Protection Division.

Justice, B., & Justice, R. (1979). *The broken taboo: Sex in the family.* New York: Human Science Press.

Katan, A. (1973). Children who were raped. *Psychoanalytic Study of the Child, 28,* 208–224.

Katz, S., & Mazur, M. (1979). *Understanding the rape victim: A synthesis of research findings.* New York: Wiley.

Kaufman, I., Peck, A. L., & Taguiri, C. K. (1954). The family constellation and overt incestuous relations between father and daughter. *American Journal of Orthopsychiatry, 24,* 266–277.

Kelly, R. J. (1982). Behavioral reorientation of pedophiliacs: Can it be done? *Clinical Psychology Review, 2,* 387–408.

Kelly, R. J. (1984). *Gender and incest factors in reactions to adult–child sex.* Dissertation Abstract International, *45,* 2692B–2693B. (University Microfilms No. 84–26055).

Kelly, R. J. (1985, August). *Child sexual abuse and homophobia.* Paper presented at the 93rd Annual Convention of the American Psychological Association, Los Angeles.

Kelly, R. J., & Kaser-Boyd, N. (1985, April). *Outpatient group therapy for adolescent sex offenders.* Paper presented at the 65th Annual Convention of the Western Psychological Association, San Jose.

Kelly, R. J., & Tarran, M. J. (1983, April). *Gender differences in childhood sexual experiences and subsequent attitudes toward child sexual abuse.* Paper presented at the 54th Annual Convention of the Eastern Psychological Association, Philadelphia.

Kelly, R. J., & Tarran, M. J. (1984, April). *Negative homosexuality bias in reactions to adult–child sex.* Paper presented at the 64th Annual Convention of the Western Psychological Association, Los Angeles.

Kempe, C. H. (1978). Sexual abuse, another hidden pediatric problem. *Pediatrics, 62,* 382–389.

Kentucky prosecutors' manual on child abuse and neglect (1984). Frankfort, KY: Office of the Attorney General.

Kerns, D. (1981). Medical assessment of child sexual abuse. In P. B. Mrazek & C. H. Kempe (Eds)., *Sexually abused children and their families.* London: Pergamon Press.

Kinsey, A. C., Pomeroy, W. B., & Martin, C. E. (1948). *Sexual behavior in the human male.* Philadelphia: W. B. Saunders.

Kinsey, A. C., Pomeroy, W. B., Martin, C. E., & Gebhard, P. H. (1953). *Sexual behavior in the human female.* Philadelphia: W. B. Saunders.

Kleven, S., & Krebill, J. (1981). *The touching problem.* Bellingham, WA: Soap Box Productions.

Kluft, R. B. (Ed.). (1985). *Childhood antecedents of multiple personality.* Washington, DC: American Psychiatric Press.

Knittle, B. J., & Tuana, S. (1980). Group therapy as primary treatment for adolescent victims of intrafamilial sexual abuse. *Clinical Social Work Journal, 8,* 236–242.

Korbin, J. E. (1977). Anthropological contributions to the study of child abuse. *Child abuse and neglect, 1,* 7–24.

Korbin, J. E. (1979). A cross-cultural perspective on the role of the community. *Child abuse and neglect, 3,* 9–18.

Korbin, J. E. (1980). The cultural context of child abuse and neglect. *Child abuse and neglect, 4,* 3–13.

Korbin, J. E. (1981). *Child abuse and neglect: Cross-cultural perspectives.* Berkeley: University of California Press.

Kraft, A. (1973). *Are you listening to your child?* New York: Walker.

Krieger, M. J., Rosenfeld, A. A., Gordon, A., & Bennett, M. (1980). Problems in psychotherapy of children with histories of incest. *American Journal of Psychotherapy, 34,* 81–88.

Kroth, J. (1979). *Child sexual abuse: Analysis of a family therapy approach.* Springfield, IL: Charles C. Thomas.

Landis, C. (1963). *Sex in development.* College Park, MD: McGrath.

Landis, J. (1956). Experiences of 500 children with adult sexual deviation. *Psychiatric Quarterly Supplement, 30,* 91–109.

Leaman, K. M. (1980). Sexual abuse: The reactions of child and family. In K. MacFarlane, B. M. Jones, & L. L. Jenstrom (Eds.), *Sexual abuse of children: Selected readings* (DHHS Publication No. OHDS 78-30161). Washington, DC: U.S. Government Printing Office.

Leaman, K. M., & Knasel, A. L. (1980). Developmental sexuality. In K. MacFarlane, B. M. Jones, & L. L. Jenstrom (Eds.), *Sexual abuse of children: Selected readings.* (DHHS Publication No. OHDS 78-30161). Washington, DC: U.S. Government Printing Office.

Libai, D. (1969). Protection of the child victim of a sexual offense in the criminal justice system. *15 Wayne Law Review, 977,* 955, 1010–1018.

Lindholm, K. (1984). *Trends in child sexual abuse: A study of 611 reported cases in Los Angeles County.* Paper presented at the 64th Annual Convention of the Western Psychological Association, Los Angeles.

Lindholm, K., & Willey, R. (1983). *Child abuse and ethnicity: Patterns of similarities and differences* (Occasional Paper No. 18). Los Angeles: UCLA Spanish Speaking Mental Health Research Center.

Lukianowicz, N. (1972). Incest: I. Paternal incest: II. Other types of incest. *British Journal of Psychiatry, 120,* 301–313.

Lustig, M., Dresser, J. W., Spellman, S. W., & Murray, J. B. (1966). Incest: A family group survival pattern. *Archives of General Psychiatry, 14,* 31–40.

MacFarlane, K. (1978). Sexual abuse of children. In J. Chapman & M. Gates (Eds.), *The victimization of women.* Beverly Hills: Sage Publications.

MacFarlane, K. (1979). *Issues in intervention and treatment of sexual abuse.* Paper presented at the Fourth National Conference on Child Abuse and Neglect, Los Angeles.

MacFarlane, K., & Bulkley, J. (1982). Treating child sexual abuse: An overview of current program models. In J. Conte & D. Shore (Eds.), *Social work and child sexual abuse.* New York: Haworth Press.

MacFarlane, K., Jones, B. M., & Jenstrom, L. L. (Eds.). (1980). *Sexual abuse of children: Selected readings* (DHHS Publication No. OHDS 78-30161). Washington, DC: U.S. Government Printing Office.

MacFarlane, K., & Korbin, J. (1983). Confronting the incest secret long after the fact: A family study of multiple victimization with strategies for intervention. *Child Abuse and Neglect, 7,* 225–240.

Machotka, P., Pittman, F. S., & Flomemhaft, K. (1967). Incest as a family affair. *Family Process, 6,* 98–116.

MacVicar, K. (1979). Psychotherapeutic issues in the treatment of sexually abused girls. *Journal of the American Academy of Child Psychiatry, 18,* 342–353.

Maisch, H. (1972). *Incest.* New York: Stein & Day. (1973). London: Andre Deutsch.

Martin, M. J., & Walters, J. (1982). Familial correlates of selected types of child abuse and neglect. *Journal of Marriage and the Family, 44,* 267–276.

Masson, J. M. (1984). *The assault on truth: Freud's suppression of the seduction theory.* New York: Farrar, Straus and Giroux.

May, J. G. (1977). Sexual abuse, the undercover problem. *Current Problems in Pediatrics, 7,* 1–43.

Meiselman, K. C. (1978). *Incest: A psychological study of causes and effects with treatment recommendations.* San Francisco: Jossey-Bass.

Melton, G. B. (1981). Children's competency to testify. In *Law and Human Behavior, 5,* 75.

Melton, G. B. (1983). Procedural reforms to protect child victim/witnesses in sex offense proceedings. In J. Bulkley (Ed.), *Child sexual abuse and the law.* Washington, DC: National Legal Resource Center for Child Advocacy and Protection, American Bar Association.

Minuchin, S. (1974). *Families and family therapy.* Cambridge, MA: Harvard University Press.

Molnar, B., & Cameron, P. (1975). Incest syndromes: Observations in a general hospital psychiatric unit. *Canadian Psychiatric Association Journal, 20,* 373–377.

Mrazek, D. A. (1981). The child psychiatric examination of the sexually abused child. In P. B. Mrazek & C. H. Kempe (Eds.), *Sexually abused children and their families.* New York: Pergamon Press.

Mrazek, P. B. (1980). Sexual abuse of children. *Journal of Child Psychology and Psychiatry and Allied Disciplines, 21,* 91–95.

Mrazek, P. B. (1981). The nature of incest: A review of contributing factors. In P. B. Mrazek & C. H. Kempe (Eds.), *Sexually abused children and their families.* New York: Pergamon Press.

Mrazek, P. B., & Bentovim, A. (1981). Incest and the dysfunctional family system. In P. B. Mrazek & C. H. Kempe (Eds.), *Sexually abused children and their families*. New York: Pergamon Press.

Mrazek, P. B., & Mrazek, D. A. (1981). The effects of child sexual abuse: Methodological considerations. In P. B. Mrazek & C. H. Kempe (Eds.), *Sexually abused children and their families*. New York: Pergamon Press.

Naitove, C. E. (1982). Arts therapy with sexually abused children. In S. M. Sgroi (Ed.), *Handbook of clinical intervention in child sexual abuse*. Lexington, MA: Lexington Books.

Nakashima, I. I., & Zakus, G. (1979). Incestuous families. *Pediatric Annals, 8*, 300–308.

National Center on Child Abuse and Neglect. (1978). *Child sexual abuse: Incest, assault and exploitation* (DHHS Publication No. OHDS 79-30166). Washington, DC: U.S. Government Printing Office.

Neinstein, L., Goldenring, J., & Carpenter, S. (1984). Nonsexual transmission of sexually transmitted diseases: An infrequent occurrence. *Pediatrics, 74*, 67–75.

Oaklander, V. (1978). *Windows to our children*. Moab, UT: Real People Press.

O'Brien, S. (1980). *Child abuse: A crying shame*. Provo, UT: Brigham Young University Press.

Orr, D. P. (1979). Emergency management of sexually abused children. *American Journal of Diseases of Children, 133*, 629–631.

Parker, J. (1982). The rights of child witnesses: Is the court a protector or a perpetrator? *New England Law Review, 17*, 643–717.

Paul, D. M. (1977). Medical examination in sexual offenses against children. *Medical Science Law, 17*, 251–258.

Paulson, M. J. (1978). Incest and sexual molestation: Clinical and legal issues. *Journal of Clinical Child Psychology, 7*, 177–180.

Pelton, L. H. (1978). Child abuse and neglect: The myth of classlessness. *American Journal of Orthopsychiatry, 48*, 608–617.

People v. Buckey et al., No. A753005 and A750900 (Los Angeles County Municipal Court, 1984–85).

Perlmutter, L. H., Engel, T., & Sager, C. J. (1982). The incest taboo: Loosened sexual boundaries in remarried families. *Journal of Sex and Marital Therapy, 8*, 83–96.

Peters, J. J. (1973). Child rape: Defusing a psychological time bomb. *Hospital Physician, 9*, 46–49.

Peters, J. J. (1974). The psychological effects of childhood rape. *World Journal of Psychosynthesis, 6*(5), 11–14.

Pittman, F. S., III. (1976). Counseling incestuous families. *Medical Aspects of Human Sexuality, 10*, 57–58.

Porter, F. S., Blick, L. C. & Sgroi, S. M. (1982). Treatment of the sexually abused child. In S. M. Sgroi (Ed.), *Handbook of clinical intervention in child sexual abuse*. Lexington, MA: Lexington Books.

Powell, G. E., & Chalkley, A. J. (1981). The effects of paedophile attention on the child. In B. Taylor (Ed.), *Perspectives on paedophilia*. London: Batsford.

Reimer, S. (1940). A research note on incest. *Americal Journal of Sociology, 45*, 565–571.

Riggs, R. S. (1982). Incest: The school's role. *Journal of School Health, 52*, 365–370.

Righton, P. (1981). The adult. In B. Taylor (Ed.), *Perspectives on paedophilia*. London: Batsford.

Rist, K. (1979). Incest: Theoretical and clinical views. *American Journal of Orthopsychiatry, 49*, 680–691.

Rogers, C. M. (1982). Child sexual abuse and the courts: Preliminary findings. In J. R. Conte & D. A. Shore (Eds.), *Social work and child sexual abuse*. New York: Haworth Press.

Rosenfeld, A. A. (1976). Case report LVIII—a case of sexual misuse. *Psychiatric Opinion, 13*, 35–42.

Rosenfeld, A. A. (1977). Sexual misuse and the family. *Victimology: An International Journal, 2*, 226–235.

Rosenfeld, A. A. (1978). Sexual abuse of children. *Journal of the American Medical Association, 240*, 43.

Rosenfeld, A. A. (1979). Incidence of a history of incest among 18 female psychiatric patients. *American Journal of Psychiatry, 136*, 791–795.

Rosenfeld, A. A., Nadelson, C. C., & Krieger, M. (1979). Fantasy and reality in patients' reports of incest. *Journal of Clinical Psychiatry, 40*, 159–164.

Rosenfeld, A. A., Nadelson, C. C., Krieger, M., & Backman, J. J. (1977). Incest and sexual abuse of children. *Journal of the American Academy of Child Psychiatry, 16*, 327–339.

Ruch, L. O., & Chandler, S. M. (1982). The crisis impact of sexual assault on three victim groups: Adult rape victims, child rape victims, and incest victims. *Journal of Social Service Research, 5*, 83–100.

Rush, F. (1983). Foreword. In E. Bass & L. Thornton (Eds.), *I never told anyone*. New York: Harper & Row.

Russell, D. E. H. (1983). The incidence and prevalence of intrafamilial and extrafamilial sexual abuse of female children. *Child Abuse and Neglect, 7*, 133–146.

Russell, D. (1984). *Sexual exploitation: Rape, child sexual abuse and harassment*. Beverly Hills: Sage Publications.

Sagarin, E. (1977). Incest: Problems of definition and frequency. *Journal of Sex Research, 13*, 126–135.

Saltman, V., & Solomon, R. S. (1982). Incest and the multiple personality. *Psychological Reports, 50*, 1127–1141.

Sanford, L. T. (1980). *The silent children*. New York: McGraw-Hill.

Sarafino, E. (1979). An estimate of nationwide incidence of sexual offenses against children. *Child Welfare, 58*, 127–134.

Saries, R. M. (1982). Sexual abuse and rape. *Pediatrics in Review, 4*, 93–97.

Schachter, M. (1979). Long term prognosis for prepubescent victims of sexual aggression. *Gaceta Neuro-Psiquiatrica, 3,* 11–19.

Schecter, M. D., & Roberge, L. (1976). Sexual exploitation. In R. E. Helfer & C. H. Kempe (Eds.), *Child abuse and neglect: The family and the community.* Cambridge, MA: Ballinger.

Schoettle, U. C. (1980). Child exploitation: A study in child pornography. *Journal of the American Academy of Child Psychiatry, 19,* 289–299.

Schutz, W. (1967). *Joy.* New York: Grove Press.

Sgroi, S. M. (1975). Sexual molestation of children: The last frontier in child abuse. *Children Today, 4,* 18–21.

Sgroi, S. M. (1977). Kids with clap: Gonorrhea as an indication of child sexual assault. *Victimology, 2,* 251–267.

Sgroi, S. M. (1978). Comprehensive examination for child sexual assault: Diagnostic, therapeutic, and child protective issues. In A. W. Burgess, A. N. Groth, L. L. Holmstrom, S. Sgroi (Eds.), *Sexual assault of children and adolescents.* Lexington, MA: Lexington Books.

Sgroi, S. M. (1982a). A conceptual framework for child sexual abuse. In S. M. Sgroi (Ed.), *Handbook of clinical intervention in child sexual abuse.* Lexington, MA: Lexington Books.

Sgroi, S. M. (Ed.) (1982b). *Handbook of clinical intervention in child sexual abuse.* Lexington, MA: Lexington Books.

Sgroi, S. M., Porter, F. S., & Blick, L. C. (1982). Validation of child sexual abuse. In S. M. Sgroi (Ed.), *Handbook of clinical intervention in child sexual abuse.* Lexington, MA: Lexington Books.

Shaw, V. L., & Meier, J. H. (1983). *The effect of type of abuse and neglect on children's psychosocial development.* Unpublished manuscript, Children's Village U.S.A.

Simari, C. G., & Baskin, D. (1982). Incestuous experiences within homosexual populations: A preliminary study. *Archives of Sexual Behavior, 11,* 329–344.

Simpson, C. A., & Porter, G. L. (1981). Self-mutilation in children and adolescents. *Bulletin of the Menninger Clinic, 45,* 428–438.

Sloane, P. S., & Karpinsky, E. (1942). Effects of incest on the participants. *American Journal of Orthopsychiatry, 12,* 666–673.

Specktor, P. (1979). *Incest: Confronting the silent crime.* Minneapolis: Minnesota Program for Victims of Sexual Abuse.

Spencer, J. (1978). Father–daughter incest: A clinical view from the corrections field. *Child Welfare, 57,* 581–590.

Star, B. (1979). *Research perspectives on the impact of sexual abuse.* Paper presented at the Fourth National Conference on Child Abuse and Neglect, Los Angeles.

Steele, B. (1975). Working with abusive parents: A psychiatrist's view. *Children Today, 4,* 3–5.

Steele, B. F., & Alexander, H. (1981). Long term effects of sexual abuse in childhood. In P. B. Mrazek & C. H. Kempe (Eds.), *Sexually abused children and their families.* New York: Pergamon Press.

Stein, S. B. (1974). *Making babies*. New York: Walker.

Stember, C. J. (1980). Art therapy: A new use in the diagnosis and treatment of sexually abused children. In K. MacFarlane, B. M. Jones, & L. L. Jenstrom (Eds.), *Sexual abuse of children: Selected readings* (DHHS Publication No. OHDS 78-30161). Washington, D.C.: U. S. Government Printing Office.

Stern, M. J., & Meyer, L. C. (1980). Family and couple interactional patterns in cases of father–daughter incest. In K. MacFarlane, B. M. Jones, & L. L. Jenstrom (Eds.) *Sexual abuse of children: Selected readings* (DHHS Publication No. OHDS 78-30161). Washington, D.C.: U.S. Government Printing Office.

Summit, R. (1978). *Sexual abuse, the psychotherapist and the team concept* (in Vol. 2). Chicago: National Committee for Prevention of Child Abuse.

Summit, R. (1983). The child sexual abuse accommodation syndrome. *Child Abuse and Neglect, 7*, 177–193.

Summit, R., & Kryso, J. (1978). Sexual abuse of children: A clinical spectrum. *American Journal of Orthopsychiatry, 48*, 237–251.

Swift, C. (1979). The prevention of sexual child abuse: Focus on the perpetrator. *Journal of Clinical Child Psychology, 8*, 133–136.

Terr, L. (1983). Chowchilla revisited: The effects of psychic trauma four years after a school bus kidnapping. *The American Journal of Psychiatry, 140*, 1543–1550.

Terrell, M. E. (1977). Identifying the sexually abused child in a medical setting. *Health and Social Work, 2*, 112–130.

Topper, A. B., & Aldridge, D. J. (1981). Incest: Intake and investigation. In P. B. Mzarek & C. H. Kempe (Eds.), *Sexually abused children and their families*. London: Pergamon Press.

Tsai, M., Feldman-Summers, S., & Edgar, M. (1979). Childhood molestation: Variables related to differential impacts on psychosexual functioning in adult women. *Journal of Abnormal Psychology, 88*, 407–417.

Tsai, M., & Wagner, N. N. (1978). Therapy groups for women sexually molested as children. *Archives of Sexual Behavior, 7*, 417–427.

Tufts New England Medical Center, Division of Child Psychiatry. (1984). *Sexually exploited children: Service and research project* (Final report for the Office of Juvenile Justice and Delinquency Prevention). Washington, DC: U.S. Department of Justice.

Vander Mey, B. J., & Neff, R. L. (1982). Adult–child incest: A review of research and treatment. *Adolescence, 17*, 717–735.

Van Gijseghem, H. (1975). Father–daughter incest. *Vie Médicale au Canada Francaise, 4*, 263–271.

Victor, J. S. (1980). *Human sexuality: A social psychological approach*. Englewood Cliffs, NJ: Prentice-Hall.

Virkkunen, M. (1974). Incest offenses and alcoholism. *Medicine, Science and the Law, 14*, 124–128.

Walters, D. R. (1975). *Physical and sexual abuse of children: Causes and treatment*. Bloomington: Indiana University Press.

Weinberg, S. (1955). *Incest behavior.* New York: Citadel Press.

Weiner, I. (1962). Father–daughter incest. *Psychiatric Quarterly, 36,* 607–632.

Weiss, J., Rogers, E., Darwin, M. R., & Dutton, D. E. (1955). A study of girl sex victims. *Psychiatric Quarterly, 29,* 1–26.

Wells, L. (1981). Family pathology and father–daughter incest: Restricted psychopathy. *Journal of Clinical Psychiatry, 42,* 197–202.

Westermeyer, J. (1978). Incest in psychiatric practice: A description of patients and incestuous relationships. *Journal of Clinical Psychiatry, 39,* 643–648.

Winnicott, D. W. (1971). *Therapeutic consultation in child psychiatry.* New York: Basic Books.

Woodling, B., & Kossoris, P. (1981). Sexual misuse: Rape, molestation and incest. *Pediatric Clinics of North America, 28,* 481–499.

Wright, K. (1982). Sociocultural factors in child abuse. In B. Bass, G. Wyatt, & G. Powell, (Eds.), *The Afro-American family: Assessment, treatment and research issues.* New York: Grune & Stratton.

Wyatt, G. E. (1985). The sexual abuse of Afro-American and White-American women in childhood. *Child Abuse and Neglect, 9,* 507–519.

Wynne, J. M. (1980). Injuries to the genitalia in female children. *South African Medical Journal, 57,* 47–50.

Yates, A. (1982). Children eroticized by incest. *American Journal of Psychiatry, 139,* 482–485.

Yorukoglu, A., & Kemph, G. (1966). Children not severely damaged by incest with a parent. *Journal of the American Academy of Child Psychiatry, 5,* 111–124.

INDEX

Italicized page numbers indicate material in figures or tables.